THE BIG ASTON VILLA BOOK OF THE EIGHTIES

80

Legends Publishing

E-mail **david@legendspublishing.net**
Website **www.legendspublishing.net**

Dedicated to the memory of
Paul Stephen Abbott
1968 - 2008

FOREWORD

The Eighties would begin with unimagined success for Aston Villa Football Club. The winning of the First Division and the European Cup brought untold joy to the supporters, players and club.

Ron Saunders had finally assembled a team capable of challenging for honours and an historical permanence in Aston Villa folklore. The disappointments of the late 1970s were now forgotten as new heroes grabbed the headlines and shone brightly. Shaw, Gibson, Williams, Deacy, Cowans and Spink would be added to the experienced squad and with the signing of Peter Withe, this was our time.

No other team would have to play in fourteen derbies; we had to against Midlands teams. We won eleven of them and drew the three others. This was a major factor in winning the Championship. So for the first time since 1910, we had achieved our first goal, now for the European Cup. Could we win it at our first attempt to earn the title "Kings of Europe?"

The campaign started well with a comprehensive defeat of the Icelanders, FC Valur. Tougher games would prevail against two Eastern European giants, Dynamo Berlin and Dynamo Kiev. The semi-final against Anderlecht was won with a solitary goal from Tony Morley in the first-leg at Villa Park.

The countdown beckoned against Bayern Munich. Who gave us a chance to win the game? We did, from Peter Withe's right shin.

The world's greatest club prize was lifted in the Rotterdam Stadium, what a journey these last two seasons were for Aston Villa F.C. the fans and not least the players.

This was the pinnacle of any player's career. Unfortunately we couldn't repeat it the following season and no Villa team has been able to achieve since. We will be remembered and reported in the annuls of Aston Villa history. It makes us proud to be Villans.

Dennis Mortimer

INTRODUCTION

The advent of the '80s decade for Aston Villa began with a stability and continuity that had begun back in June 1974 with the appointment of Ron Saunders, the club's eleventh manager. The former Manchester City and Norwich boss had been entrusted to awaken the slumbering aristocrats of English football.

Villa hadn't entered a decade with such optimism since the 1930s. The 40s was non-existent due to the war years. The following decade opened without a manager in place until mid-December 1950 (George Martin appointed); the club failing to replace the departed Alex Massie - he left in July 1949, seventeenth months previously! The swinging 60s opened with Villa back after a year's stint in the Second Division but would suffer the ignominy of not one but two relegations in the space of four seasons to plunge Aston Villa into the wilderness of Third Division football. What a scenario for a club of their stature to welcome in a new decade.

When Ron was handed the job he inherited the most decorated side in the country and by some considerable margin. Manchester City, Manchester United, Liverpool, Arsenal, Chelsea, all of them, the teams that today's generation gravitate towards and fully expect to land the silverware, they all trailed the Villa who were the envy of all with their collective 14 trophies. The red half of Merseyside were the best of the rest on eleven in the summer of 1974. Liverpool's dominance of the 1970s at home and abroad would see them leapfrog Villa at the top of the trophy charts by the beginning of the 1980s.

Saunders knew what he wanted and with backing from the board he achieved it. Promotion from the Second Division at the first time of asking and a League Cup victory thrown in for good measure was the ideal way to celebrate 100 years of Aston Villa Football Club. Two years further on and Villa were very close to taking their first title in 67 years. Injuries to key players plus a hectic Cup schedule of 14 matches (exactly a third of the League season) resulted in only the one piece of silver, in the shape of the League Cup, finding its way to Villa Park where three had been more than achievable. In 1976/77 Villa could easily have been the first team to land the domestic treble, according to one of the leading players at the club and many supporters share that sentiment.

The remaining seasons of the 70s were a disappointing anti-climax to the legions of Villa fans. Injuries again played a part, big name players sought pastures new whilst all the time Saunders kept tinkering away, fine tuning this team of players he was quietly assembling. Many columns have been written about Peter Withe being the final piece of the jigsaw. This is indeed correct but a jigsaw is only as good as it sum total of parts or put another way the picture isn't complete without all the pieces.

This first piece of this puzzle was acquired in December 1975 and was referred to 'as a present to the fans.' Dennis Mortimer was that present. Other pieces were picked up and put into place. Only five weeks later in February the name of Gordon Cowans appeared in the first team, albeit from the Maine Road bench. It would take another two years to assemble more of that puzzle in the shape of Jimmy Rimmer from Arsenal, Everton's Ken McNaught and Dunfermline striker Allan Evans. Gary Shaw, Gary Williams and Colin Gibson, youngsters coming through the ranks, further parts. Kenny Swain arrived from Chelsea, he could play in either a midfield role or as a centre-forward.

It's not just having the pieces to a puzzle, they have to go in exactly the right place, Saunders changed his pieces and found Swain slotted in perfectly at full-back. As for Evans he seemed to fit better next to McNaught in central defence.

In the last season of the decade Tony Morley, a tricky right-footed left-winger arrived from Burnley, he only lasted six games before he went missing injured. His first game out saw the debuts of Scot Des Bremner, a grafting midfielder from Hibernian and David Geddis a scorer from Ipswich Town. A young Irish lad Eamonn Deacy would get a bit of game time under his belt before the curtain came down on the 1979/80 campaign.

The puzzle was nearing completion, there was only one piece left to put in, but where was it? The answer lay in Newcastle. Peter Withe a 28-year-old Merseysider turned down Gordon Lee at Everton to sign for Ron Saunders and Aston Villa. The £500,000 fee for the craggy centre-forward was Villa's biggest ever outlay on a player. Would it prove to be money well spent? Time would tell.

The Villa's first game of the season would kick-off at Elland Road, the home of Leeds United, a cauldron of noise and a white hot gladiatorial atmosphere, certainly not the easiest of places but nowhere near as intimidating as it had been a few years previously.....the 80s was here. Let the games begin!

Colin J Abbott

[Right] Gary Shaw scores against Crystal Palace in September's win at Selhurst Park

1980–81

[Back Row] Eamonn Deacy, Ken McNaught, Nigel Spink, Jimmy Rimmer, David Geddis, Gary Williams [Middle Row] Jim Williams (Physiotherapist), Des Bremner, Colin Gibson, Tony Morley, Gordon Cowans, Roy MacLaren (Coach) [Front Row] Allan Evans, Gary Shaw, Ron Saunders (Manager), Dennis Mortimer, Kenny Swain, Peter Withe.

Football League	Division One
Manager	Ron Saunders
Coach	Roy MacLaren
Physio	Jim Williams
Captain	Dennis Mortimer
Final Position	First
F.A. Cup	Third Round
League Cup	Third Round
Leading Goalscorer	Peter Withe 21 goals

Countless words had been written about Villa's final piece of the jigsaw in the local press, the Nationals weren't touting Villa as title candidates. Bob Paisley had stated that complacency wouldn't be tolerated as he'd strive for a third successive crown for his Liverpool side.

Dave Sexton at Manchester United had seen his side finish runners-up, they were by all accounts only a defender and midfielder away from being a championship winning side. Ipswich Town who'd finished third under Bobby Robson were expected to be there or there abouts with his team full of internationals.

Villa opened the campaign with a fine win at Leeds United, having come back from a dubious penalty within two minutes, they outplayed the home side in the second half. With three wins and a draw in the opening month Villa were one of three sides on seven points.

Back to back losses were recorded in September at Portman Road (where Villa put in possibly their best performance of the entire season) and home to Everton. The same month Villa were out of the League Cup at the hands of Cambridge United.

Six wins and a draw (from seven) saw Villa head the table for the first time in half a century with a 4-1 over Brighton. The unbeaten sequence was ended with a 1-2 reversal at Anfield, Villa went into the match with a four point cushion.

David Geddis in only his second start of the season scored two in the 3-0 demolition of Birmingham City. Villa saw the

continued >>>

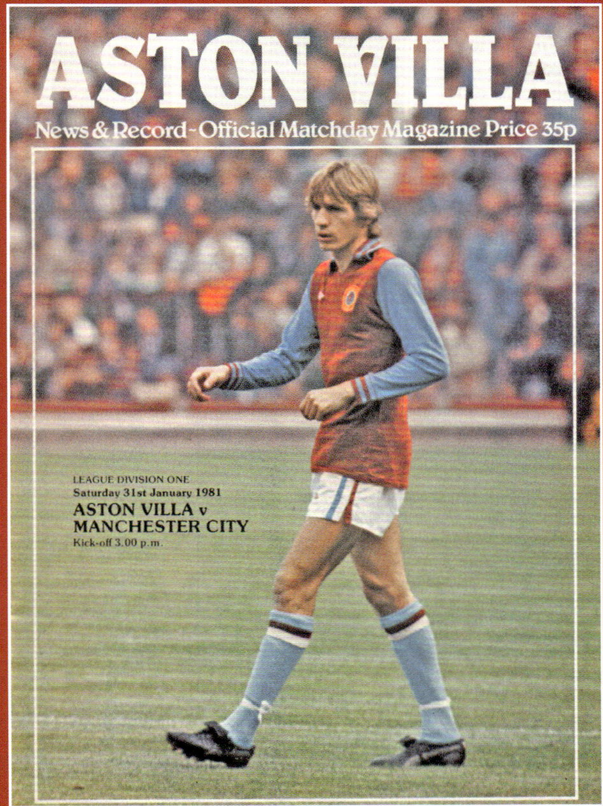

Total Home League Attendances 716,465
Average Home League 34,117
Highest Home League 47,960
Lowest Home League 25,673

		P	W	D	L	GF	GA	DIF	PTS
1	Aston Villa	42	26	8	8	72	40	32	60
2	Ipswich Town	42	23	10	9	77	43	34	56
3	Arsenal	42	19	15	8	61	45	16	53
4	West Bromwich Albion	42	20	12	10	60	42	18	52
5	Liverpool	42	17	17	8	62	42	20	51
6	Southampton	42	20	10	12	76	56	20	50
7	Nottingham Forest	42	19	12	11	62	44	18	50
8	Manchester United	42	15	18	9	51	36	15	48
9	Leeds United	42	17	10	15	39	47	-8	44
10	Tottenham Hotspur	42	14	15	13	70	68	2	43
11	Stoke City	42	12	18	12	51	60	-9	42
12	Manchester City	42	14	11	17	56	59	-3	39
13	Birmingham City	42	13	12	17	50	61	-11	38
14	Middlesbrough	42	16	5	21	53	61	-8	37
15	Everton	42	13	10	19	55	58	-3	36
16	Coventry City	42	13	10	19	48	68	-20	36
17	Sunderland	42	14	7	21	52	53	-1	35
18	Wolverhampton Wanderers	42	13	9	20	43	55	-12	35
19	Brighton & Hove Albion	42	14	7	21	54	67	-13	35
20	Norwich City	42	13	7	22	49	73	-24	33
21	Leicester City	42	13	6	23	40	67	-27	32
22	Crystal Palace	42	6	7	29	47	83	-36	19

year out with a win at home to Stoke followed the next day with a 2-2 draw at Forest. Villa were level on 34 points with leaders Liverpool.

In the New Year Villa would have the distraction of the F.A. Cup removed by losing at title contenders Ipswich. Ron's boys would bounce back the following week with a confidence boosting 2-0 win over the reigning champions, this would start a run of seven wins on the bounce, culminating in a 2-1 victory at Roker Park. Villa were second to Ipswich, level on points but they'd played a game extra.

A 3-3 draw at home to Manchester United was followed by a rare defeat (White Hart Lane) before three fine wins, Saints (H), Leic (A) and WBA at Villa Park saw Villa open up a three point gap. Ipswich came to Villa and took both points in a 2-1 win, their post-match antics that night suggested they were going to win the League, it only served to strengthen Villa's resolve. Victories at home to Forest and Boro with a draw at the Victoria Ground sandwiched between meant Villa had to take a single point from Highbury in their final match to land their first title in 71 years.

As is well known, Villa lost on the day 0-2, they failed to show but thanks to a certain Bosco Jankovic, his two goals for Boro meant Villa got to finish as leaders. Ipswich would lose their final game at home to Saints 0-3. Villa won it by four points, their 26 victories, three more than the runners-up managed. The title was lifted with only fourteen players, seven of those ever present!

[Right] Peter Withe on his League debut for Villa in the victory at Elland Road

1980-81

Sat 16th August **Leeds United (A)**
Won 2-1 **Att 23,401**
Morley, Shaw

New signing, centre-forward Peter Withe spearheaded the attack. Leeds were ahead from a penalty with only 90 seconds on the clock, Deacy upending Flynn. Leeds failure to turn chances into goals signalled Villa, inspired by wideman Tony Morley, to seize the initiative. A fine show of individual skill saw Morley beat Lukic with a shot from 25-yards. Leeds were lethargic following the equaliser, from then on only one team was in it. Good work from Morley, the ball crossed in at pace, Withe mis-kicked but the unmarked Gary Shaw was at the far post to sweep in the winner.

Wed 20th August **Norwich City (H)**
Won 1-0 **Att 25,970**
Shaw

Confidence was high following Elland Road as Villa always did OK at home to the Canaries (won 4, drawn 1 in last 5). It turned out a sterile encounter, a defensive-minded Norwich offered little, the odd times they ventured forward McNaught and Evans took it in their stride. Gordon Cowans still only 21 and described as 'the nearest to perfect midfield all-rounder in the country' by Ipswich boss Robson pulled the strings in the middle of the park. Shaw who bagged the Leeds winner pounced again on 76 minutes when he fired home left-footed to complete a move started by Withe and Morley.

Sat 23rd August **Manchester City (A)**
Drew 2-2 **Att 30,017**
Withe 2

Record signing Peter Withe scored his first goals for the club. On nine minutes, he was given time and space by City's inexperienced

defenders to chest down Morley's cross and volley home off the left upright. City's midfield created numerous chances for the forwards but their good work was in vain. It was 2-0 with 15 minutes remaining when Withe nodded in from a Cowans free kick. Villa were coasting. City were awarded a penalty for a hand-ball during a goalmouth scramble, Tueart stroked it in. With only minutes left the blue side of Manchester found an unlikely equaliser in Ray Ransom to deny Villa.

Wed 27th August — **Leeds United (H)** League Cup 2nd round 1st leg
Won 1-0 — **Att 23,622**
Morley

Wideman Morley volleyed Villa in front on nine minutes. Withe and Colin Gibson combined to release Dennis Mortimer, his cross was met 15-yards out, Tony finishing in devastating fashion. Leeds should have been buried in an avalanche of Villa chances, Withe leading the attack skilfully. A Des Bremner effort bounced off the post and into Lukic's arms. One paper declared the scoreline 'an absurd reflection of a one-sided game.' It was all still to play for in the 2nd leg.

Sat 30th August — **Coventry City (H)**
Won 1-0 — **Att 26,050**
Shaw

Villa had to play second-fiddle to their younger rivals for most of the first period. An Andy Blair long range shot skidded just wide of Rimmer's post. The improvement after the break was down to the inspirational Mortimer and it was the captain's corner that led to the 63rd minute winner. As the ball was curled into a crowded box Shaw climbed to glance a header inside the far post. Coventry played their part in a fiercely contested derby and ex-Villaman Steve Hunt went close to snatching a point for the Sky Blues. It's the club's finest post-war start!

Wed 3rd September — **Leeds United (A)** League Cup 2nd round 2nd leg
Won 3-1 — **Att 12,236**
Withe, Shaw 2

Villa doubled their aggregate lead on six minutes through Withe. Just as it looked like it was going to get embarrassing for the hosts they made a game of it when they snatched a goal back via Arthur Graham. Rimmer pulled off two vital stops to prevent United leading. Shaw struck in first-half injury time to put the visitors back ahead on the night and then sealed the win on 72 minutes. "The victory was fashioned by excellent teamwork with some exceptional individual performances," the verdict of one reporter.

Sat 6th September — **Ipswich Town (A)**
Lost 0-1 — **Att 23,163**

Villa travelled to leaders Ipswich separated only by Southampton and goal difference, all three sides on seven points. The fact that they went back to Birmingham empty handed was a travesty, they totally outplayed their hosts. Shaw could have had a hat-trick, he hesitated or chose to pass. Town cleared off their line more than once. The Ipswich goal was the result of a half-hit attempt from Thijssen, despite Allan Evans' desperate lunge. Such was Villa's play a journalist wrote, "If it's any consolation I'll forecast now that Villa will finish the season with a major trophy. It could even be the League Championship."

Sat 13th September — **Everton (H)**
Lost 0-2 — **Att 25,673**

Everton had gone 25 away games without a win. Villa started lively, Morley just offside from a Mortimer through ball. Another break saw Withe denied by the centre-backs. Des Bremner tried his luck from distance only for his shot to be deflected for a corner. It was all the home side. Everton then broke free from their defensive chains and scored just after the half hour. Four minutes later Villa's central defence was ripped apart again as Everton headed home another. This would be the only time this campaign that Villa suffered back-to-back defeats, they plummeted to tenth in the table.

Sat 20th September — **Wolverhampton Wanderers (H)**
Won 2-1 — **Att 26,881**
Own goal, Geddis

David Geddis scorer of a mid-week Central League hat-trick was in for Shaw. Villa went for the jugular from the kick-off determined to overrun Wolves. After four minutes of torrential pressure Villa were in front when Hughes was struck as Palmer attempted to hack Morley's shot clear. By half time Villa should have had the game sewn up such was their dominance; they didn't and Wolves pulled level. Geddis still trying to win the terrace boo boys over struck with an 84th minute header, just reward for a courageous display.

Tue 23rd September — **Cambridge United (A)** League Cup 3rd round
Lost 1-2 — **Att 7,608**
Morley

Morley was on target after only six minutes, he dispossessed Smith, cut inside and unleashed a low drive. Cambridge who'd knocked holders Wolves out in the last round had their work cut out! Within two minutes the tie was all even when Finney scored with a firm header. On 18 minutes the little ground was rocking when the unsighted Rimmer was beaten by a 25-yard volley. Villa's frustration was plainly visible as Mortimer and then Gibson's names went in the ref's book. Shaw came on for Morley on 64 minutes and despite a spirited second-half rally Villa couldn't penetrate as Cambridge defended ferociously.

Sat 27th September — **Crystal Palace (A)**
Won 1-0 — **Att 18,885**
Shaw

This was a game of few chances so when Shaw missed early on it looked like Villa were destined to take only a point from the team rooted to the foot of the table. Villa competed well in midfield and Evans and McNaught were solid on the few times they needed to be. Withe tended to lay the ball off to others rather than run at goal and the entire team were more workmanlike than spectacular. Shaw made amends for his earlier sloppiness in front of goal when he took possession at the near post, flicked the ball up and then caught it with a right-footed volley to fire in on 84 mins.

Sat 4th October — **Sunderland (H)**
Won 4-0 — **Att 26,914**
Evans 2, Morley, Shaw

Central-defender Allan Evans showed glimpses of his past as a centre-forward, his brace helped Villa beat a Sunderland side previously undefeated on the road. His first, a volley, came on the stroke of half-time, his second a roaring header from a Cowans corner, to seal a 4-0 victory. Sandwiched between them Morley fired in on 59 mins after taking a side pass and then Shaw stroked the ball home for his seventh of the season with quarter of an hour remaining.

Wed 8th October — **Manchester United (A)**
Drew 3-3 — **Att 38,831**
Withe, Cowans (pen), Shaw

Fourth placed Villa were two places above their hosts. Repeatedly Villa tore United to shreds without breaking the deadlock. This changed in the 15th minute, Withe was bundled down on the edge of the box, Cowans glided free-kick found Peter to put Villa in front. United were level from the penalty spot when Evans handled and 60 seconds later they were ahead through Coppell from six-yards out. Villa equalised on 55 minutes courtesy of a Cowans spot-kick only to concede two minutes later. A Kenny Swain cross left United keeper Bailey in two minds, as he looked on Shaw rose to head home.

Sat 11th October — **Birmingham City (A)**
Won 2-1 — **Att 33,879**
Cowans (pen), Evans

In what could be described as a 'thriller' Blues dominated early on yet fell behind to a Cowans penalty after Mark Dennis had handled. Villa edged the second-half only for City to level via Worthington, also from the spot after Ainscow had gone down in suspect fashion. Six minutes from time McNaught lofted a free-kick into the area, his defensive partner Evans, with his back to goal turned and dinked the ball into the top corner, "the best goal I've ever scored," said Evans.

Sat 18th October — Tottenham Hotspur (H)
Won 3-0 — Att 30,940
Morley 2, Withe

Great determination was shown by winger Morley to reach a lost cause (Perryman's ill-fated back-pass) and put Villa ahead late in the first half. Tony added his second with only 34 second-half seconds on the watch with a delightful curling shot after a Mortimer cross was only partly cleared by ex-Villa full-back Gordon Smith. Withe notched the third with a simple tap-in on 84 minutes. Villa should have scored double!

Wed 22nd October — Brighton & Hove Albion (H)
Won 4-1 — Att 37,367
Mortimer, Withe, Bremner, Shaw

Sitting on the shoulder of leaders Ipswich a win would take Villa to the top. Ex-Villan John Gregory gave the Seagulls a 27th minute lead. A Mortimer goal before the break turned the game in Villa's favour. In the second half Villa ran riot. A left foot shot from Withe found the back of the net, Bremner made no mistake from close range and then Shaw scored number four after a clever one-two with Colin Gibson. The last time Aston Villa moved to the top of Division One – exactly 48 years ago to the day, 22nd Oct 1932.

Sat 25th October — Southampton (A)
Won 2-1 — Att 21,239
Morley, Withe

Aston Villa maintained their impressive start to the season, helped by an early Tony Morley goal; also that the inspirational Kevin Keegan was struggling to shake off a first-minute Evans challenge (which required stitches). Saints equalised on the hour and put Villa under a period of pressure. Within eight minutes Villa had their noses back in front to silence 'The Dell,' Mortimer slid the ball to Evans whose raking cross was tucked away by Withe. McMenemy left his seat to gesture to the home support to get behind their team – to no avail.

Sat 1st November — Leicester City (H)
Won 2-0 — Att 29,953
Shaw, Cowans

Leicester came to B6 looking to settle for a point and it looked likely until Gary Shaw broke the stalemate with a crashing right-foot shot. Peter Withe's headed pass set up the young striker. Only four minutes later Withe again rose to steer a header towards Gordon Cowans who beat Mark Wallington with a sharp shot inside the near post. It wasn't a fluid display by Saunders men but their sheer hard work had paid dividends, five wins on the bounce.

Sat 8th November — West Bromwich Albion (A)
Drew 0-0 — Att 34,195

With so much at stake the accent was very much safety first with both defences very much on top. Gary Williams back for the first time since the opening day put in a steady shift. In a dour game of few chances a McNaught shot from the edge of the 18-yard box sailed harmlessly over the bar, Withe headed narrowly wide while Williams and Cowans were denied by Godden. Rimmer was called on a few times, parrying a Brown shot and later closing down Moses.

Wed 12th November — Norwich City (A)
Won 3-1 — Att 16,388
Shaw 2, Evans

In spite of Ipswich's defeat at Brighton last night Villa lacked desire. One paper likened their display as a real 'Jekyll & Hyde' performance. But, a devastating late rally ensured Villa remained unbeaten in 11 games after trailing to a Paddon goal on 24 minutes. It needed the efforts of Rimmer and McNaught to stay in touch as Norwich threatened to add to their slender lead. Villa were back on equal terms just after the hour from a Shaw header. It wasn't until seven minutes to go that the visitors took the lead also through Shaw. Gary then turned creator for Evans to nod home from close range.

[Above] Gary Shaw battles with Tottenham's Steve Perryman

Sat 15th November **Leeds United (H)**
Drew 1-1 **Att 29,106**
Shaw

Leeds took an 11th minute lead through a fluke goal by Alex Sabella. It cannoned off a defender and looped over Rimmer. They then threw up a defensive barricade. Villa deservedly levelled with nine minutes left in the first period when Shaw stuck his foot out to ensure Morley's goalbound shot evaded Lukic. On 77 minutes Villa thought they'd snatched a lead when Morley teed up Shaw but the referee ruled the goal out for an infringement.

Sat 22nd November **Liverpool (A)**
Lost 1-2 **Att 48,114**
Evans

Saunders named an unchanged starting XI. Villa burst forward from the whistle with a Mortimer shot cannoning off the back of Souness. Liverpool then attacked, this pattern continued throughout a goalless first-half. Williams cleared off the line and Bremner responded when Rimmer failed to gather a cross. Dalglish put the hosts in front on 65 mins. Villa were level 13 minutes later when a McNaught free kick was partially cleared, Evans caught it first time to curl the ball beyond Clemence. The referee was looking at his watch ready to blow for time when Dalglish positioned on the right of the Villa box somehow managed to thread the ball between defenders' legs and into the net.

Sat 29th November **Arsenal (H)**
Drew 1-1 **Att 30,140**
Morley

The Gunners were so defence conscious, England winger Rix almost partnered full-back Sansom. Saunders half-time talk must have been as brutal as the arctic conditions, his team came out and threatened to take the game by storm. Villa got their break when Morley fired them into a deserved lead. Mortimer, set up by Cowans watched on as his shot beat Jennings but thundered off the bar. Ten minutes after this let off Arsenal scored, a Sunderland cross was met by Talbot who steered the ball beyond Rimmer. Villa's lead at the top was cut to two points.

Sat 6th December — Middlesbrough (A)
Lost 1-2 — Att 15,721
Shaw

Villa did well to survive the most intense 45 minutes pressure they'd met this season. Their only chance fell to Cowans, beaten by Platt's bravery. The second-half was a different story. Geddis in for the suspended Withe was felled on the edge of the area, Morley's free kick deflected wide. Shaw saw a shot turned round the post and then Geddis tried his luck from 35-yards which skidded the wrong side of the upright. Johnston put Boro ahead on 83 mins but Shaw responded 60 seconds later. A goal for the hosts two minutes from time ensured Villa were knocked off top spot but level on points with Liverpool.

Sat 13th December — Birmingham City (H)
Won 3-0 — Att 41,101
Geddis 2, Shaw

Blues started the stronger and only after a Curbishley goalbound shot blocked by Cowans did Villa finally stir. Geddis still in the side had a dream 'derby.' He scored twice, the first as he raced on to a Mortimer through ball before slotting home and then squeezing a shot into the bottom corner from an Evans head down. The former Ipswich striker had a big hand in the second goal too, it was his shot that had Wealands beaten only to see the ball come back at pace off the upright, Shaw firing in the rebound. With Liverpool drawing 1-1 at Portman Road the Villa were back at the summit.

Sat 20th December — Brighton & Hove Albion (A)
Lost 0-1 — Att 16,429

Villa failed to compete with their usual tenacity and their casual and almost lethargic passing was their downfall. Even Brighton's goal on 15 minutes was handed to them on a plate, Swain's weak back-pass to Rimmer intercepted by Robinson, who fired in. Cowans was also having an uncustomary nightmare, he gave the ball away cheaply but Ritchie could only fire against the bar. To rub salt in Wolves had lost at Anfield!

Fri 26th December — Stoke City (H)
Won 1-0 — Att 34,658
Withe

Peter Withe marked his return from suspension with the only goal in a bruising Boxing Day encounter. Shaw and Withe tested Stoke's defence throughout against determined defending. Rimmer kept the visitors at bay with two outstanding saves. Late in the first half Villa were ahead, wizardry by Morley on the wing, the ball crossed in for Shaw to fire in, Fox parried but only as far as Withe who squeezed the ball home. Villa went all out for a second goal in the closing stages but couldn't muster one, they were still behind the leaders but only on goals scored. The goal difference was the same.

Sat 27th December — Nottingham Forest (A)
Drew 2-2 — Att 33,930
Own goal, Shaw

Villa started tremendously and were ahead on the quarter-of-an-hour. A Mortimer corner, Gunn swung his boot, the ball struck Larry Lloyd and in it went 1-0 to the Villa. Francis pulled one back for Forest just before half time. Shaw bagged his 16th of the season as Villa looked to be heading for a deserved victory. A freak deflection robbed Villa, Martin O'Neill was the villain of the piece as he made it 2-2.

[Right] Tony Morley being held by Forest's Viv Anderson

Sat 3rd January **Ipswich Town (A)** FA Cup 3rd round
Lost 0-1 **Att 27,721**

Villa were spared a drubbing thanks to the defiance of Evans and McNaught. Thijssen and Muhren were rampant in Town's midfield eclipsing Mortimer, Bremner and Cowans. Mariner scored the game's only goal in the 13th minute. Saunders claimed his side monopolised the second half, Cooper only had one save to make - with two minutes to go - when he had to gather a Cowans deflected free kick.

Sat 10th January **Liverpool (H) Won 2-0**
Att 47,960
Withe, Mortimer

This was the acid test to see if Ron's boys could make a valid claim for the title. For the first half hour Villa were quicker and more determined than the League leaders and it was during this spell that Scouser Withe fired Villa in front. Morley weaved past his marker slipped the ball to Shaw whose shot was palmed away by Clemence only as far as the bearded one. Liverpool applied pressure with Rimmer denying Kennedy, McDermott and Souness. Villa went further ahead on 82 minutes via Merseyside born captain Mortimer. Villa were back on top, a point clear of Ipswich.

Sat 17th January **Coventry City (A)**
Won 2-1 **Att 27,094**
Morley, Withe

There should have been goals in the first half, Morley clipping a post came the nearest. Villa's wideman sparked his side's supercharged start after the break setting up both Withe and Bremner with chances. Tony also saw a clever lob beat a defender who managed to clear at the second attempt. No surprise for guessing who broke the stalemate? He outsprinted the defence to shoot beyond Sealey. It was a Morley cross that Withe stooped to head home ten minutes later. Hateley scored a consolation for City.

[Left] Peter Withe on the ball at home to Manchester City

Sat 31st January **Manchester City (H)**
Won 1-0 **Att 33,683**
Shaw

With the game only minutes old Paul Power wilted under an Allan Evans challenge, his Corrigan bound header was too soft and Shaw honed in to jab the ball over the line. Villa were full of running but had to counter-attack at one stage as City won five corners in a two minute spell. Villa also cleared twice off the line. McNaught went off with a heavily strapped knee (eight stitches) on the hour but Bremner plugged the gap. On one occasion Des dived straight in front of Kevin Reeves, to deny a certain goal.

Sat 7th February **Everton (A)**
Won 3-1 **Att 31,480**
Morley, Mortimer, Cowans (pen)

With talk of Morley being dropped he had a point to prove. This he did, with three minutes on the clock Shaw fed Tony on the left almost on the half-way line, the winger took only four touches running at speed and cutting in before unleashing a rocket from the edge of the box into the top corner. This would be voted Goal of the Season. Everton levelled before Mortimer's 42nd minute effort regained the lead for the Villa. A Cowans penalty after Lyons had dragged Shaw back sealed the win, Villa remained second.

Sat 21st February **Crystal Palace (H)**
Won 2-1 **Att 27,203**
Withe 2

With Peter Withe scoring on four minutes it looked like the visitors, fielding a weakened side, were ripe for the picking. Unfortunately Villa struggled against bottom-placed Palace's 'let's-give-it-everything-we've-got' attitude. Withe took the sting out of the game with his second on 70 minutes but plucky Palace came straight back with a goal 60 seconds later through Hinshelwood. Picking points up on the back of poor performances is the mark of champions.

Sat 28th February **Wolverhampton Wanderers (A)**
Won 1-0 **Att 34,693**
Withe

Andy Gray battled furiously all afternoon in this reunion. With Rimmer beaten Gray blazed over from 10-yards out, his chance to win it gone! A Morley tackle on Daniel saw an ambulance summoned pitchside and the wrath of the crowd from that point on for the winger. Withe popped up to grab the decisive goal less than a minute later. The 83rd minute header, his 13th goal of the season. Ipswich boss Robson was quoted as being a 'little disappointed' with Villa's late winner.

Sat 7th March **Sunderland (A)**
Won 2-1 **Att 27,278**
Evans, Mortimer

The Villa had to survive a serious examination of their championship pedigree at Roker Park despite taking a first minute lead through Evans. A brilliant Cowans through-ball set up skipper Mortimer to thump in Villa's second. The Black Cats should have reduced the deficit shortly after but Bowyer headed over. The Roker Roar went up for the start of the second half and the hosts responded. Inspired by Stan Cummins they got a goal back, the midfielder was brought down, the free kick headed home by Hinnigan.

Sat 14th March **Manchester United (H)**
Drew 3-3 **Att 42,182**
Withe 2, Shaw

Playing their most attractive football of the season, Villa were two goals to the good at half-time. Both courtesy of their No 9, the first a header from Swain's cross, the second, turning deftly, to meet a ball helped on by Joe Jordan's head. Jordan then scored in the 46th and 66th minutes (both headers) to drag Utd level only for Shaw to restore Villa's lead two minutes later. With time almost up Coppell went over the leg of the prostrate Williams; McIlroy converted from 12-yards. "We went to sleep in certain areas and lost concentration," stated Ron Saunders.

Sat 21st March **Tottenham Hotspur (A)**
Lost 0-2 **Att 35,091**

Villa's ineffectiveness or the absence of the suspended Withe? Either way they slumped to defeat. Spurs went ahead through Crooks. A point blank miss by Geddis was then followed by a rare Cowans penalty miss. Sid held his head in his hands as the ball landed amongst the Villa crowd. When an acrobatic Archibald twisted and somersaulted to head past Rimmer it was painstakingly clear the Villa were going home empty handed. Ipswich's defeat at Old Trafford kept their lead at the top to a point. "Ipswich losing too cushions it a little bit, but doesn't alter the fact we didn't play" lamented Saunders.

Sat 28th March **Southampton (H)**
Won 2-1 **Att 32,467**
Morley, Geddis

Third-placed Southampton would prove a tough nut to crack, not helped when Evans put into his own net. It took a scoreboard announcement that Ipswich were trailing at home to for Villa to burst into life. A Cowans through ball was flicked on by Geddis into the path of an offside looking Morley who didn't hesitate. Despite McMenemy arguing, the goal stood. The celebrations hadn't subsided when Williams ran at length with the ball before slipping it to Geddis, the striker cut into the box before planting a stunning shot into the bottom corner. Ipswich won 4-1.

Sat 4th April **Leicester City (A)**
Won 4-2 **Att 26,032**
Withe 2, Bremner, Morley

City took a 15th minute lead through a Lynex penalty after McNaught had flattened Young. Defensive errors at the other end led to Villa

[Right] Kenny Swain running at the Spurs defence during Villa's defeat at White Hart Lane

Gary Williams, Tony Morley and Gary Shaw celebrate a goal against Southampton at Villa Park

taking a brief lead; Withe heading home a Cowans free kick and then Bremner popping up to score. Leicester equalised on the stroke of half time. Within four minutes of the second half Swain burst forward before putting an exquisite ball over for Withe to head home. Evans cleared off his own line before the game was finally put to bed when Morley made it 4-2 in the 55th minute. The Baggies had beaten Robson's outfit - Villa were back on top.

Wed 8th April **West Bromwich Albion (H)**
Won 1-0 **Att 47,998**
Withe

The main talking point - Geddis replaced Shaw. On a greasy pitch mistakes were inevitable, a Cowans back pass was sloppy but Villa went unpunished and within a minute a Regis header had Rimmer beaten but flashed just wide. Third placed Albion looked the livelier, Villa's strength was McNaught and Evans in defence and Withe was causing problems up front. The game suddenly changed with ten minutes remaining when Godden tipped away a Mortimer piledriver. Villa piled on the pressure, Batson misplaced his backpass, Withe stole in to scoop the ball over the advancing Godden. The victory put Villa three points above Ipswich.

Tue 14th April **Ipswich Town (H)**
Lost 1-2 **Att 47,495**

This was the big one! With only four minutes on the clock the visitors were in front. McNaught was caught with the ball at his feet waiting for Rimmer to come and collect, as time stood still Mariner didn't, he saw the opportunity, rushed in and stroked the ball home. Villa were more positive after the interval, Shaw and Withe had chances to level the game. A penalty appeal was turned down when Shaw went down from an Osman tackle. As Villa threatened again Ipswich countered through Mariner, he fed Gates who made no mistake. Shaw pulled one back with a brilliant volley but it counted for nothing.

Sat 18th April **Nottingham Forest (H)**
Won 2-0 **Att 34,707**
Cowans (pen), Withe

Villa's response - a resilient display. They should have had a penalty when a Morley centre was handled. With news that Arsenal were leading at Portman Road, Villa upped their game. Bremner was pushed in the box as he met Morley's centre. This time the ref pointed to the spot, cue Sid, who slotted the ball past Shilton. Into injury time, Morley breezed down the flank, picking out Withe to head home. This was the fifth time the team had responded with a win following defeat. Ipswich had lost; the gap at the top was back to three points.

Mon 20th April **Stoke City (A)**
Drew 1-1 **Att 23,537**
Withe

Allan Evans was back following suspension. Withe settled Villa nerves when he headed home Mortimer's free-kick. Stoke's defenders caused Villa concern from set pieces - they equalised via a corner. Shaw missed an early second-half chance and was replaced by Deacy. With Ipswich's defeat at Norwich the point gained took Villa a step nearer to the title, a fact not lost on Bobby Robson, "The only way we can win the championship now is if Villa do what we did and give it away. We are four points behind with only one game in hand"

Sat 25th April **Middlesbrough (H)**
Won 3-0 **Att 38,018**
Shaw, Withe, Evans

Villa put on a show, with wave after wave of attack it was surprising it took til the 23rd minute to get ahead. Gibson's free-kick was headed on by Evans to Withe who fired across goal for Shaw to lash in. Six minutes into the second period Villa doubled their lead. Cowans turned the ball to Morley who centred for the No 9 to nod

2
3
4
5
6
7
8
9
10

in. Evans rounded off the scoring when he fired home a Mortimer corner. Boro a bogey team over the years had been well and truly battered. Ipswich beat Man City.

Sat 2nd May **Arsenal (A)**
Lost 0-2 **Att 57,472**

Villa started brightly though The Gunners took the lead through Young. This led to unrest among Villa fans. Peter Nicholas was running the midfield, Mortimer and Cowans having an uncustomary off day. Whilst Evans and McNaught were up field for a corner Villa were caught short when Jennings punched the set-piece to Nicholas who promptly fed McDermott. He evaded Swain and Gibson before scoring. Villa were more determined after the break though their first shot on target - 71 minutes! The home side held out and won the battle but Villa had won the war. Their first title since 1910!

[Left] The Clock End, Highbury, with celebrating Villa fans being (unsuccessfully) held back by the Metropolitan Police – their team may have lost the match, but they had won the title

PRE-SEASON

• Centre-forward Peter Withe arrives from Newcastle United. His £500,000 fee a new club record. The last piece of the jigsaw according to Ron Saunders.
• Peter Withe (in claret and blue for the first time) is on target in the 1-0 win over Second Division German side FC Bocholt in Dusseldorf as Villa open their three match pre-season tour of Germany.

AUGUST

• Villa lose at Nuremburg in temperatures reaching 93. Two down at the break, Morley scores in the 1-2 loss.
• Villa round off their pre-season games when they host VFL Bochum at B6. Villa win 2-1 with Morley and Shaw scoring, defender Williams is stretchered off.
• Gordon Cowans is described by Ipswich Town and future England manager Bobby Robson as, "the nearest to perfect midfield all-rounder in the country." High praise indeed.
• Aston Villa kick-off the new season in fine style with a 2-1 victory at Elland Road.
• Three wins and a draw give the Villa their best post-war start to a season.

SEPTEMBER

• Villa start the month poorly with back-to-back defeats against Ipswich and Everton. It is the only time this campaign that it will occur.
• Transfer listed Alex Cropley and Gary Shelton both feature for the reserves in the Central League match with Derby County.
• David Geddis grabs a Central League hat-trick at Huddersfield.
• Second Division Cambridge United knock Villa out of the League Cup at the second round stage. Utd disposed of holders Wolves in the previous round.
• The Villa's youngsters start the defence of their Southern Junior Floodlit Cup with a 2-0 win over Oxford United.

OCTOBER

• Coming back from a goal down at home to Brighton & Hove Albion, Villa sit proudly at the top of the table. Exactly 48 years to the night they were last in that position!
•Of the club's six fixtures during the month, Villa win five and draw one.
• For the Central League fixture with Sheff Utd, Villa field 10 players with first-team experience.
•Colchester United are beaten 3-0 in the F.A. Youth Cup. Paul Birch is on target.
• Saunders is voted 'Manager of the Month.'

NOVEMBER

• Eamonn Deacy dislocates his left shoulder in the home fixture versus Leicester City.
• Villa's youth side fight out a goalless draw at Fulham in the SJFC. Brian McClair (later of Man Utd) stands out in claret and blue.
• A strong Aston Villa side (Poole, Bremner, Swain, Withe, McNaught, Blake) win the prestigious Daily Express Five-A-Side competition at Wembley Arena. Spurs (2-0) and Man Utd (2-0) are seen off before Arsenal are thumped 7-1 in the semi. Geoff Hurst's Chelsea are beaten 3-0 in the final. Swain scores in every game.
• Apprentice Mark Walters is invited to train with the England Youth set-up at Lilleshall.
• Midfielders Mortimer and Cowans are selected for the England B

squad for the Australia match at St Andrews.

• Mortimer is captain on the night as England B win 1-0, Cowans and Morley are also on duty.

DECEMBER

• Peter Withe receives a three match ban. He misses the Boro, Blues and Brighton matches.

• Mark Walters, a name for the future, scores two as Villa overcome Sheffield United 3-2 in the F.A. Youth Cup. The teams had drawn 2-2 at Bramall Lane five days earlier.

• End of the line in the F.A. Youth Cup. Walters put Villa ahead at Shrewsbury but Keith Leonard's young charges lose 1-3. Dean Glover was sent off in the ill-tempered match.

JANUARY

• A new electronic scoreboard arrives at Villa Park to replace the old one used since 1946 (where the numbers were slotted next to letters).

• Despite what is described as one of their best performances so far the Villa go out of the F.A. Cup at the first hurdle away to Ipswich. A blessing in disguise perhaps?

• Villa go top, jumping above Liverpool after beating them 2-0 at Villa Park. Not quite the same 5-1 scoreline from 1976/77 but equally emphatic!

• Centre-half McNaught suffered a badly gashed knee in the Man City home win. The Scot was back in the side the following weekend and would end up as one of seven ever presents over the campaign.

[Left] Peter Withe collects his 5th booking of the season during the home draw with Leeds United. Captain Dennis Mortimer tries to calm him down.

FEBRUARY

- Tony Morley so close to being dropped from the Goodison Park encounter set Villa on their way to a fine 3-1 win. His goal is voted 'Goal of the Season.'
- On the 2-1 win at home to Crystal Palace Saunders said, "Considering all the walking wounded I am delighted with the result."
- The Villa fielding the same 11 (with Williams back) win all three games played in the month, just as well because Robson's Ipswich Town do likewise.
- Peter Withe is named 'Sports Argus Player of the Month.'

MARCH

- Flu-ridden boss Saunders misses out on the trip to the north east as Villa win at Sunderland's Roker Park. It's the team's seventh straight successive victory. McNaught left the field with a suspected broken ankle, it was later learned it was ligament damage.
- Villa took to the field at home to Manchester United looking to equal the club's post-war record of eight consecutive league victories (achieved 1974/75). The game ended up all square, 3-3.
- Withe sits out the White Hart Lane encounter due to his latest suspension. He watches from the dugout.
- Mortimer (groin) and Shaw (hamstring) withdrawn from England B party for the match against Spain in Granada.

APRIL

- A shocked Gary Shaw is dropped for the Albion encounter. "He's struggled with his stamina and it would not be in his or the team's best interests to ask any more of him at this stage," was Saunders statement to the media.
- Following a 1-2 defeat at home to nearest title rivals Ipswich Town boss Ron Saunders comes out with the immortal line, "Does anyone want to bet against us?"
- Villa take a hard fought point at Stoke while Ipswich lose at local rivals Norwich. "From now on it's all about 11 men grafting as hard as they possibly can. We are top for one reason – we work for each other" said Saunders as the gap at the top stretched to four points, Town with only one game in hand.
- Saunders receives the Evening Mail's 'Sports Personality of the Month' award.

MAY

- Over seventy coaches are organised by the Villa Travel Club for the Highbury clincher.
- On the day of the decider the Brazilian Pele is paraded before the bumper crowd, no doubt reminded of Villa's fanatical support having seen it first hand at B6 with his travelling Santos side.
- After initially early pressure Villa fell away to two first-half goals that they failed to recover from. It was enough to land the coveted First Division title as Ipswich Town crashed 1-2 at Ayresome Park. Boro's Bosko Jankovic becoming a cult hero around B6 scoring both goals.
- Peter Withe plays for England in the 0-0 draw with Wales at Wembley.

[Right] More celebratory scenes at Highbury, Villa's first title win in 71 years

POSTSCRIPT

• Villa land the championship trophy having used only 14 players, seven of which are ever presents, Rimmer, Swain, McNaught, Mortimer, Bremner, Cowans and Morley, Shaw missed only two while Evans missed three.

• On summing up the season 'Manager of the Year' Ron Saunders claimed, "Winning the championship is all about consistency over the whole of the 42 games. We won 26 matches so anyone who says we don't deserve the title does not know what they are talking about,"

• Gary Shaw is voted 'Young Player of the Year' by the Professional Footballers' Association. Centre-half Allan Evans and right-back

Kenny Swain were named alongside Shaw in the 'Best First Division Side' by fellow players. Dennis Mortimer lands the 'Sportsco-Sports Argus Man of the Match awards for the 1980/81 season.

• In excess of 100,000 supporters turn out to salute the Aston Villa team as they make their way through the City Centre en route to a civic reception. As they stood on the Town Hall balcony Kenny Swain stated, "Now I know what the Beatles felt like."

[Left] Villa players celebrate winning the title in the Highbury dressing room [Right] Open top bus ride around Birmingham with the First Division trophy held by Mike Pejic and Tony Morley

[Left] Ron Saunders and the team arrive at the Council House [Above] The start of 1981-82 season and the scoreboard says it all

[Right] Villa and Spurs share the Charity Shield

1981-82

[Back Row] Eamonn Deacy, Jimmy Rimmer, Ken McNaught, Nigel Spink, Allan Evans [Middle Row] Jim Williams (Physiotherapist), Des Bremner, Gary Williams, Robert Hopkins, Brendan Ormsby, Colin Gibson, Gordon Cowans, Roy MacLaren (Coach) [Front Row] Tony Morley, David Geddis, Dennis Mortimer, Ron Saunders (Manager), Kenny Swain, Peter Withe, Gary Shaw.

Football League	Division One
Manager	Ron Saunders/Tony Barton
Coach	Roy MacLaren
Physio	Jim Williams
Captain	Dennis Mortimer
Final Position	Eleventh
F.A. Cup	Fifth Round
League Cup	Fifth Round
Leading Goalscorer	Peter Withe 17 goals (inc Charity Shield)

The only new signing was the arrival of Andy Blair from Coventry City. Villa got the campaign underway, held to a 2-2 Wembley draw with Tottenham Hotspur in the Charity Shield. The League season didn't start as the Champions had hoped, humiliated at home by newly promoted Notts County. Villa then lost at Sunderland, the first time since 1969/70 they'd lost the opening two fixtures. A win was followed by six consecutive League draws, though Villa had seen off FC Valur 7-0 on agg to negotiate the first hurdle of the European Cup. Now with 3 points for a win Villa had already lost ground as they languished in 16th position.

Late October proved kind for the Villa, they progressed against Wolves in the League Cup, gained back-to-back League victories and had returned from Dynamo Berlin with a valuable 2-1 win. They would finish that particular job in the opening week of November though they lost to the East German outfit 0-1 at home.

Aston Villa would see the New Year in with a resounding 6-0 win at Notts County (a Geddis hat-trick) in the F.A. Cup Third Round. With the postponement of the Sunderland home game Villa's next fixture was back at Meadow Lane for the League encounter, Villa lost 0-1! Four days later WBA won 1-0 at Aston to end Villa's League Cup interest.

Three days after Villa had gone down 1-4 at Old Trafford Ron Saunders walked out of the club, backroom politics at play. The official line - Saunders had terminated his contract. Tony Barton was handed the reins as caretaker manager. Within nine days Saunders would take up the manager's job at rivals Birmingham City.

continued >>>

Total Home League Attendances 562,388
Average Home League 26,780
Highest Home League 41,098
Lowest Home League 19.916

		P	W	D	L	GF	GA	DIF	PTS
1	Liverpool	42	26	9	7	80	32	48	87
2	Ipswich Town	42	26	5	11	75	53	22	83
3	Manchester United	42	22	12	8	59	29	30	78
4	Tottenham Hotspur	42	20	11	11	67	48	19	71
5	Arsenal	42	20	11	11	48	37	11	71
6	Swansea City	42	21	6	15	58	51	7	69
7	Southampton	42	19	9	14	72	67	5	66
8	Everton	42	17	13	12	56	50	6	64
9	West Ham United	42	14	16	12	66	57	9	58
10	Manchester City	42	15	13	14	49	50	-1	58
11	Aston Villa	42	15	12	15	55	53	2	57
12	Nottingham Forest	42	15	12	15	42	48	-6	57
13	Brighton & Hove Albion	42	13	13	16	43	52	-9	52
14	Coventry City	42	13	11	18	56	62	-6	50
15	Notts County	42	13	8	21	61	69	-8	47
16	Birmingham City	42	10	14	18	53	61	-8	44
17	West Bromwich Albion	42	11	11	20	46	57	-11	44
18	Stoke City	42	12	8	22	44	63	-19	44
19	Sunderland	42	11	11	20	38	58	-20	44
20	Leeds United	42	10	12	20	39	61	-22	42
21	Wolverhampton Wanderers	42	10	10	22	32	63	-31	40
22	Middlesbrough	42	8	15	19	34	52	-18	39

White Hart Lane was the end of the line where the F.A. Cup was concerned but late February/mid-March proved particularly productive for the Villa; back-to-back wins lifted them in the table while Dynamo Kiev were eliminated over the two legs 2-0 on agg.

Seven goals were shipped over two away defeats before Villa came back from a goal down to defeat Albion on home turf. The victory raised morale for the forthcoming European Cup semi-final first leg, a Tony Morley goal put Villa in the driving seat. Three consecutive League wins propelled the side to twelfth and the momentum continued with an all-important 0-0 draw in Brussels, Villa were in the Final!

With one eye on Rotterdam the season ran down with mixed results. Leeds took the points in a 4-1 win at B6, WBA were beaten at the Hawthorns whilst high flying Swansea City were comprehensively turned over 3-0, five days before the showdown with the crack German outfit Bayern Munich.

On a balmy evening in Holland's busy shipping port Aston Villa, in their change kit of all white, put on a show Real Madrid would have been proud of. A young lad by the name of Nigel Spink became a man. Villa only scored one - via the shin of their No 9 Peter Withe, it was enough!

1981-82

Sat 22nd Aug **Tottenham Hotspur (Wembley)** **Charity Shield**
Drew 2-2 **Att 92,500**
Withe 2

Spurs pairing of Ardiles and Villa were pulling the strings in midfield yet Aston Villa found their feet and took the lead. Ray Clemence fumbled a Morley corner and Withe fired in from close range. Spurs then had Villa on the back foot and levelled through Falco. The same player put Spurs ahead when he met a cross and lashed it in with his left foot. New boy Blair and Gibson combined to set Morley up, the winger's centre was met superbly by Withe who nodded it in.

Sat 29th Aug **Notts County (H)**
Lost 0-1 **Att 30,097**

The afternoon started with Villa parading the coveted League title trophy and Charity Shield, it ended with the players walking off the pitch dejectedly following a crushing 0-1 defeat at the hands of newly promoted County. In fairness luck wasn't on Villa's side, Morley saw a shot ricochet off the crossbar on six minutes, McNaught hobbled off only three minutes later and then at the other end they conceded a goal best described as sloppy.

Wed 2nd Sep **Sunderland (A)**
Lost 1-2 **Att 29,372**
Donovan

Villa were without McNaught, Shaw and Geddis, Terry Donovan and Brendan Ormsby drafted in. Donovan put Villa ahead on 23 minutes. Villa appeared vulnerable in the aerial duels - Clarke rose to head on a free kick for Ritchie to equalise nine minutes before the break. Two minutes after the interval the hosts took the lead. Rimmer parried a Ritchie header only as far as Rowell. Villa are finding out defending the title may well be more difficult than winning it?

Sat 5th Sep **Tottenham Hotspur (A)**
Won 3-1 **Att 31,265**
Donovan 2, Mortimer

Villa's championship form returned with a vengeance as the side played with control and composure. Colin Gibson celebrating his England U-21 call up outpaced Spurs defence before slipping the ball to Donovan to stab home. Villa added to their tally when a Morley corner was helped on by Withe, Mortimer caught the ball perfectly to send a thunderous volley beyond Clemence. On the stroke of half time Morley and Withe did well to set Gibson away down the flank, the full-back crossed perfectly for Donovan to add his second. Spurs pulled one back but the damage was already done.

Sat 12th Sep **Manchester United (H)**
Drew 1-1 **Att 37,661**
Cowans

Villa flew out of the traps. United had no answer as a Mortimer first-time shot sailed over the bar, Donovan's audacious overhead kick struck a post while Withe saw his shot saved brilliantly. Villa broke the deadlock when McQueen failed to cut out a cross, Withe laid it on for Cowans who cracked it in with confidence. Stapleton tapped in from close range to equalise five minutes before the break. In the second half Albiston wrapped his arms around Donovan's neck, everybody saw it, apart from the referee. United had got out of jail, even their boss Atkinson agreed his side were fortunate.

Wed 16th Sep **FC Valur Reykjavik (H)** **European Cup 1st round 1st leg**
Won 5-0 **Att 20,481**
Morley, Withe 2, Donovan 2

Villa comfortably saw off the threat from the brave amateurs from Iceland. They were one-up after only six minutes, Morley fired in low to beat Haraldsson's dive. Fans had to wait half an hour to then see two goals in a three minute spell, Withe and Donovan ensuring Villa held a 3-0 advantage at the interval. Withe put his side four up on 67 minutes and Donovan added his second two minutes later. Villa could have been into double figures but for wayward finishing.

Sat 19th Sep **Liverpool (A)**
Drew 0-0 **Att 37,474**

McNaught was back in the side. Villa battled every inch of the way, showing the desire, and hunger from last year. Jimmy Rimmer also played his part, making valuable first-half saves from Neal, Hanson and McDermott. Grobbelaar was equally as busy keeping Withe, Morley and Donovan from breaking the deadlock. Evans who'd cleared two efforts off his own line and booked for a challenge on Dalglish was the victim of a late Ray Kennedy assault which saw the Reds player sent off.

Wed 23rd Sep **Stoke City (H)**
Drew 2-2 **Att 25,637**
Withe 2

Neither side could find a rhythm in a match interrupted constantly by free-kicks. Stoke came close then Cowans had a shot turned round the upright by Fox. Villa finally got their noses in front due to yet another Stoke foul, Mortimer's lofted free kick was met by Withe who outjumped the goalie to head home. Within 29 seconds of the second half Peter made it two-nil, his first shot was blocked but he followed through to slam in the loose ball. Stoke hit back on 64 minutes and moments later made it 2-2 via a penalty after McNaught had handled.

Sat 26th Sep **Birmingham City (H)**
Drew 0-0 **Att 41,098**

With Shaw, Geddis and Donovan all injured Cowans was played up front. This nearly paid dividends when Sid was put through but shot wide. It was one of Villa's first chances as they'd been on the back foot for long periods. Rimmer had saved Villa after only four minutes, Evans fouled Gemmill but the keeper blocked the goal-

The Enfield
EACH WEEK
TELEPHONE
807 7001
FOR FULL DETAILS

bound drive following a cleverly worked free kick. Blair who had a fine game tested their keeper, shortly after Villa had a spot-kick appeal turned down when Cowans was sent sprawling in the area.

Wed 30th Sep **FC Valur Reykjavik (A)** European Cup 1st round 2nd leg
Won 2-0 **Att 3,500**
Shaw 2

Gary Shaw was back, out since playing in Villa's pre-season games in Greece. Valur had only been beaten at home once in European competition. A Mortimer free-kick found the blonde striker who struck on 24 minutes. Shaw also saw efforts thud against the woodwork and cleared off the line by Sveinsson before he added his second. He collected a loose ball before calmly bending it beyond Haraldsson. Rimmer had only one save to make the entire match while Andy Blair in midfield had a stormer!

Sat 3rd Oct **Leeds United (A)**
Drew 1-1 **Att 21,065**
Shaw

The game was only eight minutes old when a Shaw drive took a deflection to put Villa one-up. Bottom placed Leeds offered little and Villa's dominance reached embarrassing proportions. United levelled on 62 minutes in a game which saw six bookings yet Withe, Cherry and Hart - the guiltiest - stayed out of the book. Shaw who felt twinges during the game was replaced by Morley. With three points for a win this fifth successive draw meant Villa were nine points behind leaders Ipswich. Saunders backed skipper Dennis who said Villa had thrown it away!

[Left] Dennis Mortimer (almost hidden) scores to put Villa two goals up during the 3-1 win at White Hart Lane

Wed 7th Oct **Wolverhampton Wanderers (H)** League Cup 2nd round 1st leg
Won 3-2 **Att 26,353**
Bremner, Blair, Morley

Andy Gray once the darling of the Holte Enders, back in his first game at B6, gave Wolves a 1-0 lead. It could have been so different had Bremner's shot not been cleared off the line. Early in the second half Gray was sent off for a lunging tackle on Mortimer. Despite this Wolves doubled their advantage moments later but tempers flared as Rimmer was fouled by Richards. Villa then hit two goals in a three minute spell, Bremner scoring our first, an Andy Blair volley brought about an equaliser. Morley scrambled Villa in front deep into injury time.

Sat 10th Oct **Coventry City (A)**
Drew 1-1 **Att 16,306**
Shaw

Geddis was back in the starting XI for the first time since the opening day loss. Rimmer was doubtful with a shoulder injury. Villa still struggling to recapture their form of last season went in front through Shaw,against the run of play. They then had chances to take command of the game but didn't take them, they missed the leadership qualities of Withe. In the end they were lucky to take a point, Rimmer was all that stood between Villa and an overwhelming defeat, saving from Jacobs, Whitton, Thompson and then Hateley.

Sat 17th Oct **West Ham United (H)**
Won 3-2 **Att 32,064**
Morley, Geddis, Mortimer

Villa trailed Ipswich by 11 points and fourth placed WHU by eight points. The Hammers were the only side unbeaten on the road and it looked set to continue when they scored early on. Villa were then helped by keeper McAlister; out of position as Morley fired in from a Mortimer free kick, and then an innocuous Mortimer shot rolled between his legs and Geddis stole in to nudge it over the line. Dennis did get his name on the scoresheet as he hooked home Villa's third. West Ham pulled one back but the points belonged to the hosts.

Wed 21st Oct **Dynamo Berlin (A)** European Cup 2nd round 1st leg
Won 2-1 **Att 25,000**
Morley 2

A two goal salvo from winger Morley stunned the East Germans. A superbly struck volley by Tony, coupled with an Ormsby goal-line clearance gave Villa a half-time advantage. A Hans-Jurgen Riediger header left Rimmer helpless. In the 68th minute sub Ivor Linton conceded a penalty. Ullrich's spot-kick came back off the post and struck Rimmer's foot keeping the ball active, the rebound was kept out by Jimmy and the ball looped over the bar. In the closing stages Morley picked up a headed Withe clearance following a Dynamo corner, ran the entire length of the pitch before slotting home.

Sat 24th Oct **Wolverhampton Wanderers (A)**
Won 3-0 **Att 19,942**
Shaw 2, own goal

Withe was back. Wolves without Gray and Hibbitt had Villa defending in numbers for the first half hour. Rimmer did well to keep a clean sheet. Villa then created a goal from nothing, Morley fed Withe who cheekily back-heeled into the path of Shaw who drilled it into the bottom corner. A minute before the break it was 2-0 to the visitors when a Shaw back-header was turned in by defender Palmer. Shaw bagged his sixth in five games, two minutes into the second half. Villa unbeaten in 13.

Tue 27th Oct **Wolverhampton Wanderers (A)** League Cup 2nd round 2nd leg
Won 2-1 **Att 19,491**
Cowans 2 (1 pen)

The opening goal, which put Villa two-up on aggregate, was well worked, Shaw chested the ball down to Sid who cut inside Carr before executing a superb right-footed chip over Bradshaw. Withe later had the ball in the net but it was disallowed for handball. Wolves had a few chances before they fashioned an equaliser on 73 minutes through sub Richards. A Cowans penalty 90 seconds from the end restored Villa's advantage after Morley had been sent tumbling.

[Above] Dennis Mortimer storms past Ipwich Town's Terry Butcher during the defeat at Villa Park

Sat 31st Oct **Ipswich Town (H)**
Lost 0-1 **Att 32,652**

The match was only nine minutes old when Ormsby conceded a corner, Muhren floated it over and the unchallenged Osman glanced his header beyond Rimmer. Villa had suffered defeat at the hands of Town in last season's Villa Park encounter due to defensive errors. Villa held territorial advantage over their opponents for much of the game yet failed to test Cooper in goal – not one shot on target! The nearest, a Shaw header which flashed marginally wide.

Wed 4th Nov **Dynamo Berlin (H)** **European Cup 2nd round 2nd leg**
Lost 0-1 **Att 28,175**

Anxious to put their first defeat in 15 to bed the Villa started well and tested 6' 7" keeper Rudwaleit, Morley was foiled with two attempts. Sid Cowans was also denied by the goalie's lightning quick reflexes. Kenny Swain blocked a Schultz shot on the line but the Villa defence were unable to prevent the impressive Riediger from supplying a telling cross which Frank Terletzki put away with confidence. Villa came back, a Williams header cleared on the line and a Shaw effort ruled out, offside. With Dynamo sneaking the 1-0 win Villa had made it through the tie by virtue of the away goal.

Sat 7th Nov **Arsenal (H)**
Lost 0-2 **Att 27,316**

Williams replaced Ormsby. With only one league win at home supporters openly criticised the team following what was their worst performance thus far. Jennings was called on once, to stop Colin Gibson shooting Villa in front. The game changer was when Rix put Arsenal ahead. From then on it was all the visitors, a second goal followed before the half-time whistle, Talbot firing in at the near post. Villa had no answer. The press had a field day calling them 'one season wonders!'

Wed 11th Nov **Leicester City (A)** **League Cup 3rd round**
Drew 0-0 **Att 19,806**

Villa without a goal in three games were put under the cosh against their Second Division opponents. Leicester went all out to get an early goal, a Melrose shot lacked power and when the same player slipped the ball under Rimmer, Gibson was on hand to boot the ball clear. Villa's first threat, close to the break, was superbly crafted, involving Swain, Withe and Cowans, ending when Sid's close range shot was blocked well by Wallington. Gibson denied Lineker a minute into the second half. At least Saunders side had lived to fight another day!

Sat 21st Nov **Middlesbrough (A)**
Drew 3-3 **Att 12,522**
Own goal, Cowans, Shaw

Eamonn Deacy started his first game since February. Both sides attacked from the start. Villa took the lead when Peter Withe's shot struck McAndrew on the way in. The Boro player redeemed himself when he fired in a (disputed) penalty after Ross had been fouled (outside the area). Cowans fired Villa into the lead on the hour and Shaw made it 3-1 four minutes later. Ashcroft pulled two back to make it 3-3. Further goals were averted only by the heroics of Platt and Rimmer in what the newspapers claimed was a sparkling match.

Wed 25th Nov **Leicester City (H)** **League Cup 3rd round replay**
Won 2-0 **Att 23,136**
Cowans (pen), Withe

Mortimer was still out injured so Deacy remained in the side. Eamonn was booked for a challenge on Lineker before he himself was brought down for a penalty in the 16th minute, Gordon Cowans from the spot 1-0. Chances were missed by both sides before Withe put Villa firmly in the driving seat when he found himself unmarked and nodded in Gibson's cross from the left. Wallington showed what an outstanding keeper he was as he kept Withe, Shaw and Morley at bay.

Sat 28th Nov **Nottingham Forest (H)**
Won 3-1 **Att 26,847**
Bremner 2, Withe

Clough's Forest were sitting fifth, ten positions and ten points higher than the hosts yet the form book was turned on its head as Villa finally reproduced their title winning form. Villa Park was brought back to life as the fans roared their approval on what was a flawless display. Bremner started the ball rolling when he fired in an angled shot on six minutes, his second a low drive through a crowd of players after Shilton had parried Cowans free kick. Forest reduced the deficit but the two goal cushion was restored when Withe scored.

Tue 1st Dec **Wigan Athletic (A)** **League Cup 4th round**
Won 2-1 **Att 15,362**
Cowans (pen), Withe

Fourth Division Wigan were up for it. Villa gave them respect, playing the same starting XI that beat Forest. Before the visitors could settle into a rhythm the home side were in front. Peter Houghton scored with a delicate lob from outside the box. Saunders side were visibly rocked and were still trailing at the break. Shaw won a penalty on 55 minutes which Cowans put away with ease. A Shaw strike 10 minutes from time struck the Wigan keeper and Withe pounced to hit it home from all of three yards out.

Sat 5th Dec **Manchester City (A)**
Lost 0-1 **Att 32,487**

Despite a shaky start Villa fought magnificently, Corrigan did well to deal with a stinging shot from Morley. The keeper then parried a Shaw shot and ex-Villan Bobby McDonald had to deal with it before the striker got to the rebound. Rimmer was well protected by Evans and Williams as Corrigan had to deal with shots from Cowans and Evans. City went ahead through Tueart but the Villa players weren't happy. In the build up the ref allowed the hosts to take a quick free kick even though Bremner was laid prone on the half-way line having clashed heads with teammate Gary Williams.

Tue 15th Dec **Swansea City (A)**
Lost 1-2 **Att 15,191**
Own goal

Withe was suspended so Geddis led the line. The Swans were in front with only a dozen minutes on the clock, a headed goal by Robbie James. The lead was short lived, Villa were level within two minutes, Thompson attempted to clear Gibson's low hard cross but only succeeded in turning the ball beyond Dai Davies. The Welsh side immediately hit back forcing two splendid saves. Villa under continuous pressure fell behind again James bagging his second of the night. Linton replaced Deacy mid way through the second half, it was Ivor's last appearance.

Sat 19th Dec **Everton (A)**
Lost 0-2 **Att 16,544**

Villa went into the game two points above the drop zone. Terry Bullivant, Noel Blake and Donovan all started as Saunders attempted to shake things up. It failed miserably, Villa put up a wretched performance. Then the inevitable happened when Lyons totally unchallenged headed home from a corner. Villa chances were few and far between and weren't helped when Geddis and Donovan repeatedly chased the same ball. The only surprise of the afternoon was it took Everton until the 89th minute to score their second.

Mon 28th Dec **Brighton & Hove Albion (A)**
Won 1-0 **Att 24,259**
Morley

Mortimer was back having missed the last eight. Brighton started the better but couldn't find a way through Villa's rugged defence, the partnership of Evans and Williams excelling. Villa took the lead just after the hour, Bremner crossed from the right, Geddis miskicked but Morley didn't, smashing the ball home. Albion were playing with centre-back Steve Foster (later to sign for Aston Villa) as a striker, he was unfortunate when he headed a Case cross against the crossbar. Saunders admitted his side had weathered the storm.

Wed 5th Jan **Notts County (A)** FA Cup 3rd round
Won 6-0 **Att 12,312**
Own goal, Shaw, Geddis 3, Cowans (pen)

County were behind with only 58 seconds on the clock, an own goal, Mair cleared his lines but the ball struck Richards, in it went. On nine minutes it was two when Geddis was instrumental in the build up that resulted in a tap in for Shaw. On the half hour Geddis rose to make it 3-0. Four minutes later a Gibson cross was only half cleared and Geddis pounced to get his second of the evening. The hat-trick was realised in the 69th minute after impressive work between Morley and Shaw. Cowans made it six when he fired home from the penalty spot.

Sat 16th Jan **Notts County (A)**
Lost 0-1 **Att 9,590**

Withe was back, three goal hero Geddis was out. Villa boss Saunders was horrified the game even went ahead, he would be even more shocked at the final whistle. Neither side had a chance to display any skill, it took all the players' efforts to remain upright. Avramovic made two fine saves but control became more difficult as the game wore on. Trevor Christie stunned Villa with his late goal when he met Masson's corner.

Wed 20th Jan **West Bromwich Albion (H)** League Cup 5th round
Lost 0-1 **Att 35,197**

The game opened at a frenetic pace. Robertson was carded only three minutes in when he flattened Mortimer. Shaw 21 today should have put Villa ahead but squandered a glorious chance, slicing wide with only Grew to beat. Statham put Albion in front just after the half hour. Tony Morley never came back out after the break nor was there any sign of the sub, Morley had received his marching orders in the tunnel for swearing at a linesman, remonstrating as Albion had handled twice in their own area and gone unpunished both times.

Sat 23rd Jan **Bristol City (A)**
Won 1-0 **Att 20,279**
Shaw

City were lively but the visitors containment policy whilst not pretty, was effective. Withe, Shaw and Morley were all off form, the bearded No 9 did see his side's best chance fly over the bar. City also carved out openings. After the break Villa upped the tempo and Blair had the ball in the net only to see it chalked off, Cowans offside. Late on the deadlock was broken, a Cowans corner was met by Shaw, he hit the ball firmly and the keeper seemed to have it covered but it struck an outstretched leg and diverted the ball into the opposite corner.

Sat 30th Jan **Liverpool (H)**
Lost 0-3 **Att 35,947**

Villa were simply battered. Ian Rush struck on three minutes and it was 2-0 only 20 minutes later through McDermott. Villa came out for the second half and put Liverpool on the back foot for 10 minutes or so, in this time a Cowans strike was close, and then Bremner's first-time snap-shot went narrowly wide. Blair came on for Williams. Once the Reds had weathered the storm they grew in stature, a third followed (McDermott) with quarter of an hour remaining. Villa sat 17th three points above the drop.

Tue 2nd Feb **Sunderland (H)**
Won 1-0 **Att 19,916**
Geddis

Dropping Morley (one paper described as 'erratic') meant the inclusion of Gary Shelton. Bremner was moved to a back four place. This was further exasperated when the ever-present left-back Colin Gibson had to go off injured. Villa got their noses in front in the 51st minute, Withe headed on a Bullivant cross for Geddis to lash in right-footed. It could have been his second of the night as moments earlier he was forced to shoot wide by keeper Barry Siddell. Villa made heavy work of it though Bremner was superb in filling in.

Sat 6th Feb **Manchester United (A)**
Lost 1-4 **Att 43,184**
Geddis

Villa went into this fixture without a win at United's ground since 1954, a run of 19 games. Playing Withe and Geddis upfront Villa snatched an early lead through the latter. Bailey had no chance with the stunning drive. United's reply came in first-half stoppage time. Villa totally capitulated after the interval; Bryan Robson put the hosts in front. Only three minutes later Coppell made it 3-1. Hard-working Geddis went close with two half chances, Withe was described in one report as totally ineffective. A Moran headed rounded off the scoreline.

Wed 10th Feb **Southampton (H)**
Drew 1-1 **Att 24,287**
Withe

It was impossible to ignore the atmosphere inside Villa Park, created by yesterday's resignation by boss Saunders. Pro-Saunders chants rang out aimed at chairman Bendall. Villa playing their best football for months were causing unlikely division leaders Southampton great difficulty. A Geddis shot was scrambled away by the keeper's legs, Withe from six yards out lifted the ball over the bar. Even though the return of McNaught brought composure to the defence Saints snatched a lead through Keegan. Evans and Mortimer combined to set Withe away but the goalie saved bravely at the striker's feet. In the 67th minute a Bremner shot struck ex-Villa player Chris Nicholl and fell to Peter to score.

Sat 13th Feb **Tottenham Hotspur (A)** FA Cup 5th round
Lost 0-1 **Att 42,950**

Even though Spurs were buoyant Villa proved their equals. They played with style and spirit – Evans went close - and were only let down in the final third of the park. Withe and Geddis weren't mixing well. Rimmer pulled off two outstanding saves before a momentary lack of concentration in the Villa rearguard allowed Falco to head home. Tony Morley brought back in by caretaker manager Tony Barton was full of trickery and was denied by defenders' lunges or the coolness of Clemence.

Wed 17th Feb **Tottenham Hotspur (H)**
Drew 1-1 **Att 23,877**
Withe

Gary Shaw was back. Mortimer was unlucky not to give his side a lead, his volley flashed just the wrong side of the upright. Withe then through on goal mis-cued straight to Clemence. Right-back Swain played a beautiful ball over the Tottenham defenders but Shaw's on-target header was held by the goalkeeper. Villa piled on the pressure in the second 45 minutes but the Villa crowd was silenced when Spurs took the lead very much against the run of play. Within ten minutes Withe levelled the scores with a neat header.

Sat 20th Feb **Birmingham City (A)**
Won 1-0 **Att 32,817**
Withe

The match was never likely to be a classic and so it proved, though Villa threatened to tear City apart for the first 25 minutes but didn't. It was more a tough battle for possession and it took an error in the 57th minute to break the stalemate. A Morley pass lofted in the direction of Withe was missed by Geoff Scott, the player struggling due to an injury picked up moments earlier. Withe aware of the player's plight pounced at the opportunity and coolly fired past Jones in goal.

Sat 27th Feb **Coventry City (H)**
Won 2-1 **Att 24,474**
Cowans (pen), Shaw

The match was barely two minutes old when Garry Thompson gave City the lead. Mark Jones making his Villa debut made a fine run down the right, squared the ball to Bremner who played it to Shaw, as Gary met it he was pushed in the area. Cowans calmly

[Above] Des Bremner goes on a run watched by Tottenham's Garth Crooks during the F.A. Cup defeat at White Hart Lane

stroked the penalty home. A thundering 30-yarder was pushed onto the bar by Rimmer before Jones having a great day prduced a perfect cross for Withe to nod down for Shaw who drilled in a volley. Thompson was given his marching orders for kicking Evans.

Wed 3rd Mar **Dynamo Kiev (A)** **European Cup quarter-final 1st leg**
Drew 0-0 **Att 20,000**

Oleg Blokhin (later to become the USSR National Championship's all-time leading goalscorer with 211 goals) hit the post after just four minutes but any advantages Kiev had hoped for were torn from their grasp by the resourcefulness of Mortimer and Cowans in midfield. Villa were ruthless in the tackle against the Russians and remorseless in both attack and defence. Blokhin was well shackled by the centre-half pairing of McNaught and Bremner (for the injured Evans). Yevushenko had the ball in the net but it was ruled out for offside.

Sat 6th Mar **West Ham United (A)**
Drew 2-2 **Att 26,894**
Cowans, Withe

Blair remained in midfield, Bremner playing deeper. Villa started in style and went deservedly ahead on 17 minutes through a Cowans goal. He seized on a mistake played a one-two with Peter Withe and then ran through to beat the goalie. Brooking was judged to have been fouled by Bremner, Stewart scored from the spot. Villa were trailing seven minutes into the second half when Van Der Elst headed home. Villa upped the tempo and were back on terms when Blair rolled a pass to Shaw, he crossed and Withe did the rest with his trusty head.

Sat 13th Mar **Wolverhampton Wanderers (H)**
Won 3-1 **Att 26,790**
Donovan, Morley, Shaw

Villa improving by the week were aided by clumsy Wolves defending. A shot by Shaw struck Parkin, instead of putting it into the stands he hesitated and Donovan rushed in to jab it over the line. Morley added a second 11 minutes later. Wayne Clarke's goal saw Villa lead at the interval 2-1. Gary Shaw added a third for the Villa to the delight of the Holte Enders, it was only his second at home yet he'd notched up nine on his travels.

Wed 17th Mar **Dynamo Kiev (H)** **European Cup quarter-final 2nd leg**
Won 2-0 **Att 38,579**
Shaw, McNaught

The Villa were rampant from the start – Shaw was on target four minutes in; McNaught's free-kick was hoisted into the area, Withe chested to Cowans, he found Gary who waltzed past three defenders and slotted in with his left from an acute angle. Villa maintained their attacking momentum. Shortly before the half-time interval Cowans curled in a corner from the right, McNaught outjumped Withe and the Kiev keeper to plant the ball just inside the post. Chanov pulled off saves to deny Morley and Shaw after the break and Withe somehow missed from two yards out following neat work by Bremner.

Sat 20th Mar **Ipswich Town (A)**
Lost 1-3 **Att 21,106**
McNaught

With Bremner and Mortimer out injured and Withe suspended, Villa started with Blair and Bullivant for only the second time. It would be Terry Donovan's last game in claret and blue. Ipswich took a lead mid-way through the first half before a McNaught header was grabbed off the line by Sivell. In injury time of the first period it was 0-2 when Rimmer was beaten by a fierce McCall drive. Alan Brazil, miles offside added a third before McNaught bagged a consolation.

Sat 27th Mar **Arsenal (A)**
Lost 3-4 **Att 24,756**
Shaw, Morley, Heard

The game was littered with defensive mistakes and with Mortimer and Bremner still not back Arsenal looked capable of scoring at will.

[Above] Terry Bullivant clatters into Birmingham's Pat Van Den Hauwe during Villa's win at St. Andrews

Notwithstanding that, half time was reached with the scores finely balanced at 2-2. Gary Shaw had scored Villa's first to level the game at 1-1. Tony Morley known more for his exploits on the left flank scored Villa's second when he stole in on the blind side to head home from an impressive height. The Gunners added two more before Pat Heard added Villa's third on 64 minutes. A bemused Tony Barton added, "The game could easily have ended 9-8!"

Tue 30th Mar **West Bromwich Albion (H)**
Won 2-1 **Att 28,440**
Shaw, Withe

Even without Regis Albion looked a threat. They were ahead before ten minutes was showing on the board, through Nicky Cross. As at Arsenal on Saturday Villa employed Morley on the right to add shape and pressure young Webb. It took until four minutes into the second period before Villa were level. Shaw scoring as he turned in a Swain cross at the near post. Peter Withe put Villa ahead on 70 minutes when he connected with a Cowans free kick to head powerfully past Mark Grew in goal.

Wed 7th Apr **Anderlecht (H)** **European Cup semi-final 1st leg**
Won 1-0 **Att 38,539**
Morley

Anderlecht made their intentions clear from the start, with leading scorer Willy Guerts on the bench they were going to defend en masse. Time after time Villa were shut out in Anderlecht's offside trap. To make matters worse when Villa escaped the clutches of the Belgian's defence they squandered their chances, a Shaw header bounced on the roof of the net and Morley hooked a shot wide. Five minutes later Morley made amends for his glaring mistake, Cowans flicked on a crossfield ball from Shaw and off Tony set on another run. This time his shot rocketed in. Cowans put Morley through on goal but his diving header was saved by Jacques Munaron.

Sat 10th Apr **Southampton (A)**
Won 3-0 **Att 22,801**
Own goal, McNaught, Morley

Third placed Southampton had won more games at home than anyone else. Rimmer had a routine save to make from Channon in a dull first half. The second was everything the first wasn't. Chris Nicholl started the rout turning the ball into his own net as Cowans free kick flashed across the face of goal before Saints failed to cut out a corner and McNaught made no mistake from close range. Rimmer was called on to save from Keegan, Ball and Wallace before Southampton conceded a third in the final seconds from Morley.

Mon 12th April **Brighton & Hove Albion (H)**
Won 3-0 **Att 22,731**
Geddis 2, Evans

Geddis in for Shaw, he'd scored in his last two outings. The first-half showing was poor with Rimmer an almost spectator, Villa's attack were no better. The second-half kicked into life very early on, Withe well harnessed by Foster was able to get to Pat Heard's long ball and set his partner up to score off the crossbar. With Foster upfield searching to equalise Geddis took advantage of the centre-back's absence to head Withe's cross into the net for his second. Evans got his head to a Cowans free kick to round off the scoring.

Sat 17th Apr **Middlesbrough (H)**
Won 1-0 **Att 21,098**
Evans

Andy Blair started for the first time in five. Evans followed up last Monday's goal with a fine header on 27 minutes when he out-jumped the Middlesbrough defence to meet Cowans corner kick. Villa had been in control up to that point, they never looked likely to surrender their lead thereafter. The scoreline should have been more emphatic had Boro keeper Platt not been in such inspired form, he made two particularly fine saves to deny Pat Heard. Blair did beat the goalie but his delicate chip grazed the top of the bar.

[Above] Tony Morley gets up to head past Arsenal goalie George Wood during the goal feast defeat at Highbury

Wed 21st Apr **Anderlecht (A)** European Cup semi-final 2nd leg
Drew 0-0 **Att 38,040**

Villa played with purpose, a long ball from Swain was lost by Muneron as Withe thundered in but as the striker attempted to square to Shaw it was blocked. Williams set Shaw away, his centre met by Evans who headed wide. Villa's best chance, saw a cross-field ball from Swain beat the offside trap, Shaw hit a tremendous shot which the keeper parried, Morley lofted it back in but the goalie recovered to smother the attack. Withe succeeded in getting the ball into the net but to his dismay the flag was up for offside. Play was held up as fans from the Villa end poured onto the pitch. At the games conclusion Aston Villa had made it to the biggest final in domestic football.

Sat 24th Apr **Nottingham Forest (A)**
Drew 1-1 **Att 18,213**
Cowans (pen)

Villa were cool and composed yet were let down by their less than clinical finishing. A momentary lapse in the visitors defence saw Forest gifted a goal in the 12th minute. Villa should have been two-up by that stage had Shaw and Withe not missed by inches. Villa's equaliser came from the ever reliable Gordon Cowans from the spot, Bowyer having pulled Mortimer back in the box. Villa momentum suffered when Dennis had to leave the field injured. With quarter of an hour left to play Blair was tripped by the advancing Peter Shilton, his teammates were up in arms as the referee let play continue.

Wed 28th Apr **Leeds United (H)**
Lost 1-4 **Att 20,566**
Geddis

Relegation bound United fell behind in the 9th minute. Withe and Morley combined on the left to release Cowans, who moved forward before unleashing a piledriver that Lukic could only turn away – into the path of Geddis. Leeds were back in the frame when Worthington created for Graham to score. To further rub salt in the visitors scored two blistering goals within 12 minutes of the second half starting. Villa looking anything but European Cup finalists conceded a fourth on 63 minutes.

Sat 1st May **Manchester City (H)**
Drew 0-0 **Att 22,150**

After a slow opening Man City went close as they won three corners in a minute. The strong wind was causing havoc with high balls for Rimmer in the box. In the dying seconds of the first half Shaw slipped an inch perfect ball to Heard, instead of shooting Pat rolled the ball to Morley 12-yards out who shot high into the stand. City missed a sitter four minutes into the second half, Power headed straight into Rimmer's arms with the goal at his mercy. Jimmy was then forced into saving from Hartford. Villa took control for the last 20 minutes but couldn't break the deadlock.

Wed 5th May **Stoke City (A)**
Lost 0-1 **Att 10,363**

Evans and Mortimer were back. A Bracewell goal in the 16th minute was sufficient to inflict defeat though Villa weren't helped in that Morley and Shaw seemed to have lost their golden touch. Tony Barton admitted his side were fortunate to go in just trailing by the one at the break. Morley's play was indecisive before he hobbled out of the game on 55 minutes with a thigh strain. After witnessing the one goal reversal one press man suggested Villa could be on the receiving end of a five-goal drubbing by Bayern Munich.

Sat 8th May **West Bromwich Albion (A)**
Won 1-0 **Att 19,556**
Heard

The game started at a decent pace, both sides looking to draw first-blood. Rimmer rushed out to thwart Regis and handled outside his area, he was booked for his trouble. Shaw and Mortimer had been denied at the other end by Godden. Cowans did get beyond

[Above] Anderlecht goalie Jacques Munaron saves with Villa's Allan Evans set to pounce

the keeper only to see his shot hacked off the line by Statham. After the interval, Regis tested Rimmer before seeing red following an altercation with McNaught. Albion then watched as Williams cleared his lines after a swerving shot had beaten Rimmer. Pat Heard's last-gasp strike blasted Villa ahead, a fine reward after such a solid display.

Sat 15th May **Everton (H)**
Lost 1-2 **Att 20,446**
Cowans

Graeme Sharp fired The Toffees ahead after seizing on a ball that fell awkwardly between McNaught and Williams. The first half climaxed by a glorious equaliser from man of the match Cowans. Shaw controlled a headed clearance, spotted Sid's dash into the area and flicked an intelligent pass into the midfielder's path, who unleashed a clinical shot accurately past Southall. The host's inability to punish Everton cost them the game when Sharp hit a second just before the hour mark.

Fri 21st May **Swansea City (H)**
Won 3-0 **Att 18,294**
Morley, Bremner, Withe

Villa Park was treated to two goals of the highest order. For the first Withe fed the closely marked Morley, with consummate ease he chipped the ball right-footed, it rose and then dropped a mere inch under Sander's crossbar. Swansea boss Toshack: "It is impossible to legislate for the instinctive skill Morley showed." The next equally impressive, Peter flicked the ball up, back-heeled it, Mortimer threaded a perfect pass for Bremner to hit at full stride. After the interval Villa went round, over and through their opponents but could only add the one. Withe turned from provider to scorer.

[Left] Villa lining up prior to the European Cup final [Right] Dennis Mortimer, Tony Barton and Peter Withe celebrate winning the European Cup

Wed 26th May **Bayern Munich** **(Rotterdam) European Cup final**
Won 1-0 **Att 39,776**
Withe

Nine minutes in Rimmer left the field with a shake of his head. In an atmosphere only a European final can generate, Nigel Spink, with a look of sheer bewilderment ran to take his place in goal. He let no one down, he dived, he climbed, he remained calm as the German's prodded and probed. A full stretch save from Durnburger and then two minutes later a save to deny Karl Heinz Rummennigge. Villa had chances, Evans stumbled as he ran at their goal, Shaw then hit a beauty of a ball across the goalmouth but there was no one to finish. With Bayern threatening to swamp the Villa, Barton's men worked the ball from the middle to the left channel and Morley, he turned this way and that before delivering a low, hard cross, Withe ran in, stuck out his right peg, the ball glanced in off his shin, beyond the despairing reach of the keeper and in off the upright. The place erupted, Villa were in front! Swain later headed off his line, Spink kept defying the odds and when all else failed the lineman came to the rescue to wave Hoeness offside as the German found the back of the net. From the 67th minute when the goal arrived, time stood still, four hours later (or so it seemed) the ref blew up – Aston Villa were 'Kings of Europe!'

PRE-SEASON

• The draw for the 27th European Cup competition is made in Zurich. Aston Villa are paired with relative unknowns FC Valur Reykjavik of Iceland.
• The players report back for training a week before most teams due to participation in the Charity Shield. Training is done on the slag heaps at Kingsbury.
• Villa host Rotherham United (last season's Division Three champions) in a match at Bodymoor Heath. Andy Blair a potential signing watches as Villa run out 2-1 winners.

AUGUST

• Terry Donovan stars in the Villa reserve team that beat Mansfield Town's senior side 3-0.
• Andy Blair's transfer fee from Coventry City is settled by an independent tribunal. A figure of £300,000 is agreed with further to pay should Villa sell within his four year contract.
• Aston Villa take in a 10-day pre-season tour of Switzerland and Greece. They play two matches in each country.
• Ken McNaught is a doubt for the coming campaign as he limps out of the win at FC Frauenfeld with a reoccurring knee injury.
• Villa approach Middlesbrough keen to sign England U-21 striker Dave Hodgson but it comes to nothing.
• Shaw is out for the start of the campaign with a possible stress fracture in his foot.
• Newspaper articles appear that the club are interested in Nottingham Forest's Trevor Francis, "I have nothing to report yet and it is not my style to talk in the Press about any possible action I may take on the transfer market" says Saunders.

SEPTEMBER

• Injured Gary Shaw has to pull out of next week's England U-21 match v Norway in Oslo.
• Villa's defence of their title takes a blow as they suffer defeat at Sunderland. Played two – lost two! Terry Donovan shows he still has goals in him as he gets on the scoresheet in what is his first game for 17 months.
• Full back Colin Gibson makes his England U-21 debut in the goalless draw against Norway.
• Andy Blair scores for the Scottish U-21 side as they defeat their Swedish counterparts at Easter Road.
• The Villa youth team crush Plymouth Argyle 4-1 as they start their defence of the Southern Junior Floodlit Cup.
• Peter Withe replaces Mariner on 75 minutes as England lose 1-2 in a World Cup qualifier in Norway.
• The Villa are drawn against Wolverhampton Wanderers in the League Cup. The first leg to be played at Villa Park.
• Aston Villa have their first taste of European Cup football as FC Valur Reykjavik are comprehensively beaten 5-0 at Villa Park.

OCTOBER

• Villa agree to sell midfielder Willie Young to Torquay United for £100,000.
• Two 18-year olds, Kevin Rogers and Ray Walker sign pro terms having served two year apprenticeships. Both started out as midfielders, Rogers is now playing at left-back while Walker has been converted to a central defensive role and is capped at Schoolboy and Youth level for England .
• Aston Villa Football Club's AGM takes place Oct 13th.
• ATV put on a private screening of Nottingham Forest v Dynamo Berlin (two seasons ago) for the Villa squad.

[Above] Shaw in his England under-21 shirt in November 1981

• Aston Villa's youngsters attempting to win the Southern Junior Floodlit Cup for the fourth successive time trounce Bournemouth 6-0. Tony Rees bags a hat-trick.
• Kenny Swain who missed the win over WHU last weekend is pronounced unfit for duty for the Villa's game behind the Iron Curtain.

NOVEMBER

• Donald Bendall (son of Villa Chairman Ron) is appointed Vice-Chairman in place of departing Harry Kartz.
• Aston Villa and Liverpool create history by becoming the first two English sides to reach the last eight of the European Cup in the same season. They are joined by Bayern Munich, CSKO Sofia, Anderlecht, Craiova, Red Star Belgrade and Dynamo Kiev. The draw will be made Dec 11th.
• On getting through to the European Cup quarter-finals a delighted Saunders said, "It was so tense, but a truly wonderful game that provided a great night for Aston Villa. We made history for the club and the supporters."
• Peter Withe and Tony Morley are named in Ron Greenwood's squad of 22 for the Wembley World Cup qualifier versus the Hungarians.
• The Wigan Athletic secretary personally delivers £10,000 of tickets to Villa Park for the Cup clash to be played at Springfield Park next week. It remained to be seen who would be selling them, Villa or Leicester City.

DECEMBER

• Centre forward Peter Withe is reacquainted with his old Forest roommate, Larry Lloyd, now manager of League Cup opponents Wigan Athletic. Withe scored the winner!
• Geddis starts for the three games Withe is suspended.

• Following the coldest night since records began the Villa/Albion derby game is postponed.
• The draw for the European Cup is made. Villa face Russian side Dynamo Kiev. Ties to be played Mar 3rd and Mar 17th.
• Both Ivor Linton and Noel Blake make their last appearances in the claret and blue.
• Villa lose their first three league games of the month, luckily they won't lose three on the spin for the remainder of the season.

JANUARY

• Villa win 6-0 at Meadow Lane in the F.A. Cup 3rd round. It's the club's biggest away victory in the competition since 1929. On that occasion Villa beat Clapton Orient 8-0 having drawn 0-0 at Villa Park.
• David Geddis becomes the first Villa player to bag an F.A. Cup hat-trick since Ron Wylie's at Everton in 1959.
• Due to postponements their next fixture – Notts County at Meadow Lane. Villa contrive to lose this one 0-1.
• The Albion League Cup tie is hit by the weather. An estimated 400 tons of snow settled on the Villa Park pitch and terraces during the blizzards.
• With missing the Ashton Gate cup-tie Des Bremner ends an unbroken spell of 120 consecutive matches, stretching back to Sep '79.
• Gary Shaw gets plastered. Finding fluid on the knee Gary's leg is put into a plaster cast as a protective precaution.

FEBRUARY

• UEFA intervene and set a time-limit on the Russians in order for the Villa to know where their quarter-final tie will take place. Eventually the destination is arranged, Simferopol in the Crimea.

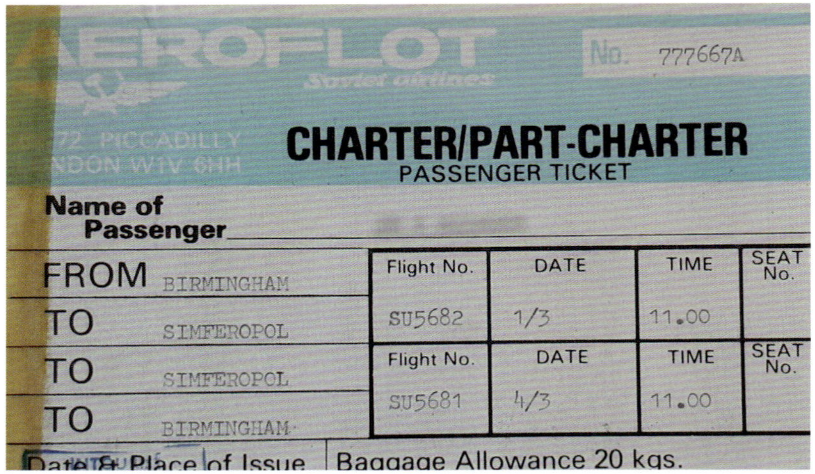

[Above] A flight ticket to Ukraine and Soviet security for the match against Dynamo Kiev [Right] Tony Morley and Tottenham's Glenn Hoddle on England duty

• Ron Saunders walks out at Villa Park. One comment to the stunned press, "If I'm going to manage then I want to be manager, not office boy!"
• Reports appear that winger Tony Morley wants to leave the Villa.
• Villa play at White Hart Lane in an F.A. Cup 5th round tie. They then play Spurs at Villa Park four days later, if not in a replay in a league fixture.
• Ron Saunders sat in the St Andrew's directors' box for the Villa game at Birmingham City. He was due to be unveiled as new Blues manager on Monday. The Villa fans chanted, "You must be mad Saunders!"
• Tony Morley makes his full England debut in the 4-0 win over Northern Ireland.

MARCH

• Villa begin the month with a satisfying nil-nil draw in the European Cup quarter-final 1st leg away to Dynamo Kiev. This result wouldn't do Tony Barton's chances of becoming full manager any harm at all.
• With the Kiev game looming, immediately after the Wolves match two wagon loads of sand are poured across the centre of the pitch to reduce the muddy consistency, the result of torrential rain over Birmingham.
• Terry Donovan plays his last first-team game in the defeat at Portman Road.
• Villa go down 3-4 at Arsenal. Terry Bullivant makes his last appearance in the claret and blue.

APRIL

• A Tony Morley goal is all that separates Villa and Anderlecht in the semi-final at Villa Park.

• Villa preparations for the semi-final 2nd leg go far smoother than could be hoped. Three wins, nine points, no goals conceded!
• Villa players get their hands on the huge European trophy; it travels with the club to Brussels having been in Liverpool's possession. Let's hope it returns with them next month!
•Villa's youngsters beat rivals Birmingham City 2-1 in the Southern Junior Floodlit Cup semi-final. Mark Walters bagged the winner.
• Violent outbreaks on the terraces at Anderlecht sour the club's celebrations as they draw 0-0 to reach the final. It transpires the fans that encroached the pitch were English soldiers stationed in nearby Germany.
• Following the Belgian 'riots' quotes abound. One paper prints one such article from the Villa vice-chairman Don Bendall but names him as John Blundell.
• UEFA fine the club £15,000, it is the biggest imposed by their disciplinary committee on any club since 1978. Villa are also ordered to play their next European tie at home behind closed doors.
•Geddis plays against Leeds as Shaw is on England U-21 duty

MAY

• It's a bit of a mixed bag in the build up to the Rotterdam final on 26th May, the team draw one, lose two and win two.
• Allan Evans is named in Scotland's World Cup party of 40.
• Aston Villa defeat the German giants Bayern Munich in Feyenoord's De Kuip Stadium. The win courtesy of a Peter Withe goal ensures the European Cup stays in England for the sixth successive year.
• Villa's youngsters play in two West German tournaments and win them both. In Mannheim they beat Red Star Belgrade 3-0 in the final and then they travelled on to Salem, where they beat Kaiserslautern 1-0 in that final. Mark Walters was named 'Player of the Tournament.'

[Above] Villa players waiting for the trouble to stop at Anderlecht before resuming play [Right] The Villa team check out the condition of the Anderlecht pitch

g.heylens
adidas

ASTON VILLA FC
SUPER VILLA
ASTON VILLA
COME ON YOU LIONS
ASTON VILLA
LEAGUE CHAMPIONS
EUROPEAN CUP FINALISTS
ASTON VILLA
VILLA
ASTON

[Left] Villa fans at the Final [Above] Captain Mortimer and goalscorer Withe bring the European Cup back to England

[Right] Fans look from amongst the trees to get a glimpse of the behind closed doors match against Besiktas in September 1982

1982-83

ASTON VILLA

[Back Row] Eamonn Deacy, Dean Glover, Mark Hutchinson, Ray Walker, Robert Hopkins, Mark Jones, Colin Gibson, Allan Evans, Ken McNaught, Pat Heard, Martin McKenzie, Tony Rees, Paul Kerr, Noel Blake, [Standing] Bryan Jones (Youth Coach), Brian Little (Youth Coach), Paul Williams (Physiotherapist), Kevin Rogers, Gordon Cowans, Andy Blair, Nigel Spink, Kevin Poole, Jimmy Rimmer, David Geddis, Gary Williams, Mark Walters, Roy MacLaren (Coach), Bill Shorthouse (Reserve Coach) [Seated] Tony Morley, Des Bremner, Kenny Swain, Tony Barton (Manager), Dennis Mortimer, Peter Withe, Gary Shaw, [On Ground] Paul Birch, Tim Langford, Darren Bradley, Leigh Palin, Tony Obi, David Norton, Stephen Barnes.

Football League	Division One
Manager	Tony Barton
Coach	Roy MacLaren
Physio	Jim Williams
Captain	Dennis Mortimer
Final Position	Sixth
F.A. Cup	Quarter-finals
League Cup	Second Round
Leading Goalscorer	Gary Shaw 24 goals

The Champions of Europe kicked off the new season against a Sunderland team that had narrowly avoided the drop. Cowans gave Villa a half time lead, but they lost 1-3! A 0-5 thumping at Goodison Park was followed by defeat at The Dell, the first time since 1964/65 the club had lost their first three League fixtures. Villa were the only team on 'nil points' as they say in European parts.

Villa found their legs, Luton were beaten 4-1, Forest by the same score, then a remarkable result, a 1-0 win at Maine Road against the joint leaders. Swansea were also beaten, Villa were up to tenth. Following the game against the Welsh club Villa held on to a 0-0 draw in Turkey to put Besiktas out of the European Cup 3-1 on agg. The Villa Park game had been played behind closed doors on the order of UEFA following last season's semi-final scenes at Anderlecht.

Notts County progressed at Villa's expense in the League Cup winning both ties yet in between Villa hit Watford for three. The Hornets had just been promoted but would go on to finish the season in a highly respectable third position under the guidance of Graham Taylor. Dynamo Bucharest were beaten in front of 80,000 on their patch by a Gary Shaw brace, and in the 4-2 second-leg Shaw got a hat-trick. Another run of four successive wins elevated the team to third place, same points as Manchester United but three shy of leaders Liverpool. This form bode well with Villa going to Tokyo to face Penarol in the World Club Championships. Barton's boys failed to become the first British side to lift the trophy as they went down by two goals to the Uruguayans.

continued >>>

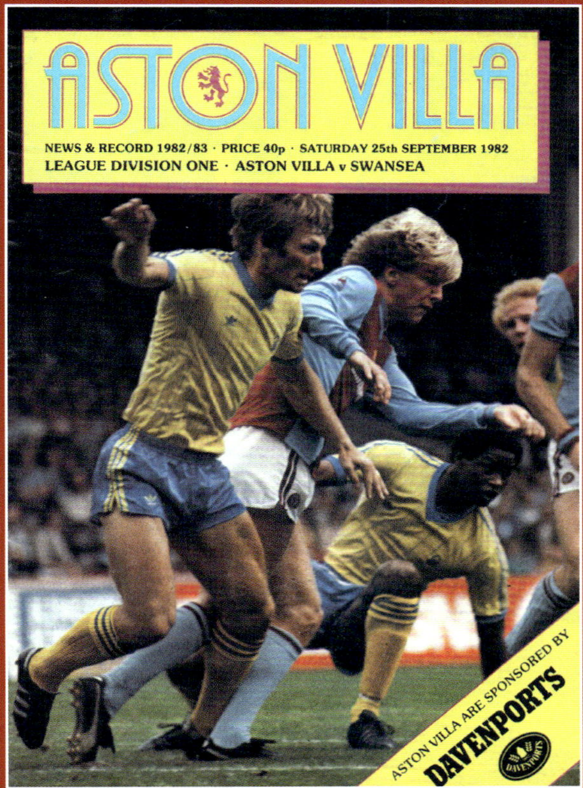

Total Home League Attendances	**498,712**
Average Home League	**23,748**
Highest Home League	**40,897**
Lowest Home League	**17,452**

		P	W	D	L	GF	GA	DIF	PTS
1	Liverpool	42	24	10	8	87	37	50	82
2	Watford	42	22	5	15	74	57	17	71
3	Manchester United	42	19	13	10	56	38	18	70
4	Tottenham Hotspur	42	20	9	13	65	50	15	69
5	Nottingham Forest	42	20	9	13	62	50	12	69
6	Aston Villa	42	21	5	16	62	50	12	68
7	Everton	42	18	10	14	66	48	18	64
8	West Ham United	42	20	4	18	68	62	6	64
9	Ipswich Town	42	15	13	14	64	50	14	58
10	Arsenal	42	16	10	16	58	56	2	58
11	West Bromwich Albion	42	15	12	15	51	49	2	57
12	Southampton	42	15	12	15	54	58	-4	57
13	Stoke City	42	16	9	17	53	64	-11	57
14	Norwich City	42	14	12	16	52	58	-6	54
15	Notts County	42	15	7	20	55	71	-16	52
16	Sunderland	42	12	14	16	48	61	-13	50
17	Birmingham City	42	12	14	16	40	55	-15	50
18	Luton Town	42	12	13	17	65	84	-19	49
19	Coventry City	42	13	9	20	48	59	-11	48
20	Manchester City	42	13	8	21	47	70	-23	47
21	Swansea City	42	10	11	21	51	69	-18	41
22	Brighton & Hove Albion	42	9	13	20	38	68	-30	40

A Johan Cruyff-esque goal from Mark Walters - still talked about today – overcame a defiant Northampton Town in the F.A. Cup Third Round. Silverware was won, well a wooden plaque to be precise according to skipper for the night Ken McNaught, in the form of the Super Cup. Villa turned over a 0-1 loss in Spain to conquer Barcelona 3-0 at a bouncing Villa Park, Shaw, Cowans and McNaught goals inflicting the damage. Wolves were also defeated in the Cup that had eluded the club since 1957.

League wins throughout February and March kept Villa in contention for a UEFA Cup spot whilst they missed out on reaching the semis of two competitions, Arsenal in the F.A. Cup after Villa had disposed of Watford in the previous round; Juventus progressed in the Euro Cup with a 5-2 agg win to knock the holders out, Cowans and Withe finding the net.

April derbies against Birmingham City, West Bromwich Albion and Stoke City yielded maximum points. A creditable 1-1 draw in the penultimate match at Anfield was bettered when Villa beat Arsenal 2-1 at home to finish the campaign in sixth, it was the final game in the claret and blue for both McNaught and Geddis.

Villa's League placing ensured European football was on the agenda for next season.

1982-83

Sat 28th Aug **Sunderland (H)**
Lost 1-3 **Att 22,945**
Cowans

Villa fielded the European Cup final team with the exception of Shaw, his place taken by youngster Mark Walters. The midfield were in control, Withe was his aggressive best and Walters shone every time he got the ball. Cowans opened the scoring in the 22nd minute. Villa reshuffled after the break, Withe didn't come back out, Morley moved inside with Heard playing wide. The second half was a different scenario, on the hour West equalised, five minutes later Villa were caught napping and fell behind. Sunderland hit them with a third late in the game.

Tue 31st Aug **Everton (A)**
Lost 0-5 **Att 24,029**

Villa fell behind after eight minutes, Adrian Heath heading over the static defence. Mortimer prompted a number of moves but Villa went further adrift, Heath again. Andy King sent Villa in at half time trailing 0-3. It stayed that way until five minutes remained, Graeme Sharp then added two. Only keeper Jimmy Rimmer emerged with any credit. The central defence was appalling, between them, mis-hit back passes, wild kicks hitting their own woodwork, a penalty given away, and a booking. In the end Villa were fortunate to get away so lightly.

Sat 4th Sep **Southampton (A)**
Lost 0-1 **Att 17,943**

Villa's third successive defeat yet Peter Shilton pulled off numerous magnificent saves to thwart Villa. Saints took the lead within two minutes, shortly after Mark Jones hooked away a goalbound

Fashanu header. From then on the hosts were backpedalling, a 26th minute Withe header looked inevitable but somehow Shilton parried the shot before scrambling it away. Four minutes later the keeper was at it again to deny the Villa forward who'd got on the end of Mortimer's centre. The entire team grew but to no avail.

Wed 8th Sep **Luton Town (H)**
Won 4-1 **Att 18,823**
Mortimer, Withe, Cowans 2 (2 pens)

The Villa were back to something resembling their best form. Dennis Mortimer scored the opener, Blair started the move winning a heading duel, he found Withe who squared to his captain 1-0. Withe converted a simple tap-in on 21 minutes and when Antic fouled Morley in the box it was more or less game over. Cowans, gave former Villan Jake Findlay no chance. Even when the Hatters pulled one back in the 54th minute it was nothing more than a token as the margin was restored when Sid struck his second spot kick of the night to make it 4-1, Kellock climbing all over Withe.

Sat 11th Sep **Nottingham Forest (H)**
Won 4-1 **Att 21,224**
Mortimer, Withe 2, Cowans (pen)

Their second victory in the space of four days. Mortimer opened the scoring with a fierce right-footed shot. Villa raced further in front, following a precise build up between Blair, Cowans and Mortimer, Withe was left with the easy task of firing in from close range. Forest were awarded a penalty and scored from it when Heard felled Hodge. Cowans restored the two-goal cushion from the spot, Shaw brought down by Willie Young. Ten minutes remaining the game was put to bed when Withe notched his second of the afternoon. Forest had Bowyer sent off!

Wed 15th Sep **Besiktas (H)** **European Cup 1st round 1st leg**
Won 3-1 **Att app 250** **(played behind closed doors)**
Withe, Morley, Mortimer

Villa's defence of the trophy was played out in an empty stadium, the penalty for the trouble at Anderlecht in the semi-final. A Williams cross on six minutes was met by Withe to tap in. Tony Morley scored his first of the campaign to make it 2-0 with only nine minutes played. Dennis hitting a purple patch hit his third in only eight days when his shot went through Rasim's hands. Villa were coasting. Besiktas pulled one back when a fumbled shot rolled beyond Rimmer. Necdet volleyed wildly over on 86 minutes.

Sat 18th Sep **Manchester City (A)**
Won 1-0 **Att 28,650**
Shaw

Villa totally dominated, superior up front, hard as steel in defence. Shaw's attacking instincts were back as he helped himself to a 36th minute winner, created by the equally sharp Withe. Morley was a livewire and showing the signs that terrorised defenders last season while Allan Evans was singled out by boss Barton following his powerful contribution in defence. They had to weather occasional storms but City seldom had the capacity to match them. Williams in goal denied Shaw of a certain hat-trick.

Sat 25th Sep **Swansea City (H)**
Won 2-0 **Att 21,246**
Mortimer, Evans

Villa helped themselves to a fifth consecutive win. Mortimer fired a stunning volley past Dai Davies to break the deadlock in the 32nd minute. Mark Jones started the move, robbed Hadziabdic, played in Withe, took the return and running at speed crossed a good ball for his captain. On the stroke of half time Mortimer and Cowans linked up at a free kick, Sid sent it over and the onrushing Allan Evans headed it in with power. Swansea offered very little, Villa keeping them penned in their own half for long spells.

Wed 29th Sep **Besiktas (A)** European Cup 1st round 2nd leg
Drew 0-0 (agg 3-1) **Att 45,000**

Villa expecting a cynical confrontation didn't have to extend themselves. The host's only contribution to the game was the hostile atmosphere created by their supporters. Mortimer and his players paced themselves in the steam bath heat and whilst content to hold the ball the Villa pushed forward as gaps appeared, Mortimer, Bremner and Cowans had attempts go wide. McNaught and Jones made timely tackles and Rimmer was called on just a couple of times.

Sat 2nd Oct **West Bromwich Albion (A)**
Lost 0-1 **Att 25,165**

Villa conceded territory to a lively Albion in the first half, restricted to two chances in the first 45 minutes; a Morley volley struck Batson and a smart move down the wing ended with Mortimer unable to get on the end of a perfectly executed chip from Shaw. West Brom had control of the midfield and the final third of the pitch. Villa fell behind to an error by Cowans, his backpass was woefully weak, Nicky Cross snapped it up and made no mistake.

Wed 6th Oct **Notts County (H)** League Cup 2nd round 1st leg
Lost 1-2 **Att 16,312**
Withe

Villa should have built a commanding lead, they were cruising until they went in front on 22 minutes when Withe finished off a slick move involving Mortimer and Shaw. After that the Villa players took their foot off the gas. Jones who'd performed well was taken ill at the interval and replaced by Pat Heard. County short on ability came out and started playing, plugged away and were level on 75 minutes. The set-back had no effect on the Villa and they fell behind with five minutes left. Their work cut out for the second leg.

[Right] Gordon Cowans is first to the ball during the defeat to Notts County at Meadow Lane

Sat 9th Oct **Notts County (A)**
Lost 1-4 **Att 8,977**
Shaw

Robert Hopkins debuted for the axed Morley, McNaught out through injury. Rimmer had already saved twice to deny Christie when County opened the scoring. Eight minutes later Villa were two down. Cowans visibly struggling had to continue as Villa had used their substitute. County went 3-0 up before Shaw gave the Villa fans something to cheer when he pulled one back. Just when it looked like there may be a revival of sorts Withe was red carded for arguing, he was in the tunnel when number four went in.

Sat 16th Oct **Watford (H)**
Won 3-0 **Att 21,572**
Withe, Morley 2

Colin Gibson was No 3 in place of Williams. Villa made their intentions clear within five minutes when a Withe header hit the post. Withe then twice missed the target as did Cowans. The big lad made amends when he thundered a shot past Sherwood. It took until the second half to add to their goals tally, Morley tied the right-back in knots before unleashing a shot from the edge of the box into the far corner. His second came from great work from Cowans, all the winger was left to do was steer it into the net.

Wed 20th Oct **Dynamo Bucharest (A)** European Cup 2nd round 1st leg
Won 2-0 **Att 80,000**
Shaw 2

Tony Morley was back to his best while Withe and Shaw fought a ferocious battle up front. The first goal arrived on 11 minutes, full back Gibson started the move from his own box, laid it to Morley, his pinpoint cross was headed on by Withe for Shaw to deliver an unstoppable strike. Dynamo threw numbers forward but they succeeded in playing into Villa's hands. Villa were captivating the huge appreciative crowd with their controlled and compelling football. Dynamo fell further behind when Shaw got a second.

DAVENPORTS
TOYOTA
TOYOTA

SIGNS

Sat 23rd Oct **Norwich City (A)**
Lost 0-1 **Att 14,986**

Below par Villa created little in a game that was destined to be a low scoring affair. Former Villa favourite John Deehan got the goal; he burst past McNaught but was sent sprawling and took the penalty himself. Moments later Chris Woods brought down Cowans in full flight, Sid hit the spot kick, but it only rattled the woodwork. Evans limped off just before the hour, replaced by Williams. In the dying seconds Gibson and Bertschin were sent off for nothing more than handbags.

Tue 26th Oct **Notts County (A)** League Cup 2nd round 2nd leg
Lost 0-1 (agg 1-3) **Att 6,921**

The first half was devoid of any creativity. Villa were brighter after the break. Deacy on for Jones at the interval. Geddis looked at his best while operating on the right while Cowans worked tirelessly in the centre of the park trying to create openings. Shaw had a half chance but Avramovic dived bravely at the forwards feet, injuring himself in the process. The ref waved play on and as Villa attacked he called a halt to play. County scored with two minutes left.

Sat 30th Oct **Tottenham Hotspur (H)**
Won 4-0 **Att 25,992**
Cowans 2 (1 pen), Morley, Shaw

Villa welcomed back Withe. Spurs would have been out of sight had it not been for the brilliance of Rimmer, making six superlative saves. Villa took a 57th minute lead from the 12-yard spot, Cowans after Withe had been shoved. As Tottenham pushed forward a Mortimer pass was met by Sid who hit an unstoppable shot from 25-yards. A minute later Morley made it 3-0 when he swept in the rebound from a Gary Shaw shot. Shaw then had one ruled offside, before making it four just 30 seconds later.

[Left] Gary Shaw stoops to head home the first of his hat-trick against Dynamo Bucharest

Wed 3rd Nov **Dynamo Bucharest (H)** European Cup 2nd round 2nd leg
Won 4-2 (agg 6-2) **Att 22,244**
Shaw 3, Walters

Gary Shaw who'd scored in Romania was at it again within five minutes of the start. A spectacular goal, he flung himself full-length to get his head on Morley's cross. Dynamo levelled through Multescu. A disastrous blunder by goalkeeper Moraru let Shaw in to head Villa 2-1 in front. On 67 minutes a Shaw volley got him his hat-trick, he was replaced moments later to a standing ovation. Iordache hit a long-range strike to make it 3-2. Substitute Walters capped his European debut when he made it 4-2 on the night.

Sat 6th Nov **Coventry City (A)**
Drew 0-0 **Att 12,199**

The two sides played their part in an enthralling derby though Villa had the clearer chances. A combination of the woodwork, carelessness in front of goal and the impressiveness of the Sky Blues rearguard denied Villa from going joint third in the table. In the 7th minute Shaw's curling left-footed effort hit the post. In the second half Shaw was denied, Sealey pulling off a smart point-blank save. Bremner had a clear shot at goal but again the City stopper came out on top. Man-of-the-match Gordon Cowans produced a glittering display.

Sat 13th Nov **Brighton & Hove Albion (H)**
Won 1-0 **Att 18,834**
Withe

Villa seemed intent on attacking down the left flank (though Mortimer, Bremner and Cowans controlled the midfield) but Brighton's Foster and Gatting were wise to it. The visitors played with only one up front and packed their defence, this meant Villa were restricted to shooting from distance. Graham Moseley (on-loan at Villa Park in the early '70s) was inactive apart from getting an arm to a stooping Gary Shaw header. When it looked unlikely Villa were going to be unable to penetrate, up popped Withe, escaping the clutches of Foster, to head home at the far post.

Sat 20th Nov **Manchester United (H)**
Won 2-1 **Att 35,487**
Shaw, Withe

Villa's seventh straight home win was achieved by one thing – passion! United were excellent but Villa were sharper. Shaw set them on their way. A Cowans corner kick was met by Mortimer who diverted the ball to Evans, Allan fired goalwards but Shaw nipped in to change its direction and beyond Bailey. Stapleton's goal eight minutes later made it 1-1. Withe outjumped the United centre-backs to regain the lead. Villa had now lost only once at home to The Red Devils in 13 league meetings.

Sat 27th Nov **Stoke City (A)**
Won 3-0 **Att 18,797**
Own goal, Shaw 2

Stoke were torn apart by a quality Villa side. The first goal had a touch of fortune, Bremner produced a dashing run, his cross found the head of Cowans; the ball was going wide before it struck Parkin and trickled into the net. Prior to this it looked inevitable that City would score but Rimmer pulled off a blinding save. With Evans and Jones working well they soaked up everything Stoke could throw at them. Gary Shaw continued his rich vein of form with two goals in a 15 minute spell. His first expertly turned in with his left foot, the second a header from a corner.

Sat 4th Dec **West Ham United (H)**
Won 1-0 **Att 24,658**
Cowans (pen)

Unchanged Villa they set themselves up with numerous half-chances throughout an exciting but goalless first half. Martin and Lampard held up well against the continual threat of Withe and Shaw while Parkes did what was needed when Villa were through on goal. Mortimer had left the field on 20 minutes with a calf injury; sub Walters was put to work on the wing with Morley moving infield. Villa finally broke the stalemate with only seven minutes left to play. Withe was brought down by Martin, Cowans coolly converted, hitting his shot to the bottom right corner. Villa were up to third.

[Left] Villa's defence prepare for a Liverpool free-kick during December's defeat

Tue 7th Dec **Arsenal (A)**
Lost 1-2 **Att 17,384**
McNaught

A win would see Villa go joint top, instead they went behind on 10 minutes. Whyte taking two bites to put it away. Villa playing against the driving rain hardly got into the Arsenal half and on 30 minutes it was 0-2. Another dead ball situation, Woodcock finished it ramming the ball into the roof of the net. With Villa's first attack of the night they reduced the deficit, Heard deputising for Mortimer floated a free-kick in, Withe flicked it on and McNaught headed it in. Woods was sent off for rushing out and body-checking Withe. Stuart Robson took over the green jersey but Villa failed to trouble him.

Sun 12th Dec **Penarol (Tokyo)** **World Club Championship**
Lost 0-2 **Att 63,000**

All that stood in the way of Aston Villa from being crowned the World's best club side was Penarol, the 1982 Copa Libertadores winners. The Uruguayan side were appearing for the fourth time, winning twice. With two minutes on the clock a Gordon Cowans free-kick rattled the crossbar, an inch lower and Villa would have been in front. Four minutes later a Tony Morley shot skimmed just the wrong side of the post. For the first 20 minutes the Villa were stronger, faster and more positive than the South American outfit. How it changed... In the 27th minute Penarol were awarded a free-kick from a good 30-yards out, Jair Goncalves Prates the Brazilian forward let fly, it swerved in the air and in off the post. The second from winger Walkir Silva clipped the inside of the upright and went in.

Sat 18th Dec **Liverpool (H)**
Lost 2-4 **Att 34,568**
Shaw, Withe

Villa trailed by three goals inside 30 minutes. Each one down to confusion at dead ball situations. Rimmer could hardly stay on his feet; he slipped rather than dived as the first went in, then having saved from Rush he slid along his line as Dalglish's inswinging corner carried into the far corner. With Villa's defence skidding on the icy surface a Souness free-kick bounced off a defender to run to Kennedy, 0-3. Goals by Shaw and Withe within a two-minute spell meant they were still in the match. After the break Villa piled forward. Against the run of play Rush scored their fourth.

Mon 27th Dec **Birmingham City (A)**
Lost 0-3 **Att 43,864**

Ex Villan Noel Blake put Blues ahead when he got to Handysides rebounded shot. Due to Blake both Shaw and Withe had slim pickings as he took up his usual position. For all the extra skill and quality throughout the team Villa couldn't up their game, Coton was only troubled to make a couple of worthwhile saves. Goal number two on 70 minutes came about when Rimmer could only push the ball out for Handysides to get another crack at it. City hit a third seven minutes later. This would be Rimmer's last game.

Wed 29th Dec **Ipswich Town (H)**
Drew 1-1 **Att 21,912**
Withe

Nigel Spink between the posts for the first time since Rotterdam got a rousing reception. Villa started well. Peter Withe put them in the driving seat after 20 minutes, his shot deflecting slightly off Butcher. Villa could have taken the lead much earlier, time and again half chances were missed and clear cut opportunities were blazed wide or high. John Wark got Town's equaliser on the stroke of half time. Ipswich a pale shadow of the team under Robson and were described in one paper as 'ragged and disjointed.'

Sat 1st Jan **Manchester United (A)**
Lost 1-3 **Att 41,545**
Cowans (pen)

Villa looked lethargic. Spink was powerless to stop United going ahead through Stapleton. Within 60 seconds Villa were back in the game. Shaw turned Remi Moses in the area but was brought down, Cowans sent Bailey the wrong way. Three minutes into the second half Villa were under the cosh, Muhren hit the woodwork, McQueen flashed a header inches over and Cowans cleared off the line twice in quick succession. Villa fell behind again, through Coppell. Stapleton later bagged his second.

Mon 3rd Jan **Southampton (H)**
Won 2-0 **Att 19,925**
Cowans (pen), Evans

Morley was back, Gibson retained his place in the starting XI. It was Tony's magic that led to the Villa going in front. He gave Mick Mills a torrid time, in the end the former England captain pulled back his tormentor to give away a spot-kick. Peter Shilton dived to his right but could only look on as Gordon Cowans planted it to the keeper's left. Goal number two was a result of a corner, Sid neatly floated the ball over, McNaught flicked it on and Evans headed it home. Morley's contribution, Cowans' ingenuity and Williams magnificent defensive display proved way too much for Southampton.

Sat 8th Jan **Northampton Town (A)** **FA Cup 3rd round**
Won 1-0 **Att 14,529**
Walters

Shaw failed a fitness test so Walters was brought in. It was hard to believe Northampton were a Fourth Division outfit, they went all out with wave after wave of attacks. Thankfully McNaught and Evans were on top of their game. More than half an hour had elapsed

[Right] Gary Shaw levels the aggregate score against Barcelona at Villa Park to send the tie into extra time

before Villa managed to score, Morley operating on the left flank found Withe who flicked it inside to Walters. In the blink of an eye the youngster turned in Cruyffesque style and confidently drove into the back of the net. A goal of stunning skill!

Sat 15th Jan **Sunderland (A)**
Lost 0-2 **Att 16,052**

The Black Cats were second from bottom, with only Birmingham City beneath them. Villa had two opportunities to break the dead-lock, Morley denied when Turner pushed the ball over the bar and a Walters firm header was held by the goalkeeper. Villa then fell behind in the 27th minute. McNaught helping the ball into his own net after a Leighton James free kick. From that point on Sunderland never looked back. Spink kept Villa in the game when he saved from Stan Cummins. Within minutes of the break the Rokermen were further ahead, Worthington with a left foot drive.

Wed 19th Jan **Barcelona (A)** **European Super Cup 1st leg**
Lost 0-1 **Att 45,000**

Villa's stubbornness created anxiety in Barca's play. It took until the 52nd minute for Spink to be beaten, Marcos' drive was covered but it took a deflection off Bremner's boot. Villa had few chances to score, a Shaw header lacked power, Alonso headed the ball away as Withe moved in and Peter almost had his head taken off his shoulders as Urruti collided with him as he punched the ball away. Barton had fully expected a plethora of injuries beforehand but due to the excellent handling of the game by the Swiss referee it didn't descend into a kicking match.

Sat 22nd Jan **Manchester City (H)**
Drew 1-1 **Att 20,145**
Shaw

Villa bombarded City yet all they had to show for it was a smartly taken goal by Shaw on four minutes, he was unchallenged as he beat Joe Corrigan. The move had initially started from an Evans throw in and then Withe and Mortimer combined before feeding Gary. A Williams effort struck a post and a Shaw header bounced fractionally over the crossbar. Asa Hartford made it 1-1 driving in beyond Spink. For the last 20 plus minutes Villa picked up where they had began, Shaw had an easy chance amid a flurry of feet and then a Cowans shot, albeit mis-hit brought off an outstanding reaction save.

Wed 26th Jan **Barcelona (H)** **European Super Cup 2nd leg**
Won 3-0 (agg 3-1) **Att 31,570**
Shaw, Cowans, McNaught

The die was cast as early as the 12th minute when Alberto was booked for a late, late tackle on Blair. Nasty and niggling fouls continued and sent Villa players tumbling throughout the first half. Barcelona weren't interested in playing football. The second half started just as badly, McNaught was yellow carded before Alberto was given his marching orders. Villa desperately needed a goal and it came with only ten minutes remaining, Shaw turned brilliantly and drove the ball in to take the 'brawl' into extra-time. Walters on for Morley was hauled down in the box. Cowans spot-kick was saved by Urriti but Sid followed up to smash the rebound in. A McNaught header made it 3-0 (3-1 agg). The biggest surprise was that the Spaniards only had two sent off and five others booked!

Sat 29th Jan **Wolverhampton Wanderers (H)** **FA Cup 4th round**
Won 1-0 **Att 43,121**
Withe

The match was only 40 seconds old when former Villa favourite Andy Gray headed down for Mel Eves, fortunately his first time effort went well wide. Villa found it hard going against an impressive Alan Dodd and his fast tackling defenders but got their noses in

[Right] Villa players greet the Holte End after a tough victory over Barcelona to clinch the European Super Cup

SUNOCO

front to a stubbed shot. Shaw slipped the ball to Withe, it was more a left-footed hack that sent the ball bobbling off the upright and into the net. Villa had an exciting spell which saw Cowans bundled over in the area by Matthews but referee Hackett rejected the appeal.

Sat 5th Feb **Nottingham Forest (A)**
Won 2-1 **Att 16,352**
Withe 2

Once Villa weathered the early storm they started to assert their own pressure. Tony Morley was denied when a close-range header was blocked. The winger then sent over an inch perfect centre for Withe, who gave Sutton no chance. Forest's Wilson levelled within three minutes. Cowans missed an early second-half penalty (Morley sent sprawling by Bowyer and Swain). On the hour Withe stroked a sublime 25-yarder that sailed clean over Sutton's head. It was vintage Withe.

Sat 12th Feb **Everton (H)**
Won 2-0 **Att 21,117**
Morley, Withe

Everton had won their last five. Mortimer was back having missed three matches. Dennis put in a typically powerful performance and played a part in the opening goal. It started with Cowans in his own box, he supplied Withe who cleverly flicked it on to Shaw; Gary put Mortimer through and his cross-shot was a met at the far post by Morley - a superb all-round team goal. Everton appeared cautious as Villa attacked with flair. Villa's second goal, Gibson fed Morley whose centre was met by Withe to hit his fourth in three matches.

[Left] Colin Gibson marked by Juventus' Gaetano Scirea during the European Cup clash at Villa Park

Sat 19th Feb **Watford (H)** **FA Cup 5th round**
Won 4-1 **Att 34,330**
Shaw, Morley, Gibson, Cowans

No one would envisage the scoreline based on the first 20 minutes, Watford had chance after chance to score and could have been six-nil up. Once Villa went ahead they weren't going to be caught. Shaw started the goal fest. Morley helped himself to goal number two with a delightful lob. The third started with Shaw who created space for Cowans to get a good cross in which was met by full-back Gibson. Sid rounded off the goals when he chested down Blair's free kick before rifling it past Sherwood. Blissett pulled one back from the penalty spot.

Sat 26th Feb **Watford (A)**
Lost 1-2 **Att 19,318**
Walters

Watford started as they did in the cup-tie only this time they went in front, Blissett scoring courtesy of the underside of the crossbar. From there on in it was one way traffic, Watford's high-ball and long-ball style of play wreaking havoc in the Villa rearguard. A mix up between Sherwood and Bolton allowed Walters to slip in and equalise. After the break Villa's defence failed to close down Wilf Rostron, his 30-yard shot found its way into the right hand corner of the net.

Wed 2nd Mar **Juventus (H)** **European Cup quarter-finals 1st leg**
Lost 1-2 **Att 45,531**
Cowans

It soon became apparent that Villa's blood and sweat would be severely tested against the Italian's technique and ability. Villa were missing Evans, Bremner slotting in at centre-half. Juventus were ahead with only 46 seconds on the clock, Rossi ghosted in at the near post to steer his header wide of Spink. McNaught powered a header beyond Dino Zoff in the 14th minute but it was mysteriously ruled out. Villa were back in the tie ten minutes into the second half,

Cowans pass from the right was picked up by Gibson, his cross met by Sid who dived headlong to head in from six yards out. In the 84th minute Boniek ran between Bremner and McNaught to slot in the winner.

Sat 5th Mar **Norwich City (H)**
Won 3-2 **Att 18,624**
Withe, Deacy, Shaw

Norwich took a 19th minute lead when Barham scored from close range. Withe got his trusty head to a Cowans free kick to make it 1-1 at the half time break. City regained their advantage when Van Wyk scored. Eamonn Deacy scored his first goal in Villa colours, Withe found Deacy who smashed in his shot from distance. Villa weren't finished, Woods denied Withe before Shaw bagged the winner when he escaped the attentions of Symonds to turn in Gibson's centre.

Tue 8th Mar **Notts County (H)**
Won 2-0 **Att 17,452**
Withe, Shaw

Withe gave his side a slender interval lead with his 16th of the campaign. His partner in crime Gary Shaw went one better. By putting Villa firmly in the driving seat with the second goal of the evening, Shaw had bagged his 17th. It was only the fourth time the prolific pairing had scored in the same game this season. Had it not been for the bravery between the posts of Mick Leonard Villa could have obliterated the memory of five defeats in the previous six encounters with the Magpies before tonight. Villa were up to fourth.

Sat 12th Mar **Arsenal (A)** **FA Cup 6th round**
Lost 0-2 **Att 41,774**

McNaught dropped out just before kick-off and shortly into the game Evans was suffering with blurred vision following a fierce collision with Alan Sunderland. Villa had a few half chances but Arsenal were sharper and it was no surprise when they took the lead,

Woodcock hooking the ball in from two yards. Five minutes later Petrovic made it 2-0. Villa came more into it after the interval with Gibson pushing forward and Walters doing likewise after replacing Deacy. The closest they came was when a firm Withe header came back from the underside of the bar.

Wed 16th Mar **Juventus (A)** European Cup quarter-finals 2nd leg
Lost 1-3 (agg 2-5) **Att 70,000**
Withe

Juventus launched a search and destroy mission, backed by a partisan crowd. Bettega fired the first warning shot but luckily it struck McNaught and cannoned to safety. Villa were cruelly punished when a Platini corner was met by Rossi, his strike skidded across the greasy surface through Spink's hands. A Withe header was bravely saved by Zoff before Villa went further behind. Rossi's corner this time, played back by Gentile who set up Tardelli, 2-0 to Juve. Platini added a third on 67 minutes. Withe reduced the deficit on 80 minutes but it was a mere consolation. The holders were out.

Sat 19th Mar **Coventry City (H)**
Won 4-0 **Att 20,509**
Shaw, Withe 2, Evans

Villa shrugged off Turin with an explosive performance. Coventry weren't helped by how vulnerable their defence looked when Shaw and Withe attacked. Gary bundled the first one over the line and with less than 30 minutes played; Withe rose to give Sealey no chance as Villa made it two. City had a few half-chances that amounted to nothing. Evans cracked in the third to give Villa a commanding half-time lead. Peter Withe hammered in his second to make it 4-0.

[Left] Villa's Eire international Eammonn Deacy on the ball during the away F.A. Cup defeat to Arsenal

Wed 23rd Mar **Tottenham Hotspur (A)**
Lost 0-2 **Att 22,455**

Villa clearly lacked a cutting edge up front as Withe, Shaw and Walters were starved of service as Cowans, Mortimer and Bremner in midfield were totally dominated by Mabbutt, Perryman and Hoddle. Falco put Spurs ahead having been set up by Brazil. Clemence, apart from smothering the ball at the feet of Mortimer, was hardly troubled at all. Villa were already beaten before Falco bagged his second of the evening with 85 minutes gone. The only embarrassment for Tottenham was naming Saunders as manager in the match programme!

Sat 26th Mar **Brighton & Hove Albion (A)**
Drew 0-0 **Att 14,648**

Relegation threatened Albion were first to show, the fighting qualities that have seen them progress to the F.A. Cup semi's visibly apparent. They should have been two goals clear even without a home win in three months. Smilie fumbled one chance within 30 seconds and then new signing Connor also went close. Ex-Villa loanee Moseley held firmly to a Withe header, while between the other posts Spink was fortunate when he dropped the ball but Stevens fired over the bar.

Sat 2nd Apr **Ipswich Town (A)**
Won 2-1 **Att 20,945**
Shaw, Withe

Ipswich were ahead two minutes in when a Williams clearance rebounded into the net off McCall. Had Mortimer not been alert to clear a Butcher header off the line the scenario could have been so so different. Villa then started looking like the Villa of old and in first-half injury time Walters scampered down the wing and crossed for Shaw to level. Cowans pulled the strings in the second half and Villa were rewarded when Withe headed home the winner.

Mon 4th Apr **Birmingham City (H)**
Won 1-0 **Att 40,897**
Shaw

Villa were quick to utilise the pace of Walters; Shaw rolled the ball into the path of the speeding teenager but as Mark flew into the box he was upended by Blake. Ref Midgeley said, "Nothing doing." In typical 'derby' fashion there was little quality on show, if players lingered on the ball they ended up being taken down. It took until the 84th minute for the stalemate to finally be broken. Gary Shaw scored, he took Withe's knock-down in his stride before firing a low shot into the net. The result kept Villa on track for a UEFA Cup place.

Sat 9th Apr **Luton Town (A)**
Lost 1-2 **Att 10,924**
Shaw

Villa started well, moving the ball around, perhaps a bit too casually. Luton, serious relegation contenders were more enterprising than their placing suggested. They caught Villa's rearguard cold when they snatched a lead. Shaw, Villa's salvation in recent weeks added to his goal tally with a splendid effort, Cowans set Shaw away, the blond haired striker controlled the ball before spinning and firing. Luton appeared more in need of the points, centres rained in but Evans and McNaught remained strong. With a draw looking likely Luton snatched a last minute winner.

Tue 19th Apr **West Bromwich Albion (H)**
Won 1-0 **Att 26,921**
Mortimer

Curbishley was handed his full debut. Traditionally Albion encounters are rugged, bitterly fought out affairs, this was no exception. The opening 20 minutes was a softening up process by both sides but with Robertson and Withe booked early doors it was sufficient to keep the game from spilling over. WBA with five men across the back proved hard to break down. Villa finally did this on the stroke of half time and in style. A brisk touch by Shaw, the cross

from Curbishley, a controlled header by Withe and Mortimer under heavy pressure was able to head home from three yards out. Villa were up to third.

Sat 23rd Apr **West Ham United (A)**
Lost 0-2 **Att 21,822**

Villa were on the back foot from the start, Spink who'd already saved from Swindlehurst and Van der Elst was powerless to prevent the Hammers first goal. He did well to claw Goddard's header away but Swindlehurst reacted sharpest and jabbed the loose ball in. Villa lacked punch up front, their two best chances falling to left-back Colin Gibson. His first, a rising shot Parkes did well to turn over the crossbar, the second an angled drive after the defender had cut in from the touchline. A Villa revival sank without trace when West Ham added a second with just over a dozen minutes remaining.

Sat 30th Apr **Stoke City (H)**
Won 4-0 **Att 20,944**
Cowans, McNaught, Morley, Evans

Villa strangely employed the long target ball tactics even though Withe was missing, Shaw and Walters up front. This failed immediately with Stoke mopping up everything. Cowans who'd played well for England in the week started the rout when he latched on to a Mortimer shot that Fox spilled and chested the ball over the line. Sid then had a hand in all three following goals, McNaught met a corner at the near post, Morley raced on to Cowans through ball to fire left-footed beyond Fox to make it 3-0 and Allan Evans rounded off the scoring with his head.

[Left] Peter Withe on the ball during the Bank Holiday derby day win over Birmingham City

Mon 2nd May **Swansea City (A)**
Lost 1-2 **Att 9,173**
Shaw

Villa again without Withe, the twin spearhead of Shaw and Walters with Morley playing a supporting role from the flank lacked understanding and penetration. High balls floated in were dealt with comfortably. Deterined Swansea were playing for their First Division lives, they scored within ten minutes. Even being harried out of possession Villa came back, McNaught floated over a free kick, partner Evans headed back across goal and Shaw darted in to side-foot a simple goal. The winner came only five minutes after the break, Gale driving low into the far corner.

Sat 7th May **Liverpool (A)**
Drew 1-1 **Att 39,939**
Shaw (pen)

Liverpool had already won the title race but wanted to put a show on for their departing manager Bob Paisley. The heavens opened before the start and when Gary Shaw slotted in a 12th minute penalty it appeared that Villa were going to rain on Paisley's parade too. Spink saved not one but two penalties from Phil Neal (the keeper adjudged to have moved) and just when it looked like Villa might take three points, Dalglish managed to reach Johnston who pounced to force the ball in.

Sat 14th May **Arsenal (H)**
Won 2-1 **Att 24,647**
Shaw, Gibson

Villa looked nervous on the greasy surface until a fluke goal by Shaw calmed the nerves. As Morley crossed Mortimer and Shaw collided, the ball spiralled off Gary's head, up and back and over the line. Villa edged closer to the win when Shaw teed up Gibson ten minutes into the second half with a tremendous crossfield ball, Colin ran on, connected and sent a shot past Jennings. Arsenal pulled one back on 69 minutes. The game marked McNaught's

For the first time in the club's history they will go in to a new season fighting on six fronts, the League title, F.A. Cup, League Cup, European Cup, European Super Cup and last but not least the World Club Championship.

PRE-SEASON

• Terry Bullivant moves on to Charlton Athletic, Barton wanted him to stay but without a guarantee of first-team football.
• Aston Villa had two players on World Cup duty in Spain. Allan Evans played for Scotland against Russia while Peter Withe got no further than the England bench.
• Brian Little is appointed Youth coach, succeeding Keith Leonard. Malcolm Beard is named as the new chief scout.
• The name Davenports will adorn the Villa shirts for the coming season as Birmingham's only brewery becomes the club sponsor.
• The Villa players have to report back for pre-season training a week after the majority of First Division sides. With the European Cup final played in the last week of May and then the side facing the Kuwait National Team in Morocco after that date the Villa's season didn't end until June.

AUGUST

• Villa's final offer is rejected by Ken McNaught.
• Tony Barton approaches Brighton regarding England defender Steve Foster.
• Gary Williams is sent off against Werder Bremen. It was Friday 13th.
• Villa's Germany pre-season tour results make for grim reading - three straight defeats, 11 goals conceded, three scored. They then lose at home to Czechoslovakian side Dukla Prague.
• Villa announce under 16s can get to watch Villa Park games for £1.
• Allan Evans hands in a transfer request immediately after Villa lose 1-3 at home to Sunderland.
• Sunderland's 'England B' star Shaun Elliott is linked with a Villa move.
• The disillusionment, the aftermath of the poor pre-season amongst Villa fans is evident in the fact that the Supporters' Club run only two coaches to Everton.
• Ken McNaught agrees to sign a new contract.
• Following the inept 0-5 defeat at Goodison Park it emerged Manager Barton had told them at the break, "Now you have your pride to play for!" Asked if they had he replied, "You saw for yourself, some of them didn't."
• Barton says he will make changes. Kenny Swain is the first to be dropped, Everton turns out to be his last game!

SEPTEMBER

• Stoke City's Alan Dodd is invited to train with the Villa as manager Barton contemplates signing him.
• Villa sign Australian Anthony Dorigo on apprentice forms, the youngster paid his own fare over for trials.
• Gary Shaw is sidelined, firstly with the flu and then wisdom tooth surgery.
• Despite losing at Southampton the side then go and win four consecutive league games. They also successfully negotiate the first hurdle in their defence of the European Cup.
• Noel Blake a reserve centre-half moves to Birmingham City for £35,000.
• Villa's match at home to Besiktas is played behind closed doors, part of UEFA's fine following the trouble at Anderlecht at the semi stage.
• Ken McNaught signs a new contract.
• Gary Shaw plays in England's Under-21 European Championship tie v West Germany.
• Tony Morley plays in England's 2-2 in Denmark.

[Above] Dennis Mortimer scores against Besiktas at an empty Villa Park in September 1982

OCTOBER

• Villa lose at the Hawthorns for the first time in 17 years.
• The Dynamo Bucharest hierarchy arrive from Romania to spy on the Villa at Notts County.
• Morley is selected for the England squad to meet West Germany.
• Full-back Kenny Swain moves to Nottingham Forest on loan.
• Peter Withe is to be disciplined and possibly fined for his sending off in the league match at Meadow Lane. He was dismissed for arguing with the ref, Barton said, "It was inexcusable and stupid."
• Aston Villa Football Club hold their AGM. Chairman Ron Bendall is absent through illness.
• Villa apprentice David Norton joins the England Youth party for specialist training at Lilleshall. The England coach – Graham Taylor.

NOVEMBER

• Villa's involvement in the Southern Junior Floodlit Cup comes to an end. They lose 1-2 at home to Watford.
• Barton's plans to sign Dave Swindlehurst from Derby are put on ice following the return of Peter Taylor to the Baseball Ground.
• Peter Withe's winner in the victory over Brighton was the striker's 100th League goal.
• Swain extends his loan period (a further month) at Brian Clough's Nottingham Forest.
• Tony Morley plays a part in England's 3-0 win over Greece in Salonika.
• Reading striker Kerry Dixon is on Barton's radar.
• It is revealed Aston Villa have debts of £1.6 million.
• Villa give Crystal Palace permission to talk to Geddis.
• Ron Bendall and his son Donald resign as directors of Aston Villa Football Club PLC. On the same day Doug Ellis is elected Chairman of the Club.

DECEMBER

• Villa are still yet to find out their opponents in the World Club Championship match, they will face either Cobreloa (Chile) or Penarol (Uruguay).
• Doug Ellis reveals he has bought Bendall's 42% share holding in the club.
• The Villa will learn their European Cup quarter-final opponents later in the month. The draw is announced as they are in Tokyo preparing for the World Club Championships. They will meet Italian giants Juventus.
• Pat Heard makes his last appearance in the 1-2 defeat at Highbury, Villa miss out on going joint top of the table. McNaught is captain for the evening.

• The European Cup draw is announced (they will meet Italian giants Juventus) as Villa are in Tokyo preparing for the World Club Championships.
•Tony Barton's side lose 0-2 to South American Champions Penarol. They came away with a lot of credit.
• Dave Geddis joins Luton Town on loan.
• Jimmy Rimmer bows out in the Birmingham City loss.

JANUARY

• Villa and Forest agree a fee for Kenny Swain.
• Villa's youngsters go out of the F.A. Youth Cup, 2-5 at Norwich City.
• Pat Heard joins Sheffield Wednesday for £60,000.
• Aston Villa wallop Barcelona 3-0 in the 2nd leg of the European Super Cup to land the trophy 3-1 on aggregate.
• Paul Birch lands himself a medal as he comes on for the last eight minutes of injury time against Barcelona.
• Villa go into their F.A. Cup tie with Wolverhampton Wanderers boasting the best record of any side in the competition. In winning 170 of their 225 ties they have a success rate of 66.5%.
• Terry Donovan goes out on loan to Oxford United.

FEBRUARY

• Malcolm Beard, the Villa's chief Scout, flies to Naples to cast his eye over Juventus. Celtic manager (later Villa boss) Billy McNeill also provides excellent info on the Italian side as his side faced them last season.
• The Villa squad head down to Devon for a three day break. It was thought the players might benefit from a change of environment.
• Sid Cowans wins his first England cap in the 2-1 win over Wales, to add to his Youth, Under-21 and 'B' caps.
• Villa's 2-1 victory at Forest's City Ground ensures their first League double of the campaign.
• After disposing of Watford in the F.A. Cup 5th round Villa are drawn to play at either Middlesbrough or Arsenal. Both bogey sides!
• Full-back Mark Jones is put in plaster. His ankle injury far worse than first expected.
• Villa reserves head the Central League table following victory over Everton res.

MARCH

• When Paolo Rossi scores for Juventus in 46 seconds Villa find themselves trailing in a European Cup tie for the very first time. Juve win 2-1 at B6.
• Gordon Cowans is linked with Juventus.
• A quote heard from the Villa Park Press box during the Notts County match, "County's offside trap is about as ragged as Jimmy Sirrel's teeth!"
• Negotiations break down, Tony Barton fails to sign David Swindlehurst from Derby County.
• Barton lands his first signing, Alan Curbishley from Birmingham City. The fee £100,000 plus Robert Hopkins moving in the opposite direction.
• Apprentice David Norton travels to Israel with the England Youth party.
• Aston Villa sign 14-year old Mark Burke on associate schoolboy forms.
• Terry Donovan moves to Burnley in a £20,000 deal.
• Villa lose 0-2 at Highbury in the F.A. Cup quarter-finals.
• Villa's hold on the European Cup is over as they crash out to Juventus 1-3 in Turin (2-5 agg).
• Gary Shaw gave Gentile his shirt after the Juve match, "You've been in it all night, so you might as well take it home with you!"
• Jimmy Rimmer decides he still has a future at B6 following talks with Ellis and Barton.

APRIL

• Ray Walker makes his debut at West Ham United.
• England manager Bobby Robson has been paying particular attention to Gary Williams. Perhaps international honours could be forthcoming?
• Aston Villa are linked with Celtic star Charlie Nicholas.
• Villa reserves notch up their biggest win of the season, 8-0 at home to Stoke City. Geddis and Morley each get a brace.
• Gary Shaw's goal in the loss at Luton means he has beaten his best goal tally for a season. His Kenilworth Road goal puts him on 21.
• The Villa reserves beat Sheff Utd 6-1 to go back top of the Central League.
• David Norton plays for the England Youth versus their Belgium counterparts.
• Peter Withe and Gordon Cowans star in England's 2-0 win over Hungary at Wembley.

MAY

• Despite ending the season on a winning note (Arsenal H) to secure sixth place Villa still need Man Utd to lift the F.A. Cup to ensure UEFA Cup football.
• Gordon Cowans receives the Evening Mail Footballer of the Year Trophy [pictured left] from chairman Doug Ellis before the last game of the season at home to Arsenal.
• Villa Park is to host the England v USSR European Youth Championship match.

JUNE

• Gordon Cowans scores England's second goal in the 2-0 victory over Scotland at Wembley. The player admits the paper talk of a possible move to Italian side Naples is true. He has spoken with them and is definitely interested.

[Right] Paul Rideout gets a shot on target during the match at Watford

1983–84

IVECO
mita
IVECO
IVECO TRUCK

[Back Row] Tony Morley, Paul Rideout, Mark Walters, Andy Blair, Allan Evans, Alan Curbishley, [Middle Row] Jim Williams (Physiotherapist), Ray Walker, Mark Jones, Nigel Spink, Colin Gibson, Gary Williams, Gordon Cowans, Roy MacLaren (Coach) [Front Row] Ken McNaught (moved to WBA), Des Bremner, Steve McMahon, Tony Barton (Manager), Gary Shaw, Peter Withe, Dennis Mortimer.

Football League	Division One
Manager	Tony Barton
Coach	Roy MacLaren
Physio	Jim Williams
Captain	Dennis Mortimer
Final Position	Tenth
F.A. Cup	Third Round
League Cup	Semi-finals
Leading Goalscorer	Peter Withe 22 goals

Villa got the season off to a flyer beating WBA complete with their new signing Ken McNaught by the odd goal in seven. Brendan Ormsby who filled the centre-half berth scored the second-half winner. They would also win their next game at home to Sunderland.

In the UEFA Cup Portuguese side Vitoria Guimaraes inflicted a one-nil defeat but Villa came back in the second leg to destroy them, Withe bagging three in the 5-0 rout.

After ten League games Villa were sitting ninth, they had the best home record in the division, having won all five and conceding only three goals in the process. They were also through to the next round of the League Cup having got past Portsmouth 5-4 over the two legs.

When Villa brought back a commendable 2-2 draw from their game at Spartak Moscow, another Walters wonder goal, it looked like job done, it wasn't - the Russians over-turned a half-time deficit to go through 2-1 in Brum.

When Arsenal came to Aston it was a foregone conclusion, The Gunners had only two away wins to their name. Had Tony Woodcock stayed at home perhaps Villa would have ran out 2-1 winners, he didn't, he played, he also scored five goals and Villa were resoundingly beaten 2-6 and dropped five places. Their next game - Old Trafford! Villa hadn't won there in 22 attempts, United were two points clear at the summit. Peter Withe scored twice to shake up the table with a surprise 2-1 victory.

continued >>>

		Total Home League Attendances	448,790
		Average Home League	21,370
		Highest Home League	39,318
		Lowest Home League	13,052

		P	W	D	L	GF	GA	DIF	PTS
1	Liverpool	42	22	14	6	73	32	41	80
2	Southampton	42	22	11	9	66	38	28	77
3	Nottingham Forest	42	22	8	12	76	45	31	74
4	Manchester United	42	20	14	8	71	41	30	74
5	Queens Park Rangers	42	22	7	13	67	37	30	73
6	Arsenal	42	18	9	15	74	60	14	63
7	Everton	42	16	14	12	44	42	2	62
8	Tottenham Hotspur	42	17	10	15	64	65	-1	61
9	West Ham United	42	17	9	16	60	55	5	60
10	Aston Villa	42	17	9	16	59	61	-2	60
11	Watford	42	16	9	17	68	77	-9	57
12	Ipswich Town	42	15	8	19	55	57	-2	53
13	Sunderland	42	13	13	16	42	53	-11	52
14	Norwich City	42	12	15	15	48	49	-1	51
15	Leicester City	42	13	12	17	65	68	-3	51
16	Luton Town	42	14	9	19	53	66	-13	51
17	West Bromwich Albion	42	14	9	19	48	62	-14	51
18	Stoke City	42	13	11	18	44	63	-19	50
19	Coventry City	42	13	11	18	57	77	-20	50
20	Birmingham City	42	12	12	18	39	50	-11	48
21	Notts County	42	10	11	21	50	72	-22	41
22	Wolverhampton Wanderers	42	6	11	25	27	80	-53	29

Manchester City and West Bromwich Albion were brushed aside in the League Cup before Villa fell to another heavy defeat at Meadow Lane, last season it had been 1-4, this time round 2-5!

Villa's 2-1 win at home to QPR on the last day of December meant they entered the New Year in seventh position. January brought no League wins but it did include three encounters with Norwich City in the space of eleven days. Honours shared, Villa went through to the League Cup semis whilst The Canaries progressed in the F.A. Cup after a replay.

The first League win of 1984 came courtesy of bottom-placed Wolverhampton Wanderers, Withe 2, Birch and Walters in the 4-0 caning. Back-to back wins - for the first time since the opening games - over Forest and Sunderland both 1-0, lifted Villa to eighth; only to fall to defeat at Blues who were now four points behind and in tenth (amazingly Birmingham would only collect four more points from their remaining eight fixtures and would drop with Notts County and Wolves).

Wins over Watford and Notts County at home continued at West Ham United where Villa recorded only their third away win of the campaign. Mortimer's goal kept Villa eighth with two games remaining. Villa's home record was better than champions elect Liverpool at that moment.

Aston Villa would finish the campaign in tenth place after losing their last two fixtures, home to Everton 0-2 and away to Ipswich Town 1-2.

[Right] Gary Shaw on the ball during the season curtain raiser victory over West Brom

1983-84

Sat 27th Aug **West Bromwich Albion (H)**
Won 4-3 **Att 30,590**
Evans, Walters, Shaw, Ormsby

Albion scored first through Zondervan on five minutes. McNaught now playing for the Baggies failed to spot Evans make a late run to get his head on to Gibson's centre. Villa new boy Steve McMahon presented Withe and Shaw with chances but both were unable to take them. Shaw then set up Walters, the youngster dummying keeper Barron. WBA were back on level terms through Garry Thompson before Shaw got in on the act, 3-2. Regis fired in on the stroke of half time to send both teams in all even. Brendan Ormsby bagged the winner.

Mon 29th Aug **Sunderland (H)**
Won 1-0 **Att 21,969**
Walters

McMahon and Mortimer were out Blair and Birch in. Villa's players looked tense against a stubborn but lively team and let them stroke the ball about far too much. Birch and Walters had shots saved by Turner. The tempo raised after the interval and as Villa gained in momentum Sunderland wilted. Withe had a 20-yard drive headed off the line by Venison, the keeper saved from Shaw (twice), Blair and Birch in a frenetic period. Birch was quick to exploit the gaps and set up Walters with a great pass for the winger to volley in.

Sat 3rd Sep **Queens Park Rangers (A)**
Lost 1-2 **Att 16,922**
Withe

Villa went behind after four minutes, hindered by the wind and the ball's awkward bounce. Stainrod bagged the goal. Spink was alert to pull off three spectacular saves while McMahon was proving to be a powerhouse in the midfield, Walters was also a threat with his

skilful running. McMahon had the ball in the net but was offside. Withe then saw a header cleared. On 67 minutes the ball spun off Peter's head but it was into his own net, Rangers in the driving seat. Withe scored in the dying seconds - too little, too late.

Wed 7th Sep **Nottingham Forest (A)**
Drew 2-2 **Att 16,379**
Withe, Shaw

Forest were first out of the blocks though Villa started to gain composure. On 17 minutes the visitors made the breakthrough, Gibson pinpointed one such set piece at Withe who headed beyond van Breukelen. Davenport made it 1-1 four minutes before the interval. Wallace clear through forced a fine save from the advancing Spink before Villa regained their lead. Gibson was hauled down, Shaw took the spot kick but the keeper moved too soon. Gary retook it only to see the keeper block this attempt too, luckily he scooped in the rebound. Birtles snatched a dramatic equaliser five minutes from time.

Sat 10th Sep **Norwich City (H)**
Won 1-0 **Att 18,887**
Mortimer

Paul Rideout, making his first start, linked up with Withe to set up Mortimer to open the scoring. City stopper Woods was caught in no-man's land and with the defence waving for offside Dennis coolly lobbed the stranded keeper. Mortimer who many thought was on his way out of B6 slotted into Villa's new midfield of McMahon and Curbishley with ease. The game should have been killed off when a Rideout shot hit the side-netting, seconds later the youngster was denied again when Watson hacked another of his efforts away.

Wed 14th Sep **Vitoria Guimaraes (A)** **UEFA Cup 1st round 1st leg**
Lost 0-1 **Att 28,750**

The Portuguese looked decidedly amateurish as Withe out-foxed their offside-trap within five minutes of the start, his volley expertly saved by Silvino. Their forward line fared little better as they struggled to trouble Villa's rearguard. Evans missed a golden chance to put his side ahead and was equally guilty when he did the same in the second half. With it looking likely Villa would go home with a satisfactory draw Paquito got into the area on the wrong side of McMahon, as they brushed he went down, the ref didn't hesitate, pointing to the spot. Gregorio beat Spink to initiate wild scenes.

Sat 17th Sep **Liverpool (A)**
Lost 1-2 **Att 34,246**
Gibson

Liverpool started in style, Spink saving from Rush and Lee. He then went one better keeping out Johnston's volley. Villa had a few first-half chances but none compared to the one Walters was gifted; he raced on to a deflected cross yet placed the ball wide of the upright. Villa were less of an attacking force after the interval though Evans and Gibson put in exemplary displays to withstand the bombardment. Dalglish scored on 72 minutes, eight minutes later Rush made it two driving in from 25-yards out. Gibson pulled one back with six minutes remaining. McMahon was dismissed with 10 seconds to go for retaliating to Souness.

Sat 24th Sep **Southampton (H)**
Won 1-0 **Att 21,209**
Withe

Morley was reinstated on the flank, Walters moving infield to cover the absent Shaw. Mark was in splendid form, he was well supplied by his hardworking midfield and terrorised the towering Southampton defenders as Villa destroyed the visitors in the first half. All they had to show for their domination was a solitary goal, Walters setting up big Withe to simply sidefoot home. Morley grew in confidence as the match progressed but Villa were unable to open the floodgates. They were up to sixth.

[Right] Allan Evans heads toward goal during the rout of Vitoria Guimaraes at Villa Park

ANSELLS BITTER
Bristol Street Motors

Wed 28th Sep **Vitoria Guimaraes (H)** UEFA Cup 1st round 2nd leg
Won 5-0 (agg 5-1) **Att 23,732**
Withe 3, Ormsby, Gibson

Villa were constantly caught slumbering in the first half in spite of Withe scoring after 115 seconds, his headed goal from six-yards out after Morley skipped past two tackles to deliver the perfect cross. Whatever Barton said at half time worked. Villa came out and gave a superb show. A Withe header on 49 minutes was fumbled over the line by the goalkeeper; Ormsby then glanced in a Mortimer corner to make it 3-0 on the night. Gibson charged through to slide in the fourth. Murca was sent off following an outrageous tackle on Walters. Withe drove home his third and Villa's fifth.

Sat 1st Oct **Luton Town (A)**
Lost 0-1 **Att 12,747**

In the first half Villa were far superior but floundered around the box and totally collapsed inside it. In the 50th minute Frank Bunn who'd spent the game falling down outside the penalty area finally went down the other side of the 18-yard line. In fairness to Gary Williams he had little choice, his fellow defenders were caught square and too far upfield from the long hopeful ball and it took two charges to fell Bunn. Moss took the spot-kick and gave Spink no chance. Morley made way for Shaw but couldn't provide a cutting edge to his side's blunt attack.

Tue 4th Oct **Portsmouth (A)** League Cup 2nd round 1st leg
Drew 2-2 **Att 18,484**
Gibson, Evans

Portsmouth caused all sorts of trouble for the Villa. Spink could only watch as a Hateley header struck the crossbar, Biley then hit a high cross that Nigel managed to turn around the upright. Knight denied Evans from scoring before Hateley found the back of the net when his angled shot was well placed. Pompey went two-up when Gibson sliced a corner into his own net. Only four minutes were remaining when Gibson pulled one back against the run of play. With 60 seconds left Evans fired in a shock equaliser.

Sat 15th Oct **Birmingham City (H)**
Won 1-0 **Att 39,318**
Withe

The wet, greasy surface didn't help, nor did the player's losing their heads. Evans was brought down twice in the opening five minutes by brutal efficiency. Hopkins chopped Walters down to suffer the wrath of the supporters. The goal that decided this 90 minutes of mayhem arrived in the 29th minute, Withe chased down a half-hearted backpass, Coton in goal fumbled and Peter neatly rolled it in from an acute angle. Even the men in black were at risk, a Blake sliding tackle took a linesman clean out. Gibson received his marching orders and Spink saved a Blake penalty.

Wed 19th Oct **Moscow Spartak (A)** UEFA Cup 2nd round 1st leg
Drew 2-2 **Att 50,400**
Gibson, Walters

It was vintage Aston Villa, discipline was impressive and the defence tackled with great authority to keep the game scoreless at the break. Within 90 minutes of the re-start Gibson controlled a Morley pass, outstripped Sochnov and drove left-footed beyond Desayev. Five minutes later Spartak replied through Gavrilov. Walters fired Villa back in the lead, though closely marked by Podzniakov he swivelled, flicked the ball inside and hit a swirling shot that gave keeper Desayev no chance. With play almost up the ref blew when Soshnomov tumbled in front of Ormsby. To much Soviet laughter a penalty was given, Gavrilov calmly stepped up to make it 2-2.

Sun 23rd Oct **Wolverhampton Wanderers (A)**
Drew 1-1 **Att 13,202**
Withe

Withe and Walters were marked out of the game by Coy and Dodd though the former evaded the close attention to get on the end of a Walters cross to score his eighth of the season with a stooping header. Villa rightly felt like the victims of bad refereeing when Wolves levelled; Mortimer stopped fully expecting the whistle when he was tugged back twice by Rudge, instead the teenager was allowed to continue and centre for Clarke to back-heel past Spink.

Wed 26th Oct **Portsmouth (H)** League Cup 2nd round 2nd leg
Won 3-2 AET (agg 5-4) **Att 20,898**
Evans (pen), Withe, Walters

Portsmouth were in front after just six minutes. Notwithstanding the fact the game sparkled it took until the 52nd minute for Villa to level the tie. Dillon handled Bremner's close range shot and Evans scored from the spot. When Dillon chipped Spink on 79 minutes it looked like Villa were out. With four minutes remaining Mortimer powered down the left and crossed for Withe to head home. It took a goal in the 102nd minute of extra time to seal the match, Walters getting on the end of a beautifully threaded pass from McMahon to slot it in.

Sat 29th Oct **Arsenal (H)**
Lost 2-6 **Att 23,678**
Morley, Evans (pen)

Villa looked wrong from the kick-off, Woodcock put The Gunners in front within a few minutes, he then headed home the second goal as Arsenal raced into a commanding 4-1 lead by half time. The only bright spot a delicately chipped goal by Morley. An Allan Evans penalty made little difference as Arsenal added two more in the second 45 minutes to record a comprehensive 6-2 victory, Woodcock bagging five!

Wed 2nd Nov **Moscow Spartak (H)** UEFA Cup 2nd round 2nd leg
Lost 1- 2 (agg 3-4) **Att 29,511**
Withe

Villa scored after just two minutes. Mortimer started the move in midfield, fed Morley whose cross fell perfectly for Withe at the far post. Villa had Spink to thank, for keeping them in the tie making numerous saves. Within a minute of the second half Spartak were back in it, Villa's defence was split wide open and Cherenkov made no mistake. The Russians kept piling on the pressure, won numerous corners and in the very last minute Cherenkov's hopeful low ball into the crowded goalmouth took a wicked deflection beyond Spink.

Sat 5th Nov **Manchester United (A)**
Won 2-1 **Att 45,077**
Withe 2

Villa ran, tackled and harried their star-studded opponents; Wilkins wasn't allowed to settle while Evans and Ormsby shackled Stapleton. They went ahead when Withe collected a loose ball and his hopeful volley caught the unsighted Bailey by surprise, 1-0. The second, after the interval, was a result of Withe's sheer determination, Gibson challenged Duxbury, his back-pass was anticipated by the craggy centre-forward who sprinted ten yards behind the defence and clinically placed his shot past the keeper. Robson pulled one back four minutes later.

Wed 9th Nov **Manchester City (H)** League Cup 3rd round
Won 3-0 **Att 23,922**
Gibson, Evans, Mortimer

Gibson now playing wide-left got the ball rolling when he opened the scoring on 18 minutes, his strike giving Williams no chance. McMahon, Mortimer and Birch were running the midfield but no further goals arrived before the interval. Just after the hour mark and with City's central defenders caught cold skipper Allan Evans was left to head home Birch's right-sided corner kick. The brilliance of Withe and Rideout created Villa's third goal, scored by Dennis Mortimer.

Sat 12th Nov **Stoke City (H)**
Drew 1-1 **Att 19,272**
Withe

Mervyn Day was in for Spink. Fox did well to deny McMahon in the ninth minute but from then on Stoke asked all the questions as Barton's new 4-4-2 system struggled in the first-half. It was Stoke who took an interval lead, through Chamberlain. Gibson injured minutes before the half-time whistle failed to emerge for the second period, replaced by

Walters. Rideout went close but Fox managed somehow to get his hands to the ball. The Villa striker had the last laugh, moments later he withstood a vigorous challenge to meet a Birch cross and send Withe through to notch the side's equaliser on 54 minutes.

Sat 19th Nov **Leicester City (H)**
Won 3-1 **Att 19,024**
Withe, Rideout, McMahon

Leicester City stretched Villa from start to finish yet the hosts went ahead when Withe rose unchallenged to head a Walters cross past Wallington. Paul Birch's initial running made the goal. City still dangerous on the break fell further behind, Williams crossed a perfect ball for Rideout to claim his first senior goal when he nodded home at the far post. The visitors pulled one back on the stroke of half time when Spink gave a penalty away, Lynex converted. McMahon's goal in the 70th minute gave Villa the breathing space they needed.

Sat 26th Nov **Notts County (A)**
Lost 2-5 **Att 8,960**
Mortimer, Evans (pen)

Alan Curbishley was back for the first time in six games. Notts hadn't won at home since the opening day but were two up by 17 minutes, Christie and Chiedozie doing the damage. Mortimer scored with a 25-yard drive following decent work by Gibson. Villa were unlucky when a Brendan Ormsby header was cleared off the line. Notts then made it 3-1 on 68 minutes and then added another from the penalty spot. A poor back pass from Ormsby let Chiedozie in though Villa pulled it back to 2-5 when Evans scored from the spot, substitute Walters fouled in the box.

Wed 30th Nov **West Bromwich Albion (A)** **League Cup 4th round**
Won 2-1 **Att 31,114**
Walters, Mortimer

Villa went through after an angry confrontation. Walters put them ahead on five minutes with a tap-in following a blocked Rideout

[Above] Brendan Ormsby in an aerial duel with Dave Swindlehurst during Villa's home win against West Ham

header. A clash between Robertson and Rideout resulted in the Villa forward leaving the field for treatment. Villa were down to ten men when Albion forced a Regis equaliser five minutes later. McNaught was booked for a tackle on Withe that left him limping. Owen was red carded before the interval. Peter was a no show for the second half, taken to hospital with a suspected broken leg. Mortimer's goal in the 71st minute proved decisive.

Sat 3rd Dec **West Ham United (H)**
Won 1-0 **Att 21,297**
Rideout

Rideout led the front line, five internationals missing including Withe. The cause further hampered when Gibson pulled a hamstring and was replaced by Deacy. As the game progressed West Ham pushed forward - Spink pulled off two outstanding saves to deny second-placed United – and it left gaps for Villa to counter attack. Teenager Rideout shackled throughout found space, outjumped the defence to head home a Williams cross. Mortimer and Morley should have added goals and then in the dying seconds a Swindlehurst shot was kicked off the line by Villa's scorer.

Sat 10th Dec **Everton (A)**
Drew 1-1 **Att 15,814**
Rideout

Even with Spink added to the list of sick and injured, Villa had little difficulty containing a disappointing Everton side. With few chances to show on either side Paul Birch burst into life on the hour. He began the move, feeding Walters who in turn put a telling pass into the path of Rideout to score. On 79 minutes the referee awarded Everton a penalty, Ormsby harshly adjudged after winning the ball fairly from Heath. Sheedy blasted over, justice done. In the 89th minute Andy Gray struck at the far post, his goal coming out of nothing.

Sat 17th Dec **Ipswich Town (H)**
Won 4-0 **Att 16,548**
Withe, Rideout, McMahon, Evans (pen)

Villa took a third minute lead when Ian Cranson under pressure from Withe headed into his own net, Withe was somehow credited with the goal. Spink denied the visitors an equaliser on two occasions. Paul Rideout scored following good work by Williams and Withe. This set off a dazzling 20 minute period where Villa added two more goals, the unstoppable McMahon strode in to score on 68 minutes and Evans fired home a penalty after Walters had been tackled by O'Callaghan.

Mon 26th Dec **Watford (A)**
Lost 2-3 **Att 18,276**
Curbishley, Walters

Villa went behind in the first minute, Spink distracted as a free kick came over, tapped in from two yards. On 20 minutes Williams failed to clear a Steve Sims free kick, Barnes stole in to make it two. Villa fell further behind nine minutes into the second half. Just after the hour Deacy was shown red for a second offence. Only then did Villa start playing; Curbishley hit his first goal for Villa from 20-yards out and Walters added a second with ten minutes remaining when he tapped-in from McMahon's centre.

Tue 27th Dec **Tottenham Hotspur (H)**
Drew 0-0 **Att 30,125**

Tony Barton was visibly relieved to escape with a point in a match that amazingly ended in a 0-0 draw. Deacy gave the ball away with alarming ease. On another day Alan Brazil could have bagged a hat-trick, hesitating and shooting wide was Villa's fortune. Clemence had little to do other than two world-class saves; Withe conjured up a cunning chip on 74 minutes, moments later Walters was denied from the same range. Villa's No 9 did get the ball in the net but it was ruled out for offside.

Sat 31st Dec **Queen's Park Rangers (H)**
Won 2-1 **Att 19,978**
Evans (pen), McMahon

Gary Shaw, out for nearly three months showed he still had it, playing a part in both goals. Shaw, twisting on McMahon's pass following superb work by Deacy was tripped by Fenwick - penalty. Skipper Evans placed it in the corner to equalise, Villa having gone behind to a Jeremy Charles goal after 53 minutes. Steve McMahon made it 2-1 with a wonderful goal, he took Shaw's pass with one touch before curling the ball high beyond Hucker.

Mon 2nd Jan **Southampton (A)**
Drew 2-2 **Att 18,963**
McMahon, Shaw

Villa blew their best chance of a second win on their travels. Steve McMahon opened the scoring with a cracking low shot inside Shilton's right post, having been set up by Withe and Mortimer. Villa dominated the midfield forcing Southampton into mistakes and as they ploughed on in the atrocious conditions Shaw nipped in to further their lead. In what was rough justice for the Villa, they let the hosts off the hook as the Saints pulled back two goals in the last eight minutes.

Sat 7th Jan **Norwich City (H)** **FA Cup 3rd round**
Drew 1-1 **Att 21,454**
Withe

After a scrappy start it turned into a typical cup-tie, hard running and tough tackling. Norwich took the lead when former Villa favourite John Deehan calmly side-footed in. Villa were on level terms on 34 minutes, Mortimer chipped in a free kick from 30-yards for the unmarked Withe to get a touch with his left foot and beat Woods. A Gary Shaw snap shot was almost over the line before Devine kicked it clear.

[Above] Mark Walters crosses under the watchful eye of Norwich City's Dave Watson during the F.A. Cup draw

Wed 11th Jan **Norwich City (A)** FA Cup 3rd round replay
Lost 0-3 **Att 16,420**

It was a surprise it took six minutes for the Villa to go behind, it should have been 0-3 at that stage! Channon got the first from a rebound. Villa failed to put Norwich under any pressure and an out of form Shaw was replaced by Rideout, who livened things up briefly. Villa soon fell into disarray and masterminded by Channon Norwich added further goals through Mendham and Bertschin. "We were given a lesson," said Barton.

Sat 14th Jan **West Bromwich Albion (A)**
Lost 1-3 **Att 20,359**
Shaw

Villa masters of give-away points on opposition grounds looked to have broken the spell when Shaw scored from point-blank range in the opening minute of the second half. Villa held on til the 84th minute and then they crumbled. Firstly Thompson lobbed Spink; less than three minutes later Thompson added his second as he stretched and put his header wide of the keeper. The nightmare wasn't quite over, as Bremner slipped, Regis strode forward to slot home number three.

Tue 17th Jan **Norwich City (A)** League Cup quarter-final
Won 2-0 **Att 21,568**
Shaw, Rideout

Villa played for a semi-final place like their lives depended on it. Rideout served notice of Villa's intentions forcing Woods into a save after three minutes. Villa got their noses in front mid-way through the first half when Shaw jabbed the ball in from a Mortimer header. A little over a dozen minutes later Mortimer and McMahon combined, Rideout 20-yards out, swivelled and swung his right boot at it, Woods was beaten. Barton was delighted; "The lads were totally committed, and they played some good football out there."

Fri 20th Jan **Liverpool (H)**
Lost 1-3 **Att 19,566**
Mortimer

Conditions were treacherous and it was questioned whether the game should have been played. Villa protecting the best home record in the division skated ahead in the 15th minute. The move started with Williams and Curbishley, Rideout flicked the ball past the Liverpool defence, Mortimer timed his run to perfection and placed the ball beyond the prone keeper. Liverpool were level only 15 seconds into the second half; Lawrenson pumped the ball forward from the kick-off, Ian Rush powered past Bremner and left Spink helpless. Rush volleyed a second, and chipped his third.

Sat 4th Feb **Luton Town (H)**
Drew 0-0 **Att 18,656**

Without a home win this year the Villa struggled against a Luton side intent on defending in numbers and hitting on the breakaway. They were unfortunate when a Rideout shot was deflected wide by an arm, instead of a penalty they were given a corner. McMahon had two attempts go close, one skimming the bar, the other flying inches wide. Sealey only had one real save to make, that was to deny Rideout in the 80th minute.

Sat 11th Feb **Norwich City (A)**
Lost 1-3 **Att 13,658**
Shaw

Spink, McMahon and Withe the notable casualties. Perhaps it was the fifth meeting of these sides that made the Villa appear bored to death, hence, Norwich had the edge. Mervyn Day kept Villa in the game up to half time through good luck and good saves. Norwich hit the post and had two goalbound efforts cleared off the line before scoring twice in a nine minute spell through Deehan and Channon. Deehan got his second before Evans pulled one back.

Wed 15th Feb **Everton (A)** League Cup semi-final 1st leg
Lost 0-2 **Att 40,006**

In an unsavoury match of free kicks Villa fell behind on 28 minutes to a fluke goal as Spink and Mortimer let the ball run between them. When it looked like Villa would be taking a narrow one goal deficit into the 2nd leg Everton scored a second with only eight minutes remaining, Richardson given time to control the ball before firing it in. With only seconds left Gary Shaw saw his shot turned away by Richardson's arm, Villa players appealed and were horrified when the ref waved away their calls for a penalty. TV replays proved it was indeed a handball.

Sat 18th Feb **Arsenal (A)**
Drew 1-1 **Att 26,640**
Evans (pen)

Arsenal went in front on 11 minutes; Rix spotted Spink on the far post so he drove his free kick at the near, and it worked. Villa didn't sit back, driven on by Evans and Mortimer who was making his 300th appearance. The only thing their attacks lacked was punch. Mortimer clear through following a telling McMahon pass was hauled down by Talbot. Allan Evans calmly sent Jennings the wrong way scoring his fifth of the season from the spot.

Wed 22nd Feb **Everton (H)** League Cup semi-final 2nd leg
Won 1-0 (agg 1-2) **Att 42,426**
Rideout

Villa came to within a whisker of making it to the Final at the expense of an Everton side unbeaten in 14 matches. Villa pressed for that vital early goal but were thwarted by Southall and his defenders. Desperation saw the introduction of Rideout early in the second half. Within four minutes Paul had found the back of the net, an earth shaking roar went up. From that moment there was a belief and for the remaining half hour Villa threw everything at Everton who were pushed back to the brink – but ultimately held on.

Sat 25th Feb **Wolverhampton Wanderers (H)**
Won 4-0 **Att 18,257**
Withe 2, Birch, Walters

Rejected in the week by England and without a goal in eight games, Peter Withe threw the Wolves defence into disarray with two goals, in the 23rd and 61st minute; his first after he'd controlled Mortimer's angled shot. John Burridge saved twice from Mark Walters before Birch gave him no chance with a short range shot to make it 3-0. Frustrated by having to play wide to keep his place in the side, Walters scored a brilliant individualist goal in the last minute to give Barton food for thought.

Sat 3rd Mar **Manchester United (H)**
Lost 0-3 **Att 32,874**

New signing Steve Foster sitting in the stands would have seen a Villa central defence repeatedly bamboozled by the constant running of United's forwards. Spink had already prevented three goals before Colin Gibson wrong-footed his Villa teammates with a misjudged header that Remi Moses swept in from close range. An Ormsby header wide of the mark was Villa's sum total in the first period. When Whiteside put United further ahead it was obvious there was no coming back for the Villa. And so it proved, Bryan Robson fired in the third and within minutes the Holte End had half emptied.

Sat 10th Mar **Stoke City (A)**
Lost 0-1 **Att 13,968**

Villa should have been well ahead in this encounter, what with Paul Birch in sparkling form making intelligent runs and Mortimer and McMahon bossing the midfield. Mark Walters curling shot was narrowly wide. As his side kept pressing for the lead they overstretched

[Right] Allan Evans disputes a decision with referee Keith Hackett during Villa's League Cup home leg semi-final against Everton

their rearguard. A Maguire ball split the Villa defence, Painter out-sprinted Ormsby and put off initially by the advancing Spink, the youngster kept his cool and calmly planted the ball low into the net.

Tue 13th Mar Coventry City (A)
Drew 3-3 Att 11,106
Evans (pen), Withe, Rideout

Coventry were in front on ten minutes when Daly scored with a cheeky free kick. Walters was tripped from behind only a minute later, Evans scoring from the spot. Withe unmarked made it 2-1 when he powered home a header on 22 minutes. Allardyce at fault for giving Peter too much space made amends when he ensured the game was level at the break. Within a minute of the restart Rideout spotting Suckling off his line, chipped the keeper with his right foot. Coventry equalised once Withe was in goal, in place of the injured Spink.

Sat 17th Mar Nottingham Forest (H)
Won 1-0 Att 16,270
McMahon

A feature of Villa's play, the accurate long range kicking from Mervyn Day that caused mayhem in the Forest defence. McMahon peppered Forest's goal all afternoon with efforts from all angles, some high, wide, some requiring the intervention of van Breukelen. One finger-tip save being world class. Just when it seemed destined to be 0-0 Rideout chased a deep ball, pushed it to Birch who crossed perfectly for the on-running McMahon to tuck it in at the near post.

Sat 24th Mar Sunderland (A)
Won 1-0 Att 11,908
Walters

The sodden pitch meant mistakes were understandable and frequent even though the goalmouth incidents were few and far between. McMahon had possibly his best display in a Villa shirt. The only goal came just before the interval when Walters pulled a Withe header down, in one slick move he flicked the ball between his legs, spun round, then drilled a low shot wide of Turner. Thanks to an exhausting victory Villa rekindled their hopes for a place in Europe.

Sat 31st Mar Birmingham City (A)
Lost 1-2 Att 23,993

In spite of Ron Saunders packing his Birmingham midfield with three left-backs and a central defender they still metered out a sound beating. The tone of the match was set in the first minute when Hopkins (ex-Villa but a staunch Bluenose) crashed through Gibson. Blues took the lead, Coton then saved from Evans and McMahon but Villa were level when Withe got on the end of Rideout's cross to head home his 20th of the campaign. The hosts won through a goal scored only 36 seconds into the second half.

Sat 7th Apr Coventry City (H)
Won 2-0 Att 15,318
Ormsby, Birch

Aston Villa pride was restored when a weakened XI – Gibson, Curbishley, Withe and Rideout missing - were able to beat Coventry with plenty to spare. Andy Blair tested the City keeper twice before Villa went in front when Paul Birch's shot was headed home by the unmarked Ormsby. Birch bagging his second of the season put Villa in the driving seat. McMahon beat three defenders but his shot didn't trouble Suckling in goal.

Sat 14th Apr Leicester City (A)
Lost 0-2 Att 13,366

The scoreline was no reflection on what transpired on the pitch. Yes, Leicester went ahead on 17 minutes but for the heroics of Mark Wallington in goal Villa would have put the game out of reach. For 20 minutes of the second half the Leicester keeper denied all with his acrobatic, twisting and tumbling. Allan Evans and Des Bremner saw certain goals saved. As Villa ran out of steam Leicester bagged a second with five minutes to go.

Wed 18th Apr **Tottenham Hotspur (A)**
Lost 1-2 **Att 18,668**
Walters

Villa never looked like adding to their two away wins even though they went in front from a Mark Walters goal. Their lead was held for only three minutes, Mabbutt was left totally unmarked to head in. As the first-half came to a close an Archibald centre struck Williams and a penalty was given. The Villa players were livid, McMahon threw the ball at the referee and was booked, though he was lucky not to be shown red. Roberts hammered the ball past Mervyn Day.

Sat 21st Apr **Watford (H)**
Won 2-1 **Att 16,110**
Mortimer, Foster

Dennis Mortimer making his 400th League appearance marked the occasion with a second minute goal, driving in hard his shot took a deflection off Bardsley. Watford were level five minutes later. The only other action of note, McMahon clearing off his line. Villa displayed renewed urgency after the break. Sherwood kept Withe and Walters efforts out but was beaten by Steve Foster who was making his home debut.

Sat 28th Apr **Notts County (H)**
Won 3-1 **Att 13,052**
Walters 2, Withe

Mark Walters lit up Villa Park with a dazzling display despite Notts County taking a 20th minute lead. Eight minutes later the scores were even, Mortimer's carefully placed cross picked out Walters to head beyond the keeper. Mark's second on 57 minutes was even better, turning one way then swivelling before unleashing a thumping left-hand drive. Mortimer and Walters combined to set Withe up for number three only four minutes later.

Sat 5th May **West Ham United (A)**
Won 1-0 **Att 17,393**
Mortimer

Villa picked up only their third victory on their travels, ably assisted by Steve Foster who organised, shouted, headed and tackled; showing why Villa had parted with £200,000 to land him. West Ham were beginning to gain momentum when Villa scored in the 19th minute. Withe picked out Mortimer who'd timed his run to perfection, before slotting the ball beyond Parkes and into the far corner. One paper referred to Foster as "Villa's chief among the Indians in Villa's defence."

Mon 7th May **Everton (H)**
Lost 0-2 **Att 16,792**

Villa's final chance to impress their disgruntled fans failed miserably – their lethargy was rampant. Paul Kerr making his full debut as a striker saw little of the ball and was spared when he was substituted just after the hour with Bremner coming on. Efforts by McMahon and Withe were Villa's sum total on the evening. Richardson and Sharp did the damage in the second half.

Sat 12th May **Ipswich Town (A)**
Lost 1-2 **Att 19,985**
Withe

With nothing at stake it was a credit to the players on both sides that they served up such an enjoyable game. Villa made a promising start yet fell behind to an Eric Gates goal. They only trailed for six minutes when Peter Withe challenged Steve McCall for a loose ball and managed to poke it over the line for his 22nd of the season. A Walters' effort came back off the woodwork and fell into the keeper's arms. Ipswich found the winner with 15 minutes remaining.

PRE-SEASON

Gordon Cowans suffers a double fracture of his right leg breaks in the FC America game during a tournament in Spain. Villa draw the game 2-2 and lose on penalties.

AUGUST

• Despite Nigel Spink putting pen to paper on a new five year deal the club sign Mervyn Day.
• Midfield warrior Steve McMahon joins from Everton for £250,000.
• Paul Rideout a centre-forward arrives from Swindon Town. Villa saw off competition in the shape of Liverpool to secure the youngster.
• Villa kick-off the season with a seven-goal thriller at home to WBA. McNaught is in the Albion side, his replacement Brendan Orsmby scores the winner in the 4-3 derby.

SEPTEMBER

• Villa are the opponents for the first Division One fixture played on QPR's plastic pitch.
• Mark Walters is selected for the England U21 squad.
• Gary Shaw damages ligaments in the game at Forest. He won't start another game until 31 December.
• Villa overcome Portuguese side Vitoria Guimaraes 5-0 at home in the UEFA Cup having lost 0-1 in the first-leg. European Cup final scorer Withe bags a hat-trick.

OCTOBER

• Nigel Spink and Peter Withe are called into the England squad for the forthcoming Hungary match in Budapest.

• Villa beam their Russian UEFA Cup-tie at Spartak Moscow to Villa Park for their supporters.
• Eamonn Deacy departs for Derby County on loan.
• The club post a loss of nearly £500,000 in their annual report.

NOVEMBER

• Villa's fist win in six on their travels – Old Trafford. Withe bags both goals in the fine 2-1 victory.
• The club are prepared to listen to offers for Des Bremner and Tony Morley.
• Villa progress in the League Cup (Milk Cup) beating Albion 2-1.

[Above Back Row L-R] Rideout, Palin, Ormsby, Evans, Day, Walters [Front Row] Gibson, Williams, Birch, Blair prior to The Birmingham Six-a-side's

[Left] Villa's pre-season included a game of cricket or two

DECEMBER

• Deacy recalled from Derby due to spate of injuries at the club.
• Tony Morley signs for West Bromwich Albion.

JANUARY

• Villa's youngsters fall 1-2 at the quarter-final stage of the F.A. Youth Cup to Arsenal.
• A 2-0 win at Carrow Road ensures Villa's place in the League Cup semi-final.

FEBRUARY

• Aston Villa announce Mita are the new shirt sponsors.
• The Highbury match signals Dennis Mortimer's 300th League appearance.
• Everton defeat Villa in the semi-finals, exacting revenge for 1977.

MARCH

• Centre-half Steve Foster arrives from Brighton & Hove Albion.
• Villa are pegged back in the 3-3 draw after Nigel Spink is forced off injured. Withe took his place between the posts.
• Before the month is out Foster requires surgery for a trapped nerve.

APRIL

•Villa beat Coventry City 1-0 at Villa Park. The Sky Blues search for their elusive first win at B6 continues.
•Villa record back-to-back wins for only the third time this campaign. They also win their next game but that's the following month.

MAY

• Dennis Mortimer's goal at West Ham United in the 1-0 win is his last for the team.
• Peter Withe's goal in the 1-2 defeat at Portman road is his 22nd of the campaign. His best ever in the Villa colours.
• Tony Dorigo is the 24th player used in the season when he turns out at Ipswich Town.

[Right] New Villa boss, Graham Turner, poses with his team ahead of the 1984/85 campaign

1984-85

GC
MW
DB

[Back Row] Ray Walker, Alan Curbishley, Nigel Spink, Steve Foster, Mervyn Day, Paul Rideout, Brendan Ormsby, [Middle Row] Jim Williams, Steve McMahon, Mark Walters, Gary Shaw, Dennis Mortimer, Eamonn Deacy, Colin Gibson, Gordon Cowans, [Front Row] Paul Birch, Gary Williams, Allan Evans, Graham Turner (Manager), Peter Withe, Des Bremner, Tony Dorigo.

Football League	Division One
Manager	Graham Turner
Coach	Malcolm Beard
Physio	Jim Williams
Captain	Allan Evans
Final Position	Tenth
F.A. Cup	Third Round
League Cup	Third Round
Leading Goalscorer	Paul Rideout 15 goals

Tony Barton had gone before the end of June. Shrewsbury manager Graham Turner was handed the job. He did his credentials no harm with the team winning their first two games, Coventry 1-0 at home and Stoke away 3-1, only to see the Villa lose heavily at newly promoted Newcastle. Worse was to come - a 0-5 scoreline at Forest.

By the end of September Villa were 14th in the table having suffered four League defeats in the month. The one saving grace, they had overcome Scunthorpe United in the Second Round of the League Cup winning 3-2 away and 3-1 at VP. Des Bremner was transferred to Birmingham City during the month.

Frenchman Didier Six one of their European Championship winning stars gave a sparkling performance as he debuted at home to Manchester United. Ron Atkinson's side were two points behind leaders Tottenham but Villa put three past them, Withe, Evans and Rideout on target.

Queens Park Rangers ended Villa's involvement in the League Cup during a sequence of seven Division One fixtures without a win, the five goal drubbing at Filbert Street the most damaging. Sadly Dennis Mortimer had played his last game in the 2-2 draw at Villa Park when he came on to replace Steve McMahon.

Villa's only other victories in the calendar year would be at home to the two North East sides, Sunderland and Newcastle United, won 1-0 and 4-0 respectively. A Paul Rideout hat-trick helping in the demolition of The Magpies. Wins were as thin on the ground as Steve Foster appearances; signed only last April from Brighton he played seven games last season and only ten this time round before packing his Luton bound bags.

continued >>>

Toal Home League Attendances 384,683
Average Home League 18,318
Highest Home League 37,132
Lowest Home League 10,874

		P	W	D	L	GF	GA	DIF	PTS
1	Everton	42	28	6	8	88	43	45	90
2	Liverpool	42	22	11	9	68	35	33	77
3	Tottenham Hotspur	42	23	8	11	78	51	27	77
4	Manchester United	42	22	10	10	77	47	30	76
5	Southampton	42	19	11	12	56	47	9	68
6	Chelsea	42	18	12	12	63	48	15	66
7	Arsenal	42	19	9	14	61	49	12	66
8	Sheffield Wednesday	42	17	14	11	58	45	13	65
9	Nottingham Forest	42	19	7	16	56	48	8	64
10	Aston Villa	42	15	11	16	60	60	0	56
11	Watford	42	14	13	15	81	71	10	55
12	West Bromwich Albion	42	16	7	19	58	62	-4	55
13	Luton Town	42	15	9	18	57	61	-4	54
14	Newcastle United	42	13	13	16	55	70	-15	52
15	Leicester City	42	15	6	21	65	73	-8	51
16	West Ham United	42	13	12	17	51	68	-17	51
17	Ipswich Town	42	13	11	18	46	57	-11	50
18	Coventry City	42	15	5	22	47	64	-17	50
19	Queens Park Rangers	42	13	11	18	53	72	-19	50
20	Norwich City	42	13	10	19	46	64	-18	49
21	Sunderland	42	10	10	22	40	62	-22	40
22	Stoke City	42	3	8	31	24	91	-67	17

January brought a winning four game run, Albion were beaten 3-1 at home, a 3-0 win at Highfield Road meant Coventry City had failed to beat Villa on their own ground in 11 attempts, a 2-1 over Ipswich was then followed by the same result at Upton Park. These dozen points only lifted Villa to tenth in the table. Still it wasn't Aston Villa's year for the F.A. Cup, Liverpool saw to that at Anfield winning easily 3-0.

With defeat at B6 to Leicester City, Villa had won only 50% of their home games, the following home fixtures gleaned only two more points from draws with Arsenal and Champions elect Everton. Six was on target when Villa overcame Stoke City at Villa Park 2-0, two other wins followed, Tottenham away 2-0 and Sheffield Wednesday 3-0. Villa were tenth in the League.

Bizarrely three defeats on the bounce and all away from home, West Brom, Chelsea and Southampton and yet Villa remained in exactly the same position. Nine goals were scored over the next two games, QPR were thumped 5-2 at home (the first time a Villa Park crowd had seen that many scored since Arsenal 5-1 in April 1979) and Sunderland were beaten at Roker Park. Peter Withe's goal - his 92nd in all competitions - to make it 4-0 on Wearside would be his last in the famous Villa No 9 jersey.

Luton Town inflicted Villa's fourth home defeat before the curtain came down at Anfield where Villa lost 1-2.

[Right] Des Bremner challenges for the ball with Coventry City's Stuart Pearce during the opening day win over the Sky Blues

1984-85

Sat 25th Aug | **Coventry City (H)**
Won 1-0 | **Att 20,970**
Bremner

Gordon Cowans was back after a year in the wilderness following his leg break. Villa were close to taking an early lead, after a succession of neat passes Colin Gibson stormed in but saw his scooped shot go narrowly wide. Steve Foster then saw his header go marginally high of the bar. Mark Walters assisted in breaking the deadlock, he outsmarted Peake three times before gently arcing a centre for Des Bremner to head home a comfortable chance. Sid's passing especially with his left was still as exquisite as ever.

Mon 27th Aug | **Stoke City (A)**
Won 3-1 | **Att 12,505**
Walters 2, Withe

It had been a long time since an Aston Villa team had played with such verve away from home as they did against a spirited Stoke side. Villa's win was down to the delicate touch of Cowans, the brilliance of Walters and the amazing revival of both Mortimer and Bremner. Walters crashed the first goal high into the net on 14 minutes. His second in the 41st minute was even better, a mazy run around defenders ended with the ball hitting the post and finishing in the far corner. Stoke pulled one back before the break but Withe hit the third after a McMahon shot was blocked.

Sat 1st Sep | **Newcastle United (A)**
Lost 0-3 | **Att 31,591**

Both teams were on maximum points, the only two in the division. Villa were enjoying the best of the first-half play; Foster's volley shaved the outside of the upright whilst the defence stifled Newcastle so well Mervyn Day was a mere spectator. How Turner's men collapsed after the break. Waddle put Utd ahead within three

mita

minutes. Walters saw Villa's only opportunity saved by Carr only for the home side to score two further goals.

Wed 5th Sep **Nottingham Forest (H)**
Lost 0-5 **Att 17,730**

The Villa were at sixes and sevens and the midfield totally disjointed from Walters and Withe upfront. Forest on the other hand played intelligently and as a coherent unit. It was a surprise it took Clough's side 33 minutes to get ahead, a 20-yarder from Bowyer. The Villa bench squirmed in humiliation after the break as goals were literally walked in. Christie helped himself to a hat-trick and Hodge got number five. Villa fans chanted "What a load of rubbish."

Sat 8th Sep **Chelsea (H)**
Won 4-2 **Att 21,494**
Withe 2, Foster, Rideout

Villa couldn't have asked for a better start, only six minutes in and a Cowans-Walter move ended with Villa in front as Withe met the latter's centre. Peter was at it again when he powered in Sid's free-kick on 26 minutes. Eight minutes later Cowans was provider for Steve Foster to glance past Niedzwiecki to go in at half time 3-0 up. Chelsea scored in the 54th but Rideout restored the advantage meeting Withe's headed cross. Credit to Villa - even though Chelsea pulled another goal back on 75 minutes – their heads didn't drop.

Sat 15th Sep **Watford (A)**
Drew 3-3 **Att 16,440**
Foster, Withe, McMahon

Villa twice coming back from a trailing position to show they possessed character and skill. Two behind on 40 minutes Villa hit back immediately; an outstanding save denied McMahon, from the corner Foster outjumped everybody to plant a header firmly into the back of the net. Withe was presented with an easy goal when Sherwood dropped the ball at the striker's feet. Blissett scored on 76 minutes but Villa came back through McMahon.

Sat 22nd Sep **Tottenham Hotspur (H)**
Lost 0-1 **Att 22,409**

Peter Withe was out through illness. Williams took over at right-back with Gibson moving to midfield in a makeshift 4-4-2 side. Villa defended the Holte End furiously with Spurs looking to go top, Foster, Evans, Dorigo and Williams managed to keep them out. Rideout and Walters worked hard but were easy meat for the Tottenham defenders. The visitors got the only goal of the afternoon when Chiedozie scored with an easy chance in the 72nd minute. Villa were tenth.

Mon 24th Sep **Scunthorpe United (A)** **League Cup 2nd round first-leg**
Won 3-2 **Att 6,212**
Kerr 2, Gibson

Gordon Cowans and Mark Walters linked in an attack down the left to let Paul Kerr sweep Villa in front on 17 minutes. The expected easy ride didn't materialise when McMahon was taken-out by a Whitehead tackle, he went off for over five minutes then didn't show for the second half, Dorigo on in his place. Scunthorpe with two points from six games levelled on 49 minutes. Three further second half goals, two for the Villa, through Kerr and Gibson were enough to ensure the win.

Sat 29th Sep **Ipswich Town (A)**
Lost 0-3 **Att 15,378**

Villa conceded in the 11th minute but were close to equalising through Cowans and then Birch, both denied by Cooper saves. Early in the second half Rideout had the ball in the net but was flagged for offside, he gestured to the lineman. Immediately the already booked Withe was sent off in a case of mistaken identity. Within a minute Gibson was shown red, his second yellow, for what was little more than a rash challenge - very harsh. With only nine men Villa had no chance and fell further behind to goals from Gates and Osman.

[Above] Peter Withe and Steve McMahon battle for the ball during the home win over Manchester United

Sat 6th Oct **Manchester United (H)**
Won 3-0 **Att 37,132**
Withe, Evans, Rideout

French international Didier Six had a debut that could be best described as magnifique! His presence certainly brought out the best in his teammates. Villa dominated from the start and were leading within 20 minutes. Six left Duxbury for dead before chipping a magnificent ball for Withe to head in. Only five minutes later Withe headed on a Cowans centre for Evans to sweep the ball into the net. Villa's third goal underlined their superiority, a Cowans corner poked home by Paul Rideout. Villa should have had six!

Wed 10th Oct **Scunthorpe United (H)** League Cup 2nd round second-leg
Won 3-1 (agg 6-3) **Att 11,421**
Cowans, Rideout, Gibson

Villa progressed to the Third Round but left it late to dismiss gallant Scunny. Following Saturday's mauling of Manchester United the fans could expect another goal feast when Cowans scored just after the half hour, his first for 18 months. But Scunthorpe, full of fight, hit back. Gibson restored the lead with a close-range shot and Rideout made it 3-1 hooking the rebound in from Withe's blocked shot.

Sat 13th Oct **Everton (A)**
Lost 1-2 **Att 25,043**
Withe

Turner left Steve Foster out, Evans paired with Ormsby. Everton took a first-half lead through Sharp but Withe cancelled it out on the stroke of half time with a stunning header. The hosts put on a show after the interval when they exploited Villa's defensive frailties. Dorigo in for the suspended Gibson was given a torrid time and was unlucky when a penalty was awarded against him, Sharp dived in the area. Day saved it. McMahon, Dorigo and Williams all cleared off the line but were powerless when Heath chipped Mervyn in the 75th minute.

mita

Sat 20th Oct **Norwich City (H)**
Drew 2-2 **Att 14,149**
Withe 2

Two outstanding goals from Peter Withe saved Villa from an embarrassing defeat. Deehan put the visitors in front on 11 minutes. It took seven minutes for Villa to be on even terms. Woods in goal for Norwich saved from Six, Cowans and a deflected Gibson drive before his team regained the lead within seconds of the half-time whistle. Villa playing the second half with the wind beind them finally pegged Norwich back in the 69th minute. Withe this time scoring with a curling left-foot shot from 20-yards out.

Sat 27th Oct **Leicester City (A)**
Lost 0-5 **Att 11,885**

Villa looking for a new centre-half were two down after a dozen minutes. Another 21 minutes on the clock and Gary Lineker had already bagged his hat-trick due to another error by transfer-listed Ormsby. To complete Brendan's nightmare he then brought down Lineker for Lynex to make it 0-4. Villa's unprofessionalism was further emphasised with the bookings of McMahon, Gibson and Evans, all totally unnecessary. Eastoe scored a fifth with 11 minutes left.

Tue 30th Oct **Queens Park Rangers (A)** **League Cup 3rd round**
Lost 0-1 **Att 12,547**

This defeat was hard to swallow because for once Villa did everything right. They were tighter in defence, battled enthusiastically in the middle and were well-drilled with QPR's offside trap. Withe was denied by a superb save from Hucker. Cowans cursed his luck when he followed up Birch's rebound off the crossbar, the flag was raised for offside. Just as Rangers were struggling to hang on up popped John Gregory in the 64th minute, he caught the ball perfectly, from 25-yards out, Mervyn Day had no chance.

[Left] Didier Six who scored his first of the season during the home draw with Southampton

Sat 3rd Nov **West Ham United (H)**
Drew 0-0 **Att 15,709**

As the Hammers soaked up a mountain of pressure Villa's downward spiral towards the drop zone continued. Villa had the lion's share of possession but no one to share the burden of goalscoring with their craggy No 9. Paul Kerr rattled the bar with a 20-yarder, McMahon was determined in midfield but Didier Six was a luxury outwide. Villa's desperation left gaps at the back and were fortunate that West Ham didn't snatch a victory on the break.

Sat 10th Nov **Arsenal (A)**
Drew 1-1 **Att 33,193**
Birch

Villa were given the best start when Paul Birch latched on to Paul Kerr's cross with only ten minutes gone. It should have been 2-0 but Jennings kept out a Didier Six half-shot on 36 minutes. Arsenal were back in it when Mariner scored from a suspect position with half-time looming. The home side pushed on after the interval, Evans and Ormsby were solid in stopping them. In the closing stages Mervyn Day acrobatically saved from Nicholas, Mariner and Anderson within a 20 second sequence.

Sat 17th Nov **Southampton (H)**
Drew 2-2 **Att 13,397**
Withe, Six

For Villa the result was unjust in every way, having dictated the play for long periods. A trademark Withe headed goal gave Villa the lead when the striker got on the end of Birch's free-kick. A magnificent volley by the French Six on half time saw Villa with a two goal advantage. The second half was a different story, Southampton unbeaten in 11 matches came out turned it into an over-aggressive clash. Wright, Williams, Jordan and Wallace went into the book. Jordan scored almost identical goals in the 56th and 84th minute. Villa two points above the drop.

Sat 24th Nov **Queen's Park Rangers (A)**
Lost 0-2 **Att 11,689**

Villa made their own problems when they gifted John Gregory a goal 11 minutes in. Day prevented Rangers from building on their advantage on half a dozen occasions. The keeper was still at it in the second period, turning a low Stewart shot wide and then watching Gregory hit a post. The defence left him unprotected when Bannister headed in from a centre on 54 minutes. Villa managed one shot on target. A seventh League game without a win.

Sat 1st Dec **Sunderland (H)**
Won 1-0 **Att 14,669**
Rideout

After a non-entity of a first half Steve McMahon refused to let his teammates settle for the draw. He came out after the interval fired up and within four minutes he had Turner diving low to keep out his volley. Walters started to grow into the game and managed to get the ball into the net only to see it chalked off, one of Villa's forwards had strayed offside. The one-man assault continued and Turner had to save from McMahon at the second attempt and then watch as the Villaman struck the inside of the post. Rideout came to the rescue as he turned in Gibson's corner.

Sat 8th Dec **Luton Town (A)**
Lost 0-1 **Att 7,696**

Mervyn Day was dropped, Nigel Spink was in. Turner's men threatened but couldn't carve out any chances, not waking up until the second half. During Villa's best spells Luton were held together by Foster who'd left the Villa just over a week ago. With the in-form McMahon having to go off with what looked a serious injury Villa were blunted somewhat. Luton scored the only goal of the game through ex-Walsall's David Preece.

Sat 15th Dec **Liverpool (H)**
Drew 0-0 **Att 24,007**

Colin Gibson was denied a fourth minute goal when his shot was cleared by the knee of Grobbelaar. Curbishley teed up Rideout but the youngster's header was cleared on the line by Kennedy. Mark Walters sublime cross was met by Withe but his effort was marginally over the angle of the upright and bar. The second-half saw Grobbelaar makes two outstanding saves from Walters and Gibson. Spink also made clever saves but was well served by his half-backs Evans and Ormsby.

Sat 22nd Dec **Newcastle United (H)**
Won 4-0 **Att 14,491**
Evans (pen), Rideout 3

England U21 striker Paul Rideout grabbed a hat-trick as Villa destroyed early pace-setters Newcastle United. Skipper Evans opened the scoring from the spot after Rideout had been upended by Carr. Rideout added a second before the break, a low shot at the far post. Man-of-the-match Gibson supplied the cross for Paul's second in the 62nd minute. His third also courtesy of Colin who left Rideout with the easiest of chances to beat Carr. Newcastle were woeful. Villa were up to 15th.

Wed 26th Dec **Sheffield Wednesday (A)**
Drew 1-1 **Att 30,971**
Rideout

Villa performed far better than a side with only two away wins from 12 League games. They went in front through Rideout four minutes before the half-time whistle as he bundled the ball over the line with his backside. They all count! On the few occasions Wednesday threatened Spink was in commanding form. Villa looked set for all three points until two minutes to go. Mike Lyons shook off the attentions of Withe to blast home a point saver.

[Above] Villa goalie Nigel Spink plucks the ball off the head of Sheffield Wednesday striker Lee Chapman

Sat 29th Dec **Nottingham Forest (A)**
Lost 2-3 **Att 17,676**
Gibson, Rideout

Villa played with tremendous determination and deservedly led through Gibson on 17 minutes when he took a through pass from Tony Dorigo. The lead was further extended through Rideout following good work by the Australian defender and Withe. Davenport reduced the arrears in the 42nd minute. McMahon, Gibson and Birch worked tirelessly in midfield yet Forest drew level on 84 minutes. Villa were cut to the quick when Ormsby tragically handled in the dying minutes. Davenport put the penalty away.

Tue 1st Jan **West Bromwich Albion (H)**
Won 3-1 **Att 31,710**
Gibson, Birch, Rideout

Villa were a goal down to a Statham penalty, a result of Williams untidy tackle on Valentine. Gibson's goal, a low shot from Walters back heel and Godden making three amazing saves saw the teams go off level at the break. On 58 minutes Williams free-kick was helped on by Rideout for Paul Birch to push the ball beyond the Albion keeper. Rideout headed his sixth goal in four games after Withe back-flicked a Walters' corner. David Cross headed against the Villa post before later walking away from a poleaxed Evans who was stretched off.

Sat 5th Jan **Liverpool (A)** **FA Cup 3rd round**
Lost 0-3 **Att 36,877**

With only 17 seconds on the clock Gary Williams cleared in desperation after Spink had pushed away MacDonald's shot. Five minutes later a Gibson back-pass to his keeper was intercepted by Dalglish who crossed for Rush to prod home from a yard out. Four second-half minutes in Rush turned provider for Wark, his shot spinning in off Spink's feet. With Cowans and McMahon outmanoeuvred in midfield it was a question of time before more goals appeared. Only the one, another for Rush, though it could have been six.

Sat 19th Jan **Coventry City (A)**
Won 3-0 **Att 15,290**
Walters 2, Rideout

David Norton and Dean Glover were handed their First Division debuts. Coventry had never beaten Villa in this division but came close to taking the lead twice, a Peake header landing on top of the net and a sparkling run by Regis. Walters showed City how to put the ball in the net, surging past Peake he got on the end of McMahon's pass to score his third of the season. McMahon shot a yard wide, Walters just failed with a positive touch before Rideout struck, his seventh in six matches. City fell asleep, five of their defenders watched as a Gibson corner came in and Walters was there to nod in from a yard away.

Sat 2nd Feb **Ipswich Town (H)**
Won 2-1 **Att 15,051**
Cowans, Gibson

Cowans having scored against Scunthorpe in the cup, found his first League goal since his horrific leg-break. His side had dominated the game before the breakthrough in the 38th minute as he nipped through to hit the ball past Paul Cooper. In spite of Ipswich showing more urgency in the second half, Cowans a late replacement for the virus hit Birch, sent a brilliant chipped through ball for Gibson to volley home having raced round Butcher. Osman's 87th goal came too late to prevent Villa moving 12 points clear of the relegation zone.

Sat 23rd Feb **West Ham United (A)**
Won 2-1 **Att 14,855**
Walters, Ormsby

Brendan Ormsby celebrated his new two-year contract with the most incredible goal he or any other Villa player is likely to score this season. With 75 minutes showing he won a tackle on the half-way line strode into West Ham's half and unleashed a fierce drive from a full 40-yards out that scorched in like a guided missile. The Hammers had taken a second-half lead, three minutes in, through Goddard. Walters levelled on 58 minutes, driving a low shot from an impossible angle.

Sat 2nd Mar **Leicester City (H)**
Lost 0-1 **Att 16,285**

Villa took time to get into the game and were let off when Lineker went sprawling in the box, luckily the referee waved away the forward's appeals. A Walters curling shot was all the hosts had to show for their first-half endeavours. Birch saw a goal bound effort brilliantly saved by keeper Andrews and Gibson was furious as his shout for a penalty was dismissed after O'Neill handled his centre. Leicester who Graham Turner said could present a setback to Villa's New Year revival did exactly that when Alan Smith scored early in the second half.

Sat 9th Mar **Norwich City (A)**
Drew 2-2 **Att 21,120**
Evans 2 (2 pens)

Villa carved out numerous chances in the first half, McMahon and Gibson way off target and Withe failing with an attempted header from Walters cross. McMahon was replaced by Darren Bradley just after the half hour. Two second-half penalties from skipper Allan Evans looked to have done enough to secure all three points; Kerr was flattened for the first and Channon impeded Williams for the second. Norwich pulled one back between Villa's goals and a mistake by Evans was punished with five minutes to go when Rowell poached an unlikely point.

Wed 13th Mar **Arsenal (H)**
Drew 0-0 **Att 15,487**

Paul Kerr in for Rideout, worried the Arsenal back four. No one did more in an enterprising first half than young Ray Walker thrown into midfield for his first senior game of the season, his tackling and willingness to get forward caused Arsenal all sorts of problems. He was unfortunate to see a rasping drive beat Lukic but go narrowly wide. Gibson also rattled a post. On the few occasions the visitors threatened Spink was impenetrable.

[Right] Villa's Brendan Ormsby clears under pressure from West Ham's Paul Goddard during the win at Upton Park

writers
KODAK COPIERS
mita
mita
mita

Sat 16th Mar **Everton (H)**
Drew 1-1 **Att 22,625**
Evans (pen)

Aston Villa were fortunate to salvage a point from a game best described as "forgettable." A rare mistake by Steve McMahon let his former club take an interval lead, Kevin Richardson in the 42nd minute. Allan Evans saved his side yet again from the penalty spot, awarded when Stevens fouled Walters. Didier Six came on for his first game since Boxing Day and almost produced the winner. Walters and Dorigo swapped passes, Mark supplied the cross, Six caught it firmly but it was too straight to trouble Southall.

Sat 23rd Mar **Manchester United (A)**
Lost 0-4 **Att 40,941**

An eight minute hat-trick by Mark Hughes put paid to Villa's lingering European hopes. Other than pick the ball out of the net Nigel Spink had little else to do. The Villa's best chance fell to Colin Gibson, a header from Gordon Cowans firmly-driven corner which he miscued beyond the upright. The visitors played their three midfield players directly in front of the defence, allowing United acres of space on the flanks. Whiteside added the other on 54 minutes.

Wed 27th Mar **Stoke City (H)**
Won 2-0 **Att 10,874**
Own goal, Six

Uninspiring? Villa Park's lowest League crowd for 19 years thought so as they booed and slow-handclapped throughout an inept first-half display. The only applause came when Six was in possession of the ball, which wasn't very often. Villa finally got their noses in front, George Berry deflecting Withe's shot into the corner of the net. It looked like one goal would be enough as Stoke had nothing about them. With five minutes remaining Gibson swung and missed at Walters' free-kick, but Six was alert and he didn't miss, his smartly hit shot rifled in.

Sat 30th Mar **Tottenham Hotspur (A)**
Won 2-0 **Att 27,971**
Rideout, Walters

Spurs were level on points with leaders Everton so this was going to be a tough nut to crack, not helped with Spink and Evans out, Kevin Poole and Dean Glover deputising. As it was Turner's boys cast aside their recent indifferent form and put on a display few thought possible. Not least their North London opponents. When Rideout scored after 21 minutes – despite appeals for offside - Villa grew more confident. Walters also avoided the Spurs defensive tactics of playing forward hoping to catch him offside, the flag stayed down, he shot past the advancing Clemence, 2-0.

Sat 6th Apr **Sheffield Wednesday (H)**
Won 3-0 **Att 18,308**
Rideout, Ormsby, Evans (pen)

Wednesday who employed a steel-sprung offside trap were caught with ease. Only five minutes in Peter Withe hit a post. Walters took advantage of a Morris mistake, jinking outside him and centring for Rideout to head past Hodge. A Cowans corner was deflected by Villa old boy Shelton for Orsmby to make it two-nil. Three minutes later Rideout was grounded by Hodge. A bit harsh on the keeper but it bothered Allan Evans not one bit as he struck his penalty firm and true. The Wednesday keeper kept out certain goals from Six, McMahon and Williams.

Mon 8th Apr **West Bromwich Albion (A)**
Lost 0-1 **Att 20,936**

In a game that simmered for the first hour and then boiled into sense-scalding excitement, Villa won everything but the points! Albion took the lead on ten minutes when Steve Hunt found Val-

[Right] Villa's Colin Gibson is surrounded by Manchester United defenders during the heavy defeat at Old Trafford

entine, who nudged it past Poole. Godden's only action of the first half was to turn away Williams weak shot from 20-yards. The second-half was everything the first wasnt' - it was a battle. McMahon crashed drives against the bar and post, Ray Walker hit the bar not long after. Villa attacked relentlessly with possibly a dozen attempts on goal. Three of these in the last five minutes with Godden denying Walters, Gibson and Williams.

Tue 16th Apr **Chelsea (A)**
Lost 1-3 **Att 13,267**
Walters

The home side were ahead through a Bumstead goal on 13 minutes. Allan Evans added to their lead when he could only backhead a Nevin corner beyond his teammate Spink. In spite of the setback Villa refused to abandon their attacking policy. When Gary Williams hauled down Nevin for Thomas to score from the penalty spot it was game over. Walters with a touch of impudence pulled one back with ten minutes remaining but Villa would rue the missed opportunities of earlier. The Chelsea boss John Hollins conceded that the scoreline flattered his side.

Sat 20th Apr **Southampton (A)**
Lost 0-2 **Att 15,736**

Winger Tony Daley made his debut. Graham Turner's much reshaped side made a hesitant start and in this period the visitors took the lead through Moran. Villa started creating chances, Birch hit the crossbar, Walker went desperately close and Daley saw a header go fractionally wide. Evans and Ormsby set a marvellous example in containing Saints' attack; the midfield of Gibson, Walker and Birch showed style after the early lapses and Withe and Rideout produced promising and threatening runs. Regardless, they couldn't find the equaliser. Spink saved a 75th minute penalty but Southampton scored a second goal moments later.

[Above] Steve Foster gets in a solid header towards the Watford goal during the Villa Park draw

Wed 24th Apr **Watford (H)**
Drew 1-1 **Att 11,493**
Walters

Aston Villa had little to play for, European aspirations were dead and their performance wore that distinctly end-of-season look. Fans were keen to see young Daley make his home debut but it was the other winger, Walters who provided the moments of cheer with his repertoire of twists and turns. It was Mark who scored Villa's goal. The ball was cleared from defence to Withe, who flicked the ball to Gibson, his pass found Walters, he turned Taylor inside out before beating Coton. This cancelled out Nigel Callaghan's earlier sloppy goal.

Sat 27th Apr **Queens Park Rangers (H)**
Won 5-2 **Att 12,023**
Rideout 2, Withe 2, Walters

Villa cut Rangers to ribbons with their first five-goal salvo in the League for six years. Rideout converted at the far post to make it 1-0 on 16 minutes. QPR levelled four minutes later via Bannister. Wicks and Chivers hesitated when Ormsby's free-kick floated in and Rideout nipped in to take advantage. The Villa Park crowd reserved their biggest roar of the afternoon for old warhorse Withe when he scored his first in 24 games. Further goals from Walters and Peter put the Villa 5-1 ahead and Bannister rounded out the scoring in the 61st minute.

Sat 4th May **Sunderland (A)**
Won 4-0 **Att 12,467**
Gibson, Walters, McMahon, Withe

Villa turned Roker Park into a playground, one paper saying it was like taking candy off a baby! With Sunderland's lack of urgency Villa strode into a two-goal half-time lead without getting out of first gear. The only surprise was it took until the 21st minute for Villa's first to arrive, courtesy of Gibson. Thirteen minutes later Walters added the second with as much ease. The Black Cats were already buried before McMahon drilled in a brilliant finish. Peter Withe rounded off the scoring, volleying in from close range. It would be his last goal in the famous colours.

Mon 6th May **Luton Town (H)**
Lost 0-1 **Att 14,130**

With only Liverpool away to play Villa brought the curtain down on matches in B6. It was one not to remember. When Stein stormed in to hit a right-footed shot past Kevin Poole you could sense that the points were heading south. Les Sealey was required to make three saves but Villa relied too much on the ariel prowess of Peter Withe but for once the veteran target man was unable to deliver, Steve Foster who joined Luton from Villa was the game's outstanding figure.

Sat 11th May **Liverpool (A)**
Lost 1-2 **Att 33,001**
Birch

The game ended in defeat for the Villa but not before they gave the former League champions a scare. Gibson and Withe were both guilty of missing easy chances, Villa should have been two-up at the break. Instead Liverpool took the lead on 67 minutes through Whelan. Ian Rush then grabbed his 24th of the season to make it 0-2. Villa's response was an 85th minute goal from substitute Paul Birch, his 35-yard strike a spectacular affair.

PRE-SEASON

• Tony Barton is sacked two years after leading Aston Villa to their finest hour.
• Graham Turner at only 36-years of age becomes the new manager – and the youngest ever.
• Villa play both Bayern Munich and Boca Juniors in a pre-season tournament in Barcelona.

AUGUST

• Andy Blair joins Sheffield Wednesday.
• Villa win their opening two matches for the second consecutive season.

SEPTEMBER

• Dennis Mortimer plays in the first-team for the last time in the 0-5 defeat at Forest.
• Des Bremner joins Birmingham City.
• Paul Birch plays against Scunthorpe United in the League Cup, hoping Rotherham will finish the job off against Stoke City to meet Villa. His elder brother Alan scored in The Millers 2-1 win in the first-leg.

OCTOBER

• French Euro Championship winner Didier Six joins on loan from Mulhouse and has an outstanding debut in the 3-0 home win over Manchester United.
• Dennis Mortimer plays in the first-team for the last time in the 2-2 Carrow Road draw.

NOVEMBER

• Steve Foster with only 17 appearances and three goals to his name jumps ship for Luton.
• The team start the month with three draws, West Ham, Arsenal and the Saints.
• Villa's reserves beat champions elect Liverpool 5-1 in the Central League, Walters 2, Rideout 2 and Tony Daley do the damage.

DECEMBER

• Paul Rideout scores a hat-trick in the 4-0 victory over Newcastle United.
• Alan Curbishley moves to Charlton Athletic.

JANUARY

• Villa are out of the F.A. Cup at the first hurdle going down 0-3 at Anfield.
• On a happier not the Villa win both their League games in the month; WBA 3-1 and away to Coventry City 3-0 where David Norton is blooded.

FEBRUARY

• Mervyn Day's stay is a short one at B6. He moves to Leeds United 1 February.

MARCH

• Two Allan Evans penalties at Carrow Road earn a share of the points in the 2-2 draw. Darren Bradley makes his first-team debut replacing McMahon.
• Villa's youngsters bow out to Portsmouth after a second-replay in the Southern Junior Floodlit Cup.

APRIL

• Villa hammer Huddersfield Town 9-0 in the Central League. Leigh Palin grabs a hat-trick and the matchball.
• Speed merchant Tony Daley makes his first-team debut at The Dell
• Villa beat QPR 5-2. It's almost six years to the day since Villa scored five in the League. They beat Arsenal 5-1 in April '79.

MAY

• Peter Withe scores his 92nd and last goal for the club when he finds the net at Roker Park.
• Paul Rideout and Withe play their last for the Villa in the defeat at Liverpool 11 May.
• George Best appears in the famous claret and blue, in aid of the Bradford City fire disaster.

[Left] Gary Williams, Nigel Spink, Brendan Ormsby and Steve McMahon getting the drinks in as part of a new sponsorship deal

[Right] Steve Hodge in action during the festive period draw with West Brom at Villa Park

1985-86

mita

[Back Row] Tony Dorigo, Andy Gray, Nigel Spink, Kevin Poole, Brendan Ormsby, Dean Glover, [Middle Row] Jim Williams (Physiotherapist), Paul Birch, David Norton, Mark Walters, Gary Shaw, Steve McMahon, Gary Williams, Malcolm Beard (Coach), [Front Row] Tony Daley, Darren Bradley, Allan Evans, Graham Turner (Manager), Ray Walker, Colin Gibson, Paul Kerr.

Football League	Division One
Manager	Graham Turner
Coach	Malcolm Beard
Physio	Jim Williams
Captain	Allan Evans
Final Position	Sixteenth
F.A. Cup	Fourth Round
League Cup	Semi-finals
Leading Goalscorer	Simon Stainrod 21 goals

Andrew Mullen Gray was back at Villa with a championship medal in his pocket. Would he still be as effective? The season would only be ten days old when Steve Hodge arrived from Nottingham Forest.

A 0-4 loss at Manchester United on the opening day hardly inspired confidence. The 2-2 draw at home to Liverpool did! Villa had to wait until their fifth match to collect all three points, Luton were beaten 3-1, Mark Walters, Steve Hodge and David Norton, and then Albion were made to suffer on their own patch as Villa coasted to a 3-0 win.

October was nothing short of disastrous in the League, four consecutive defeats. Exeter City were beaten 8-1 at Villa Park in a League Cup Second Round second-leg tie to add to last month's 4-1 win at St James Park where Simon Stainrod bagged all four having signed the day before from Sheffield Wednesday. Leeds United were also put out of the competition.

A win at home to Oxford United lifted Villa from their lowly 17th place but after the next two draws Villa lost four on the spin, Chelsea, Spurs, Liverpool and Manchester United and were now only one place above the relegation positions.

West Brom bottom of the table and with a solitary victory from 17 League games held Villa to a 2-2 draw in the League Cup. Albion had led at half time. A week later Villa got the job done at The Hawthorns going through 2-1 on the night.

December wasn't very festive for Turner's team, they won only one, QPR 1-0 and lost three. The 1-1 draw at home to Albion three days after Christmas was particularly galling, Villa were expected to

continued >>>

Total Home League Attendances 319,981
Average Home League 15,237
Highest Home League 27,626
Lowest Home League 8,456

		P	W	D	L	GF	GA	DIF	PTS
1	Liverpool	42	26	10	6	89	37	52	88
2	Everton	42	26	8	8	87	41	46	86
3	West Ham United	42	26	6	10	74	40	34	84
4	Manchester United	42	22	10	10	70	36	34	76
5	Sheffield Wednesday	42	21	10	11	63	54	9	73
6	Chelsea	42	20	11	11	57	56	1	71
7	Arsenal	42	20	9	13	49	47	2	69
8	Nottingham Forest	42	19	11	12	69	53	16	68
9	Luton Town	42	18	12	12	61	44	17	66
10	Tottenham Hotspur	42	19	8	15	74	52	22	65
11	Newcastle United	42	17	12	13	67	72	-5	63
12	Watford	42	16	11	15	69	62	7	59
13	Queens Park Rangers	42	15	7	20	53	64	-11	52
14	Southampton	42	12	10	20	51	62	-11	46
15	Manchester City	42	11	12	19	43	57	-14	45
16	Aston Villa	42	10	14	18	51	67	-16	44
17	Coventry City	42	11	10	21	48	71	-23	43
18	Oxford United	42	10	12	20	62	80	-18	42
19	Leicester City	42	10	12	20	54	76	-22	42
20	Ipswich Town	42	11	8	23	32	55	-23	41
21	Birmingham City	42	8	5	29	30	73	-43	29
22	West Bromwich Albion	42	4	12	26	35	89	-54	24

take the three points and register their third home win against a side who'd lost nine and drawn two on the road.

The New Year would see Villa progress on both cup fronts initially. Portsmouth were beaten 3-2 after extra-time in an F.A. Cup Third Round replay, only for the Villa to fall to Millwall in the next round, after another replay. In the League Cup, red hot favourites Arsenal were overcome 2-1 at Highbury after a 1-1 draw at Villa Park.

The two-nil away defeat by Everton dropped Villa into the relegation places; they were without a win in seven and then lost heavily at home to Arsenal. Either side of The Gunners match Villa squared up to Oxford in the semi-finals, drawing at home 2-2 and losing 1-2 at the Manor Ground. Stainrod's goal at the Villa Park tie was his ninth in the competition.

It took until 19 March for Villa to finally register their first victory of the calendar year, 2-1 at home to West Ham, Hodge getting both. Four more wins - Leicester, Watford, Ipswich and Chelsea - in the last ten fixtures ensured Villa finished three points above the drop zone.

Albion went through the trapdoor as did Birmingham City who'd only just come back up! Ipswich who Villa had recently beaten followed them.

[Right] Luton Town defender Mitchell Thomas cannot stop Steve Hodge's shot going over the line, Villa's second goal in the 3-1 August win

1985-86

Sat 17th Aug **Manchester United (A)**
Lost 0-4 **Att 49,743**

United hit the Villa with a carbon-copy victory of last season's win at Old Trafford. Villa began the match in style but their demise could be pinpointed to the 30th minute when the lively Colin Gibson and Gary Bailey collided outside the area, when it looked likely the midfielder was going to score. He failed, but worse, he was carried off for his troubles. Villa were rocked with two goals in a two minute spell and never recovered. Hughes got his second after 75 minutes and United got a fourth seven minutes later. Gray and Shaw were given no space by Hogg and McGrath.

Wed 21st Aug **Liverpool (H)**
Drew 2-2 **Att 20,197**
Shaw, Walters

Villa took the lead when Grobbelaar was caught out by the bounce of Walters' outswinging centre, Gary Shaw was on hand to score his first Villa Park goal in just under two years. Ian Rush hit back in the 38th minute. Tony Daley came on for the injured Gary Williams, his speed immediately troubling Liverpool. Villa's other wideman Walters regained the advantage when he stroked the ball wide of the keeper in the 77th minute. Jan Molby scored seven minutes later. Two minutes from time Spink saved a Rush penalty kick.

Sat 24th Aug **Queens Park Rangers (H)**
Lost 1-2 **Att 11,896**
Walters

Villa missing experienced players didn't play with the fluency they managed against Liverpool. Indeed they were trailing with only 180 seconds on the clock, Bannister heading his side in front. The home side's plight not helped when Steve McMahon hit a penalty too tamely

EXIT

giving Hucker all the time in the world to get down. Villa's hopes of a scrambled point were raised when Walters found the back of the net on 68 minutes. A minute from time Bannister got his second.

Tue 27th Aug **Southampton (A)**
Drew 0-0 **Att 14,220**

McMahon was out due to his impending Liverpool transfer. Shaw was rested. New signing Steve Hodge making his debut, looked neat and tidy in everything he did. The Villa created few chances though Andy Gray forced Shilton into making a finger-tip save on 25 minutes. Darren Bradley in for McMahon was always in the thick of the action, none more so when being trampled by Mark Wright then flattened by Jimmy Case in the closing stages. Case was off having received a yellow earlier for a crunching tackle on Daley.

Sat 31st Aug **Luton Town (H)**
Won 3-1 **Att 10,524**
Walters, Hodge, Norton

Masterminded by new boy Hodge Villa ripped into Luton for 45 minutes. Fielding a team of mostly youngsters the lack of experience was masked by enthusiasm. Walters gave them the perfect start after three minutes, an overhead kick. The tempo never dropped and the second on 16 minutes came following the trickery of Tony Daley; he fed Hodge on the edge of the six-yard area who in turn rounded the keeper before slotting it low into the net. The third equally impressive, a pinpoint pass found Walters, his centre was met by David Norton to drive in first time. Luton pulled one back in the second half but the damage had been done.

Wed 4th Sep **West Bromwich Albion (A)**
Won 3-0 **Att 17,267**
Evans (pen), Daley, Walters

Allan Evans, Gary Williams and Andy Gray returned from injury. Villa totally upstaged Albion at the Hawthorns. Always in control, Villa went ahead from an Evans penalty after Hodge had been pushed. Tony Daley then popped up to fire a superb second goal from 20 yards. Villa confirmed their superiority when they added a third against a woeful Baggies side. Gray latched on to a poor Anderson back-pass, flicked the ball on and Walters side-footed in.

Sat 7th Sep **Birmingham City (A)**
Drew 0-0 **Att 24,971**

An injury to Darren Bradley clearly upset the Villa's midfield movement, Hodge had a subdued game. Villa's central-defenders were the real heroes, Geddis, Kennedy and Clark, well shackled by Evans and Ormsby. Spink made a blinding save with ten minutes remaining to deny Dicks, and with only seconds left he prevented Hopkins from handing Blues a win. Villa often under severe pressure held on to achieve an honourable draw.

Sat 14th Sep **Coventry City (H)**
Drew 1-1 **Att 12,198**
Hodge

Coventry without a win at Villa Park came desperately close to pulling off a shock victory. Villa were a goal behind five minutes in when Williams was punished for a weak back-pass to Spink. Steve Hodge equalised for Villa after Gray headed an Evans up-field clearance into the midfielder's path. Villa looked off-colour and displayed few ideas up front, their few moves stemming from the lively Hodge and Paul Birch. Play went from bad to worse after the interval.

Sat 21st Sep **Ipswich Town (A)**
W 3-0 **Att 11,882**
Walters, Hodge, Birch

Villa already looked the far better team long before their opening goal in the 13th minute. Tony Dorigo swung over a centre from the left, Gray headed it perfectly for Walters to steer it in with clinical control. Ipswich went close but Dozzell's shot rebounded off the legs of Spink. Villa pressed forward, four men against Town's three - the result, Hodge set up by Birch for an easy goal. Bradley came on for

Gray in the second half and within minutes the game was cut and dried when Birch made it three with his glorious 47th minute goal.

Wed 25th Sep **Exeter City (A)** League Cup 2nd round first-leg
Won 4-1 **Att 5,325**
Stainrod 4

Simon Stainrod signed the day before from Sheffield Wednesday crowned an unbelievable debut for Villa with four goals. His opener on 11 minutes when he pounced first to head home a Birch corner, his second came only six minutes later, beating two defenders and rounding the keeper before slotting the ball in from close range. Exeter made an adventurous start after the interval, Kellow volleying past Spink, to reduce the deficit. Cue Stainrod, who snatched further goals in the 56th and 70th minutes. Darren Bradley and Exeter's Gale were sent off on 80 minutes for fighting.

Sat 28th Sep **Everton (H)**
Drew 0-0 **Att 22,048**

Villa dominated the first 30 minutes and in this time Simon Stainrod could and should have had Villa sitting easy with a goal advantage; he saw a header glance off Southall's left-hand upright with the keeper beaten. In the second half Birch found him as he galloped goalwards in space, Southall saw the danger, rushed out and smothered the ball as Stainrod attempted to lift it over him. Gray's stooping header was turned round the post by the goalkeeper. At the other end Spink had to fling himself at the feet of Lineker and a Sheedy shot bounced off the top of the crossbar.

Sat 5th Oct **Arsenal (A)**
Lost 2-3 **Att 18,869**
Stainrod, Walters

Tony Woodcock put the Gunners ahead but Villa were level within two minutes. Simon Stainrod opened his League account driving the ball home after Mark Walters had done splendidly well to set him up. Arsenal were back in front in the 18th minute, Anderson out-jumped the defence to head Rix's cross. Hodge then forced a smart save from Lukic. Villa were back on an even footing on 70 minutes when Walters caught the opposition by surprise. Stainrod hit the woodwork moments before Whyte scored the winner in the 86th minute.

Wed 9th Oct **Exeter City (H)** League Cup 2nd round second-leg
Won 8-1 (agg 12-2) **Att 7,678**
Gray 2, Stainrod, Ormsby 2, Williams 2, Birch

It was a ridiculously easy affair, Villa six goals to the good before half time. Gray started the rout with a fine left-foot shot, Hodge having paved the way. Three minutes later the midfielder again provided the Scot with his second simple goal. Stainrod scored the third after Evans had knocked on a Birch corner. Ormsby squeezed the fourth in; Williams hit a superb shot a minute later for his first goal for Villa and three minutes before the interval Gary got his second. Exeter found the back of the net on 49 minute before Birch and Ormsby completed the 12-2 aggregate demolition.

Sat 12th Oct **Nottingham Forest (H)**
Lost 1-2 **Att 15,351**
Gibson

It was tough luck on Villa to go behind to an Ormsby own-goal (whilst trying to kick clear he only succeeded in finding his own net) having created a hatful of chances, especially in the first half. Villa fought back with Colin Gibson scoring a cheeky equaliser, rounding Pearce and then chipping Sutton. Nigel Clough's headed goal in the 72nd minute proved to be the winner though Forest should have had a penalty when Hodge and Davenport came together in the box. To everyone's amazement the ref waved play on.

Sat 19th Oct **West Ham United (A)**
Lost 1-4 **Att 15,034**
Stainrod

Although Villa had their fair share of the play they had nothing to match The Hammers strikers. Villa made the more promising start and were in front thanks to a clinical piece of finishing from Stainrod. He'd already been denied a goal by the splendid Phil Parkes. West Ham were level on 24 minutes when McAvennie lashed in from close range. Eleven minutes later it was Cottee's turn. Villa attempted to hit back but were caught on the break and ruthlessy punished twice, first by Cottee and then McAvennie.

Sat 26th Oct **Newcastle United (H)**
Lost 1-2 **Att 12,633**
Gray

Manager Turner has admitting the defence needed strengthening, and it was easy to see why. Villa had a nightmare opening ten minutes, they were one down but it could have been three. The gloom finally lifted in the 16th minute; Ray Walker drove a long ball forward, Stainrod turned it into the path of Gray to head his first League goal of the season. A Thomas save denied Walters a goal. Shortly afterwards Beardsley drove home from ten yards. The defeat meant Villa had won only once in front of their own fans.

Wed 30th Oct **Leeds United (A)** **League Cup 3rd round**
Won 3-0 **Att 15,444**
Walters, Stainrod 2

Dean Glover played a crucial role as Villa battled their way to victory at Elland Road. Leeds youngsters threw everyone forward and had it not been for the strength of Villa's defence it could have been a different story. Villa took the lead on 15 minutes, Stainrod finding Walters for his fifth of the campaign. Hodge should have doubled the advantage, as should Evans who hit a second-half penalty straight at Day in goal. The Villa defenders held firm against a flurry of attacks, before Stainrod scored in the 62nd minute and added his second nine minutes later from a tight angle.

Sat 2nd Nov **Oxford United (H)**
Won 2-0 **Att 12,922**
Evans (pen), Stainrod

Ray Houghton and John Aldridge went close to scoring for Oxford before Simon Stainrod was upended by the keeper. Allan Evans - with only three first-half minutes showing - gave Hardwick no chance driving in an unstoppable shot. Walters still had time to see his shot smack the outside of the post before the interval. The League points were assured on 56 minutes; Stainrod chased down Dorigo's long pass, shrugged off Shotton before beating the goalkeeper with a curling left-foot shot.

Sat 9th Nov **Watford (A)**
Drew 1-1 **Att 14,085**
Gray

It took Villa until five minutes before the break to finally have a goal stand, Gray throwing himself headlong onto Tony Dorigo's cross. Andy had already put the ball in the net, with what Turner described as a "tremendous goal" only to see it ruled out for Walters being called offside (but not interfering with play). Mark had also seen a goal chalked off by the official. Talbot equalised in the second half, with Blissett offside in the six-yard area, a decision that upset the Villa lads.

Sat 16th Nov **Sheffield Wednesday (H)**
Drew 1-1 **Att 13,849**
Gibson

Villa were described in one paper as "a team of much potential, but little achievement." Villa started with promise, Walters, Daley and Hodge making lively runs. Spink was the first keeper tested, having to save an Andy Blair shot on 18 minutes, only to fumble the ball into his own net following a dangerous Hart header across the goalmouth. A Walters centre caught Wednesday's defenders off guard and Gibson met it with a powerful downward header. With skipper Evans producing his best performance of the season Wednesday never looked like pinching a winner.

[Above] Villa's Simon Stainrod is marshalled by Sheffield Wednesday's Paul Hart during the Villa Park draw

Wed 20th Nov **West Bromwich Albion (H)** League Cup 4th round
Drew 2-2 **Att 20,204**
Evans (pen), Stainrod

Garth Crooks lit the fuse by opening the scoring in the third minute. Varadi was denied when Spink tipped his header past the post. Stainrod twice beat Bradshaw in goal only to see Thomas clear off the line; the Villa forward also had a 12-yard drive saved spectacularly by the keeper. Albion extended their lead in the 52nd minute. Villa hit back and were awarded a penalty following an altercation between Hodge and Steve Hunt. Evans made no mistake from the spot. Stainrod levelled the tie when he followed through after Williams shot had only been parried.

Sat 23rd Nov **Chelsea (A)**
Lost 1-2 **Att 17,509**
Gray

Villa fell behind on the half hour mark when Kerry Dixon outpaced Evans to a long clearance. Villa weren't trailing for long, and when Gray equalised it looked like Villa would extend their unbeaten run. A second-half goal line clearance robbed Andy of his second of the afternoon while Stainrod and Bradley were denied by Wood with Niedzwiecki beaten both times. Speedie got the better of Dean Glover to snatch the winner with seven minutes remaining.

Wed 27th Nov **West Bromwich Albion (A)** League Cup 4th round replay
Won 2-1 **Att 18,629**
Hodge, Walters

Aston Villa outgunned old enemies Albion as Steve Hodge set them on their way with a quite brilliant opening goal; Gray knocking the ball into his path having been picked out by Dorigo. Bradshaw denied Villa more first-half goals as he made saves from Birch, Hodge and Dorigo. Walters added a second goal after Stainrod back-headed a clever Birch cross from the right. Villa target Steve Hunt scored with a smart left-footed strike in the 73rd minute.

Sat 30th Nov **Tottenham Hotspur (H)**
Lost 1-2 **Att 14,099**
Walters

Even though Villa started reasonably well, they still slumped to a fourth Villa Park defeat, they missed Gray. Paul Birch hit a post in the 11th minute and Clemence had to be alert to save from Hodge. Tottenham didn't have to perform particularly well; they took the lead through Mabbutt on 52 minutes and were gifted a second when Dean Glover mis-hit a back pass to Spink, enabling Falco to nip in and score. Shaw was taken off to be replaced by Daley. Villa hit a consolation with two minutes left to play when Clemence was only able to palm Hodge's effort into the path of Walters.

Sat 7th Dec **Liverpool (A)**
Lost 0-3 **Att 29,418**

Paul Elliott made his debut. Villa were in the game for one minute and 37 seconds, that's all it took for Jan Molby to open the scoring. Andy Gray unsettled the Liverpool back four and when Grobbelaar was unable to hold one of his stinging shots Hansen was there to tidy up. Walters was also denied by the keeper. Paul Walsh made it two and Macdonald made it three with nine minutes remaining. Ian Rush missed five chances.

Sat 14th Dec **Manchester United (H)**
Lost 1-3 **Att 27,626**
Hodge

Villa were unable to prevent United opening a five points gap at the top of the table. Graham Turner's men trailed when Bradley diverted an Olsen free-kick beyond his keeper. For 15 minutes the Villa reacted with spirit and were rewarded with an equaliser when a Hodge shot rebounded off a defender and past Turner. It was all-even at the break. Poor control by Evans allowed Stapleton to send Strachan racing through to beat Spink and then Mark Hughes rose unmarked to head in on 68 minutes. Villa dropped three places to fourth from bottom.

Tue 17th Dec **Queens Park Rangers (A)**
Won 1-0 **Att 8,237**
Birch

With only five minutes played Paul Birch took advantage of an error by Fereday to pounce on the loose ball and coolly chip a stunning goal over goalkeeper Paul Barron. QPR on the back of three defeats were clearly short of confidence, Villa stand-in keeper Kevin Poole didn't help when he stopped Fillery with an outstanding save on 29 minutes. A minute later opposing physios, Villa's Jim Williams and Rangers' Dave Butler clashed on the pitch as they tended Gray and McDonald, who'd banged heads. The QPR lad required nine stitches. Byrne looked a certainty to score but Poole clawed the effort round the post.

Thurs 26th Dec **Leicester City (A)**
Lost 1-3 **Att 13,752**
Walters

Leicester opened the scoring on 17 minutes through O'Neill. Villa gave themselves some hope just after the half hour when Walters nudged home a firm, low Hodge cross. With four minutes til the interval the home side regained the lead through Smith from two yards. Walters, fouled in the box, took the penalty kick in the absence of Evans but aimed it straight and tamely at Andrews. Osman nodded home a third. Villa conceded all three goals from corners, Turner said; "that was criminal."

Sat 28th Dec **West Bromwich Albion (H)**
Drew 1-1 **Att 18,796**
Kerr

Turner made five changes to the team that lost at Filbert Street. Villa soaked up the early pressure and started getting a foothold in the match. When transfer-listed Paul Kerr lashed Villa into a 43rd minute lead it looked like Albion were heading for their 17th defeat of the campaign. Robertson was on hand to keep an Evans back-header from creeping in at the near post following a Hodge corner. When

[Above] The referee attempts to separate the Villa and Leicester City players during the Boxing Day defeat at Filbert Street

Paul Elliott could only half block a McKenzie shot Steve Hunt was on hand to grab the 77th minute equaliser.

Wed 1st Jan **Manchester City (H)**
Lost 0-1 **Att 14,215**

Jeers and cat-calls for the manager's head rang out at Villa Park yesterday after the latest disappointing performance. On a treacherous surface Villa's defence was reduced to tatters as Mark Lillis and Paul Moulden posed the problems. Steve Hodge put a shift in keeping City at bay whilst Andy Gray back in the team, missed two glorious opportunities to put his side ahead. The slow hand clap that echoed around the ground started long before City grabbed the winner in the second half.

Sat 4th Jan **Portsmouth (A)** FA Cup 3rd round
Drew 2-2 **Att 17,732**
Kerr, Birch

Portsmouth laid siege to the Villa goal for the entire first half yet it was the visitors who took an interval lead. Kerr raced in to connect with a fine header after a Paul Birch 25-yard shot cannoned off the crossbar. Noel Blake headed an equaliser at the far post on 56 minutes. An angry exchange between Gilbert and Stainrod led to the Pompey player being sent off. Villa then fell behind to a penalty awarded for obstruction though TV replays would show that wasn't the case. In an explosive match Villa grabbed a last minute equaliser through Birch as he managed to get his toe to Walters' left-wing cross. Villa lived to fight another day.

Sat 11th Jan **Coventry City (A)**
Drew 3-3 **Att 10,326**
Stainrod, Gray, Elliott

It took only 73 seconds for Villa to go in front from a Stainrod volley. For the next 20 minutes it was all Villa, they should have increased their lead. Then a dramatic turnaround as Coventry hit three goals first-half goals in a 22 minute spell as the Villa defence was walked through. Gray pulled one back when he headed in a Birch free kick. Villa then pressed forward, Evans missed a penalty in the 67th minute but with 11 minutes remaining Elliott forced the ball home from close range to force a 3-3 draw.

Mon 13th Jan | **Portsmouth (H)** FA Cup 3rd round replay
Won 3-2 AET | **Att 14,958**
Evans (pen), Stainrod 2

For the second time in this Cup saga Villa would hold an interval lead. Allan Evans from the penalty spot after Walters had been upended. Andy Gray missed a sitter on 50 minutes. With seven minutes left on the watch the promotion-chasers were level from Stanley's 20-yard volley. Extra-time was now required to separate the teams. Villa were back in front when Knight failed to hold Kerr's shot, Hodge squared to Stainrod to score his first. His second came seven minutes later when he headed into the unguarded net. Pompey pulled it back to 3-2 when Stanley stroked home a penalty.

Sat 18th Jan | **Luton Town (A)**
Lost 0-2 | **Att 10,217**

Villa matched Luton in the middle of the park, the differences were at the back and upfront. Villa fell behind when Paul Elliott failed to put power into his clearance, then Birch compounded the error by mis-cueing; Stein gratefully picked up the loose ball and fed Newell, 0-1. Mark Walters had opportunities to run at the defence but little came of them. With quarter of an hour remaining David Norton was robbed of the ball with a powerful tackle by Stein who tucked the ball under Spink.

Wed 22nd Jan | **Arsenal (H)** League Cup 5th round
Drew 1-1 | **Att 26,093**
Glover

Villa started well and had Arsenal on the back-foot as efforts from Birch and Walters served an early warning. Seconds after keeper Wilmot held a Gray short-range header The Gunners went ahead, Villa's defence caught by a ball over the top. A goal down and increasingly frustrated by the Arsenal's seemingly impregnable defence Dean Glover turned the game on its head. With 15 minutes to play Glover got on the end of Gray's controlled pass to force home his low drive – his first senior goal in claret and blue.

Sat 25th Jan | **Millwall (H)** FA Cup 4th round
Drew 1-1 | **Att 12,205**
Hodge

Villa's players found it difficult to raise their game on a tricky playing surface, the conditions didn't bother the opposition who showed more determination and aggression. Millwall went in front from a dead-ball situation, Evans having fouled Fashanu, the kick was floated over and McLeary fired home at the second attempt, his first shot rebounding off the woodwork. Hodge worked tirelessly rallying his teammates and it was his goal from a Williams pass that took the tie to a replay.

Wed 29th Jan | **Millwall (A)** FA Cup 4th round replay
Lost 0-1 | **Att 10,273**

Steve Hodge had to miss representing England in Egypt due to this Cold Blow Lane replay. Millwall were more at home on a pitch the papers described as a "mud heap" and could count themsleves unlucky when Lovell's volley flashed narrowly over the angle of the woodwork. Poole in for the injured Spink made a fine save from the penalty spot to deny Millwall a deserved lead. Villa were fortunate to go off at the break level. Fashanu a constant menace scored the only goal of the game in the 57th minute.

Sat 1st Feb | **Southampton (H)**
Drew 0-0 | **Att 8,456**

Graham Turner survived his latest crisis when his much-changed side showed a steely determination to earn a point. Williams, Walters and Stainrod were axed for Shaw, Kerr and Bradley. Saints played with a sweeper and that stifled Andy Gray. There were few goalmouth thrills

[Above] Millwall's Micky Nutton challenges Simon Stainrod during the F.A. Cup 4th round draw at Villa Park

though Paul Elliott playing his best game since his move from Luton forced Shilton into a diving save. Villa deserved their point and might have won had their finishing been a little sharper.

Tue 4th Feb | **Arsenal (A)** League Cup 5th round replay
Won 2-1 | **Att 33,091**
Birch, Evans

Following last week's F.A. Cup defeat the Villa produced a superb comeback. After a quick-fire raid down the left involving Dorigo and Kerr, Paul Birch fired in to give Villa a 30th minute lead. Birch had a hand in the second, floating a free-kick towards the far post for Evans to head past Lukic. Poole was outstanding in goal, handling with confidence, but was powerless to prevent Mariner's deflected shot off Evans in the 77th minute. Without doubt Villa's best performance of the season.

Sat 1st Mar | **Everton (A)**
Lost 0-2 | **Att 32,171**

Villa battled bravely against the League leaders and a point looked likely as Evans and Elliott subdued the Everton forwards. Villa held out until 15 minutes from the end. Graeme Sharp collected a pass from Lineker, his first shot came back off Evans' legs but he made no mistake at the second time of asking. Provider then turned scorer when Lineker hooked Steven's free-kick onto the post before knocking it in as it came back to him. Villa were in the bottom three and had played a game more than those above.

Tue 4th Mar | **Oxford United (H)** League Cup semi-final 1st leg
Drew 2-2 | **Att 23,098**
Birch, Stainrod

Aston Villa's dreams of an easy passage to Wembley were shattered by Oxford as they were forced to fight every inch of the way. John Aldridge was chief tormentor, his brilliantly taken goal gave the visitors an eighth minute advantage. He also clipped the bar in the 22nd minute. Paul Birch then conjured up a goal from nothing, beating Judge from 25-yards. A Simon Stainrod header gave Villa the lead but it was held for only 60 seconds. Aldridge was fouled by Evans, brushed himself down and calmly converted it.

Sat 8th Mar **Arsenal (H)**
Lost 1-4 **Att 10,584**
Walters

Turner's side had relegation written all over them as they conceded four ridiculous goals. Villa actually took the lead in the 49th minute, Walters scoring his 11th of the season. This stirred Arsenal, Elliott deflected a Rix shot into his own net and Nicholas scored the second on 73 minutes. The Villa defence then collapsed, Hayes scored a simple tap-in and then Rocastle added a fourth on 89 minutes. Villa still with only two League wins in five months.

Wed 12th Mar **Oxford United (A)** **League Cup semi-final 2nd leg**
Lost 1-2 **Att 13,989**
Walters

Two lapses in the Villa rearguard cost the team a place at Wembley for the League Cup final, though the attack rarely troubled the home side's dominance. The opening goal arrived on 57 minutes, Les Phillips driving under the unprotected Spink. The second Oxford goal killed Villa off. Jeremy Charles header past the keeper in the 73rd minute effectively put the outcome to bed. Hodge cleared a Slatter effort off the line before Walters found the net with three minutes to go – too little, too late.

Sat 15th Mar **Nottingham Forest (A)**
Drew 1-1 **Att 12,933**
Walters

Ex Villa players Andy Blair and Steve Hunt were back in claret and blue, hopefully their experience could help stave off relegation. Between them, other old boy Gray and Hodge, gave Villa direction and purpose. Villa took an early grip with Hunt dictating, a Gray header went wide and Shaw's chip was straight at Segers. Forest took the lead just after the hour, Clough took the penalty after being brought down by Evans. Villa heads didn't drop and they were rewarded, Blair's corner helped on by Elliott for Walters to force the ball home.

Wed 19th Mar **West Ham United (H)**
Won 2-1 **Att 11,567**
Hodge 2

With the game less than two minutes old West Ham were ahead, Steve Hunt chested the ball down only to see it roll between Spink's legs. Hodge scored a superb 38th minute equaliser, getting on the end of Andy Gray's header across the area. It was that man Hodge again, Blair knocked a clever ball over the West Ham defence and Steve, in space, volleyed in from six yards. What a way to celebrate his latest England call-up. His finishing touches could yet keep Villa in the top flight.

Sat 22nd Mar **Birmingham City (H)**
Lost 0-3 **Att 26,694**

Two years ago Turner discarded Des Bremner, the Scot came back to haunt the Villa boss as he helped inspire a Blues win. Birmingham's use of a sweeper baffled Villa. A long clearance by Seaman was missed by Elliott, Clarke met it and it was 1-0 to the visitors. Seven minutes later Clarke was at it again after Evans had been forced into an error by Bremner. Spink was then beaten for the third when he was caught in no-man's land and Whitton got on the end of Ranson's long-headed clearance.

Sat 29th Mar **Manchester City (A)**
Drew 2-2 **Att 20,935**
Hodge, Stainrod

City started at a storming pace, Villa had Hodge, Hunt and Blair helping out in their own box. The visitors then began to impose themselves as Hunt found space. They went in front when Hodge lashed the ball in from a Blair corner. The lead only lasted until the 63rd minute, McNab's shot into the top corner giving Poole no chance. The young keeper was beaten again, a Lillis shot was blocked but the rebound fell to Wilson. In a frantic finish Villa rescued a point with Stainrod guiding the ball into the net.

Mon 31st Mar **Leicester City (H)**
Won 1-0 **Att 12,200**
Stainrod

Villa's fourth League win at home against a very average Leicester side was a desperately close affair. Smith and Banks both squandered good chances whilst Dorigo had to react to a Laurie Cunningham dropped corner. Hodge and Blair worked tremendously hard against Mauchlen and McAllister. Villa's goal in the 50th minute, a header from Simon Stainrod was the result of their most decisive raid of the afternoon. Villa were now only in the bottom three on goal difference.

Sat 5th Apr **Oxford United (A)**
Drew 1-1 **Att 11,406**
Stainrod

It's not hard to see why Villa have lost only one of their six games since Andy Blair and Steve Hunt signed, their running and effort providing more strength and resilience to the midfield. Villa dominated the first half with nothing to show for it. A Charles goal put Oxford undeservedly ahead but Villa's response was immediate. Hodge started the move, in space on the right, Hunt then fed Walters before Stainrod dived bravely into a crowded area to head home. At least Oxford, directly above in the table hadn't pulled clear.

Wed 9thApr **Newcastle United (A)**
Drew 2-2 **Att 20,435**
Daley, Hunt

Prior to kick-off Daley was pencilled in for the injured Gray. Newcastle got their noses in front through Whitehouse on 17 minutes but Daley justified his inclusion ahead of Gary Shaw when he scored a splendid equaliser just after the half hour. Relegation fears were intensified when Tony Dorigo was harshly sent off for an innocuous though late first-half offence. In the 80th minute Norton fouled Beardsley, Gascoigne thumped home the free-kick, the three points seemingly destined for Tyneside. Two minutes from time Hunt atoned for a glaring miss volleying home a Walters cross.

Sat 12th Apr **Watford (H)**
Won 4-1 **Att 12,781**
Dorigo, Evans (pen), Gray, Stainrod

Aston Villa's players left the field to a standing ovation, the club were out of the relegation zone for the first time in two months. Yet things had looked so different at the interval with Watford leading through Sinnott's 11th minute goal. It took Villa two second-half minutes to draw level, Dorigo recording his first goal. Evans made it two from the penalty spot, the referee refusing to play advantage when Talbot used his hands to deflect Hodge's centre into the net. In less than a minute Andy Gray added a third. Stainrod rounded off the scoring with ten minutes left.

Wed 16th Apr **Ipswich Town (H)**
Won 1-0 **Att 13,611**
Hodge

Luckily for Villa, Ipswich Town's finishing didn't match their eagerness. Poole made two saves and another effort was wide of the mark. Villa's only chance of note in the first half saw Stainrod's close-range effort blocked by Cooper. After the break Villa got more into the game, more so with the arrival of Daley in place of Walters. The teenage winger played a part in the goal; he hit a tremendous dipping shot that Cooper could only tip away, the ever alert Hodge dived in to grab his tenth of the season. Steve's goal virtually guaranteed safety.

Sat 19th Apr **Sheffield Wednesday (A)**
Lost 0-2 **Att 19,782**

Turner's side battled bravely but were always going to be second best to a powerful Sheffield Wednesday outfit. Megson put the Owls

VAUXHALL
BEDFORD
furnishing

in front on the half hour. Dorigo went agonisingly close to an equaliser with a 30-yard dipper. Villa struggled on the heavily sanded pitch and on 64 minutes Gray hobbled off with an ankle injury to be replaced by Glover. Within two minutes Sterland put the home side ahead with a free-kick from 25-yards. Daley had to come off injured leaving his teammates a man short. There was no way back.

Sat 26th Apr — **Chelsea (H)**
Won 3-0 — **Att 17,770**
Norton, Hunt, Stainrod

The win guaranteed Villa wouldn't be joining West Bromwich Albion and Birmingham City through the relegation trap door. Kevin Poole played a huge part, pulling off three outstanding saves before Villa led through David Norton. Chelsea equalised on 71 minutes from the penalty spot. Hunt volleyed Norton's cross to put Villa 2-1 up. Stainrod sealed the points with an injury-time third.

Sat 3rd May — **Tottenham Hotspur (A)**
Lost 2-4 — **Att 14,854**
Stainrod, Elliott

Simon Stainrod prodded Villa in front with only 95 seconds having elapsed. Spurs were on level terms within a minute, Falco scrambling the ball beyond Poole's left hand. Kevin then produced some sparkling first-half saves as Tottenham dominated but couldn't stop them going in front five minutes after the break. The hosts extended their lead with 74 minutes gone but still Villa competed. With six minutes remaining Elliott rose to head beyond the reach of Clemence. As the visitors pressed for an equaliser they were hit by a breakaway Allen goal.

[Left] Sheffield Wednesday's Mel Sterland scores their second of the afternoon at Hillsborough

PRE-SEASON

• The Villa Park revolving doors are kept busy, Withe, Mortimer, Six, Rideout and Cowans all exit whilst fans' favourite Andy Gray returns.

AUGUST

• The new Henson kit isn't a big hit with the supporters, the shirt carries no badge other than the initials AVFC. Forty years on the fans can't get enough of it - they love it!
• Despite the comings and goings Villa lose heavily 0-4 on the opening day at Old Trafford.
• Gary Shaw plays the first three games of the new season. His last first-team action was February 1984.
• Steve Hodge arrives at Villa Park from Nottingham Forest. Don't blink you'll miss him!

SEPTEMBER

• Steve McMahon gets his move to Liverpool.
• Four Aston Villa players are selected for international games. Mark Walters and Steve Hodge for the England U21s; Andy Gray for Scotland and Tony Daley with the England Youth side.
• Simon Stainrod has a dream debut scoring four goals in the 4-1 win over Exeter City in the League Cup 2nd round 1st leg.
• Four of Villa's ten clean sheets in the League come in this month.

OCTOBER

• Not a great month for League points with none collected in the four fixtures played.
• It's a different story in the League Cup as Villa finish the job they started with Exeter City, winning 8-1 (agg 12-1) and then seeing off Second Division Leeds United 3-0 at Elland Road.
• Brendan Ormsby plays the last of his 140 games in the Villa first-team.

NOVEMBER

• The month starts with a win over Oxford United. This follows four straight defeats.
• Colin Gibson is sold to Manchester United for £275,000.

DECEMBER

• Villa's first win in seven comes mid-month as QPR are beaten by a Paul Birch goal. The team then go nine League games without victory.

JANUARY

• Brian Little resigns as youth team coach to be replaced by another Villa Park legend Ron Wylie.
• Villa get beyond the F.A. Cup third round for the first time in three seasons, defeating Portsmouth 5-4 after a replay but fall to Millwall 1-2, having also required a replay.

FEBRUARY

• The 8,456 crowd for the Southampton match is Villa's lowest for a League game in nearly three decades!
• Villa shock their own supporters by beating Arsenal 2-1 at Highbury in the League Cup quarter-final replay having been held at Villa Park 1-1.

[Above] The Villa team mean business wearing bowler hats and carrying briefcases and brollies

MARCH

• Former players Steve Hunt and Andy Blair are brought back to the club for their vast experience.
• Darren Bradley plays his last in the first-team at home to Arsenal.

APRIL

• Steve Hodge is picked for England's World Cup squad for Mexico.
• Villa go out at the semi-final stage 3-4 over two legs to eventual League Cup winners Oxford United.

MAY

• Villa end the 1985/86 season as they opened it, conceding four goals but at least they manage two at the other end in the 2-4 loss at White Hart Lane.

[Right] Tony Cottee and Frank McAvennie, left like statues by Warren Aspinall during the win over West Ham

1986-87

[Back Row] Martin Keown, Paul Elliott, Nigel Spink, Kevin Poole, Garry Thompson, Simon Stainrod [Middle Row] Paul Birch, Gary Williams, Tony Dorigo, Andy Blair, Steve Hunt, Steve Hodge, [Front Row] Neale Cooper, Allan Evans, Graham Turner (Manager), Ron Wylie (Coach), Andy Gray, Tony Daley.

Football League	Division One
Manager	Graham Turner/ Billy McNeill
Coach	Ron Wylie
Physio	Jim Williams
Captain	Allan Evans
Final Position	Twenty-second
F.A. Cup	Third Round
League Cup	Fourth Round
Leading Goalscorer	Allan Evans 8 goals

Aston Villa invested heavily, in came Villa fan Garry Thompson from Sheffield Wednesday, Aberdeen midfielder Neale Cooper and Martin Keown an Arsenal defender.

Three losses off the cuff including an opening day horror show where Spurs won 3-0 at Villa Park and a trip to Plough Lane for the first top-flight match at Wimbledon saw Villa and Manchester United the only teams with no points on the board. Luton were beaten 2-1 by substitute Paul Kerr's brace then more defeats; home to Oxford and then a 0-6 hammering at Nottingham Forest. Graham Turner was relieved of his post within 24 hours.

Ron Wylie was caretaker for the Norwich City match, Villa lost 1-4 in front of a sparse 12,000 Villa Park crowd. Billy McNeill was named new manager, he oversaw Villa draw at Reading in the Second Round first-leg of the League Cup, even better was the surprise 3-3 draw at Anfield against third placed Liverpool. Momentum gathered pace, two League wins with a 4-1 win over Reading in the Cup sandwiched between them. Back-to-back wins followed a Vicarage Road loss.

Derby County of the Second Division provided stiff opposition as Villa made progress in the League Cup though a replay was required. During a League run of seven games that harvested only four points Villa were eliminated in the Fourth Round by Southampton. In front of 5,125 at Villa Park Derby were beaten in the Full Member's Cup 4-1, only for Villa to go out at the next hurdle to Ipswich.

continued >>>

Total Home League Attendances 381,611
Average Home League 18,171
Highest Home League 32,093
Lowest Home League 12,304

		P	W	D	L	GF	GA	DIF	PTS
1	Everton	42	26	8	8	76	31	45	86
2	Liverpool	42	23	8	11	72	42	30	77
3	Tottenham Hotspum	42	21	8	13	68	43	25	71
4	Arsenal	42	20	10	12	58	35	23	70
5	Norwich City	42	17	17	8	53	51	2	68
6	Wimbledon	42	19	9	14	57	50	7	66
7	Luton Town	42	18	12	12	47	45	2	66
8	Nottingham Forest	42	18	11	13	64	51	13	65
9	Watford	42	18	9	15	67	54	13	63
10	Coventry City	42	17	12	13	50	45	5	63
11	Manchester United	42	14	14	14	52	45	7	56
12	Southampton	42	14	10	18	69	68	1	52
13	Sheffield Wednesday	42	13	13	16	58	59	-1	52
14	Chelsea	42	13	13	16	53	64	-11	52
15	West Ham United	42	14	10	18	52	67	-15	52
16	Queens Park Rangers	42	13	11	18	48	64	-16	50
17	Newcastle United	42	12	11	19	47	65	-18	47
18	Oxford United	42	11	13	18	44	69	-25	46
19	Charlton Athletic	42	11	11	20	45	55	-10	44
20	Leicester City	42	11	9	22	54	76	-22	42
21	Manchester City	42	8	15	19	36	57	-21	39
22	Aston Villa	42	8	12	22	45	79	-34	36

The next League victory wasn't until Boxing Day; that match brought Villa face to face with Charlton Athletic who were above them in the table. The 2-0 win enabled Villa to leapfrog the London side and also clear of the relegation berths. The day after Villa lost 1-4 at Stamford Bridge and on New Year's Day it was the turn of Champions to be Everton to take all three points and push Villa back into the mire.

The distraction of the F.A. Cup didn't improve confidence, Villa were held at home to Chelsea before being dumped out 1-2 in the replay. No wins were chalked up in the months of January or February and only three points from a possible 21 were collected. The one positive that gave the fans some hope to cling to was the gutsy showing in the 2-2 draw at home to Liverpool when Villa came back from conceding in the first minute. Warren Aspinall made his debut.

March wasn't any kinder, Wimbledon shared the points in a 0-0 stalemate; Villa then travelled north to meet bottom placed Newcastle United who'd lost their last three. The Geordies won 2-1. The writing was on the wall within two minutes at the Dell, Villa were already two down and would go on to ship another three.

Villa's first League win in 13 attempts was lucky for some, just not Coventry City. Paul Birch scored the only goal, the Sky Blues wait for a B6 win continues! Villa's biggest win of the season arrived 25 April when West Ham were soundly beaten 4-0, it would also be Villa's last. The defeat at Hillsborough in the penultimate match sealed the club's fate. It had been on the cards a long time. There's an old saying "Things have to get worse before they get better... things had just got worse!

[Right] Villa's Allan Evans and QPR's Robbie James expect to get clattered during the Loftus Road defeat

1986-87

Sat 23rd Aug — Tottenham Hotspur (H)
Lost 0-3 — Att 24,712

Garry Thompson was the only debutant, Martin Keown and Neale Cooper both ruled out. Villa could sense trouble when Clive Allen put Spurs ahead within four minutes. The second also came in the first half when Allen got on the end of a Hoddle free-kick. Elliott stood firm in defence and Hodge nearly pulled one back when he hit the crossbar. Spurs substitute Paul Allen headed off the line from Thompson and Stainrod also went close. Clive Allen bagged his hat-trick when he side-footed home.

Tue 26th Aug — Wimbledon (A)
Lost 2-3 — Att 6,372
Evans (pen), Thompson

Wimbledon playing their first home game in the top flight took the lead on ten minutes, Hodges swept Gary Williams aside to score from 18-yards. Williams was dismissed three minutes later for a retaliatory kick on Hodges. Allan Evans levelled from the spot after Hodge had been tripped by Winterburn. John Fashanu restored the Wombles lead heading in a Kevin Gage corner. Wimbledon extended their advantage when Gage scored with an 89th minute penalty. Thompson scored his first in Villa colours deep into injury time.

Sat 30th Aug — Queens Park Rangers (A)
Lost 0-1 — Att 10,011

Having shipped six goals in two games it was no surprise Turner opted to play with a sweeper in a five-man defence. It made the Villa compact at the back with Blair and Dorigo able to move forward. Hodge missed a golden opportunity while Poole saved from both Fereday and McDonald. With Villa stretched Sammy Lee missed a great chance as did Martin Allen. A Bannister goal was sufficient to bring about Villa's third successive defeat though Keown had a solid debut.

Wed 3rd Sep **Luton Town (H)**
Won 2-1 **Att 13,122**
Kerr 2

The turning point came when Andy Blair came off following a clash with Ricky Hill, Paul Kerr came on in his place. Villa's first goal came from a Stainrod crossfield pass, Kerr jinked past the retreating defenders before firing an unstoppable shot wide of Les Sealey. His second goal came 60 seconds after the half-time break, the result of a strong raid down the left by Thompson and Daley, Stainrod missed Daley's cross at the far post but Kerr was on hand to squeeze the ball home. Still Villa lived dangerously, in the 87th minute they were punished by a Stein header.

Sat 6th Sep **Oxford United (H)**
Lost 1-2 **Att 14,668**
Stainrod (pen)

Villa never looked comfortable against a hard-working Oxford team. Villa's cause not helped with Evans having to go off having been involved in a collision with Charles earlier. The first half was a scrappy affair, Villa offering very little. The visitors went in front on 67 minutes and doubled their lead only three minutes later, Aldridge and Leworthy doing the damage. Stainrod briefly raised hopes from the penalty spot after being tripped by Briggs.

Sat 13th Sep **Nottingham Forest (A)**
Lost 0-6 **Att 17,045**

Villa's expensive team were cut to ribbons by a young and exciting Forest side. The Villa defence was non-existent as Evans and Elliott were given the run-around. Carr started the goal blitz on eight minutes, Clough added a second mid-way through the half. The manager's son bagged his brace within 30 seconds of the interval. Webb made it four after Poole had only half saved a Clough header. Birtles wrapped up a fifth in the 64th minute and Webb stole in with only moments remaining. Graham Turner was sacked within 24 hours!

Sat 20th Sep **Norwich City (H)**
Lost 1-4 **Att 12,304**
Stainrod

Manager-less Villa hit an all-time low when they slumped to the bottom of the division. First-team coach Ron Wylie demanded more, the performance was as bad as the mauling at the City Ground. Phelan put the visitors ahead with Biggins scoring just before the half-time whistle. Gordon made it 0-3 on 55 minutes. Steve Bruce made it four with the simplest of goals. Not even Stainrod's consolation goal two minutes from time relieved the gloom in the stadium.

Wed 24th Sep **Reading (A)** League Cup 2nd round 1st leg
Drew 1-1 **Att 9,363**
Hodge

Villa's new manager Billy McNeill suffered a nightmare start to his job when Reading opened the scoring with less than two minutes on the watch. Spink brought in for his first game of the season hadn't touched the ball before he was lifting it out of the net. Villa hit back with transfer-seeking Steve Hodge. Evans' free-kick was flicked on by Stainrod, enabling Hodge to steal in behind the defence and squeeze a shot into the far corner. Villa's defence took the strain in the second half though Birch struck the Reading bar with a header on 75 minutes.

Sat 27th Sep **Liverpool (A)**
Drew 3-3 **Att 38,322**
Hodge, Thompson, Evans (pen)

Hodge silenced the Kop with a fourth minute goal, only for Wark to equalise just after 20 minutes from the penalty spot. Garry Thompson headed in when Grobbelaar misjudged Hunt's aerial cross, the Liverpool bench were on their feet complaining their keeper had been obstructed! Indecision at the back let Wark in to level the scores before the break. Hansen pulled Hodge down before the hour, Evans sent Grobbelaar the wrong way. Villa were denied all three points when McMahon struck with seconds remaining.

Sat 4th Oct **Coventry City (A)**
Won 1-0 **Att 19,047**
Thompson

Aston Villa maintained their marvellous record over the Sky Blues but it wasn't without drama. Cyrille Regis was desperately unlucky with three headers. Nigel Spink tipped one over the bar, saw another flash just the wrong side of the upright and then watched as Steve Hunt cleared one off the line. Thompson scored his third of the season though it was hotly disputed by City's players, claiming he was a yard offside. Gray came on for Stainrod, he looked extremely sharp and twice went close to scoring.

Wed 8th Oct **Reading (H)** League Cup 2nd round 2nd leg
Won 4-1 (agg 5-2) **Att 12,484**
Hodge, Gray 2, Walters

Villa's revival under McNeill continued, they started like an express train. Hodge put Villa ahead in the sixth minutes after Thompson had seen his shot blocked. They were two-up after Gray scored at the far post. In spite of it being one-way traffic Reading pulled one back on 28 minutes with Spink at fault. In the second half Walters set Hodge away down the left and from his deep centre Gray headed in. Walters got on the scoresheet with a fourth from a low drive.

Sat 11th Oct **Southampton (H)**
Won 3-1 **Att 16,211**
Elliott 2, Evans (pen)

Paul Elliott fired his side in front in the 22nd minute, Walters took the corner kick, Evans flicked it on and Elliott supplied the killer touch. Shilton prevented further goals in the half. Four minutes into the second half and Villa looked to have secured the victory. Thompson's aerial power beat Wright to Dorigo's free-kick and forced a hand ball from Bond. Evans gave Shilton no chance. Villa celebrations were cut short moments later when a hopeful long ball was collected by Clarke, he drew Spink before setting up Wallace for an easy goal. Villa were somewhat shaky until Elliott notched his second on 64 minutes.

[Above] Paul Elliott looks focussed during the defeat at Watford

Sat 18th Oct **Watford (A)**
Lost 2-4 **Att 16,420**
Walters, Stainrod

Walters swept Villa in front – against the run of play - with a low left-foot shot from Garry Thompson's pass, then they collapsed dramatically. Falco grabbed his first from a Nigel Callaghan centre. Two minutes later Elliott and Spink collided as they went for a Barnes cross, leaving Falco with a free header. The Villa keeper hesitated to come for a cross, Falco headed on for Jackett to score a simple goal. Again Spink was caught in no-man's land when Blissett crossed for Falco to bag his hat-trick. Stainrod on for Keown found the back of the net on 66 minutes.

Sat 25th Oct **Newcastle United (H)**
Won 2-0 **Att 14,614**
Hodge 2

Newcastle produced a rousing first half that tested the Villa defence to the full, Martin Keown responding perfectly to Cunningham's aggressive forward play. Steve Hodge – so often the scorer of vital goals – served up two more against the Geordies. The first, Keown turned the ball back into the box from Hunt's corner kick, Hodge met it with a left-foot volley that tore into the roof of the net. His second took a deflection off McDonald's foot after Thompson had headed a Norton free-kick into his path. Villa then had goals chalked off either side of half time, both for offside.

Wed 29th Oct **Derby County (A)** League Cup 3rd round
Drew 1-1 **Att 19,374**
Daley

McNeill's injury hit squad were without Gray and Thompson. Villa took a lucky 15th minute lead through Tony Daley, the winger ending a move started by Birch when he ran from the half-way line before rifling the ball under goalkeeper Wallington. The second half was a different story with Derby showing more adventure. The equaliser was still something of a tragedy for Villa, Evans headed out a corner but the ball fell kindly for Harbey who promptly volleyed past Spink giving the keeper no chance.

Sat 1st Nov **Leicester City (H)**
Won 2-0 **Att 14,529**
Stainrod 2

In a frantic first 45 minutes Villa struggled to deal with Leicester's attacks, mostly revolving around Alan Smith. Spink had to leap acrobatically to tip round a long range effort from Mauchlen, then reacted brilliantly to beat out a Smith shot, and then coming out bravely to deny McAllister. In the second half Hunt was upended in the box, as he fell he flicked the ball up, Stainrod reacted quickest and threw himself backwards to execute a perfect bicycle kick, 1-0. It was Stainrod again seven minutes later starting a Villa attack with a probing run, finishing it with a fierce shot.

Tue 4th Nov **Derby County (H)** League Cup 3rd round replay
Won 2-1 **Att 19,477**
Birch, Thompson

Villa looked to be in command when Paul Birch broke the deadlock within 11 minutes, Hodge and Daley provided the opening for the midfielder to fire a spectacular shot into the far corner. But Derby riding high in the Second Division refused to panic and were level on 24 minutes. Garry Thompson steered Villa into the last 16 with a brilliant 61st minute goal. He chested down a superb 25-yard crossfield pass from right-back Norton to rifle past Wallington, finally breaking Derby's resistance in the process.

Sat 8th Nov **Manchester City (A)**
Lost 1-3 **Att 22,875**
Daley

With McNeill returning to Manchester City Villa were given the hot reception they expected. Villa's good early start was wrecked in the 26th minute when Moulden was presented with his first goal. City then ran the show and went further in front, Varadi from close range. Villa regained the initiative and Daley whipped round three lunging challenges to blast an unstoppable shot past Suckling. City fans started taunting McNeill even more when they realised their 81st minute goal had won the points.

Wed 12th Nov **Derby County (H)** Full Members' Cup
Won 4-1 **Att 5,124**
Shaw 2, Evans, Daley

Gary Shaw given his first start of the season saw his name up in lights as he rolled back the years, scoring twice. His first arrived on 19 minutes, a genuine piece of goal-scorers finishing as he slid in to meet Stainrod's centre. Allan Evans scored Villa's second with a header on 32 minutes. Derby pulled one back through Micklewhite five minutes later but Daley restored the two-goal cushion on the stroke of half time. Shaw's second goal showed another side of his talents with a magnificently judged 25-yard lob in the 59th minute.

Sat 15th Nov **Chelsea (H)**
Drew 0-0 **Att 17,737**

Shaw's midweek goalscoring was rewarded with his first League start, it's a shame it was a game of no goals, not a lot of entertainment and a total lack of attacking ideas. Villa's only chances fell to Norton and Shaw though the full-back earned credit for his long probing runs. Chelsea came out for the second half and threw men forward, Rougvie heading wide, Jones shooting inaccurately and Dixon over the bar. Nigel Spink threw himself at a Dixon shot deep into stoppage time to deny Chelsea the three points.

Tue 18th Nov **Southampton (A)** League Cup 4th round
Lost 1-2 **Att 13,402**
Evans (pen)

Crucial decisions cost Villa. On 16 minutes Garry Thompson forced the ball over the line from Stainrod's centre, neither referee nor linesman saw it so it wasn't given. Seven minutes before the interval Mark Dennis, already booked, went in two-footed to crumple Stainrod, the result – only a lecture. Saints then went down the other end and scored. Clarke drilled a shot past Poole on 64 minutes. Evans made it 1-2 converting a penalty. Kerr thought he'd equalised but the ref claimed Thompson had pushed Wright. Dennis and Keown clashed, both were off. Williams followed soon after.

Sat 22nd Nov **West Ham United (A)**
Drew 1-1 **Att 21,959**
Thompson

West Ham took a ninth minute lead with a counter-attacking goal by Cottee. It actually came from a Villa corner cleared by McAvennie. Inspired by the Heroics of Spink, saving from McAvennie and Keen, Villa began to force their way back. The pressure paid off, on 62 minutes Daley came on for Hunt, with his first touch of the ball the winger got the equaliser. Norton impressed in midfield with a display of tremendous energy he was unfortunate to see a shot blocked on the line by Gale.

Sat 29th Nov **Arsenal (H)**
Lost 0-4 **Att 21,658**

Despite Martin Keown's own goal to put the League leaders in front, Villa overcame the setback and created chances for Williams and Daley. Kerr was replaced at the break by Walters, McNeill's intention of grasping the midfield. The strategy failed, on the hour Arsenal went two-up; Hayes shot caught Spink on the arm and bounced into the goal by way of the post. From then on the visitors were unstoppable. Groves made it three on 71 minutes and still they weren't finished, Rocastle rolled the ball casually past Spink to score the fourth.

Tue 2nd Dec **Ipswich Town (A) Full Members' Cup**
Lost 0-1 **Att 8,244**

A place for the quarter-finals in the Cup that nobody wants! Second Division Ipswich fielded a bunch of raw youngsters, though they performed like men when they realised Villa were not going to be as tough as they expected. A seventh minute save by Spink prevented Gleghorn from scoring a shock opener. Seasoned internationals Hodge and Gray missed glorious chances as Steve Hunt tried desperately to lift his teammates. Wilson put the hosts ahead on 72 minutes. Villa were denied an equaliser in the dying stages when Hallworth palmed over a tremendous drive from Thompson.

Sat 6th Dec **Sheffield Wednesday (A)**
Lost 1-2 **Att 21,144**
Evans (pen)

Villa already without Elliott, Keown and Williams currently serving three match bans were hit with more bookings as Evans, Hunt and Hodge all went in the book. They were down to their last fit 13 players and opened promisingly as Stainrod moved back to midfield. Evans gave them the perfect lift when he scored from the spot after Hodge had been brought down by the Wednesday keeper. The Owls were back on level terms on 37 minutes, a Marwood penalty after Glover was adjudged to have pushed Gary Shelton. There was a further blow for Villa when Chapman scored four minutes into the second half.

Sat 13th Dec **Manchester United (H)**
Drew 3-3 **Att 29,205**
Hodge, Thompson, Evans (pen)

In a game of rip-roaring entertainment Villa's defence was first to fall. In the 19th minute Robson opened the way for Davenport to score. Far from being discouraged Villa made United pay four minutes later, Hunt's volley beaten away by Walsh only for Hodge to score from three yards. United's second-half blast led to a Whiteside goal followed two minutes later with Davenport firing beyond Spink. Thompson got Villa's second running on to an exquisite pass from Hunt. Allan Evans completed the comeback from the penalty spot.

Sat 20th Dec **Oxford United (A)**
Drew 2-2 **Att 8,362**
Thompson, Walters

Garry Thompson put Villa into the lead after seven minutes with the Oxford defence appealing for offside. Oxford hit back, Briggs headed goal from Ray Houghton's free-kick. Villa didn't allow it to affect their total commitment and Walters scored a spectacular goal after 25 minutes to put them ahead again. Villa were placed under severe pressure in the second half but it looked like they'd hold on, until the substitute referee awarded a hotly disputed penalty.

Fri 26th Dec **Charlton Athletic (H)**
Won 2-0 **Att 16,692**
Birch, Daley

Without Steve Hodge (transferred to Tottenham), Villa's front men Gray and Thompson rarely threatened Charlton keeper Bolder. The introduction of Paul Birch for David Norton had an immediate uplifting effect on Villa. Walters hit a post before Stainrod, Williams and Keown combined to send Birch racing through, leaving the keeper stranded with a neat finish. Three minutes later Birch was there again, fastening on to a Walters cross to unselfishly set up teenager Daley for his fourth goal of the season.

Sat 27th Dec **Chelsea (A)**
Lost 1-4 **Att 14,637**
Elliott

Chelsea bottom of the table and with only four wins thrashed a Villa team whose momentum had vanished. The game was only eight minutes old when Keown and Nevin went sprawling in the area following an innocent collision. The referee interpreted it differently, Spackman scoring from the spot. Hunt hung his head when his shot cannoned off the crossbar. On the stroke of half time Dixon smashed the ball in from two yards. Villa had plenty of possession but rarely threatened. Chelsea hit two further goals before the Villa replied through Elliott

Thur 1st Jan | **Everton (A)**
Lost 0-3 | **Att 40,219**

Everton struggled throughout the first half against a battling Villa side with Allan Evans and Paul Elliott outstanding in defence. In the 47th minute Harper hit a 20-yard shot, it struck Stainrod and then Evans before bouncing tamely past Nigel Spink. Trevor Steven nipped in to drive the ball in the net from six yards and Sheedy scored the third with a Volley. It's safe to safe luck wasn't on Villa's side where the first goal was concerned.

Sat 3rd Jan | **Nottingham Forest (H)**
Drew 0-0 | **Att 19,159**

Villa Park witnessed a non-stop festival of attacking football. Villa had more of the play but Forest created the better openings. Spurred on by the presence of Neale Cooper, McNeill's unsure side played with a glittering promise. Daley and Walters controlled the wings. Twice Thompson propelled headers wide of Segers' far post. Dorigo blasted a shot that the keeper had to catch. Villa started the second half with a profusion of corners but Forest gradually forced their way back, Spink doing his job commendably. Villa were second from bottom.

Sat 10th Jan | **Chelsea (H)** **FA Cup 3rd round**
Drew 2-2 | **Att 21,997**
Cooper, Hunt

For half an hour after Bumstead had put Chelsea into a 36th minute lead McNeill's improving side were well held by the visiting defence. Only after the introduction of Birch (for Daley 60 mins) and Gray (for Stainrod 71 mins) did Villa assert a degree of pressure bound to bring goals. The gamble paid off, Cooper got the final touch in the 72nd minute goalmouth scramble. Speedie grabbed an 87th minute goal but Villa still found time to level when Hunt took Walters' short pass and fired in.

[Left] Martin Keown marks Charlton's Jim Melrose during the Boxing Day home win against The Valliants

Wed 21st Jan | **Chelsea (A)** **FA Cup 3rd round replay**
Lost 1-2 AET | **Att 13,473**
Hunt

The win was there for the taking after Steve Hunt's 13th minute goal gave them a priceless lead. It was an advantage they held until seven minutes from the end of normal time. Villa won a corner but let Chelsea break-away and Durie scored from it to take the tie into extra time. It was tough on Villa, the odd times Chelsea had got through Spink pulled off quite brilliant saves. On the 100th minute Durie won a penalty with a blatant dive, Hazard took it and scored.

Sat 24th Jan | **Tottenham Hotspur (A)**
Lost 0-3 | **Att 19,121**

A Steve Hunt pass was intercepted by Allen leaving Steve Hodge to dummy Keown and rifle a shot past Spink. Hodge who'd upset the Villa players by announcing he had to leave Villa Park in order not to damage his international prospects was on target again heading home a Hoddle corner. Claesen scored a third, the Villa defence believing he was offside, but it counted. Villa had looked good going forward, Walters constantly threatened and Villa claimed they should have had a penalty though they were already three down. They were now two points from safety!

Sat 7th Feb | **Queen's Park Rangers (H)**
Lost 0-1 | **Att 13,109**

Villa crashed to their 14th loss of the season and now only have eight home games to save themselves. This latest defeat came with a bizarre own goal from Martin Keown, he blazed Walker's shot into his own net attempting to clear. To rub salt in, Villa had waited for the offside flag that never came when Rosenoir had set Walker free. Throughout the 90 minutes Villa scarcely looked like they'd score, Hunt had a shot cleared off the line and Walters tested Seaman.

Sat 14th Feb **Luton Town (A)**
Lost 1-2 **Att 9,174**
Evans (pen)

This latest defeat bore all the worrying hallmarks of a side sliding towards the Second Division, Villa's players unwilling to show that extra edge of determination. They made a reasonable start but it wasn't until Allan Evans penalty 14 minutes from time that Villa began to show some fight. By then Villa were already trailing to Steve Foster's opener followed by a 31st minute penalty that Harford scored. Spink had to save from Grimes and Harford later on.

Sat 21st Feb **Liverpool (H)**
Drew 2-2 **Att 32,093**
Own goal, Elliott

Aston Villa gave the sort of gutsy performance that could yet see them haul clear of the relegation zone. They recovered from conceding within 40 seconds of the start by drawing level when Lawrenson scored an own goal, Grobbelaar parried a cross into his defender. Walters pulled up with thigh trouble, his replacement Daley tormented the life out of Venison. As Villa's biggest gate of the season roared their approval Paul Elliott responded by poking them into the lead, two minutes before the half-time whistle. Liverpool scored in the 61st minute and from then on Villa were penned back.

Sat 28th Feb **Norwich City (A)**
Drew 1-1 **Att 14,849**
Elliott

Elliott drew first blood on 34 minutes with a firm header from Williams' free-kick. The transfer-listed defender was a tower of strength as Villa had to defend their lead resolutely. Spink performed heroics saving magnificently from Biggins' close-range effort. Norwich gradually turned the screw and levelled matters in the 72nd minute, Phelan stabbing the ball home despite the desperate attempts of Keown to keep it out. Spink had the last word with another splendid stop.

Wed 4th Mar **Wimbledon (H)**
Drew 0-0 **Att 12,484**

Villa's frustrating inability to turn possession into goals could cost them their First Division place. For the third match in a row, their performance lacked nothing in guts but where it mattered in the penalty area they failed miserably. Warren Aspinall came closest to breaking the deadlock but his swerving drive slapped against the upright. A Steve Hunt chip struck the bar and Beasant saved from Cooper. Thompson appeared to have ended his goal famine when he nudged home Daley's corner but the goal was ruled out for a push.

Sat 7th Mar **Newcastle United (A)**
Lost 1-2 **Att 21,365**
Daley

Villa's defence was caught napping when Cunningham raced onto a ball from Anderson, the visitors appealing for offside, the linesman's flag stayed down, 0-1. McNeill's side were under considerable pressure for long periods but clawed their way back and forced an unexpected equaliser. Thompson won possession, moved the ball to Aspinall who turned it to Daley, His left-footed chip shot sailed spectacularly over Thomas. A superb finish by Beardsley decided the match.

Sat 21st Mar **Southampton (A)**
Lost 0-5 **Att 13,686**

As a competitive sporting spectacle, it was all over after three minutes by which time Villa's pathetic defence had given Saints two soft and silly goals. A lazy Elliott back pass resulted in the first, a half-cleared cross the second. After that it was a question of how many. A Clarke free-header - defenders out of position - past Spink made it three-nil on 20 minutes. A compilation of errors between Elliott and Evans let Clarke in for his second before the break. Shil-

[Right] Liverpool's Ian Rush and John Aldridge prove a handful during the Villa Park draw

mita
crown
paints

ton was beaten by Birch but Cockerill popped up to preserve his clean sheet. The only surprise was Saints only bagged one goal in the second half.

Wed 25th Mar **Watford (H)**
Drew 1-1 **Att 12,575**
Hunt

Villa's midfield was a form-less mess, their attack shot-shy and their defence tense and once again unable to find teammates with consistent accuracy. Watford hit a post and the bar before Andy Gray featured in several likely-looking moves, they amounted to nothing. In the 21st minute Villa went behind to a Falco diving header. A Walters' low shot into the stomach of goalkeeper Coton seemed all that Villa could muster. With defeat written all over them Villa secured a point when Steve Hunt scored on 81 minutes, just reward for his willingness to play with an injured knee.

Sat 28th Mar **Coventry City (H)**
Won 1-0 **Att 18,689**
Birch

Paul Birch's coolly-taken goal won three vital points for Aston Villa but it was the save of the season by Nigel Spink that rescued two of them. A rainbow fleetingly appeared over Villa Park, as if a signal for the goal Birch was about to score. He conspired with Andy Gray to produce an opening before finishing in style on 61 minutes. Villa thundered forward for the next quarter of an hour to make certain, Thompson's lob just wide, Gray shooting into the side netting and Walters heading weakly when well placed. With five minutes remaining Kilcline smashed a free-kick through the wall, the ball deflected, Spink touched the ball wide.

Sat 4th Apr **Manchester City (H)**
Drew 0-0 **Att 18,241**

Villa's strikers without a goal this year, never troubled City keeper Suckling, Nigel Spink had even less to do. Birch was Villa's most dangerous attacker but missed the chance to open the scoring when he delayed a right-foot shot, eventually opting to chip but Suckling made an easy catch. Walters found himself in front of goal but appeared nervous and half hit the ball beyond the far post. Andy Gray's inaccurate header was followed by City's first genuine assault with Varadi similarly heading wide.

Sat 11th Apr **Leicester City (A)**
Drew 1-1 **Att 11,933**
Walters

One point from an encouraging performance was again short of what is necessary for an exciting rescue act. Leicester's approach was a mixture of over-casual and over-brutal. Cooper was stretchered off on 14 minutes and reappeared nine minutes later, to be replaced by Daley in the 33rd minute. Steve Moran opened the scoring on 39 minutes when he swept in Smith's cross. The hobbling Mark Walters got on the end of an Aspinall in-swinger to beat Andrews in goal.

Sat 18th Apr **Everton (H)**
Lost 0-1 **Att 31,218**

Leaders Everton inflicted Villa's 18th League defeat as their travelling army chanted "Champions." The visitors didn't play particularly well though in fairness Villa denied them space and openings. The Everton goal came when Steve Hunt, Villa's most impressive player, fouled Reid on the half-way line. The ball was floated in for Clarke to head back for Sheedy to volley into the top corner. Villa who'd worked hard without troubling Southall were now seven points from safety.

[Right] Steve Hunt scores the equaliser during the home draw with Watford

ANSELLS BITTER
Taylorsteel
ELECTRICITY
mita

mita
mita
mita
JVC
6

Mon 20th Apr **Charlton Athletic (A)**
Lost 0-3 **Att 5,595**

Villa reserved their worst display of the season for third-from-bottom Charlton at Selhurst Park. The most galling part about the defeat was the apparent indifference of most of the players to what was happening. It could have been a different story had Gray not missed a simple chance and Aspinall hadn't fired over the bar with just the keeper to beat. Two down by 25 minutes, Villa conceded the third a minute into the second half. The Charlton manager Lawrence remarked; "I must confess how easy it was. I was surprised at their lack of fight."

Sat 25th Apr **West Ham United (H)**
Won 4-0 **Att 13,584**
Hunt, Aspinall 2, Stainrod

Starting hesitantly, Villa sensed West Ham were trying to stroll the game. Steve Hunt opened the scoring following what appeared a hand ball by Gale. Warren Aspinall gave Villa a two-goal half-time cushion when he placed an angled shot into the far corner. Kevin Poole also played his part keeping out Stewart's six yard shot. Villa then added two in as many minutes, Aspinall with a 12-yard header, Stainrod scoring at the second attempt, his first drive spinning into his path off a post.

Sat 2nd May **Arsenal (A)**
Lost 1-2 **Att 18,462**
Aspinall

Hayes pointed Arsenal to their latest victory with a 19th minute penalty after Hunt had handled. Amazingly Villa hit back five minutes later, Aspinall heading in Steve Hunt's high curled shot. Hayes then added his second going past Williams and Elliott before firing past the luckless Poole. As Arsenal pushed forward Villa held out and in the last ten minutes went close to saving the contest. Wilmot had to dive to push out a powerful Gray left-footed shot and then got his feet to a near post shot from Aspinall.

Mon 4th May **Sheffield Wednesday (H)**
Lost 1-2 **Att 15,007**
Robinson

The day relegation became a certainty, 30 years to the day Villa had just lifted their seventh F.A. Cup at Wembley. Villa began nervously and paid for it, trailing by two goals before the interval whistle. Phil Robinson, moved up to midfield when Elliott with a forehead wound remained in the dressing room after half time, delivered a right-foot volley to give Villa hope. Old warrior Andy Gray, head dripping blood from the earlier clash with Elliott, chased until he could barely take another step.

Sat 9th May **Manchester United (A)**
Lost 1-3 **Att 35,179**
Birch

Full-back Bernard Gallacher was given his debut as would Stuart Ritchie who came on as a substitute for the injured Andy Gray. Villa managed to keep the first-half scoreless. But after the interval Manchester United who'd not had to get into second gear sunk Villa with a triple blast within ten desperate minutes. Blackmore swept the ball past Spink from close range for number one, Olsen then scored from ten yards, the third, a simple header from Robson. It was left for Paul Birch to score Aston Villa's last goal of the season and in the First Division.

[Left] Arsenal's Tony Adams occupies the Villa defence at a corner during the defeat at Highbury

PRE-SEASON

• The Villa Park revolving doors are kept busy with Garry Thompson, Neale Cooper and Martin Keown arriving from Sheffield Wednesday, Aberdeen and Arsenal respectively.

AUGUST

• Villa emulate the start of the '82/83 season losing their first three.
• Aston Villa are the first opponents to visit Wimbledon's Plough Lane in the top-flight, following the host's meteoric rise from the Southern League in nine seasons.

SEPTEMBER

• Following the 0-6 capitulation at Forest, Graham Turner is invited to Doug Ellis' house to 'smell the roses' he's no longer manager when he leaves the chairman's Four Oaks home.
• Within eight days Billy McNeill is instated having left a poor Manchester City side that would suffer relegation.
• The Villa take a point from eventual runners-up Liverpool in a 3-3 draw. Had the game gone on any longer they'd have lost, Villa players trade punches with each other as they leave the field.
• A young striker by the name of Ian Olney is on target in the Southern Junior Floodlit Cup, though Villa lose at Arsenal.

OCTOBER

• Villa finally get an away win on their travels, their first in five attempts as they beat Coventry City 1-0.
• Scot Andy Gray scores his only goals (two) of the campaign in a 4-1 win (agg 5-2) over Reading in the League Cup.
• Three of Villa's eight League wins are recorded this month.

NOVEMBER

• Villa reserves beat Newcastle United 7-1 in the Central League. Mark Walters scores four of them.
• End of the road where the League Cup is concerned as Villa crash out 1-2 at The Dell.

DECEMBER

• Allan Evans scores his fifth League goal (all from the penalty spot) in the 3-3 draw at home to Manchester United. Hodge plays his 70th and last game in claret and blue.
• Steve Hodge moves to Tottenham Hotspur.

JANUARY

• Not a great month. Villa go out in the F.A. Cup third round to Chelsea after extra time in the Stamford Bridge replay. They only glean a single point from their three League fixtures.
• Neale Cooper makes his long-awaited debut at home to Nottingham Forest, the game ends 0-0.

FEBRUARY

• McNeill's only signing, Warren Aspinall arrives from Everton for £300,000. The youngster had been a prolific scorer at Wigan prior to his Goodison move.

[Right] New Villa manager, Billy McNeill, is unveiled to the press

MARCH

• Mark Burke makes his debut on 18 April in the defeat at Everton.

APRIL

• Too little too late?... Villa give their supporters hope when they convincingly beat West Ham United 4-0 at Villa Park. Warren Aspinall scores twice (his first since arriving), Hunt and Stainrod also on target.

MAY

• On 4 May Aston Villa are confirmed as relegated in the loss at Hillsborough. Thirty years to the day the famous club lifted the F.A. Cup for a record seventh time.
• Billy McNeill is sacked on 8 May. The Villa still have a match to be played.
• Frank Upton who led the Villa youngsters to F.A. Youth Cup victory in 1972 is in charge for the final game of the season, Manchester United away. Villa lose.
• Full-back Bernie Gallacher makes his debut at Old Trafford. For Gray, Dorigo, Robinson and Glover it's their last.

[Right] David Platt beats Bradford City goalie Paul Tomlinson to score the only goal of the game against The Bantams

1987-88

[Back Row] Garry Thompson, Steve Sims, Lee Butler, Allan Evans, Kevin Gage, Gareth Williams, [Front Row] David Norton, Tony Daley, Warren Aspinall, David Platt, Paul Birch.

Football League	Division Two
Manager	Graham Taylor
Coach	Steve Harrison, John Ward, Bobby Downs
Physio	Jim Walker
Captain	Allan Evans, Steve Sims, Martin Keown
Final Position	Second
F.A. Cup	Fourth Round
League Cup	Fourth Round
Leading Goalscorer	Warren Aspinall 13 goals

Billy McNeill was gone. Watford's Graham Taylor was in, within days he assessed the club was a shambles. Out went T. Dorigo, G. Williams and P. Elliott, in came S. Sims, D. Hunt, K. Gage and A. McInally. A few games in M. Lillis would arrive.

Not the start Taylor expected, only two points from a possible 12 including defeat to Birmingham City. Villa were in the bottom three. September brought three vital victories and a win at Middlesbrough in a League Cup Second Round first-leg tie. Aspinall was leading scorer with five to his name.

Away wins at Plymouth and Leeds elevated them to sixth, a vast nine points off trailblazers Bradford City. A Walters hat-trick in the 4-1 defeat of Crystal Palace plus back-to-back wins over Reading and Shrewsbury put Villa in second position. Middlesbrough and First Division Tottenham were dispatched in the cup.

Villa then won four on the spin – Oldham (A) 1-0, Bradford (A) 4-2 (Andy and Stuart Gray debuted), Swindon (H) 2-1 and Birmingham (A) 2-1. Garry Thompson scored five in the sequence, the two at Blues ensuring legend status. By now Villa were out of two cups; the Simod Cup – no loss there – and the League Cup to Sheffield Wednesday.

M. Walters, A. M. Gray and S. Stainrod were also gone; for Rangers, WBA and Stoke City respectively.

Points were dropped with three draws then Villa saw the New Year in with style, overcoming Hull City 5-0 they hit the top. January saw three further League victories to strengthen their

continued >>>

Total Home League Attendances 403,523
Average Home League 18,341
Highest Home League 36,423
Lowest Home League 11,772

		P	W	D	L	GF	GA	DIF	PTS
1	Liverpool	40	26	12	2	87	24	63	90
2	Manchester United	40	23	12	5	71	38	33	81
3	Nottingham Forest	40	20	13	7	67	39	28	73
4	Everton	40	19	13	8	53	27	26	70
5	Queens Park Rangers	40	19	10	11	48	38	10	67
6	Arsenal	40	18	12	10	58	39	19	66
7	Wimbledon	40	14	15	11	58	47	11	57
8	Newcastle United	40	14	14	12	55	53	2	56
9	Luton Town	40	14	11	15	57	58	-1	53
10	Coventry City	40	13	14	13	46	53	-7	53
11	Sheffield Wednesday	40	15	8	17	52	66	-14	53
12	Southampton	40	12	14	14	49	53	-4	50
13	Tottenham Hotspur	40	12	11	17	38	48	-10	47
14	Norwich City	40	12	9	19	40	52	-12	45
15	Derby County	40	10	13	17	35	45	-10	43
16	West Ham United	40	9	15	16	40	52	-12	42
17	Charlton Athletic	40	9	15	16	38	52	-14	42
18	Chelsea	40	9	15	16	50	68	-18	42
19	Portsmouth	40	7	14	19	36	66	-30	35
20	Watford	40	7	11	22	27	51	-24	32
21	Oxford United	40	6	13	21	44	80	-36	31

position at the summit, a six point advantage over Crystal Palace. Liverpool knocked Villa out at the Fourth Round stage of the F.A. Cup in front of 46,324, Villa Park's biggest attendance since the 1980/81 title was won. It was also the month Gary Shaw played his last game.

New boy David Platt scored at Blackburn but Villa went down 2-3, they'd also lost 1-2 at Ayresome Park the previous Sunday. The win put Rovers top by two points, a game in hand too! Wins at Bournemouth and Reading took Villa's victories on the road to 13, a new club record, Villa were top of the pile.

A catastrophic three game losing streak ensued, Stoke and Oldham at home, with an encounter at Millwall between them. They were still leaders but by a solitary point, the chasing pack had games in hand. Millwall now up to fourth would go on and win their next five matches, finding form at the best possible time.

A point at Selhurst Park dropped Villa to fifth, five points adrift of the leaders. Home wins over The Shrews and Bradford meant Villa still had an outside chance going into the final game – Swindon Town away.

Millwall weren't part of the equation. They were Champions. Middlesbrough were sitting in second a point ahead of Villa and Bradford, both on 77. With Leicester winning on Teesside and Ipswich defying the odds at Valley Parade it handed Villa the automatic place by virtue of the 0-0 draw at the County Ground.

Villa were back where they belong!

1987-88

Sat 15th Aug — **Ipswich Town (A)**
Drew 1-1 — **Att 14,805**
Own goal

Graham Taylor's new look Aston Villa came within inches of victory. Only the width of the post prevented Stainrod from heading a 77th minute winner. Villa played with discipline and determination and made a dream start when their new full-back Kevin Gage crossed powerfully and O'Donnell turned the ball into his own net. Ipswich hit back eight minutes later. Had Villa's finishing matched their quick approach work they might well have been three up by the interval.

Sat 22nd Aug — **Birmingham City (H)**
Lost 0-2 — **Att 30,870**

Villa fielded the same XI that opened the campaign. In a match that produced five bookings and 52 free-kicks Taylor accused his players of "a lack of professionalism." What could be at best described as a second city derby flop left the Villa boss embarrassed. Unfortunately Birmingham were good value for the win and after the second goal went in you sensed it wasn't going to be Villa's day. Substituted Steve Hunt was set for a move.

Sat 29th Aug — **Hull City (A)**
Lost 1-2 — **Att 8,315**
Aspinall (pen)

Despite playing their part in an entertaining contest, Villa were left chasing shadows as Hull took control in the second half. The home side took a 20th minute lead from the penalty spot, Daley bundling Daniel to the ground. Villa's equaliser nine minutes later also came from the 12-yard spot, Aspinall sent sprawling in the box got up and took the kick himself. Spink kept his side on level terms with some excellent saves but could do nothing to stop the winner in the 61st minute.

Mon 31st Aug **Manchester City (H)**
Drew 1-1 **Att 16,282**
Gage

There were encouraging signs, the players getting used to the new manager's demands. Villa had more shape against an unbeaten Manchester City side, or they did until Gage fired them into a 40th minute lead with a superbly struck 25-yarder. After the interval Mel Machin's team stepped up a gear giving Sims and Keown a nervous 15 minute spell before they inevitably scored a deserved equaliser. Five minutes from time Mark Burke was denied a Villa winner, Hinchcliffe a diving header off the line.

Sat 5th Sep **Leicester City (A)**
Won 2-0 **Att 10,288**
Walters, Lillis

Mark Walters who wants to leave Villa Park caused massive problems for Leicester, testing their keeper Andrews twice in the first seven minutes. Villa's opening goal was courtesy of the fleet-footed winger, he raced down the right flank, cut inside the full-back and sent the keeper the wrong way. City replied and gave Spink a few anxious moments. A Cool chip by Mark Lillis after Leicester failed to clear gave Villa a two-goal cushion. It also gave them vital breathing space to relax and perform til the end with no tension.

Tue 8th Sep **Middlesbrough (H)**
Lost 0-1 **Att 12,665**

Villa were beaten by a better, more controlled and composed team. In the first half Pallister and Parkinson effectively reduced the threat of Lillis and the on-loan Malcolm Allen, although Villa had chances. Steve Hunt hit the bar, Allen fired the rebound over. Spink only had to save once, from Ripley. After the interval Boro ventured over the halfway line. With ex Villaman Bruce Rioch in charge of them it was ironic the goalscorer was Paul Kerr – a scorer in Villa's last three seasons. Chants of "Ellis out, Saunders in" rang out.

Sat 12th Sep **Barnsley (H)**
Drew 0-0 **Att 12,621**

Barnsley were top of the table. If Villa had problems before the game they were left with a mountain to climb when Steve Hunt was sent-off with only ten minutes played. He'd been booked only three minutes in for two nasty late tackles. Hunt put Walters through but the winger was felled by Futcher. Claims for a penalty were justified, but not Hunt remonstrating with the referee who was given little choice. As expected Barnsley took control but Sims and Keown more than earned their keep.

Wed 16th Sep **West Bromwich Albion (A)**
Won 2-0 **Att 22,072**
Aspinall 2

Warren Aspinall returned following being dropped for two games, struck twice to hand Villa the honours in a hard-fought showdown. He chased down a Cooper through ball, Reilly missed his tackle then failed to prevent Aspinall's shot cross the line. This gave Villa the boost they desperately needed and from that point were in total control of the game. Andy Gray now in the Albion colours came closest to equalising but the shot was well saved by Spink at his near post. With the final whistle approaching Aspinall got his second, planting the ball past the advancing Naylor.

Sat 19th Sep **Huddersfield Town (A)**
Won 1-0 **Att 6,884**
Hunt S

Villa maintained their surge up the table with a third away win in a season getting brighter by the match. At Leeds Road they won this rain sodden clash with plenty to spare. Lillis tried desperately to score against his former club, Walters was brilliant too and had chances, created by his own vivid individuality. Aspinall battled with confidence, fresh from his two-goal success at Albion, Warren did get the ball in the net but the referee ruled Walters had been offside. When a Gage shot was dropped by the keeper Hunt was on hand to blast it into the net.

Wed 23rd Sep **Middlesbrough (A)** League Cup 2nd round 1st leg
Won 1-0 **Att 11,424**
Aspinall

Villa played with such disciplined resolve especially after Warren Aspinall's 25th minute goal, it would have been a tragedy if they'd lost. In defence acting skipper Steve Sims and Keown showed they were capable of handling Hamilton and Kerr. The midfield was also sound, Birch buzzing as only he can do, David Hunt providing steel and Steve Hunt the experience and guile. Lillis again led the line well, it was from his flick-on from Birch's cross that Aspinall dived in to score. Spink denied Hamilton from a penalty, David Hunt handling.

Sat 26th Sep **Sheffield United (H)**
Drew 1-1 **Att 14,761**
Gage

Villa recovered from a hesitant start to take a 21st minute lead with a superb goal from Kevin Gage, curling a 20-yard free-kick around the wall and into the bottom corner. He was almost on target when a similar effort struck the bar just before half time. Eckhart saw his 50th minute header cleared off the line by Birch. Shortly after The Blades levelled when Morris slotted home. Lillis had an effort cleared off the line while Walters twice went close.

Sat 30th Sep **Blackburn Rovers (H)**
Drew 1-1 **Att 11,772**
Aspinall

After missing the first six weeks through injury Alan McInally gave glimpses of what he can do, his strength evident, he made a vital contribution before being subbed on 75 minutes. Both goals had been scored long before then. Villa drew first blood in the sixth minute with an Aspinall header. Blackburn had already let their opponents off the hook but they weren't as charitable on 19 minutes. Barker fired a justified equaliser. Villa with only three points from 18 on home soil had to endure chants of "what a load of rubbish."

Sat 3rd Oct **Plymouth Argyle (A)**
Won 3-1 **Att 10,515**
Walters 2, Lillis

Villa's fourth League win, all coming on their travels, elevated the team up to eighth. McInally was a starring figure, on 70 seconds he collected a Spink clearance burst past a defender, his thumping shot hit the post and Walters squeezed it in from a tight angle. Plymouth had hardly recovered and Villa were two-up. The move started with a Bernie Gallacher side-step and ended with Lillis getting his head to it following Birch's intervention. Plymouth pulled one back on 13 minutes but Villa restored their advantage thanks to a quality piece of finishing by Walters.

Wed 7th Oct **Middlesbrough (H)** League Cup 2nd round 1st leg
Won 1-0 (agg 2-0) **Att 11,702**
Birch

At the seventh attempt of asking Villa finally broke their Villa Park hoodoo, got their home win, albeit not the three points but a place in the next round, and all with ten men following the sending off of McInally. The big Scot was dismissed on 23 minutes for double dissent. Birch had already put Villa ahead in the first minute and missed two further chances before the set back. Villa responded with a committed defensive display, Sims and Keown dominant, full-backs Gage and Gallacher equally effective.

[Right] Kevin Gage beats Blackburn's Steve Archibald to the ball during the home draw against Rovers

mita
copiers

Sat 10th Oct **Leeds United (A)**
Won 3-1 **Att 20,698**
Own goal, Aspinall 2

Villa penetrated Division Two's best-protected stronghold, their victory providing real hope they'll be back in the First Division next season. The visitors' defence laboured to contain a lively Leeds side. Spink kept Taylor and Sheridan efforts out but United took a 12th minute lead, Taylor heading in Snodin's corner. Villa hauled themselves back into it, Walters shot lacked power but the ball took a cruel deflection off Rennie giving Day no chance. Leeds lost their way after the break, Aspinall put Villa ahead in the 49th minute then he nipped in to turn the ball over the line from close range for Villa's third.

Sat 17th Oct **Bournemouth (H)**
Drew 1-1 **Att 15,145**
Walters

Aston Villa continue to be the great enigma of Division Two – they win at will away but can't beat anyone at home. When Walters got on the end of McInally's back-header to touch in a simple goal on ten minutes few would have realised the significance - they had just witnessed Aston Villa's 6000th League goal. Villa's midfield support for the three strikers was patchy at best and Bournemouth took advantage when they were all even 95 seconds into the second half. Ten minutes later they nearly took the lead, when O'Connor struck the post. Gary Shaw came on for the last 11 minutes.

Wed 21st Oct **Crystal Palace (H)**
Won 4-1 **Att 12,755**
Walters 3, (1 pen), Hunt S

Within three frantic minutes Aspinall had been booked and Walters had opened the scoring, Mark seizing on a Thomas pass. Palace's Andy Gray demonstrated why Villa were keen to purchase his services and his midfield looked dangerous until Villa scored again. Aspinall's penalty following a Redfearn handball was saved, as was his follow up with Wood hooking it away, only to Walters, 2-0. Wright pulled a goal back for Palace within two minutes. Steve Hunt made the result safe on 74 minutes and Walters got his hat-trick via the penalty spot with two minutes remaining.

Sat 24th Oct **Stoke City (A)**
Drew 0-0 **Att 13,494**

Taylor's team weathered a storm and scrambled a point due to the flawless goalkeeping display of Nigel Spink. Three saves came in the first half as Stoke threatened to run riot yet Aspinall missed a glaring chance in the 2nd minute after riding two tackles he put his shot well wide from 12-yards out. Gallacher had the last word before the break with a 30-yard effort which forced a sprawling save from Fox. Villa fans called out in vain for a penalty when Aspinall was wrestled to the ground on the hour.

Wed 28th Oct **Tottenham Hotspur (H)** League Cup 3rd round
Won 2-1 **Att 29,114**
McInally, Aspinall

Spurs generosity to their opponents began early. Aspinall had already worked their keeper before McInally scored his first Villa goal, a fulsome header. Walters repeatedly tried the extraordinary, the ordinary would have sufficed. Ardiles an exhibition of creative football was a constant and came up with the equaliser on 64 minutes. It was Villa who then went in search of a goal. Walter's was denied by Parks and Aspinall hooked a shot over the bar. From yet another corner, a Birch in-swinger, Parks could only palm to Aspinall to score his eighth of the season.

Sat 31st Oct **Reading (H)**
Won 2-1 **Att 13,413**
Blair, Lillis

Villa were so ineffective in the first half they failed to provide a single test for the Reading keeper. They certainly didn't look like a side unbeaten in ten League outings. Horrix opened the scoring for the visitors just before the hour after Spink's defenders had been cruelly exposed. Quality might have been missing from Taylor's team but not character, within six minutes and out of the blue Andy Blair put Villa back in the game with a rasping 20-yard drive. The winner on 78 minutes was equally as unexpected, Lillis from 25-yards!

Tue 3rd Nov **Shrewsbury Town (A)**
Won 2-1 **Att 7,089**
Keown, Aspinall

Shrewsbury missed the ideal opportunity to go in front when Leworthy mis-timed a clear header. A dozen minutes later Martin Keown got his first senior goal in what was his 65th appearance. Mark Walters was dismissed on the half hour mark, it was late and high and despite the full-backs' dying swan routine, Walters maintained he didn't touch him. Following the sending off Villa resorted to hitting on the counter. Villa's winner came five minutes into the second half when Aspinall's shot beat Perks.

Sat 7th Nov **Millwall (H)**
Lost 1-2 **Att 13,255**
Keown

Millwall in losing last week to bottom-of-the-table Huddersfield made a nonsense of the form book. The encounter was won and lost in the opening 18 minutes, Millwall exposing some hesitant Villa defending. Cascarino drove home the first, Briley made it two with disdainful ease. Villa were back in it, a Gage crossfield ball enabled Walters to cross for Keown to head past Horne's despairing lunge. The furious Villa onslaught that ensued saw Lillis and Birch efforts scrubbed for offside and despite the strong running and accurate centres whipped in by Walters, Millwall hung on.

Wed 11th Nov **Bradford City (H) Simod Cup**
Lost 0-5 **Att 4,217**

Villa were equipped to neither combat nor match the skills of the Second Division leaders. Taylor's experiment of playing Lillis at centre-back and McInally in midfield clearly backfired. Bradford romped to a three goal interval lead. Ian Ormondroyd scored the first of Bradford's second-half goals as they cruised to an easy victory. Regardless of it being a derisory competition in the fans' eyes the manager summed it up;"A team needs a 5-0 thrashing like a hole in the head!"

Sat 14th Nov **Oldham Athletic (A)**
Won 1-0 **Att 6,484**
McInally

Alan McInally scored the only goal of a disappointing game in the 36th minute but it was Villa's defenders who were the real heroes. Before and after the goal Oldham enjoyed most of the play but so resolute were Sims and Keown in the centre, ably assisted by Gage and Gallacher on the flanks that Spink hardly had a save to make. Chances fell Villa's way on the break but Gorman was equal to Aspinall and McInally – 23 of Villa's 34 point haul had come on their travels. Jumping up a place to 4th Villa were on the promotion trail.

Wed 18th Nov **Sheffield Wednesday (H)** League Cup 4th round
Lost 1-2 **Att 25,302**
Thompson

With Wednesday down to ten men following Megson's sending off in the first half, Villa threw away a golden opportunity to make the last eight of the competition. The visitors went close within two minutes, a Birch shot was then bundled away for a corner and Spink saved well from Sterland. Wednesday went in front through Chapman but Villa bounced back, Gallacher's deep cross was met by Thompson. Shortly after came the sending off incident, Lillis appeared to be punched. Villa were rocked on 71 minutes when Spink was beaten by West.

Sat 28th Nov **Bradford City (A)**
Won 4-2 **Att 15,006**
Gray S 2, Birch, Thompson

New signings, Stuart Gray and Andy Gray were the vital elements in this outstanding victory. Stuart fired Villa in front when his left-foot shot took a slight deflection. Bradford were level through a penalty

mita
copiers

after the ball hit Sims' arm, TV footage shows it was accidental. Villa regained the lead within a minute through Birch. Villa were on their way when Thompson's header flew past Tomlinson. Bradford scored via a second Futcher penalty, Sims' handling with intent. Stuart Gray saved the best til last, trading passes with his No 9 he then clipped the ball in.

Sat 5th Dec **Swindon Town (H)**
Won 2-1 **Att 16,127**
Thompson 2

A hectic and exciting game that brought numerous scares for the Villa, yet could have resulted in a five goal home win. Swindon twice cleared off the line and survived a Walters shot that struck an upright. On the other hand Villa's defence was consistently unsettled by the speed with which Swindon moved into their box. Garry Thompson's two goals put Villa in the driving seat, meeting a Birch cross with his head from 12-yards on 53 minutes; the second, out jumping everyone to loop his header over Flowers. Swindon refused to lie down and through a Quinn penalty made it a nervy ending for Villa.

Sat 12th Dec **Birmingham City (A)**
Won 2-1 **Att 27,789**
Thompson 2

Thompson's two goals in a game between between two committed sides extended Villa's run to nine wins and a draw from their last ten. Bruno's first goal came from a cleverly flighted centre from Gage, leaving Godden completely stranded. Kennedy gave the home side hope in the 18th minute, celebrated in annoying fashion with trouble already brewing on the terraces. After the break Villa started to use the pace of Walters and Birch. Thompson headed his second on 53 minutes and was only denied a hat-trick when a shot was deflected high over the bar.

[Left] Villa defending against the aerial threat of Oldham Athletic's Roger Palmer on the Boundary Park astroturf

Fri 18th Dec **West Bromwich Albion (H)**
Drew 0-0 **Att 24,437**

The game started with Villa in the ascendancy Gage, Birch and Stuart Gray all threatened Naylor's goal. It soon turned out Villa's defence were not much different to the Albion's rearguard. Reilly rammed a shot at Spink after a Steve Sims' mistake then Keown similarly erred but Spink was able to flip Kelly's chip over the bar. Tony Morley, Palmer and Burrows continued to cause problems for Ron Atknson's side. Birch came closest to scoring when he struck the inside of the upright.

Sat 26th Dec **Sheffield United (A)**
Drew 1-1 **Att 15,809**
Thompson

The pattern was set from the first minute and it was United asking the questions, Spink called on with an angled dive within 60 seconds. Again Villa were relieved when Dempsey miskicked from 10-yards out. Thompson headed just wide and The Blades were unlucky when Duffield finished weakly and straight at the keeper. Bruno put Villa in front on 65 minutes, surprisingly not with his head. A minute later Dempsey broke forward and with a modest shot from a narrow angle his effort crept under Spink.

Mon 28th Dec **Huddersfield Town (H)**
Drew 1-1 **Att 20,948**
Birch

Within the first minute Garry Thompson went close to opening the score against relegation threatened Huddersfield. Paul Birch finally made the breakthrough when he put Villa ahead on 29 minutes. Malcolm Macdonald's Terriers were only trailing for three minutes, Duncan Shearer stunning the Villa Park crowd. In a match described as untidy and wasteful seven players were cautioned, four of them Villa. Taylor's response; "I do not want Aston Villa represented this way."

Fri 1st Jan | **Hull City (H)**
Won 5-0 | **Att 19,236**
Gray S, Aspinall 2, Gray AA, McInally

Villa hit top spot as promotion contenders Hull were totally swept aside. Stuart Gray was on the pitch less than eight minutes before back injury forced him off. The only positive, for the lad he'd given the Villa a lead two minutes previously. Lillis headed off his line, Spink saved a 13th minute penalty, Dyer had a shot rattle the cross-bar. Substitute Aspinall operating on the left then struck twice, his first from three yards out, the latter, heading on Evans' flick on 64 minutes. Moments later Andy Gray drove home the fourth and Alan McInally added another through sheer persistence.

Sat 2nd Jan | **Barnsley (A)**
Won 3-1 | **Att 11,542**
Aspinall, Birch, McInally

Aston Villa made the Oakwell stage their own soaking up pressure in the first half then handing Barnsley a brutal lesson in the art of finishing. Aspinall started the ball rolling with a goal in the 36th minute. Birch beat the keeper with the most delicate of chips. Foreman pulled one back for the hosts before Alan McInally put the game to bed. Some 4,000 Villa fans chanted "Champions" and celebrated as if promotion had already been achieved.

Sat 9th Jan | **Leeds United (A)** FA Cup 3rd round
Won 2-1 | **Att 29,002**
McInally, Gray AA

Villa remained cool in the white-hot atmosphere of Elland Road. Despite Leeds providing much of the early aggression it was Villa who took the lead. A long kick by Spink was helped on by Thompson, McInally finished the move beating Day from 25-yards. Andy Gray's goal, a thundering right-footed shot put Villa in the driving seat. In the 74th minute Davison elbowed Spink as he rose to head the ball in. Villa players remonstrated but the goal stood. Roll on round four.

Sat 16th Jan | **Ipswich Town (H)**
Won 1-0 | **Att 20,201**
Keown

The mysterious home form continued. Martin Keown leapt magnificently getting on Andy Gray's 40-yard free-kick to put his side in front with only five minutes on the clock, but it didn't lead to the flurry of goals that the Villa fans expected. If anything Ipswich were unfortunate not to take a share of the points as Villa looked disjointed apart from in defence. Shaw playing on the left in place of the suspended Aspinall clearly didn't work. Before the break Town battered Villa's goal, Spink did well from Stockwell, Humes and Wark. Villa opened the second half more determined.

Sat 23rd Jan | **Manchester City (A)**
Won 2-0 | **Att 24,668**
Daley, Thompson

Teenager Tony Daley put them on their latest victory run with a clever 13th minute goal having been played through by 'Rambo' McInally. Gallacher did well to clear off the line from City's Morley, John Gidman then scuffed his shot. Villa went in ahead at the interval. Keown, Thompson, Lillis and Daley all had shots beaten out by a bemused defence. Thompson's goal midway through the second half sealed City's fate, his bullet header handing Villa their 11th win on the road.

Sun 31st Jan | **Liverpool (H)** FA Cup 4th round
Lost 0-2 | **Att 46,324**

Villa's biggest crowd since the visit of West Brom and Ipswich in the 1981 title season witnessed a very slick Liverpool side. Villa had their chances and for a 20-minute stretch McInally and Gray (A) worried their opponents into unlikely confusion. Grobbelaar had to make a scrambling save to keep Mark Lillis from opening the scoring. Spink

[Right] Alan McInally jumps with Liverpool's Alan Hansen during the F.A. Cup clash at Villa Park

also had to be alert, Beardsley and Aldridge testing him. Daley then had two shots blocked, the first by Venison, the second by the keeper. Barnes on 54 minutes got the first goal, Beardsley added a second with four minutes remaining.

Sat 6th Feb **Leicester City (H)**
Won 2-1 **Att 18,867**
Lillis, Evans

Aston Villa somehow avoided a bombardment from relegation threatened Leicester. Lillis squeezed the ball home from a narrow angle when Andrews had turned Daley's shot away. Villa doubled the lead within two minutes, Evans meeting Paul Birch's corner. McInally was close to making it 3-0 but the keeper somehow turned it over the bar. Leicester were the more enterprising even at 0-0, but after the break they carved massive holes in Villa's defence. Spink had to make a string of outstanding saves. The score certainly wasn't reflective of the game.

Sun 14th Feb **Middlesbrough (A)**
Lost 1-2 **Att 16,95**
Daley

Villa were away so it came as no shock when the visitors broke the deadlock through Tony Daley. Thompson held off Mowbray for 50-yards before putting the ball on a sixpence for the Villa winger to tap in from a few yards. Gray (A) and Lillis refused to be dominated in midfield and Bruno competed fearsomely yet they couldn't fashion another goal. Middlesbrough who flourished in patches scored in the 81st minute. The noise hadn't abated when Boro broke forward and found a winner. Villa weren't infallible on their travels.

Sat 20th Feb **Blackburn Rovers (A)**
Lost 2-3 **Att 17,356**
Platt, Thompson

A sterile, unimaginative game suddenly sprung to life when the hosts went in front a minute before the half-time whistle. Villa still hadn't started playing and were further behind when Archibald got number two on 55 minutes. From there Villa dominated virtually the whole match. David Platt, a new signing pulled one back in the 63rd minute. While Villa were searching for the equaliser Blackburn scored on the break. Thompson pressured Hendry into turning the ball over his own line and as much as Villa poured forward they couldn't prevent Rovers overtaking them at the top of the table.

Sat 27th Feb **Plymouth Argyle (H)**
Won 5-2 **Att 16,142**
Gray S (pen), Platt, Birch 2, Thompson

Within a six minute spell of the first half Villa scored three goals, just as well, they had trailed from the sixth minute due to Daley's mis-hit back pass. Tony redeemed himself, on 19 minutes when he terrorised the defence and won a penalty, Gray (S) stroked it in. Within two minutes the winger was on the rampage again, setting up Platt for the second. Birch volleyed in to make it 3-1 at the break. Thompson got amongst the goals, heading in off the post, then Birch scored after more impressive play from Daley. Argyle got one in the 82nd minute. Villa were back on top by virtue of goal difference.

Sat 5th Mar **Bournemouth (A)**
Won 2-1 **Att 10,057**
Daley, Platt

Daley was unstoppable for the second successive game. Paul Birch should have given his side a fifth minute lead but Villa's travelling thousands didn't have long to wait for the first of two magnificent goals; Daley ran through two tackles before jabbing a 15-yard shot off Peyton's right-hand post; this was matched when Platt killed the ball on the edge of the area, swivelled and chipped a shot of extreme delicacy over Peyton's head. A Cooke drive took a slight deflection to pull a goal back for the Cherries.

Sat 12th Mar **Leeds United (H)**
Lost 1-2 **Att 19,677**
McInally

Dreadful defending from two first-half corners in the 13th and 36th minutes allowed the determined Leeds outfit back into the promotion race through Swan and Taylor goals. Thompson, marking the near post, was beaten twice by Pearson. Villa never found their rhythm until it was too late but picked up slightly after the hour when McInally replaced Birch. It was the Scot who gave his side hope with ten minutes remaining. Thompson and both Grays were all denied by Day in goal.

Sat 19th Mar **Reading (A)**
Won 2-0 **Att 10,255**
Birch, Thompson

Graham Taylor's men equalled the Second Division record of 13 away wins in one season. An interval substitution turned the game in Villa's favour when McInally came on for Daley. From that point there was only one outcome. Alan only needed a minute to make his presence felt, with his first touch he met Bruno's pass to deliver a superb cross for Birch to turn past Francis. The second goal came seven minutes from time with the Scot involved again. He prodded the ball forward for Thompson to shoot in from close range.

Sat 26th Mar **Stoke City (H)**
Lost 0-1 **Att 20,392**

Villa were bright and lively for 25 minutes only to end in utter disarray. It started so well, the Stoke keeper did well to keep out Andy Gray's 25-yarder; McInally had a shot deflected wide and Thompson hooked the ball narrowly over the bar. Villa should have taken a 33rd minute lead but neither McInally nor Thompson put in an effective shot. Keown and Platt headed into Barrett's arms before Heath scored the only goal of the game.

[Right] Garry Thompson gets the better of Millwall defender Kevin O'Callaghan at The Den

Sat 2nd Apr **Millwall (A) Lost 1-2**
Thompson **Att 13,697**

Millwall's first goal was a tragedy for Villa, failing to defend a right-wing corner. It was looking bleak for Villa until Thompson put them back in the game with a determined header on the stroke of half-time. Cascarino and Sheringham rampaged through their opponents and were instrumental in the Villa's downfall. Any hopes of a revival were dismissed four minutes into the second half when Teddy Sheringham headed in what would be the winner. This was Villa's fifth defeat in eight games.

Mon 4th Apr **Oldham Athletic (H)**
Lost 1-2 **Att 19,138**
Gray S

Villa ran the show without penetrating, with openings for Birch, Platt (twice), Thompson and Keown. To the relief of the crowd Stuart Gray managed where the others had failed in the 40th minute. Seconds later Oldham were down the other end but Bunn stabbed at his shot and it hit the underside of the bar. Wright scored in the 67th minute and as Villa disintegrated Oldham hit them again - harder. Bunn making amends for his first-half miss by snatching a last minute winner.

Sat 9th Apr **Crystal Palace (A)**
Drew 1-1 **Att 16,476**
Platt

Aston Villa's promotion prospects suffered yet another setback as they were rocked by a late penalty equaliser. It was a composed performance by Villa and having weathered Palace's early storm they went ahead when David Platt gave them a 27th minute lead. Platt almost got a second but fired over from Thompson's headed pass. Birch, Platt and Gage all went close with chances before Andy Gray's lunging tackle on ex teammate Ian Wright saw Palace awarded a penalty. Wright slotted home the 83rd minute spot kick. Villa dropped down to fourth

C. H. Tay
MARTINS
BOWDEN & DO
SIGNS
021
6000

Sat 23rd Apr **Shrewsbury Town (H)**
Won 1-0 **Att 18,396**
Aspinall

Warren Aspinall came in from the cold to give Aston Villa their first win in a month. It was a far from convincing display by Graham Taylor's team. Aspinall's goal arrived in the 35th minute and had it not been for a missed penalty barely five minutes later then Villa would have cruised home. As it was Villa were ultimately grateful to Nigel Spink, he reacted brilliantly to Green's 82nd m nute bullet header to tip the ball over the bar, without him it wouldn't have been three points.

Mon 2nd May **Bradford City (H)**
Won 1-0 **Att 36,423**
Platt

Not particularly pretty but a win's a win. Quite an achievement when you consider the Villa's home form over the campaign. David Platt got the only goal of the game in the 24th minute from a header, after connecting with Gage's in swinging cross from the right, he was then the pivotal figure for the remainder of the match. The win kept Villa above Bradford on goal difference only with Middlesbrough a point ahead - a three way tie for the last automatic promotion place.

Sat 7th May **Swindon Town (A)**
Drew 0-0 **Att 10,959**

Villa should have wrapped the game up in the second half, Thompson hitting the Swindon bar with a looping header, then a scramble in the defence to clear the ball to safety. Eight minutes later Platt did exactly the same thing, the ball coming back off the angle but rebounding out of the danger area. An agonising wait of eight minutes ensued before news filtered through Boro and Bradford had both lost. Villa were out of Division Two at the first attempt.

[Left] The contrasting emotions of David Platt – dejected with the Villa team as Oldham's Frankie Bunn scores a last minute winner at Villa Park – and elated after scoring at Selhurst Park

PRE-SEASON

• Graham Taylor is announced as the latest manager in the Villa Park hotseat. His initial assessment; "It's a shambles!"
• Villa's five-match tour of Scandinavia produces four wins and a draw. Offensively, all looks promising as they score 21 goals in total.

AUGUST

• Four new signings are unveiled; Steve Sims from Watford, Kevin Gage Wimbledon, David Hunt Notts County and Alan McInally Celtic.
• Outgoings include Gary Williams to Leeds United, Paul Elliott moves to Pisa and Tony Dorigo joins Chelsea.
• Villa take a point in the opening game at Portman Road. Ipswich Town had finished fifth last season.

SEPTEMBER

• Watford's Malcolm Allen signs on loan.
• Mark Lillis, signed from Derby County makes his debut at Leicester City, scoring the second goal in the 2-0 win. Villa's first of the campaign.

OCTOBER

• In a sequence that started last month Villa win six consecutive away matches; Leic, WBA, Huddersfield, Boro LC, Plymouth and Leeds United. A feat the club last achieved 90 years ago.
• Villa's form isn't as strong at home, they have yet to win in front of their own in seven attempts. Mark Walters hat-trick sees off Crystal Palace in a fine 4-1 victory at B6.
• Graham Taylor manages an England B team to victory in Malta. This might have consequences further down the line.

NOVEMBER

• The scenario continues. Villa lose at home yet win their three away fixtures. The best of them – the 4-2 win at leaders Bradford City. New boys Andy Gray and Stuart Gray add grit to the midfield, the latter weighs in with two goals.
• The ten men of Division One's Sheffield Wednesday end any League Cup aspirations.

DECEMBER

• Recently signed Andy Gray receives a three-match ban.
• The unlucky Neale Cooper has to have his foot put in plaster. More game time lost.
• Garry "Bruno" Thompson follows up with his Bradford and Swindon Town (two) goals with a brace at St Andrews as Villa beat Birmingham City 2-0 in a cauldron of noise.

JANUARY

• The Villa's second win at Elland Road ensures the name's in the hat for the F.A. Cup 4th round.
• Over 46,000 watch as Villa fall to two second-half goals in the Cup at home to Liverpool.
• Villa go top after hitting Hull City for five. Gray S, Aspinall 2,Gray A.A and McInally the scorers.
• A day later the team continue their impressive away form as they win at Barnsley. Birch scores a peach of a chip in the 3-1 victory.
• Villa take a maximum 12 points from their four League fixtures; scor-ing 11 goals with Nigel Spink keeping three clean sheets.

[Above] Stuart Gray makes his Villa debut at Bradford City

FEBRUARY

• Gary Shaw joins Blackpool on a month's loan.
• An unknown arrives from Crewe Alexandra, his name – David Platt.
• French leaders Monaco are convincingly beaten at Villa Park, Gareth Williams, Andy Gray and Platt score the goals.
• A Nigel Spink penalty save helps Villa to a 2-1 win at home to Leicester City. They remain four points clear of Blackburn at the top.
• The team suffer back-to-back defeats, both are on their travels but bounce back with a 5-2 win over Plymouth Argyle.

MARCH

• When Aston Villa win at Reading's Elm Park it's their 13th away victory. A record for Division Two.
•The Villa lose their second home match in the month when Stoke City win by a single goal.

APRIL

• The month starts badly as Villa fall to a 1-2 defeat at Millwall, the lead now cut to two points over Boro.
• The match at home to Oldham Athletic is sadly David Norton's last first-team match.
• Andy Gray and Martin Keown retain their places in the England U21 side to face France in the Euro Champs semi-final.
Villa are five points adrift of leaders Millwall when they face Shrewsbury at a nervy Villa Park. They win 1-0 through Warren Aspinall's goal.

MAY

• A vital David Platt goal gives Villa both points in the win over fellow challengers Bradford City to keeps their slim promotion hopes alive.
• The Villa's point in the 0-0 draw at Swindon Town's County Ground turns out to be enough for the second automatic promotion berth after Boro and Bradford unbelievably lose at home to Leicester and Ipswich respectively.
• Villa and Boro finish on 78 points, their goal difference the same +27... the Midlanders are up by virtue of scoring 68 goals to Middlesbrough's 63!

[Right] Nigel Spink tips a shot round the post during the first away game win at Highbury

1988–89

[Back Row] **Martin Keown, Mark Lillis, Alan McInally, Nigel Spink, Lee Butler, Gareth Williams, Garry Thompson** **[MiddleRow]** **Bobby Downes (Coach), David Hunt, David Platt, Warren Aspinall, Paul Birch, Andy Blair, Gordon Cowans, Neale Cooper, Derek Mountfield, Steve Sims, Jim Walker (Physiotherapist),** **[Front Row]** **Tony Daley, Bernie Gallacher, Allan Evans, John Ward (Coach) Graham Taylor (Manager), Dave Richardson (Coach), Andy Gray, Chris Price, Stuart Gray.**

Football League	Division One
Manager	Graham Taylor
Coach	John Ward, Bobby Downs, Dennis Booth
Physio	Jim Walker
Captain	Allan Evans, Stuart Gray, David Platt
Final Position	Seventeenth
F.A. Cup	Fourth Round
League Cup	Fifth Round
Leading Goalscorer	Alan McInally 22 goals

Following an opening day draw with Millwall, Villa took the spoils at Highbury in a 3-2 win. It would be the only one in the first eight games, including four at home. The team were languishing in 15th position and had it not been for McInally's seven goals it could have been far worse.

On a positive note Villa had progressed at the expense of rivals Birmingham to the next round of the League Cup, the 2-0 at St Andrews bettered in the second-leg 5-0. League wins were recorded at home to both Everton and Tottenham but three losses were soon dealt. You just knew things weren't good when one of those was inflicted by Coventry City, their first win over the Villa in 52 years.

League Cup football saw Villa overcome Millwall 3-1 and Ipswich 6-2 (Platt got four) to reach the quarter-finals whilst on the Simod Cup trail Villa hit Birmingham 6-0 before bowing out at Derby County.

December saw Villa remain unbeaten until New Year's Eve when Arsenal exacted revenge winning 3-0 at Villa Park and despite wins over Norwich 3-1 and QPR 2-1, with points taken at Ayresome Park 3-3 and Kenilworth Road 1-1, the drop zone remained too close for comfort.

The January was tough on both fronts; where the cups were concerned Villa went out at home to Wimbledon in the F.A. Cup Fourth Round having overcome a two-goal interval deficit at Crewe Alexandra where the manager gave his famous half-time talk. At Upton Park, Villa fans escaped serious injury on overcrowded terracing whilst the side lost 1-2 to extinguish fur-

continued >>>

Total Home League Attendances 442,893
Average Home League 23,310
Highest Home League 41,409
Lowest Home League 15,218

		P	W	D	L	GF	GA	DIF	PTS
1	Arsenal	38	22	10	6	73	36	37	76
2	Liverpool	38	22	10	6	65	28	37	76
3	Nottingham Forest	38	17	13	8	64	43	21	64
4	Norwich City	38	17	11	10	48	45	3	62
5	Derby County	38	17	7	14	40	38	2	58
6	Tottenham Hotspur	38	15	12	11	60	46	14	57
7	Coventry City	38	14	13	11	47	42	5	55
8	Everton	38	14	12	12	50	45	5	54
9	Queens Park Rangers	38	14	11	13	43	37	6	53
10	Millwall	38	14	11	13	47	52	-5	53
11	Manchester United	38	13	12	13	45	35	10	51
12	Wimbledon	38	14	9	15	50	46	4	51
13	Southampton	38	10	15	13	52	66	-14	45
14	Charlton Athletic	38	10	12	16	44	58	-14	42
15	Sheffield Wednesday	38	10	12	16	34	51	-17	42
16	Luton Town	38	10	11	17	42	52	-10	41
17	Aston Villa	38	9	13	16	45	56	-11	40
18	Middlesbrough	38	9	12	17	44	61	-17	39
19	West Ham United	38	10	8	20	37	62	-25	38
20	Newcastle United	38	7	10	21	32	63	-31	31

ther League Cup dreams. In the League the sole win (Newcastle United) meant Villa were only three points above the bottom three.

Villa beat Sheffield Wednesday 2-0 in the first week of February, the next eight games would reap only two points, Villa had also failed to score in the last five of those. The table made for grim viewing - Villa were 15th, and only had a two point safety cushion.

April Fool's Day, serious business for Villa, they achieved only their eighth win of the campaign, the goals from Daley and Olney enough to sink Luton. A week later on Tyneside Villa managed only their second away win, by beating the Magpies 2-1 Villa gave themselves a fighting chance and pushed the Geordies further into the clart.

No more wins would follow, not even at home to the Sky Blues, that's how dire the situation was. Only three more points would come from the last four fixtures. Newcastle and Boro were gone, it was out of Villa and West Ham to join them. The Hammers had two games remaining; they would have to win both. They won at Forest, but mercifully they lost at Anfield. Villa were staying put!

European Cup winner Allan Evans had played his last, so too Keown and Sims, Alan McInally was Bayern Munich bound.

[Right] Alan McInally scored a brace in the Upton Park draw against West Ham

1988-89

Sat 27th Aug **Millwall (H)**
Drew 2-2 **Att 22,449**
Gray S (pen), McInally

Millwall created the first chance, Lawrence shooting wide from distance after 75 seconds. McInally then struck, his shot firm but directly at the keeper. Millwall with more of the midfield possession went in front, a corner was floated over and Cascarino headed in. Rambo got the ball in the Lions' net but he'd hauled a player back in the process. Cascarino scored his second within two minutes of his first. Villa with a mountain to climb hit back through a Gray (S) penalty, Gray (A) tripped by the keeper. McInally got the equaliser three minutes before the interval.

Sat 3rd Sep **Arsenal (A)**
Won 3-2 **Att 37,417**
McInally 2, Gray AA

Winterburn had a torrid time, Tony Daley at his explosive best. The Villa winger assisted McInally in both of his goals, the first a side-footed drive, the next a well-placed powerful shot three minutes into the second half. Arsenal pulled back level through Marwood and Smith but Villa were back in front within two minutes. Andy Gray's powerful free-kick going in off the post. Nigel Spink then made crucial saves to preserve Villa's lead.

Sat 10th Sep **Liverpool (H)**
Drew 1-1 **Att 41,409**
McInally

When Alan McInally scored - his fourth goal in three games – the opener in the 39th minute he was still celebrating when Liverpool re-started. Allan Evans his captain, had a word, told him to do his job and close players down. Liverpool's second-half equaliser in the 63rd minute came via a free-kick, the only problem, the kick was taken more than 10-yards from the incident. Whilst Spink was organising his defence the kick was taken and Ray Houghton lobbed the keeper. The referee allowed the goal to stand.

Sat 17th Sep	**West Ham United (A)**
Drew 2-2	**Att 19,186**
McInally 2	

Despite Villa proving they fear no one, the team need to find that killer instinct, twice now letting a two-goal lead slip. McInally took his impressive haul to six in four games with two opportunist first-half goals. This after Villa soaked up everything West Ham had thrown at them. New signing Derek Mountfield highly effective in the sweeper role, had the misfortune to concede an own goal. In a disastrous three-minute spell a mix-up between Spink and Evans presented Kelly with a gift of an equaliser.

Sat 24th Sep	**Nottingham Forest (H)**
Drew 1-1	**Att 23,029**
Gage	

Gordon Cowans gave England manager Robson food for thought with a starring role that put Steve Hodge firmly in the shade. It was 'Sid' Cowans' square pass which brought Kevin Gage's 22nd minute goal, the 20-yard shot skidding through Sutton's fingers. Another superb pass after the break should have delivered a second goal, Daley denied by the keeper's dive to push the ball around the post. Carr grabbed an 80th minute equaliser and Webb forced Spink into a magnificent diving save in the last seconds.

Tue 27th Sep	**Birmingham City (A)** League Cup 2nd round 1st leg
Won 2-0	**Att 21,177**
Gage, Gray AA	

Villa only gave brief glimpses of last season's promotion form but they did enough to establish a lead that should see them through to the next round. Revelling in his new midfield role Kevin Gage struck a superb goal within the first six minutes. Villa had that decisive edge with Gage's biting tackles and Gray (A) and Cowans sharpness. Andy hit the second goal on the stroke of half time. Villa came out after the break and Godden had to react to keep Platt out. After that Birmingham dominated but couldn't put the ball in the net.

Sat 1st Oct — Sheffield Wednesday (A)
Lost 0-1 — Att 18,301

Villa found at their cost that not all sides base their game on football's finer points. Wednesday's approach was rugged, robust and resolute and they should have been out of sight by the half-time whistle, instead of just the single goal advantage. Villa were more dominant in the second half with some powerful over-lapping runs from full-back Chris Price. But the main talking points were Stuart Gray's penalty spot failure and the sending off of Andy Gray.

Sat 8th Oct — Wimbledon (H)
Lost 0-1 — Att 15,416

Villa's poor home form of last season was repeating itself, four draws and now a loss. Villa missed the aerial threat and strength the injured Alan McInally could bring to the table, the situation made worse when Thompson went off to be replaced by Evans in the 76th minute. Mountfield gave another solid performance, looking compact and mobile. While Villa were waiting for the full-time whistle Wimbledon, ever relentless, got forward in the 87th minute to score through Scales. The win keeps Wimbledon in the bottom three but the defeat drops Villa down five places to 16th in the table.

Wed 12th Oct — Birmingham City (H) League Cup 2nd round 2nd leg
Won 5-0 (agg 7-0) — Att 19,753
Mountfield, Gage 2, Olney, Daley

Blooding young striker Ian Olney, Villa were determined to get it right in front of their own fans, serving up a storm that Birmingham could find no shelter from. The game was 45 seconds old when Mountfield headed home Cowans' cross. Gage fired in a free-kick to double the lead and six minutes later made it 3-0 with a volley. Olney's close-range shot slipped under the keeper to the delight of the youngster. Gage was a revelation, at the heart of everything. Daley wrapped the scoring up on 70 minutes.

Sat 15th Oct — Charlton Athletic (A)
Drew 2-2 — Att 7,594
McInally, Platt

Villa trudged off trailing to a solitary goal after a pedestrian 45 minutes. When Villa came out after the break McInally was on in place of Olney. What a transformation, Villa were a totally different proposition. The big Scot found his way into the referee's book for dissent before finding the back of the net, within ten minutes of his arrival. The Valiants came back with a Williams goal on 61 minutes. Rambo then went on a stunning 30-yard dribble before unselfishly passing to Platt to tap into an empty net.

Sat 22nd Oct — Everton (H)
Won 2-0 — Att 26,636
Daley, Platt

For once Villa got all the key components correct, disciplined at the back, competitive and inventive in midfield and lethal in front of goal. They got their just rewards; Tony Daley scored a spectacular volley that will be talked about for years to come. After the interval Villa were determined to build on their single goal advantage. David Platt did just that, his majestically executed second cemented Villa's most entertaining and incisive spell since their return to the top flight.

Sat 29th Oct — Tottenham Hotspur (H)
Won 2-1 — Att 26,238
Own goal, Daley

Villa were able to go a goal up and not surrender the points. Fenwick put through his own net on the hour, slicing McInally's back-header. Spurs equaliser came from the penalty spot, Fenwick making amends for his earlier error. Keown, Evans and Mountfield

[Above] Gordon Cowans scored the equaliser at Old Trafford

were dominant though Gascoigne and Stewart clearly struggled. Cowans and Gage bossed the midfield. Villa recovered from conceding when McInally got behind the Spurs defenders and crossed for Daley to tap in. Spurs dropped to bottom, Villa stayed ninth.

Wed 2nd Nov **Millwall (H)** League Cup 3rd round
Won 3-1 **Att 17,648**
McInally 2, Platt

Ruddock fired third-placed Millwall into an 11th minute lead. McInally ran forward 20-yards before unleashing an unstoppable shot from the right of the box on 17 minutes. The best was to come, Rambo picked the ball up in his own half, turned, ran, shrugged off three challenges before dispatching the ball to the right of the keeper. A truly remarkable goal! Spink made crucial saves before Platt made full use of McLeary's mistake to complete the scoring.

Sat 5th Nov **Manchester United (A)**
Drew 1-1 **Att 44,804**
Cowans

Graham Taylor's side showed they can live with the best. They were given a bit of a run-around in the first half but limited the damage to a 42nd minute Steve Bruce goal. Villa's spirited second-half fightback took Ferguson's United by surprise. Cowans' far-post shot from McInally's cross on the hour salvaged the point but with a little more power up front it could have been three points. David Platt made it a personal triumph having been released by United four seasons ago.

Wed 9th Nov **Birmingham City (H)** Simod Cup 1st round
Won 6-0 **Att 8,324**
Platt, Gallacher, Mountfield, McInally 2, Evans

Villa fans saw the enemy hit for six! Platt struck first on three minutes. Then the game kicked into gear, with three Villa goals in a frenetic five minute period. Bernie Gallacher scored his only senior goal on 34 minutes with a fierce drive; Mountfield then added a third before

McInally got on the end of a Gage cross in the 38th minute. Allan Evans rounded off the first-half scoring. McInally scored the only goal after the interval to make it 13-0 over Blues in the three games. Only Birmingham RFC have it worse one paper declared.

Sat 12th Nov **Southampton (A)**
Lost 1-3 **Att 16,107**
Daley

Villa's unbeaten run of seven matches came to an end at the Dell. Le Tissier gave the hosts the lead on ten minutes and between him and Rod Wallace they gave Mountfield the busiest 90 minutes he's had since signing from Everton. Tony Daley's 22nd minute equaliser was clinically executed, the scores even at the break. Chris Nicholl's Saints regained their lead through Le Tissier and Wallace (R) put paid to any Villa comeback in the 81st minute.

Sat 19th Nov **Derby County (H)**
Lost 1-2 **Att 23,489**
Mountfield

Aston Villa are second-half shockers according to manager Taylor as they attempted to protect their lead instead of attempting to widen the margin. Derek Mountfield planted a powerful header in on 54 minutes. Derby contained McInally and Daley with ease. The visitors drew level in the 74th minute, they hadn't created a single chance inside the Villa area prior to this. Goddard made sure his side took all three points with a 77th minute goal.

Wed 23rd Nov **Derby County (A)** **Simod Cup 2nd round**
Lost 1-2 **Att 10,086**
McInally

Villa pride was dented again as Derby ruthlessly dismissed them from the Simod Cup, found wanting on several fronts. Gallacher was turned inside-out in the build up to Derby's opener on three minutes, Micklewhite prodding it in. McInally blasted his way past two defenders to beat Shilton with a fearsome 25-yard right-footed drive in the 42nd minute. The Scot unleashed another vicious shot within minutes but the keeper tipped it away for a corner. Micklewhite's second of the game meant the end of the road for Villa in the competition.

Sat 26th Nov **Coventry City (A)**
Lost 1-2 **Att 19,880**
McInally

Villa were without defenders Gallacher and Evans. Gray (S) was back after missing three matches.Villa had never lost in Division One to Coventry so their three-match losing streak would be halted at Highfield Road? Wrong! Cyrille Regis put the Sky Blues ahead with a dozen minutes showing on the clock. Villa laboured but produced nothing before the half-time whistle. Houchen extended their lead just after the hour. Villa stirred, McInally reduced the deficit but they couldn't find a way through City's packed defence.

Wed 30th Nov **Ipswich Town (H)** **League Cup 4th round**
Won 6-2 **Att 16,284**
McInally 2, Platt 4

The Villa barnstormed their way into the last 16 of the Littlewoods Cup, totally annihilating Ipswich. Alan McInally put them on the road to victory with two well taken first-half goals. Andy Gray squandered a golden chance on 31 minutes when he scooped his shot over from six yards. Rambo was upstaged by his partner Platt after the break when the youngster bagged four in an astounding 18 minute spell. Goals from Stockwell, 83rd minute and Dalian Atkinson in the dying seconds did nothing for the outcome.

Sat 3rd Dec **Norwich City (H)**
Won 3-1 **Att 19,653**
Gage 2, Platt

Aston Villa's best home performance of the season left League leaders Norwich's impressive away record in tatters. As early as 25 seconds McInally burst past four defenders to lash a shot just over

[Above] Alan McInally celebrates another Villa goal

the crossbar. Gage broke the deadlock in the 20th minute, McInally was close to adding to it on three occasions. It was a complete surprise when Norwich equalised, winger Putney firing through a mass of defenders. Platt missed a penalty but seven minutes later coolly headed past Gunn to make it 2-1. Gage then swung his boot at Cowans' half cleared corner to bag his second.

Sat 10th Dec — **Middlesbrough (A)**
Drew 3-3 — **Att 18,096**
Gray AA, McInally 2

Villa romped into a two-goal lead within six minutes to shock the Ayresome Park crowd. Gray (A) and McInally inflicting the damage. Boro halved the deficit before the break. Four minutes into the second half the hosts were on level terms through Hamilton. Mowbary added a third to put Villa behind. They pulled it back all-square when McInally made a surging run and finished with precision from 18-yards out. Keown was sent off for two bookable offences.

Sat 17th Dec — **Luton Town (A)**
Drew 1-1 — **Att 8,785**
Own goal

The game was a non-event, the surface not fit for purpose. The ball's bounce deceived everyone. Cowans and Gray attempted to merely stroke the ball with deftest of touches, they failed. Luton's players looked no more accomplished on the astroturf, even if they did take the lead through Wegerle. Johnson also seemed an alien in his own back yard, fortunately he did for Villa what their own players couldn't do – he found the back of the net, with a 25-yard lobbed goal beyond his bemused keeper.

Mon 26th Dec — **Queen's Park Rangers (H)**
Won 2-1 — **Att 25,106**
McInally 2

Alan McInally's two festive goals fired Villa five places up the table. His goals were as different as night and day; the first a simple tap-in that he mis-hit, his second was struck with tremendous force beating Seaman, following neat work by Gray (A) and Cowans. QPR player-manager Francis scored in the 73rd minute and was close to getting a second but for the heroics of Spink.

Sat 31st Dec **Arsenal (H)**
Lost 0-3 **Att 32,486**

Leaders Arsenal were gifted two easy first-half goals. A Thomas chip drew Spink off his line to allow Smith to jump and head in. Continued pressure produced the second goal on 23 minutes, Spink punched a Marwood cross straight to Rocastle, 0-2. Villa were run ragged by The Gunners, the back four at sixes and sevens and McInally well marshalled by Tony Adams. Lukic had to make saves from Cowans, Gage and McInally before Arsenal got a third with minutes remaining.

Tue 3rd Jan **Liverpool (A)**
Lost 0-1 **Att 39,014**

Villa engineered their best two chances in the early minutes. One fell to McInally the other to Gray (S), Hooper responding with a blocking dive. The visitors were given a huge let off when Ray Houghton's cross caught Nigel Spink out, with the keeper in no-man's land and unsure whether to come out or backtrack he watched on as Aldridge promptly slipped and sent his shot wide of the empty net. Villa's defenders were disciplined enough to prevent Liverpool creating more than a couple of chances, they only needed one, that came on 65 minutes, Whelan scored!

Sat 7th Jan **Crewe Alexandra (A)** **FA Cup 3rd round**
Won 3-2 **Att 5,500**
Platt, Gage, McInally

Aston Villa came back from the dead. Crewe had nothing to lose, no expectations so they went forward looking for an unlikely goal. They found it, early on too, five minutes to be exact. Keown assisted their cause putting through his own net. At half-time the air was blue, Taylor was livid. Villa came out with Gray (A) and Olney, in place of Evans and Daley. Platt got one back on 52 minutes; Gage fired home from the edge of the box and McInally bagged a 77th minute winner from a tap-in.

Sat 14th Jan **Newcastle United (H)**
Won 3-1 **Att 21,010**
Gray AA, Daley, McInally

It's not very often Villa can play as badly yet take the points. The visitors took the lead through a 29th minute penalty put away by the Brazilian Mirandinha. Their lead cut when Andy Gray snapped up a shocking O'Brien pass. When Price went off injured Taylor changed things about; Platt moved to a central midfield role, Olney alongside Rambo. Once Daley got Villa's noses in front there was only one outcome. Three minutes later McInally slid in to make it 3-1. Villa climbed four places, Newcastle dropped one position, now rock-bottom.

Wed 18th Jan **West Ham United (A)** **League Cup 5th round**
Lost 1-2 **Att 30,110**
Platt

More remembered for the scary overcrowding on the terraces due to turnstile malfunction following a powercut, this could have been a tragedy of - the later to occur - Hillsborough magnitude. West Ham's Brady had a penalty saved by Spink before Ince opened the scoring on 14 minutes. Villa were being stretched but went close to an equaliser when a McInally shot bounced off the chest of McKnight. The Hammers extended their lead before Platt's bicycle-kick reduced the arrears with two minutes to go.

Sat 21st Jan **Nottingham Forest (A)**
Lost 0-4 **Att 22,662**

Villa once again showed their soft centre, not to mention their soft defending and soft finishing. With Gage as full-back, his presence was missed in the midfield where Cowans, Birch and Gray (A) were destroyed by Hodge and Webb. In the secoind period, Pearce, Garry Parker and Laws made it "the most inept, disgraceful display it's ever been my 'pleasure' to watch from any team I've managed" snapped Taylor.

Sat 28th Jan **Wimbledon (H)** **FA Cup 4th round**
Lost 0-1 **Att 25,043**

When things aren't going right the one team you don't want to face is Wimbledon, and so it proved. They had Young sent off; Villa created chances, Evans missed a penalty but they also gave away free-kicks, 14 to be precise. And when the Wombles get dead-balls situations they loft it in rugby style and have four giants attack the ball at once. Vinny Jones popped up with the game's only goal, it trickled under Spink and through Mountfield's legs.

Sat 4th Feb **Sheffield Wednesday (H)**
Won 2-0 **Att 19,334**
Callaghan, Platt

New boys Ian Ormondroyd and Nigel Callaghan were unleashed for the visit of Wednesday. The latter's opener on 25 minutes was a neat powerful header with 'Ormo' playing a vital role. His header prevented Wednesday clearing the ball, it broke to Gage and it was from his cross that the goal came. Ormondroyd nearly got on the scoresheet himself, diving to meet Callaghan's cross, only to feel the crack of Platt's boot on the side of his head as he flew in to score.

Sat 11th Feb **Wimbledon (A)**
Lost 0-1 **Att 6,201**

This should have been a mauling of Forest proportions. Villa were so bad Graham Taylor refused to attend the press conference. Only the brilliance of Nigel Spink, an Allan Evans goal-line clearance, and the thickness of the crossbar helped Villa survive a first-half onslaught before Fashanu stabbed home the game's only goal right on the interval. Gage and Ormondroyd were unlucky not to score, McInally and Callaghan were guilty of slack finishing.

Tue 14th Feb **Everton (A)**
Drew 1-1 **Att 20,116**
Ormondroyd

Villa's new 6' 4" centre-forward 'Ormo' or 'Sticks' scored with a 16th minute volleyed equaliser and might have added more as Villa strove to unshackle themselves of the worst away record in the First Division. Everton looked lethargic and hesitant, despite Cottee's early goal, his close-range snap shot was a cruel blow for Villa's debutant keeper Lee Butler. The Villa took only three minutes to be back level. Cowans cleared off his line before Ormondroyd countered, ran with the ball for 40-yards but shooting into Southall's arms.

Sat 25th Feb **Charlton Athletic (H)**
Lost 1-2 **Att 16,481**
Cowans

Villa weren't as outclassed as they were at the City Ground, but there wasn't a lot in it. Charlton, below Villa in the table, led by the ninth minute through Caton. Gordon Cowans well-worked 39th minute goal didn't bring Villa back into the game as such. It was only a question of time, and that was on 71 minutes, substitute Leaburn scoring. The fans turned on Spink as the scapegoat, the ball skidding underneath him, yet if it hadn't been for Nigel's agility it could have been another humiliation.

Wed 1st Mar **Tottenham Hotspur (A)**
Lost 0-2 **Att 19,090**

Villa are heading for trouble if they don't get their stall in order. This defeat was far lighter than it should have been. Had Platt put the ball away from an Ormondroyd flick-on in the 2nd minute it might have been a different outcome. Chris Price kept a Walsh effort out on the line. Chris Waddle destroyed Villa almost single-handedly, with two magnificent goals, one mid-way in the first, the other mid-second half. Villa were never in it from the first blow.

Sun 12th Mar **Manchester United (H)**
Drew 0-0 **Att 28,332**

Steve Sims and McInally were back as was Butler between the posts. This was now the fifth time Villa had failed to collect all there points. They did show purpose in their play and Jim Leighton, the United keeper had to pull off two breathtaking saves, one early on in the game, a downward header from David Platt, his second even better as he twisted in mid-air to stop McInally's vicious volley. The Villa prematurely celebrating as soon as his foot connected with the ball. Butler also made a wonderful save to deny McClair. Sims and Keown were outstanding while Platt and Gage worked tirelessly.

Sat 18th Mar **Millwall (A)**
Lost 0-2 **Att 13,206**

Villa's last three defeats – all at the hands of London clubs. After Millwall, two more teams from the capital! Villa are becoming masters of conceding the early goal. Millwall third in the table, were ahead within two minutes. From then, there was only one possible outcome as Villa were harassed at the back, overpowered in midfield and downright inept up front. All they produced for 90 minutes work were three long-range efforts from Callaghan, 'Sticks' and substitute Cowans, none on target, none testing the keeper. Villa were out long before Hurlock added number two on 80 minutes.

Sat 25th Mar **West Ham United (H)**
Lost 0-1 **Att 22,471**

Ormondroyd blamed by some fans for the side's current plight was dropped, Taylor's way of protecting him. Villa were no match for West Ham, totally outclassed. Ince got what turned out to be the only goal of the game in the 11th minute. He collected the ball from the edge of his own area and ran 80-yards with it, finishing with a 20-yard strike that flew past Butler. Villa's best efforts came from Daley who headed over within seconds of McInally lobbing over the bar. David Platt hit the bar with a fierce shot from an acute angle. "The chips are down for us now" admitted Graham Taylor.

Mon 27th Mar **Queen's Park Rangers (A)**
Lost 0-1 **Att 11,382**

Villa can't score, let alone win, they are scrapping for their First Division lives. They had no McInally or Cowans and fielded four centre-backs in the side. The excellent Platt and combatative Stuart Gray did what they could to subdue Reid and Co, while getting Ormondroyd and Olney going forward. Andy Sinton's goal was the difference between both teams on paper, the margin far greater on the pitch.

Sat 1st Apr **Luton Town (H)**
Won 2-1 **Att 15,640**
Daley, Olney

The smile was back on Graham Taylor's face; his side had recorded their first win from nine attempts and in the process opened up a four-point gap over the relegation fodder. Tony Daley gave them the perfect start, hitting Luton in only the second minute with an angled shot. The relief was immediate and visible as Villa nerves steadied. Ricky Hill got on the scoresheet on 26 minutes but Villa heads didn't drop. Ian Olney got on the end of Nigel Callaghan's smart centre from the right flank to notch his first League goal. It still needed Spink, saving from Meade to achieve the victory.

Sat 8th Apr **Newcastle United (A)**
Won 2-1 **Att 20,464**
Gray S, Platt

Allan Evans chose to play against the gale-force wind from kick-off knowing if Villa held the hosts, their fans would get on their backs. It worked a treat. Villa even went ahead, Stuart Gray with a thundering 18-yard drive. From that moment Villa were unquestionably the superior team. The workaholic David Platt rounded off a dominant spell with a goal executed brilliantly. A flamboyant finale was denied by Roeder's 81st minute effort. Villa's second back-to-back win couldn't have been better timed, seven points adrift of the dreaded drop and plunging The Magpies deeper in the mire.

Sat 22nd Apr **Norwich City (A)**
Drew 2-2 **Att 14,550**
Olney, McInally

Villa dominated the first half but had only half chances to show for their endeavour. Norwich turned the game on its head with two goals coming in a crazy 45 second spell, Dean Coney and Andy Townsend. Villa refused to buckle and set about reducing the deficit. The pressure paid dividends, Callaghan's ball flicked on by McInally for Olney to fire past the debuting keeper. The visitors equalised seconds later when Platt teed up Rambo to sweep in a low 15-yard drive.

Sat 29th Apr **Middlesbrough (H)**
Drew 1-1 **Att 18,590**
Gray S

It was an error that gifted Boro - a side with only one win in 14 - a second-half lead. With no opposition within 25-yards Steve Sims chose to nod a harmless ball out for a corner. Boro also in need of points took full advantage, Hamilton sent it over, Slaven slammed it against the bar, Davenport drove in the rebound. Taylor's head slumped. It took til the dying seconds to get back on even terms; Callaghan planted a cross into the area and Stuart Gray in a forward position stole in to head a deserved equaliser.

Tue 2nd May **Southampton (H)**
Lost 1-2 **Att 15,218**
Gray S

When Rod Wallace scored within 49 seconds you just knew where this was heading. The goal did little to inspire Villa's confidence and poor distribution from the back repeatedly let them down. Things looked a whole lot bleaker when Paul Rideout made it 0-2 when he headed past Spink. The keeper made repeated saves as Saints attacked over and over. Callaghan and Platt exchanged words, not a good sign. Gray (S) scored in the 85th but it changed nothing.

Sat 6th May **Derby County (A)**
Lost 1-2 **Att 18,121**
Platt

David Hunt was in the team for the first time this campaign, with Darryl Duffy making his debut. In glorious sunshine Villa got the vital goal they needed when David Platt headed them in front on 26 minutes from a corner. The win would more or less guarantee top-flight football next season. Dean Saunders sent the teams in level at the break when he scored ten minutes after the opener. Hebberd's goal after the interval was met with groans from the hordes of travelling Villa faithful. Their side well and truly back in the mix.

Sat 13th May **Coventry City (H)**
Drew 1-1 **Att 29,906**
Platt

Villa's draw with the Sky Blues assured them of nothing on the day. A Platt volley from a Paul Birch cross looked to have put the Villa on the road to salvation. But, they didn't reckon on Coventry City - a side who'd lost seven of their last eight encounters at Villa Park – taking a point from the second half. Villa finished the campaign on 40 points. West Ham had two games remaining, by winning both Villa would go down. The Hammers won at the County Ground five days later. Luckily they had to go to Anfield - they lost 1-5.

PRE-SEASON

- Former "European Young Player of The Year" Gary Shaw moves to KB (Kjobenhavns Boldklub) a Danish side based in Copenhagen.
- David Norton ships out to Notts County.
- Gordon Cowans returns from Bari, Italy and Chris Price (Blackburn) and Derek Mountfield (Everton) join the club.

AUGUST

- With the season not kicking off until 27 August Villa's tour of Scotland occurs during the opening weeks of the month with matches at St Johnstone, St Mirren and Morton.
- Villa get the campaign underway with a 2-2 draw at home to newly promoted Millwall. Stuart Gray and Alan McInally for Villa and a certain Tony Cascarino scores both the visitor's goals.

SEPTEMBER

- Taylor's boys return from Highbury having taken all three points off an Arsenal side strongly fancied for the title in a 3-2 victory.
- Villa and Birmingham face each other in the League Cup. Villa win 2-0 at St Andrews and 5-0 in the second-leg at Villa Park where Ian Olney scores on his debut.
- Despite leading their last three League games at the interval, Villa are held to draws.

OCTOBER

- In what is their sixth League game Villa lose for the first time. Andy Gray is sent off in the 0-1 loss at Sheffield Wednesday.
- Villa get their second win of the campaign when they defeat Everton 2-0 at Villa Park. Tony Daley's acrobatic volley puts them in front.
- Andy Blair is Northampton Town bound.

NOVEMBER

- Whilst League form is sketchy the League Cup provides scintillating displays. McInally scores a sensational individualist goal against Millwall that is still talked of today.
- Goalkeeper Lee Butler makes his debut at home to Birmingham City in the Simod Cup. He has little to do as Villa run riot winning 6-0.
- Alan McInally scores two at home to Ipswich Town in the League Cup as Villa triumph 6-2. David Platt scores the other four to equal the club record set by Tony Hateley and Simon Stainrod.
- Graham Taylor is installed as favourite by the bookmakers to succeed Bobby Robson as England boss.

DECEMBER

- Kevin Gage steals the show with a brace as Villa topple surprise leaders Norwich City 3-1 at home.
- Martin Keown is sent off at Ayresome Park as Villa are held 3-3, having led 2-0.
- Villa destroy Barnsley 7-2 in a Central League match. Gareth Williams and Ian Olney score three a-piece.
- Fans favourite Garry Thompson joins Watford for £325,000.

JANUARY

- Graham Taylor rips into his players at half time as they trail 0-2 at Crewe's Gresty Road in an F.A. Cup tie. Goals from Platt, Gage and McInally save hugh embarrassment for the club.

[Above] Allan Evans is presented with with a testimonial decanter

• Villa go out to West Ham in the League Cup quarter-finals in a game that could have been a disaster of epic proportions. Villa fans have to spill onto the pitch to avoid being crushed. A powercut left electronic turnstiles unable to accurately log the numbers gaining entry.
• Fifth from bottom Villa receive some breathing space by defeating Newcastle United 3-1 at home.

FEBRUARY

• Ian Ormondroyd at a cost of £650,000 becomes the Villa's record signing when arriving from Bradford City. He scores his first goal for the club in the 1-1 draw at Everton on St Valentine's Day.
• Nigel Callaghan arrives from Watford.
• Callaghan has a dream debut, he scores the first goal as Villa beat Sheffield Wednesday 2-0 to record their seventh win in the League.

MARCH

• Immediately after the 0-2 defeat at White Hart Lane the Villa squad leave to take in a two-match tour of Trinidad and Tobago. Here the club would strike gold in the shape of a young Dwight Yorke.
• In what can only be described as a terrible month the club fail to find the net and glean a solitary point from their five League fixtures. All four losses are at the hands of clubs from the capital, Spurs, Millwall, West Ham and QPR.
• Bryan Small is in the England squad for the European Youth Championship match in Greece.

APRIL

• Only two points above the dreaded relegation zone Villa boost their chance of survival, beating Luton Town 2-1, Daley and Olney getting the all-important goals.
• Back-to-back wins are achieved for only the second time this campaign as Villa take all three points on Tyneside. The 2-1 win pushes Newcastle United further into trouble.
• Aston Villa go unbeaten during the month as they follow the wins with an impressive 2-2 draw at high-flying Norwich City and an equally important point at home to fellow strugglers Middlesbrough.

MAY

• Villa end the season with a 1-1 draw at home to Coventry City, not knowing if their First Division status is intact.
• West Ham beat Forest but ultimately lose at Anfield to join Newcastle United and Middlesbrough in the Second Division. Villa are safe by a point!

[Right] The sublime Paul McGrath in action with Wimbledon's Dennis Wise

1989–90

[Back Row] Derek Mountfield, Gareth Williams, Dean Spink, Ian Olney, Kent Nielsen, Ian Ormondroyd, Steve Sims, Nigel Callaghan, [Middle Row] Gordon Cowans, Paul McGrath, Nigel Spink, Bobby Downes (Coach), Dennis Booth (Coach), Jim Walker (Physiotherapist), Lee Butler, Kevin Gage, Mark Lillis, [Front Row] Paul Birch, Tony Daley, Bernie Gallacher, John Ward (Coach), Graham Taylor (Manager), Dave Richardson (Coach), Stuart Gray, Chris Price, David Platt.

Football League	Division One
Manager	Graham Taylor
Coach	John Ward, Dennis Booth, Bobby Downs,
Physio	Jim Walker
Captain	Paul McGrath
Final Position	Second
F.A. Cup	Sixth Round
League Cup	Third Round
Leading Goalscorer	David Platt 24 goals

The big signings included Paul McGrath from Manchester United and Kent Nielsen from Danish club Brondby IF.

The season's opener was at the City Ground 1-1, though for some Villa fans all they saw was the inside of Nottingham train station, the police caged them when their train was late in and the terracing was full to capacity. The draw was followed by two others, Liverpool home, and Charlton away. The first time the Villa had drawn the first three fixtures since 1974/75 when they finished runners-up.

Tottenham were beaten either side of defeats and it looked like another long winter was on the cards when QPR managed by Trevor Francis won 3-1 at Villa Park, the ex Blues man getting a hat-trick. Villa were in the bottom three by virtue of goal difference.

Derby County were next up at B6. Villa were outplayed but won 1-0 due to Derby's lack of finishing and tendency at finding the woodwork. Had Villa lost that day Graham Taylor was going to walk, he'd decided! This vital win was the start of five straight victories, the last one being a 6-2 mauling of Everton. The result made people sit up and take notice at goings-on in Aston.

For the second year running the League Cup trail ended at West Ham, Villa had disposed of Wolves over two-legs in the Second Round. The Zenith Data Systems Cup offered another route to Wembley, Hull City and Nottingham Forest would be eliminated before the New Year.

Nine points were gleaned from Wimbledon, Coventry City (normal service resumed) and Forest, Villa were now level on points with

continued >>>

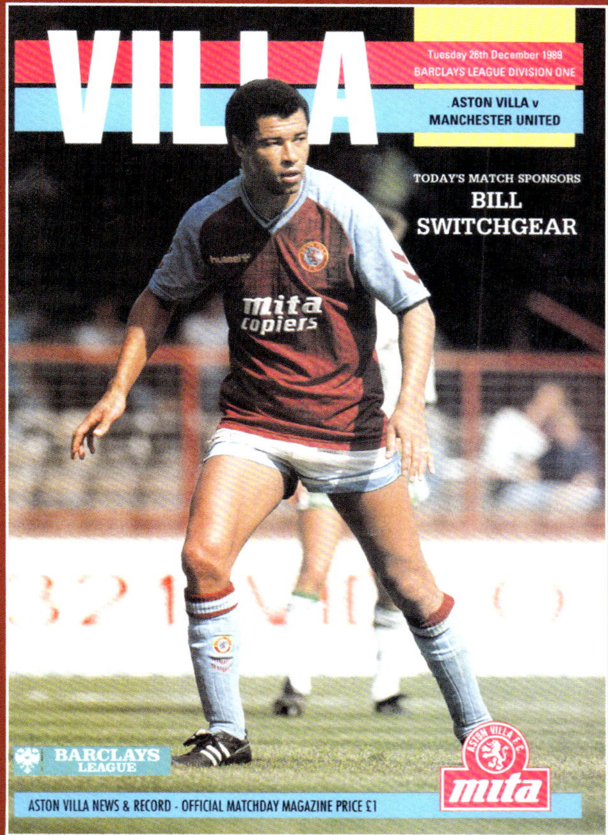

Total Home League Attendances	**485,339**
Average Home League	**25,544**
Highest Home League	**41,247**
Lowest Home League	**15,236**

		P	W	D	L	GF	GA	DIF	PTS
1	Liverpool	38	23	10	5	78	37	41	79
2	Aston Villa	38	21	7	10	57	38	19	70
3	Tottenham Hotspur	38	19	6	13	59	47	12	63
4	Arsenal	38	18	8	12	54	38	16	62
5	Chelsea	38	16	12	10	58	50	8	60
6	Everton	38	17	8	13	57	46	11	59
7	Southampton	38	15	10	13	71	63	8	55
8	Wimbledon	38	13	16	9	47	40	7	55
9	Nottingham Forest	38	15	9	14	55	47	8	54
10	Norwich City	38	13	14	11	44	42	2	53
11	Queens Park Rangers	38	13	11	14	45	44	1	50
12	Coventry City	38	14	7	17	39	59	-20	49
13	Manchester United	38	13	9	16	46	47	-1	48
14	Manchester City	38	12	12	14	43	52	-9	48
15	Crystal Palace	38	13	9	16	42	66	-24	48
16	Derby County	38	13	7	18	43	40	3	46
17	Luton Town	38	10	13	15	43	57	-14	43
18	Sheffield Wednesday	38	11	10	17	35	51	-16	43
19	Charlton Athletic	38	7	9	22	31	57	-26	30
20	Millwall	38	5	11	22	39	65	-26	26

leaders Liverpool. Villa then held the Reds to a 1-1 draw the following weekend.

Boxing Day marked the start of a remarkable run of games that are still fondly remembered today, Manchester United, Arsenal and Chelsea as well as Charlton, Saints, Sheffield Wednesday and Spurs. Villa brushed all aside and in winning at White Hart Lane they went top. A 0-3 loss at home to Wimbledon prevented them from opening a five point gap at the summit. Then shock, a 0-2 at Highfield Road.

Blackburn Rovers were beaten after a replay before Port Vale and West Brom were crushed in the F.A. Cup whilst it was Middlesbrough who made Wembley when they beat Villa over two-legs in the ZDSC Northern Area final.

Two wins then another blip with a draw and two losses. At this time Villa were unceremoniously dumped out of the F.A. Cup at Oldham, losing heavily 0-3. A rare Chris Price goal (he would score another next season) did the double over Arsenal and Chelsea were beaten at Villa Park but Liverpool were gradually pulling away.

Following a surprise loss at Old Trafford (how times have changed) Villa took maximum points for the visit of Millwall. When Villa failed to beat Norwich (3-3) the title was Anfield bound. The curtain came down at a sunbathed Goodison Park where Taylor managed his last game before taking over the England job.

1989-90

Sat 19th Aug **Nottingham Forest (A)**
Drew 1-1 **Att 26,766**
Mountfield

New defensive signings Kent Nielsen and Paul McGrath lined up alongside Derek Mountfield, the three centre-backs looked solid, a vast improvement over last season's leaky defence. Mountfield's eighth minute goal gave Villa the inspiration they needed. With McInally gone, David Platt and Adrian Heath up front didn't' quite click, there was plenty of power but not enough attacking variations. Garry Parker levelled before the hour. Villa hung on towards the end but were good value for a point.

Wed 23rd Aug **Liverpool (H)**
Drew 1-1 **Att 35,796**
Platt

Andy Comyn signed from Alvechurch made his debut - a baptism of fire. Ian Rush missed an opportunity two minutes in. Then both Venison and Callaghan had chances. On 25 minutes Barnes shimmied round Comyn not once but three times before curling a right-footed shot beyond Spink. Taylor changed things round at the break, Olney on for Callaghan, the striker deployed up front with Platt sitting behind, Birch operating down the right. It was 'Birchy' who won the corner that Platt got on the end of to crack in the equaliser.

Sat 26th Aug **Charlton Athletic (H)**
Drew 1-1 **Att 15,236**
Olney

With no wins and three straight draws Villa look to be following last season's path. They certainly look stronger in defence with the inclusion of McGrath. Again Villa conceded early but had the will and desire to come back. Ian Olney who has an uncanny knack of shielding the ball came on for Nielsen on 23 minutes, within quarter of an hour he drew his side level. Gordon Cowans put in yet another vintage display whilst Spink had his second consecutive outstanding game.

Tue 29th Aug **Southampton (A)**
Lost 1-2 **Att 14,301**
Platt

The Villa's promising, albeit tentative start disintegrated under two second-half hammer blows. Villa never really looked that dangerous until Olney and Ormondroyd were both on in the second half. By then though Villa had already conceded to a Cockerill goal. When Case added a second in the 72nd minute thoughts of last season sprang to mind. A fine shot from Platt halved the damage, 'Sticks' came close to scoring twice, a diving header and a deft flick, but Flowers was equal to both.

Sat 9th Sep **Tottenham Hotspur (H)**
Won 2-0 **Att 24,769**
Olney 2

Teenager Ian Olney who scored nearly 60 goals at junior level showed boss Taylor he is worth a regular first-team start. Kevin Gage was back, making a return after a six-month lay-off due to cartilage problems. Olney got his first of the afternoon on nine minutes, taking the ball past Butters with one touch and shooting from 12-yards, his second a simple prod-in mid-way through the first half. The Tottenham defender given a torrid time by Olney was replaced at the break. McGrath and Mountfield kept the defence tight and Birch and Platt blunted Spurs midfield.

Sat 16th Sep **Sheffield Wednesday (A)**
Lost 0-1 **Att 17,509**

Hillsborough isn't a particularly good hunting ground for the Villa, as soon as Dalian Atkinson lashed in Wednesday's tenth minute opener defeat looked inevitable. Villa can raise their game against the classier sides but drop points to sides that frequent the lower placings. They never looked like taking anything from the game and the closest they got was when Pressman kept out a Kent Nielsen drive. After six games last season Villa were a point better off.

Wed 20th Sep **Wolverhampton Wanderers (H)** **League Cup 2nd round 1st leg**
Won 2-1 **Att 27,400**
Platt, Gray S

For the opening 20 minutes Villa's one-touch passing and Nigel Callaghan's impressive passing caused Wolves' defence all sorts of problems. Platt put Villa ahead in this period when he sprinted on to a Price through ball, following a marauding charge by the full-back. Steve Bull and Andy Mutch gave the Villa centre-halves a solid work-out, the latter scored within two minutes of the second half. Bull should have put the Wolves in front, it was a let off for Villa who then took a grip of the game. Stuart Gray headed the winner from a fine pass from David Platt.

Sat 23rd Sep **Queens Park Rangers (H)**
Lost 1-3 **Att 14,170**
Platt

This was damning, the forwards aren't scoring, the defence gets breeched too often. Villa went ahead through that man Platt and are becoming a one-man band. His tenth minute opener was soon cancelled out by QPR player/manager Trevor Francis, the man the Villa faithful love to hate. Francis was at it again on the half-hour. Villa left the field to booing. Within two minutes of the game kicking-off the bloke bagged his hat-trick. Villa were in for a long winter.

Sat 30th Sep **Derby County (H)**
Won 1-0 **Att 16,245**
Platt

Villa have played far better than this and lost handsomely. Derby were far superior in every department. Dean Saunders was a handful and on any other day he would have had a couple more goals on his CV. Villa got the goal on the stroke of half time when Platt slid in from the right side to beat the prone Shilton. The visitors carried on where they left off, they were constantly testing Nigel Spink and the woodwork. Villa had luck on their side today, and the three points.

Wed 4th Oct **Wolverhampton Wanderers (A)** League Cup 2nd round 2nd leg
Drew 1-1 (agg 3-2) **Att 22,754**
Mountfield

Aston Villa with a lead from the first leg knew exactly what was required, they stuck to their task and it worked. Mountfield made the job in hand easier when he converted a Gordon Cowans' free-kick that bamboozled goalkeeper Mark Kendall. Wolves had more possession in the midfield but weren't capable of prising Villa's defence open. On 75 minutes Steve Bull showed true courage to dive in where only Andrew Mullen Gray would, he got knocked out for his trouble as Spink attempted to punch the ball but he put the ball in the net! McGrath was flattened in the same move.

Sat 14th Oct **Luton Town (A)**
Won 1-0 **Att 9,433**
Mountfield

Mark Blake was handed his debut, Gage made way. Taylor's reasoning, Blake had never encountered the plastic pitch before so he wouldn't be worried. The game was almost completely devoid of either constructive football or goalmouth action, the notable exception being Derek Mountfield's left-footed stab at Cowans' free-kick right on half-time. Neither keeper was called on much as the ball was lumped here and booted there. Mountfield, Nielsen and Cowans stood out in a tedious affair.

Sun 22nd Oct **Manchester City (A)**
Won 2-0 **Att 23,354**
Daley, Olney

Villa moved up to ninth in the table with their third successive win. They were set on their way when Tony Daley finished off a six-man move, getting on the end of Kevin Gage's superbly drilled left-wing cross. Strong performances from the centre-backs kept Villa's lead intact. With the second half only three minutes old Stuart Gray retaliated when he was elbowed in the mouth by Trevor Morley, both players were sent off for violent misconduct. Clive Allen came on for City, he hit the post and then Spink brilliantly tipped over from Paul Lake. Olney's close-range volley in the 64th minute proved a step too far for the hosts.

Wed 25th Oct **West Ham United (H)** League Cup 3rd round
Drew 0-0 **Att 20,898**

Villa failed to overcome the challenge of West Ham and seldom threatened. The visitors pushed Villa all the way but luckily didn't have the finish. Birch was replaced by Ormondroyd, his clever cross set up Olney who failed to take his chance. Gage had to clear a long punted ball over his bar. Villa showed more bite when second substitute Mark Blake entered the fray for the departing Daley. Gray and Blake worked a super opening for Platt but he lifted his shot over the bar as Parkes advanced.

Sat 28th Oct **Crystal Palace (H)**
Won 2-1 **Att 15,724**
Platt 2

The victory was launched on the solid defensive partnership of Mountfield and Nielsen. Palace, described as pedestrian matched Villa in every department, when they took the lead on 50 minutes it looked like Villa were staring defeat in the face. Had it not been for David Platt's explosive finishing then Palace would in all likelihood have clinched their first away win of the season. On the hour Platt hit a powerful close-range shot after Ormondroyd flicked-on a Nielsen's free-kick. In the final minute victory was assured when Platt hit a brilliant opportunist goal after fine work by Birch.

[Right] Ian Ormondroyd, at the heart of the action, scores his second against Coventry City

Sun 5th Nov **Everton (H)**
Won 6-2 **Att 17,637**
Cowans, Olney 2, Platt 2, Nielsen

And to think, victory would have put Everton at the top of the the table. Villa were in front within five minutes, Gordon Cowans driving in from 25-yards. Olney extended the lead firing home a rebound and Platt back-heading a Cowans' free-kick made it 3-0 at the half-time whistle. The first half wasn't a fluke, Everton were hit with two goals in three minutes through Platt and Olney. Kent Nielsen got in on the act with his first goal since arriving from Brondby with 67 minutes gone. Two late Everton goals did little to dull their embarrassment. Villa were fourth, on the same points as second placed Liverpool.

Wed 8th Nov **West Ham United (A)** **League Cup 3rd round replay**
Lost 0-1 **Att 23,833**

Villa lacked the cutting edge evident on Sunday. West Ham in only the first minute fired the first warning - a cross-shot just wide of the far post. Villa settled down and during this spell Olney headed marginally over the bar. Spink then saved a shot from the edge of the area. The hosts went in front through Dicks on 31 minutes. Comyn replaced the injured Gage. Villa did get the ball in but Platt was ruled offside. As Villa pushed forward McGrath and Olney both went close with headers.

Sat 11th Nov **Norwich City (A)**
Lost 0-2 **Att 18,186**

Norwich had clearly done their homework, Cowans was marked out of the match, as was McGrath by Andy Townsend. Villa were on the back foot long before a Mountfield own goal put the hosts ahead. Platt and Olney saw precious little of the ball and the result was never in danger even before Linighan's goal in the 69th minute. Taylor said afterwards; "We were outplayed, out-gunned and out-manoeuvred by a team who could go on and win the title." Norwich leapfrogged Villa.

[Left] Tony Daley scores to make it 2-0 at Plough Lane against Wimbledon

Sat 18th Nov **Coventry City (H)**
Won 4-1 **Att 22,803**
Ormondroyd 2, Own goal, Platt (pen)

Ian Ormondroyd's two goals in Villa's latest spectacular helped them to another exciting win over their old whipping boys, and to third place briefly. Ormo's first goal at Villa Park was a thing of beauty, a defence-splitting run by Daley then an unstoppable drive from the lanky forward. Villa went in at the break leading 2-1, Peake putting through his own net, Gynn pulling one back for City. A header from Ormondroyd put Villa firmly in the driving seat, Platt rounded off the demolition.

Sat 25th Nov **Wimbledon (A)**
Won 2-0 **Att 5,981**
Platt, Daley

Villa showed they could mix it with the working-class sides who like the rough and tumble. They matched steel with steel and their class also told, a 40-yard volleyed pass delivered by Sid Cowans was sheer poetry, it found Tony Daley who set up Platt for his 11th of the season. Nigel Spink who gallantly played on having received a bad gash whilst saving from Young, was ably protected by his three centre-halves. Daley's precision shot eight minutes from time was just reward for a scintillating performance.

Tue 28th Nov **Hull City (A)** **Zenith Data Systems Cup 2nd round**
Won 2-1 **Att 2,888**
Mountfield, Platt

The Villa team quietly slipped away from Boothferry Park with feelings of relief and embarrassment, rather than delight. They were far from impressive against the side languishing at the foot of the Second Division. It took the Villa til the 64th minute to take the lead, Mountfield rounding off a Cowans-Olney-McGrath move. When the visitors relaxed Hull hit them quick and hard, Jenkinson squeezing the ball home. Platt spared the blushes somewhat with an injury-time winner.

Sat 2nd Dec **Nottingham Forest (H)**
Won 2-1 **Att 25,757**
Olney, Platt

Kent Nielsen and Gordon Cowans on this display looked like high-class internationals. The team got the best possible start against Forest when Ian Olney fired home inside the six-yard box. Hodge needed watching, too many times he ripped through Villa's midfield. Chapman had an easy tap-in for the equaliser. Villa rose above the opposition because of Cowans and of Platt's penchant to finish with the precision of a poisonous dart.

Sat 9th Dec **Liverpool (A)**
Drew 1-1 **Att 37,435**
Olney

A visit to Anfield – always the acid test, and Villa passed with flying colours. They played really well for the first half hour and should have been further in front than by the single goal, scored by Olney in the 21st minute. Had it not been for Grobbelaar's intervention their opener would have been in the first 60 seconds. The second half was a different story, Villa had their backs to the wall, and were finally punished when Rush knocked the ball back for Beardsley to score. In knocking Dalglish's men off the top spot they revealed just how much the team as a whole have improved.

Sat 16th Dec **Millwall (A)**
Lost 0-2 **Att 10,536**

For once Taylor's tactical ploy based on three central-defenders, which has served so well in the last matches, failed to achieve the desired effect. Millwall's methods were not always legal but Platt, Cowans and Ormondroyd were rendered totally ineffective. Cascarino, recently linked with Villa, headed the first on 51 minutes. Stephenson killed the game off when he bagged a second Millwall goal. Goalkeeper Horne made his first save of the match in the 74th minute, a McGrath header.

Fri 22nd Dec **Nottingham Forest (H)** **Zenith Data Systems Cup 3rd round**
Won 2-1 **Att 6,530**
Platt (pen), Mountfield

Forest's goal resulted initially from a free-kick given away by Mountfield. They just about edged a very mediocre first half. In an eerie atmosphere with such few fans Villa came out after the break as though the League Championship was at stake. Tony Daley destroyed the visitors with a series of scintillating runs. David Platt was tripped in the box, and took the spot kick himself, 1-1. Pearce was fortunate not to see red for a vicious tackle on Daley. Villa took the lead on 74 minutes, Mountfield creeping in on the blind side to meet Sid Cowans' cross.

Tue 26th Dec **Manchester United (H)**
Won 3-0 **Att 41,247**
Olney, Platt, Gage

The first half was a case of each side weighing their opponents up. After the interval Villa pushed United back into their half and went for the jugular. Olney, from the tightest of angles, pounced in the 57th minute following a scramble when United failed to clear a Cowans' free-kick. Six minutes later Platt, as cool as you like, took the ball round Leighton to bang in a brilliant goal. It came from Cowans robbing Ince and Daley running 40-yards. Still the Villans' weren't finished, Platt laid off Daley's cross into the path of Gage who slotted it home for number three.

Sat 30th Dec **Arsenal (H)**
Won 2-1 **Att 40,665**
Platt, Mountfield

Villa fielded the same XI that overwhelmed Manchester United four days ago. League Champions Arsenal attempted to soften Villa up in the first half, they failed miserably. The intimidation backfired, a Cowans ball was lofted into the area, Ormondroyd headed it down, Platt steamed in, moved it with his left to flat foot the defender and then stroked it with precision beyond Lukic. Villa then sprung the famous Arsenal off-side trap, Daley over the top for Mountfield to crash in with his head. The London side showed their ugly side, they had been shown up and didn't like it. Adams goal on 89 minutes was too little, too late! Villa jumped over The Gunners into second.

Mon 1st Jan **Chelsea (A)**
Won 3-0 **Att 23,990**
Gage, Daley, Platt

A solid display but the scoreline flattered somewhat. Villa took a 34th minute lead through Gage but then had to stoutly defend for the remainder of the half. Chelsea missed four or five very good opportunities. Villa's second - a brilliant solo effort from speed merchant Daley - within two minutes of the second-half starting, changed the dynamics of the game, Chelsea never pressed as determinedly from then on. Platt's non-stop midfield display was his side's jewel in the crown. He added the third at the back-post from Sid's corner. Villa now trailed leaders Liverpool by two points but had a game in hand.

Sat 6th Jan **Blackburn Rovers (A)** **FA Cup 3rd round**
Drew 2-2 **Att 14,456**
Olney, Ormondroyd

Twice the Villa contrived to surrender the lead as their defence looked suddenly vulnerable. A finely crafted goal by Ian Olney, a downward header from Daley's cross was all the difference before Stapleton equalised twenty minutes later. Again Villa nosed in front, this time Ormondroyd looping a header in from a Cowans corner kick. The lead only extended to six minutes this time. Villa had Spink to thank for getting another bite at this tie, he made three outstanding saves in the last ten minutes.

Wed 10th Jan **Blackburn Rovers (H)** **FA Cup 3rd round replay**
Won 3-1 **Att 31,169**
Ormondroyd, Daley, Own goal

Blackburn were propelled into a super fast lead. Only 53 seconds were on the clock when the ball hit the back of Nigel Spink's net, the scorer Kennedy. Villa didn't panic, they played the ball around and were rewarded with two first-half goals in a five-minute spell from Ormondroyd and Daley. At the break the boss made changes, Gareth Williams was off, Birch on, Price and Gage now playing as traditional full-backs. The switch to give Villa more stability at the back, it worked like a dream. Villa extended their advantage when May put through his own goal in the last minute.

Sat 13th Jan **Charlton Athletic (A)**
Won 2-0 **Att 10,460**
Mountfield, Own goal

Centre-back Derek Mountfield gave Villa the best possible start on four minutes. It wasn't a goal of the season contender, off his shin from a yard out, but vitally important. When Charlton ventured forward they were blocked by the barrier of Nielsen and Mountfield and Paul McGrath's instinctive reading of the game. It really came down to how many Villa would score. Two in the end, an own goal on 57 minutes being suffiecient. Villa were now on level points, behind Liverpool on goal difference only, still with a crucial game in hand.

Wed 17th Jan **Leeds United (H)** **Zenith Data Systems Cup**
Won 2-0 **Att 17,543**
Gray S, Platt (pen)

This turned out to be an easy affair against a Leeds United side that are specialists of the off-side. They posed Villa the odd problem but nothing the safe hands of Spink couldn't cope with, or the bar from one Vinny Jones effort. Platt should have given the Villa a 12th minute lead, even he isn't perfect. It was down to Stuart Gray to score the first, a superb finish from Olney's ball. Platt was upended by Mervyn Day as he rounded him, but made him pay from the 12-yard spot.

Sat 20th Jan **Southampton (H)**
Won 2-1 **Att 33,118**
Daley, Gage

Southampton were fourth in the table for good reason, they are nobody's fool. Tony Daley got the game's opener in the 39th minute.

There was nothing between the sides. When Cockerill swept in the equaliser nine minutes into the second half Villa showed no signs of panic. The experience of McGrath and Co saw to it that they didn't crumble at the back. Cowans fired against the post, Ormondroyd headed off the bar but Gage got the clincher with 11 minutes to go.

Sat 27th Jan **Port Vale (H)** FA Cup 4th round
Won 6-0 **Att 36,532**
Platt, Birch 2, Olney, Gray S 2

Villa showed no mercy in a display Graham Taylor described as "a special performance." Port Vale committed suicide giving away far too many free-kicks. Platt started the rout on eight minutes getting on the end of one. The second also the result of a dead-ball situation, Birch rounding off from Mountfield's initial free-kick. Olney's strike for number three came from open play. Gray hit the next from a free-kick. Birch followed through after a Heath shot was blocked and Gray scored his second, a mirror image of the first.

Tue 30th Jan **Middlesbrough (H)** Zenith Data Systems Cup Northern final 1st leg
Lost 1-2 **Att 16,457**
Birch

When the scoring was opened in the 13th minute by Paul Birch it looked like a repeat of Saturday might be on the cards. Within two minutes Bruce Rioch's Boro side were back on level terms. As the game ran down, with draw written all over it, Kevin Gage brought down Paul Kerr from behind. From Proctor's 90th minute free-kick, Brennan fired it in with his left foot.

Tue 6th Feb **Middlesbrough (A)** Zenith Data Systems Cup Northern final 2nd leg
Lost 1-2 AET (agg 2-4) **Att 20,806**
Gray S

The game was marred with an incident in the fifth minute, Cowans and Putney challenged for the ball, Sid went in high, received a yellow for his trouble, the Boro lad was stretchered off, a fractured right tibia the outcome. It wasn't a dirty contest and one Villa should have

[Above] Tony Daley ties the Charlton defence in knots during the win at The Valley

won, Daley went close but denied by Pears. Villa broke the deadlock through Gray with a close-range header after Kent Nielsen had flicked on a corner. It took the tie into extra-time. Slaven got the first on 102 minutes. Former Villa boy Kerr hit the other eight minutes later.

[Above] Ian Olney beats Sheffield Wednesday's Nigel Pearson to the ball during the home win

Sat 10th Feb	**Sheffield Wednesday (H)**
Won 1-0	**Att 17,168**
Platt	

Dalian Atkinson should have scored after ten minutes but he hopelessly miscued. David Platt's 20th goal of the season finally broke the stalemate, it also broke their opponents, Wednesday finally buckling having been the better side. Not even the arrival on 69 minutes of nemesis Trevor Francis could tip the scales for the visitors. By their own standards Aston Villa played badly but still came up with their ninth successive home win, just one point behind Liverpool but with two games in hand.

Sat 17th Feb	**West Bromwich Albion (A)** FA Cup 5th round
Won 2-0	**Att 29,585**
Mountfield, Daley	

The goals highlighted the difference between the two sides. The classier finishing put paid to any hopes Albion had, Gary Robson breaking his leg after five minutes didn't help them either. The opening goal arrived in the 24th minute; Chris Price and Tony Daley were involved before Cowans picked out Mountfield with a long range chipped pass that the centre-back directed past Naylor. The final straw for Albion was Daley's explosive goal, a dazzling 20-yard run before rifling a low drive under the keeper.

Wed 21st Feb	**Tottenham Hotspur (A)**
Won 2-0	**Att 32,472**
Ormondroyd, Platt	

Two second-half goals swept Aston Villa to the top of the League for the first time in nine years. They achieved it with the minimum of fuss though it was comprehensive and created numerous chances in the first period. Olney had his shot blocked in the fourth minute; an Ormondroyd shot was held well by Thorstvedt; a Daley shot flew just wide of the upright. The goal finally arrived in the 51st minute, 'Sticks' firing in from 18-yards out on his weaker right foot. The second also from a Cowans free-kick, after the keeper could only palm the ball away Platt strode in to slide it home from two yards out. The Villa fans sang; "Hand it over Arsenal."

Sat 24th Feb **Wimbledon (H)**
Lost 0-3 **Att 29,325**

Nobody saw this coming. The Villa should have stamped their authority on the game early doors. More so when Daley was upended in the box with only six minutes played. David Platt reliable to a fault, stepped up the entire crowd fully expecting to see his 22nd of the season. His penalty - in one of those moments where time stands still – was straight down the middle, Segers keeping it out with his feet. Villa attacked but couldn't score. In the second half Wimbledon looked the more dangerous, they were, they also went on to hit Villa with three goals.

Sun 4th Mar **Coventry City (A)**
Lost 0-2 **Att 18,012**

Villa's best attempts all came within the first ten minutes and were from midfielder McGrath, Graham Taylor moving him forward to shadow Speedie. Those efforts sparked a positive response from Coventry but Spink was equal to them, blocking one Regis shot with his legs. In the 51st minute the deadlock was broken, Drinkell turned Mountfield and shot past Spink from six yards. Villa were still cursing the goal when Smith made it two, swerving a shot between the keeper and his left-hand upright.

Sat 10th Mar **Luton Town (H)**
Won 2-0 **Att 22,505**
Daley, Platt

Tony Daley made it a personal hat-trick; named Young Eagle of the

[Above] Kevin Gage on the ball during the defeat to Coventry

Month by Bobby Robson; a first senior England call-up and possibly your best ever goal, which also happened to put Villa back at the summit. He picked up a pass from Gareth Williams, ran 50-yards, shirked an Allpress challenge then threaded the ball between Chamberlain and the post. Villa fans stood and applauded. David Platt's goal four minutes into the second half killed the game off.

Wed 14th Mar **Oldham Athletic (A)** FA Cup 6th round
Lost 0-3 **Att 14,490**

Villa were trounced on the artificial pitch. In fact Oldham gave Villa more problems in their own area than any First Division side this season according to Taylor. Villa trailed at the break to Holden's 38th minute goal, it was superb, right into the top right corner. Ian Olney had Villa's best chance but keeper Hallworth snuffed out the threat. Chris Price put into his own net under pressure and then Redfearn made it three when he slotted home after Spink failed to hang on to a Holden shot.

Sat 17th Mar **Derby County (A)**
Won 1-0 **Att 20,062**
Ormondroyd

Tony Cascarino signed from Millwall made his debut while Nigel Callaghan was making his first start since September. It wasn't a spectacular performance by Villa but it was built on a solid base of organisation and confidence. Ian Ormondroyd came on for Callaghan for the start of the second half and got his sixth of the campaign, Kent Nielsen started the move with a superb ball from defence to Daley who kept his head and provided the low cross that 'Ormo' slid in.

Tue 20th Mar **Queens Park Rangers (A)**
Drew 1-1 **Att 15,856**
Nielsen

Villa were relieved to escape from Loftus Road with a point. QPR, with only two defeats in their last 18 games comfortably soaked up the pressure before launching their own counter offensive. Villa had one let-off when a Wegerle shot clipped Nielsen's boot and

[Above] Tony Cascarino battles for the ball with Derby County defender Mark Wright at the Baseball Ground

bounced off the crossbar for a corner. After the break Ormondroyd was thwarted by a stunning Seaman save. Clarke opened the scoring to put QPR one-up after five second-half minutes. Villa nearly went further behind, Sinton hit a post, Spink denied the same player and Clarke fired wide. Nielsen equalised driving in right-footed from a Cowans' free-kick.

Sat 24th Mar **Crystal Palace (A)**
Lost 0-1 **Att 18,586**

This was the first time in 15 League games where Villa had conceded a first-half goal. One paper suggested Villa's lethal passing game has been abandoned in favour of the long ball to service Tony Cascarino, and on this showing they had a valid point. Ex Villa player and lifelong fan Garry Thompson scored the decisive goal on four minutes, stabbing home an Andy Gray (ex Villa) long throw-in. Youngster Dwight Yorke came on for Daley.

Sun 1st Apr **Manchester City (H)**
Lost 1-2 **Att 24,797**
Cowans

Villa tossed away an early lead and the chance to regain the leadership when they surrendered against a Manchester City side fighting relegation and without an away win in four years. Villa opened the scoring against the run of play when Platt side-stepped Dibble's dive and picked out Gordon Cowans who finished with a thundering shot. City levelled before the interval and stole a winner in the second half. Villa were level on points but had played two extra games.

Wed 11th Apr **Arsenal (A)**
Won 1-0 **Att 30,060**
Price

Arsenal with an outside chance of retaining their title, were the first to threaten but Thomas chipped over the bar. Paul Birch fired a 20-yard volley but it cannoned off Dixon and went wide. Comyn then saved Villa when he hacked the ball away as Spink dropped a Dixon corner.

[Above] Paul McGrath back on the prowl at Old Trafford for the first time after leaving Manchester United

Villa through Chris Price managed to get the all-important goal with only five minutes remaining, Cascarino held the ball up before pushing a perfect pass into the path of the full-back, firing in from 15-yards.

Sat 14th Apr **Chelsea (H)**
Won 1-0 **Att 28,361**
Cowans

The biggest cheer of the afternoon was the news Liverpool had been held at home to Forest. Villa made hard work of overcoming Chelsea despite determined probing for more than an hour. A Gordon Cowans goal was all they had to show for their troubles. When Chelsea took Villa by the scruff of the neck the home side were saved by two factors; the masterful performance of the telepathic Paul McGrath and the fact the visitors were shot-shy. Villa were one point behind the Reds but had played a game more.

Tue 17th Apr **Manchester United (A)**
Lost 0-2 **Att 44,080**

Villa's title aspirations all but perished, Liverpool only require nine points from a possible 15. The Villa's reception was rapturous from their travelling support as they emerged from the tunnel. The game was there for the taking had Cascarino not squandered a glorious opportunity as United were without Leighton, Bruce and Ince. As the game progressed the home side came forward. When Mark Robins opened the scoring on 25 minutes it changed the course of the match. With only seconds left of the first half Hughes picked out Robins who curled his shot into the top corner. Villa pressed out of desperation but the defeat was inevitably.

Sat 21st Apr **Millwall (H)**
Won 1-0 **Att 21,028**
Platt

Villa had lost four and drawn one of the previous five encounters with The Lions, but Millwall's last League win was four months ago, albeit the Villa at their place. Graham Taylor's leg-weary troops were neither entertaining nor exciting. The only difference between bottom versus second from top was PFA Player of the Year David Platt. He popped up to head home at the far post after Kent Nielsen had flicked on Gordon Cowans' corner. The win ensured Villa couldn't be caught by the chasing pack, runners-up or winners it would be.

Sat 28th Apr **Norwich City (H)**
Drew 3-3 **Att 28,988**
McGrath, Cascarino, Platt

This was the day the dream ended. Fox gave Norwich a lead on the half hour. Villa then gave a glimpse of how they'd performed mid-season when they steamrolled City with three goals in a five-minute second-half spell. McGrath got the ball rolling, his first goal of the season. Cascarino followed suit when he got his first in Villa colours. There was little surprise Platt's name also appeared on the scoresheet. Mountfield put through his own net and when Rosario levelled the game at 3-3 in the 79th minute it handed the title to Liverpool.

Sat 5th May **Everton (A)**
Drew 3-3 **Att 29,557**
Cascarino, Cowans, Daley

Aston Villa were followed up the M6 by 7,000 of their faithful. Everton had an interval lead, Cascarino scoring for them. Big Cas scoring at the right end made it 1-1. Newell added a second before Southall helped the Villa cause, he carried the ball out of the area, Cowans put it straight into the top corner from the resulting free-kick. Tony Daley put Villa into the lead for the first time but it ;lasted only until the 81st minute when Sheedy stroked the ball in from the penalty spot, Mountfield fouling Cottee.

PRE-SEASON

• Alan McInally leaves for Bayern Munich and out of contract Martin Keown joins Everton.
• Paul McGrath from Manchester United, Danish international Kent Nielsen and Adrian Heath came in. Lesser known players signed included Dean Spink from Halesowen and Andy Comyn, Alvechurch.
• The club take in a five-match tour of Switzerland; losing the first two, a draw, then winning the last two in style, 6-0 (a Dean Spink hat-trick) and 9-0 (Platt 3).

AUGUST

• For the third successive season the Villa open the campaign with a point. A 1-1 draw at Forest with the team delivering a solid performance. McGrath, Nielsen and Heath all debuting.
• Andy Comyn comes in at right back for the injured Chris Price and performs well against the Liverpool attack.

SEPTEMBER

• Paul McGrath plays for Ireland in the 1-1 draw with West Germany in Dublin.
• Victory arrives at the fifth time of asking, Tottenham Hotspur beaten 2-0 at Villa Park. Ian Olney gets both goals.
• Villa suffer back-to-back defeats and are above the relegation zone by goal difference only.
• They end the month with a valuable win at home to a Derby County side who hit the woodwork numerous times and do everything but score. Had Villa lost Graham Taylor revealed much later he would have walked!

OCTOBER

• The 1-1 draw at Molineux in the League Cup second round second-leg is sufficient to see Villa go through (agg 3-2).
• The side take maximum points from their three League fixtures. They're moving in the right direction – seventh but with the same points as fourth placed Arsenal.

NOVEMBER

• Villa's youngsters put on a show beating Hednesford Town 9-0 in the F.A. Youth Cup. Liddle, Crisp and Carruthers all score two a-piece.
• Aston Villa take on an Everton side that will go top with a win. The Toffee's don't come close, Cowans gets the ball rolling with a 25-yard drive on five minutes. Villa then add another five – 6-2!
• David Platt's 88th minute goal is enough to edge past Hull City 2-1 in the Zenith Data Systems Trophy.

DECEMBER

• Aston Villa hand Dwight Yorke, who cost the club £5,000, a professional contract following his successful September trial.
• The team stay third in the table despite the loss at Millwall.
• Manchester United are soundly beaten 3-0 and four days later second-placed Arsenal leave Villa Park empty handed as Villa win 2-1.

JANUARY

• Villa's red-hot form continues as they beat Chelsea 3-0 at Stamford Bridge. Villa are second in the table, two points adrift of Liverpool but with a game in hand.

[Above] Tony Cascarino debut at Derby County

• In the Central League the reserves fight back from being 0-2 down to leaders Liverpool to win 6-3.
• Progess is made in the F.A. Cup at the expense of Blackburn (replay required) and Port Vale 6-0.
• Villa's first team fly to France to take part in the Paris St Germain six-a-side tournament, beating Nantes 3-2, losing to FC Porto 1-2, drawing with FC Porto 2-2 and a 4-6 defeat to Partizan Belgrade.

FEBRUARY

• Villa are beaten 4-2 (aet) in the Northern Area final of the ZDST by Middlesbrough.
• The team continues its winning streak in the League with a 1-0 victory at home to Sheffield Wednesday.
• In a productive four-day spell WBA are knocked out of the F.A. Cup fifth round on their own turf and Tottenham are beaten 2-0 as Villa hit top spot for the first time since landing the title.
• Two points clear at the top, a game in hand, nine successive home wins under their belts and awarded a penalty in the next game (after White Hart Lane) at home to Wimbledon. Platt fails to score, Villa lose 0-3. The midfielder admits he is still haunted about that one to this day.

MARCH

• Villa bow out meekly at Oldham in the F.A. Cup quarter-final. The 0-3 scoreline doesn't flatter the Latics.
• Villa sign Tony Cascarino, hoping his goals can get the club over the line and lift the title.
• Cascarino debuts at The Baseball Ground. Derby are beaten 1-0 thank to an Ormondroyd goal. Villa are top by five points but Liverpool have two games in hand.

APRIL

• April Fool's Day, Villa lose 1-2 at home to Manchester City.
• The dream is kept alive as Arsenal are beaten at home to a late Chris Price goal. Three days later Chelsea leave Villa Park empty handed.
• Villa lose 0-2 to a Manchester United side who have more losses than wins this season. In the minds of many this was the turning point as Villa trail by a point having played two games more.
• Cascarino opens his account but it's too little, too late... Villa are held 3-3 at home to Norwich. The dream is over, Liverpool can't be caught. Villa are guaranteed runners-up spot.

MAY

• Thousands of the Villa faithful converge on Goodison Park. Villa and Everton share a six-goal thriller. The Claret and Blue army won't leave after the whistle until the England bound GT comes to say farewell.

[Right] Ron Saunders reads chairman Ron Bendall's statement following the manager's decision to quit Aston Villa in February 1982

MANAGERS

Ron Saunders

Born: 6th November 1932
Died: 7th December 2019
Birthplace: Birkenhead
Appointed in 1974
Dismissed in 1982

Since Vic Crowe and Ron Wylie had been sacked from the club the press went into overdrive, new names being thrown in the ring on a weekly basis. Fulham refused an approach for Alan Mullery. Gordon Jago who'd resigned from QPR recently told those close to him he wasn't interested in the Villa job. Brighton chairman Mike Bamber informed the newspapers Doug Ellis had been in touch and made an inquiry for Brian Clough and Peter Taylor, to be told neither would be leaving his club. Reports suggested Sir Alf Ramsay had been offered the vacant position and rejected it.

Then the name of Ron Saunders started appearing in the papers. He'd been a goalscorer, pretty useful too, during a playing career that spanned 16 years and six clubs; Everton, Tonbridge Angels', Gillingham, Portsmouth, Watford and Charlton Athletic.

His first taste at club management was with Southern League Yeovil Town. Not exactly an easy baptism, inheriting only two players in the summer of 1967 he had to assemble an entire squad. Respectable finishes of 12th and 7th in his two seasons with The Glovers led him to struggling Division Two side Oxford United. Coming in with only 15 matches remaining Saunders steered the club safe of relegation.

His work at the Manor Ground albeit as short as it was impressed the hierarchy at Carrow Road. In his third season (1971/72) Norwich City were promoted as champions and for the first time in their history they would grace Division One. He kept them up though it was a close run affair and also led them to Wembley where they lost to Tottenham Hotspur in the 1973 League Cup final. The following season Norwich had only chalked up two League wins in 16 matches. A row between the board and manager led to his resignation in November.

Within a week managerless Manchester City lured him to Maine Road. He led the side to the League Cup final where Wolverhampton Wanderers proved victorious. League form was sketchy, only

[Right] Manager and captain hold the League Championship trophy

PRESS

[Above] The large city centre crowd share the celebrations with Ron Saunders and Dennis Mortimer

one win in 11 fixtures following their day out at Wembley earned him the sack from a board fearful of relegation. City stayed up and would finish four points clear of the drop.

Saunders hadn't applied for the £15,000 a year post but Ellis had him high on his wanted list. He'd been sacked by Manchester City in April after only five months there. It was stated that he was considering offers from Turkish champions Galatasaray and A E K of Greece though he preferred to stay in this country.

In June 1974 following a five hour board meeting chairman Ellis announced Ron Saunders was to take over the task of getting Aston Villa back into the First Division: "It was a unanimous decision by the board. I'm confident that he will do the job we want him to do."

Saunders revealed he was to sign a 'very long contract' and that he regarded the job as "The greatest thing that's happened in my career. Aston Villa are one of the greatest clubs in the game. Most managers, had they the choice, would be here."

The problem he'd encountered at Yeovil where he had no players at his disposal wouldn't be an issue at the Villa. From Crowe and Wylie going Ellis had put a ban on any transfers until a new manager was instated, meaning a cash plus Colin Harvey offer from Everton for the unsettled John Gidman who was seeking a dramatic increase in terms, meant the full-back was going nowhere. Neither was anyone else.

Saunders made only two signings in his first season at the club, Frank Carrodus coming from Manchester City and Leighton Phillips a Welsh international from Cardiff City, both influential in helping Aston Villa reclaim their place in the top flight as runners-up to Manchester United. Silverware was added in what was the club's Centenary Year when the team delivered on the League Cup when a Ray Graydon goal was sufficient to overcome Norwich City. Third time lucky for Saunders!

Villa stayed up and the following season (1976/77) they could have lifted the domestic treble with a bit of luck. They fell six points short of champions Liverpool, made the quarter-finals of the F.A. Cup and lifted the League Cup despite a glut of fixtures (14 in the cups alone) and a catalogue of injuries to key players.

Saunders busied himself assembling the pieces for an assault on the title. Again injuries played a crucial part in the side not finishing as high as they expected and the manager's job was made no easier when players with big personalities wanted out. Over the next few seasons more pieces fell into place.

Ron would achieve the distinction of leading Aston Villa to their first title for 71 years. He negotiated the first hurdles in an assault on Europe but wrangling with the board regarding his contract led to his Villa Park exit in February 1982. Chairman Ron Bendall responded publically issuing the following short statement from his Isle of Man home: "The board were surprised at Saunders' decision. The manager always had complete control over the playing side of the club."

Regarded by a generation of Villa fans as the best manager in the club's history.

Tony Barton

Born: 8th April 1937
Died: 20th August 1993
Birthplace: Sutton
Appointed in 1982
Dismissed in 1984

Tony Barton won Schoolboy and Youth honours with England before a football career that took him to Fulham, Nottingham Forest and Portsmouth. He was an outside-right who could cut in and score goals. His time at Fratton Park overlapped with a centre-forward by the name of Ron Saunders.

With medicine and treatment somewhat draconian during the 1960s Tony was forced to hang his boots up at the relatively young age of 29 due to cartilage problems. He had a year away from the game, taking a job as a salesman for a ready mix concrete company, but wasn't happy outside of football. He was invited back to Pompey, taking the role of chief scout and then later assistant manager when Ian St John replaced John Mortimore as manager.

He joined Aston Villa in late 1975 becoming Ron Saunders' assistant (he was the manager's assistant not assistant manager) already having the reputation around the Villa Park corridors as a talented spotter within the game. It was Tony Barton who'd found Villa a replacement for the career finished Keith Leonard. Barton ran his eye over Dundee United's Andrew Gray whilst in the employ of Portsmouth FC, thankfully their chairman wasn't interested, the details were then passed on to Ron Saunders who was, before Tony accepted the invitation by his former teammate to join the Villa backroom staff. His first official import was Dennis Mortimer coming to Villa Park, in fact Tony - along with his network of scouts - is credited with being responsible for the majority of the title winning side coming to B6. The exceptions being the lads who came through the youth ranks, the likes of Cowans, Williams and Shaw.

On the evening of 9 February Barton was asked by chairman Ron Bendall to take charge of the team for Saturday's forthcoming Southampton fixture at Villa Park following Saunders resignation on the same day.

"BARTON'S BRAVES" cried the Daily Mirror (11 Feb) headlines. The Aberdeen Evening News meanwhile led with the "Fergie on Villa list" heading and went on to say the Pittordrie boss has emerged as one of the favourites. Other names linked included Jack Charlton, Jock Wallace and Graham Taylor.

Coupe des Clubs Champions
Européens

CHAMPIONS
Dates fixes: 20.10.&3.11.1982
Standard de Liège
Liverpool FC
Dinamo Bucuresti
S. Sebastian
Rapid Wien
CSKA Sofia
Nendori Tirana
FC Juventus
Helsingin JK
Aston Villa
Celtic Glasgow
Olympiakos Pirée
RTS Widzew Lodz
Sporting Portugal
Dinamo Kiev

The job stayed within, Tony went from being caretaker manager to having the main job in his own right on 1 April 1982, his first game being the European Cup semi-final first leg. Before Saunders walked out the Villa had collected 19 points from their 23 League games, from Tony taking the helm the 19 remaining games yielded 23 points and more importantly the side had overcome hurdles in the European Cup in the shape of Dynamo Kiev and Anderlecht to steer Villa to a final showdown in Rotterdam.

When Aston Villa vanquished three times (in successive seasons) winners of the competition Bayern Munich many claimed it was Saunders' side that won it, Barton just happened to be there at the right time and had no right to be compared to the likes of Jock Stein. In actually fact it could be argued that it was Tony's team that won the title the previous year, and elevated Aston Villa Football Club to become Champions of Europe. They were his recommendations after all!

In Barton's first full season Villa finished a creditable sixth, achieving qualification for the UEFA Cup in the process. Under his guidance the Super Cup was also claimed at the expense of a thuggish Barcelona.

Before the 1983/84 season kicked-off Villa had dispensed with the services of Rimmer, McNaught and Geddis. Sid Cowans though still at the club was out for the foreseeable due to a nasty leg break whilst Morley was gone before the New Year. Little wonder the Villa couldn't finish higher than tenth.

On 18 June 1984 the man who guided Aston Villa to their finest hour was sacked. Ellis claiming: "The results over the last season have not been sufficiently good for Aston Villa Football Club." Tony Barton's response was of shock: "I am bitterly disappointed and astonished really because I was under no impression that this was going to happen. The chairman called me into his office and told me that the board had decided they wanted a new manager and that was it"

There had been previous issues along the way. On one occasion Tony came home saying: "That's a nail in my coffin!" then telling his family how Doug Ellis had insisted Mervyn Day don a hat and suit and chauffeur a delegation from the airport to Villa Park. Tony's reply of: Mr Ellis, he's a first-team squad player he's not your chauffeur, he's not doing it" not being very well received.

Another time Tony informed his chairman he wasn't allowed to travel on the first-team bus claiming the players wouldn't be able to relax and would be uncomfortable. That incident had Barton saying: "Another nail in my coffin."

Seen by many as a soft touch or too laid back Tony was as strong a disciplinarian as Ron Saunders was credited to be. His son Chris said: "The difference was my dad would read the riot act in the confines of the dressing room and that's where it stayed! He knew when some of the youngsters needed the tender touch whilst some of the seasoned pros wouldn't respond to kid gloves. He was a very good man manger."

A season as manager of Northampton Town was followed by three years under Chris Nicholl as assistant at Southampton. A short spell scouting at Birmingham City during Garry Pendrey's reign ended due to Tony not being paid. Barton then returned to Portsmouth where he was promised the manager's job if he kept the club up, he did, but Pompey reneged, giving the role to Jim Smith instead. Chairman Jim Gregory had apparently been told by Doug Ellis that Barton would be unable to fulfill the role because of health issues. Tony was even told to leave his Rover Sterling company car in the car park and to take a battered Mini Metro home.

However, Tony Barton remains one of a select band of managers to steer and English clubs to European Cup glory.

[Left] Tony Barton at UEFA after being drawn against Dynamo Bucharest in 1982-83

Graham Turner

Born: 5th October 1947
Birthplace: Ellesmere Port
Appointed in 1984
Dismissed in 1986

Ever since Tony Barton's June dismissal the papers were awash with stories concerning the vacant managerial post. Apparently there were in excess of 40 applicants. John Toshack was thought a probable until he chose to stay at Sporting Lisbon, Malcolm Macdonald, Malcolm Allison, Alan Durban and Gordon Lee also on the list. On 7 July the Evening Express ran the story how Ron Atkinson had been offered it, he was tempted as he feared his position at Old Trafford was under threat. Assurances were made from Martin Edwards, his manger was staying put.

Sunderland AFC had made enquiries about Peter Withe and Dennis Mortimer but they were told nothing would happen until a new manager is appointed.

On 17 July the wait was over when 36-year-old Shrewsbury manager Graham Turner was given charge of the Villa, and a five year contract. In spite of previous stories circulating Doug Ellis stated he had landed his first choice manager. Turner went on record: "A club of this size needs success. But directors can't demand it. It concerns me that there are no current internationals in the squad. I have been promised money to buy, but some players will have to leave before I can bring any in."

The new manager added: "I realise this is a big step for me as I have no First Division experience. But a lot of well-known managers have been living on reputations. I always felt I would eventually manage a top club, although this is a bit bigger and a bit earlier than I expected."

Graham Turner had played his football at the lower level of the league, Wrexham, Chester City and then Shrewsbury Town though he was a former England Youth international. As player-manager at the Shropshire club he led them to the Third Division title in 1978/79, the fact he could achieve results working to the confines of a shoe-string budget would have made his appointment even more appealing in some quarters.

The team got off to the best possible start winning their first two fixtures only to crash 0-3 at Newcastle and then four days later even heavier at Forest. Results were very inconsistent, the team

went seven games without a League victory yet would put together a four-match winning sequence during January. The tenth position finish at the end of the campaign was the very same that had led to Barton's dismissal last season.

During the 1984/85 season European Cup winners Des Bremner and Dennis Mortimer would make only nine appearances between them before being shipped out. Peter Withe would also play his last for the club, although he made it through to May.

The following season would see Villa finish only three points and four places above the relegation zone. The win at home to Watford 12 April lifted them out of the bottom three for the first time in months. The penultimate game, a 3-0 win over Chelsea finally guaranteed safety. They had unexpectedly beaten Arsenal away in a League Cup fifth round replay but would fall at the semi final stage to a struggling Oxford United. The 8,456 attendance for the visit of Southampton was the club's lowest League gate for nearly three decades.

1986/87 was only six games in when the axe fell on Villa's youngest ever manager. Villa's capitulation, to the tune of 0-6 at the City Ground, their fifth defeat already, proved a step too far. In fairness the team was always going to struggle. Experienced and big earning players can't keep being moved on with youngsters being drafted into the side but that's what was happening. It was never going to end on a good note.

Chairman Doug Ellis went on record as saying: "The decision has been very difficult for the board and for me in particular because of his high qualities as a man."

In subsequent years Turner reignited his successful managerial reputation when he guided Wolves from Division Four to Division Two. He also achieved promotion back into the Football League with conference side Hereford United.

Billy McNeill

Born: 2nd March 1940
Died: 22nd April 2019
Birthplace: Mossend
Appointed in 1986
Dismissed in 1987

The Villa Park hot seat was still moderately warm when the club's twelfth post-war manager took up position. Graham Turner had learnt his fate at the chairman's home on the morning of 14 September. Within eight days his successor was in place.

Ex Tottenham manager Keith Burkinshaw was lauded as favourite for the job with Manchester United's Ron Atkinson also a close contender, as he was prior to Turner being handed the position two years previously. Dave Bassett was the man Villa wanted according to Mirror Sport. Ron Wylie who'd previously managed West Bromwich Albion made it publicly known he had neither intention nor interest in becoming manager.

The Dundee Courier was one of the first papers to raise the name of Billy McNeill. The man was a legend in Scottish football, as player and manager, at least in the green half of Glasgow. They reported that Villa chairman Ellis had contacted Manchester City counterpart Peter Swales for permission to speak to their manager. A few days later the same paper commented that McNeill, one of the most sought-after managers in the game (McNeill led Man City to promotion from Division Two during 1984/85), could face legal action if he decides to resign and accept the challenge of reviving Villa's flagging fortunes. Swales had refused his manager to leave with McNeill adding: "The chairman has explained the position and I will go away and think it over."

On the morning of 22 September The Derby Daily Telegraph ran the heading "McNEILL OFF TO VILLA" Swales was told of McNeill's decision to leave: "I have had a long amicable meeting with the manager and he has decided to take his chance with Aston Villa. We did everything in our power to keep him here."

Speaking at Maine Road before leaving for a Villa Park press conference McNeill said: "It was a very tough decision but there is a big challenge waiting for me at Villa Park. Frankly, they made me an offer which I could not refuse. The set-up is tremendously impressive."

On McNeill taking the helm Villa had played seven games were rock-bottom with only three points, one behind Manchester United.

Villa would be unbeaten in his three League games, one of them being a 3-3 draw at Anfield, whilst the team progressed in the League Cup at the expense of Reading. Back-to-back wins were recorded at home to Newcastle and Leicester. These results saw Villa sitting in, what was for them, a lofty 16th position, fans hopes and expectations were raised. But, not for long, they wouldn't know yet that only three more wins would be registered in the last 29 fixtures as well as the 15 defeats coming the Villa's way.

In the manager's defence the Villa's dominant force was Steve Hodge and he'd orchestrated a move to Spurs in December. Villa fans had to wait until February to see the new signing (singular) when Warren Aspinall arrived from Everton. The youngster would get a dozen games under his belt and score three goals, and that from a side devoid of any confidence.

Aston Villa's relegation was confirmed with the 1-2 defeat at home to Sheffield Wednesday. McNeill was history four days later. He had been in the managerial hot seat for a total of 18 weeks and four days. At this rate the manager's office should have revolving doors. Villa and Man City shared the distinction of winning the least amount of games – eight. No other side had conceded more goals (79), Villa and Leicester both lost 22. Only twice before in their history had a Villa team lost more League games.

Billy 'Cesar' McNeill – a giant north of the border and rightly so with a playing career that yielded a European Cup winners medal, nine Scottish Championships, seven Scottish Cups and six Scottish League Cups. Management brought silverware on all three domestic fronts for the Bhoys. On returning to Celtic after his short English journey he would land another title and two cups.

Graham Taylor

Born: 15th September 1944
Died: 22th January 2017
Birthplace: Worksop
Appointed in 1987
Left to become England manager in 1990
Returned in 2002
Departed in 2003

Aston Villa Football Club had sought a new manager in 1982, 1984, 1986 and now again in the summer of 1987. It was all getting a bit tedious, the same names bandied about everytime Villa's board pulled the pin. The Sandwell Evening Mail struck first on 9 May with 'Ron Atkinson, Mr Flash of football, will be appointed manager of Aston Villa after a board meeting on Monday.' This was the third time Atkinson had been linked with the manager's job at B6.

Dave Bassett quit his Wimbledon post on 11 May fuelling the fire, he'd guided them from the Fourth to the First Division and described by the press as being among the top flight's poorest paid. The Derby Daily Telegraph claimed an approach had been made to Derby County for the Arthur Cox/Roy McFarland duo. Within days both men signed lucrative five years deals keeping them at the Baseball Ground. By 18 May Villa had their man. Graham Taylor - numerous papers claimed – quit Watford on the very day and signed for Villa immediately. The Liverpool Echo reported Taylor had agreed terms the day before but that was neither here nor there.

Taylor walked out with three years remaining on his Vicarage Road contract: "This decision will probably not make a lot of sense to some people as I am leaving a First Division club to take charge of one in the Second. But I have a reputation for not following the system and now my immediate aim is to get Villa back into the First Division as soon as possible. There is a lot of hard work to be done. I have got to restore some discipline and pride into the club."

A playing career consisting of Grimsby Town and Lincoln City, the majority played in the lower echelons of the Football League wouldn't impress the inherited Villa Park squad, but, his managerial record couldn't be quite so easily dismissed; within four years at Sincil Bank his Lincoln City side won the Fourth Division title with record points, he then moved to Watford in 1977, within five years he'd got the club to the top flight and in their first year they finished runners-up!

It's well documented the club was a shambles and Taylor wasn't prepared to stand for any interference from his chairman. Big names left and were replaced with relative unknowns. But, the right noises were coming out of Villa Park.

With only two points from the first four games this wasn't going to be the full thrust the Villa fans had hoped for, it was more a slow burn. Once the season ignited, and it did, Villa rose like champagne bubbles. From losing at home to Boro in early September the side went undefeated in the division for 12 games and then another run of a dozen games following the blip at home to Millwall. Villa remained at the summit from New Year's Day - a 5-0 demolition of Hull City - until cracks started appearing in mid-February, six defeats in a nine game sequence. At the final whistle in the 1-1 draw at Selhurst Park Villa were down to fourth. Villa took the second automatic promotion spot on the last day of the season at Swindon.

Villa hardly set the First Division alight but they remained in the top flight by a point. Birmingham City handed Villa supporters a few reasons to cheer, or thirteen to be exact, as the neighbours were beaten three times over two cup competitions; 2-0, 5-0 and 6-0.

The next season (1989/90) suggested much of the same early on with only one victory to show from seven games played. The one positive was the signing of the world class Paul McGrath. The crunch match was Derby at home. Graham Taylor saw his side win by the odd goal, only because Dean Saunders squandered numerous gilt-edged chances. The manager told reporter Rob Bishop he was going to leave had Villa lost that game. From there the side went from strength to strength. Seven straight wins on the bounce propelled the side to the top of the table. Again Villa ran out of steam towards the end, the acquisition of Tony Cascarino to help Villa cross the finishing line had an adverse effect. Villa's long run of form had taken them ahead of the pack and they finished runners-up comfortably but nine points shy of champions Liverpool.

In the last game of the season, a 3-3 draw at Goodison Park the Villa fans remained in their places at the final whistle. They wanted to applaud Graham Taylor for what he'd achieved, they knew he was off to manage England. When he was appointed Villa boss the Sandwell Evening Mail 18 May 1987 had called it correctly: "Taylor has been spoken of as a future England manager, having looked after the England youth team for several years."

[Right Manager Graham Turner behind the wheel of an Austin Montego, part of the club's sponsorship deal, surrounded by his 1985-86 Villa team

ASTON VILLA FIRST TEAM

PLAYERS

mita

DENNIS MORTIMER

When Dennis Mortimer came to Aston Villa in December 1975 as 'a present to the fans' he brought a wealth of experience to the newly-promoted side. Two-hundred first-team appearances for Coventry City – all in the top flight. A huge crowd turned out to see his Boxing Day debut at home to West Ham United and I'd wager not one fan present that day would envisage what was on the not too distant horizon. Villa fans know all about Ron Saunders' final piece of the jigsaw, what we had here in Mortimer was that very first piece, the rest would follow. Interestingly at the time of the £175,000 transfer a certain Bayern Munich were holders of the European Cup and would win it the following year, three years on the spin!

A headline appeared in one of the papers 'Currie or Mortimer to Villa for £200,000' it stated. Coventry boss Gordon Milne had expected Liverpool to come in for Dennis Mortimer a year before Villa tabled their bid, the Merseysiders opted instead for Terry McDermott from Newcastle. It was Villa's gain.

I got the nod on the Tuesday before the Bank Holiday game on the Friday. Dave Cross a teammate who had played at Norwich City under Ron Saunders had spoken to me on the Monday. He told me that Ron had been asking questions about me in a phone call. Obviously I hadn't heard anything but then funnily enough, the next day I get a phone call to go to the ground. Ron's got the money and put the bid in and I've gone to see him on the Tuesday morning. He picked me up and drove me into Villa Park. We sat down and discussed things. Ron's obviously spoken to Coventry to find out what I'm on because that's exactly what Saunders offered me, I didn't get a pay rise. You'd expect if I'd had an agent they'd be looking to get as much money for me as possible, but we didn't, we dealt with it all ourselves. I couldn't go back to Coventry, because the whole thing was about getting some money in for the club. Coventry City needed money and I was an asset.

Dennis wasn't aware at the time of signing that Saunders had earmarked him to be his captain at some stage in the future. A fact he didn't find out until Ron Saunders funeral. During a chance conversation with Alan Bennett, the Villa club secretary in 1975, he was told the story of how Bennett was sitting with Ron, before they bought Mortimer and Alan asked Ron why he had "I want him to be my captain" was the reply. He was given that role from the start of the 1978/79 season.

Having only played in the First Division all of my football career Aston Villa never come across my radar. My first impression was it's obviously a bigger ground, but it'd be interesting to see how you fill one that size. I turn up on my debut and there are 52,000 in the ground – it is filled. I'm thinking to myself what's this all about? You then see this is a big club and it's got huge potential - Liverpool didn't get those kinds of crowds.

Coming out in that game it just gave me that feeling. When Ron and I initially spoke, I can't remember exactly what was said but he never sold the club to me, not like when Peter Withe came. Ron sold the club to him, the fact that we had some really good players, both young and experienced in the side. When I came to the football club, I don't remember any conversations like that. Maybe he thought I would have known anyway I had come into a great club, with tremendous potential. That would be typical of Ron. This was his big platform and he didn't let the club down, he put the club back on the map where it belongs and from that point of view he's got to go down as one of the most successful post-war managers ever.

I got injured in only my fourth game after ten minutes against Newcastle. A clumsy challenge by Malcolm Macdonald, caught my knee and I did my ligaments again and was out for four or five weeks. That was the story of my career up to that point, all about knee ligament strains. I'd had four on the trot so I knew exactly what was wrong, I

knew what I'd done. But, it was disappointing because I played my first two games, obviously the Boxing Day then the Derby County game away the next day and I missed out on the Southampton F.A. Cup games because I hadn't been there long enough. I played in the nil-nil at Arsenal and then it was Newcastle at home. I was ready and raring to go and in ten minutes I was off. If I'm truthful about that season I didn't get back to the form I'd shown on getting the move.

Although we were training up at Bodymoor Heath there was no physiotherapist's room at the time. I was told to turn up at the ground on Monday morning. The treatment was being done in the corner of the old Trinity Road stand. "I've walked in and up the stairs, it was a dark and dismal place in those days, and I've gone up to the physio's room and obviously there's a few of the lads in there too. It was a bit of a shock actually because coming from Coventry we had one of the most progressive physiotherapists in the country, an absolutely fantastic guy called Norman Pilgrim. He was way ahead of the game, because if we got injured, we hated it, because Norman killed us. If you had an injury to your leg, he worked every other part of your body, twice a day and it was hard work, he was really up to speed on rehabilitation. So with my injuries I'd had at Coventry I'd spent quite a bit of time with him. There's me now walking into an antiquated physio room and looking around and thinking what the hell is this? Coventry's was a bright, clinical room, which looked like a place where you knew you were going to get treated correctly. I ended up sitting on the treatment table with this ultrasound on for five minutes - that was it. "What do I do now?" He said, "I'll see you this afternoon." So I immediately went up to see Ron Saunders. And I said, I'm not going to stand for this Ron. The fact that I live right next to Ryton-on-Dunsmore, if Coventry are prepared to treat me is it alright? Ron said yes and that's what happened because I knew Norman could do it. I think that was the spark for Ron to realise that he needed to get proper physiotherapy for the players.

In only Mortimer's second season Villa went from looking anxiously over their shoulder to title contenders.

When you've got players who like to run at the opposition you're always going to cause them problems because you go past one player and he might be the one who's supposed to be defending against you, so that in turn pulls another player out from his own defensive position. And that's exactly what we had in 1976/77. We had a good solid defence, Leighton's (Phillips) dropped back alongside Chris Nicholl; Johnny Robson was steady at the back, a solid defender and John Gidman, who was wasn't the greatest defender but was actually very good going forward. He used his pace to get himself out of trouble. In midfield we had myself, Alex Cropley and Frank Carrodus. When you think about Frank and I, we both liked to run at people with the ball. Alex was tremendous winning the ball for his size and a very good distributor of the ball. For his size he was a terror, he was tenacious. With Brian Little and Andy Gray upfront we wanted to move the ball forward quickly, there was no going back to the goalkeeper and passing it square, it was all about making that move forward and then getting the ball into the danger areas. Our passion and running caught a lot of teams out. We didn't need a big Peter Withe really because we had Andy who could jump and leap anyway. And then Brian who did the same as Gary Shaw would later do.

The quickness of the way we played when you read some of the reports is quite complimentary in the way we put teams under pressure. It wasn't from closing people down it came from having the ball and then putting them under pressure by the way we passed. It wasn't winning it back, it was teams struggling to get the ball the way we moved it and the way we worked it as a team.

We had a lot of energy as well, nothing to do with training hard, just players who had a natural fitness and just loved playing the game the way we did. It annoyed me when I heard people say Ron used to run us and was a very tough trainer - he wasn't tough. We trained the way we played, that was the most important thing. When we played a game in training, we made sure we replicated that kind of energy when we played a game of football. Ron got us doing that without really telling us, He just let us get on with it, because he bought the players in that he knew could do it. His training method was very much now get the ball down on the floor and let's play.

I was of the opinion we could have won the treble - the first team to do so - because I think we had the players to do it and I thought that team was good enough. We played at Man United in the sixth round and lost 1-2 having played against Everton on the Wednesday, we'd had extra time again. We had the extra replay with QPR at Highbury and lost key players at that time and we were scoring fours and fives, not many teams get those scorelines in a season. I think we were a bit like Manchester City, they score goals like that. The football we played was so quick, but controlled. Sometimes when you play quick football, it's not controlled, everything that we did was, the passing, the movement and it was all done in such a way that it complemented the players that we had. The sign of a good or a great team is when you play it complements the whole team.

We were never able to achieve for the following seasons. When you consider the goals Andy Gray and Brian Little scored in the season of 76/77 we weren't getting those now. The goalscoring dried up because they were in and out. So you think of the goals you're missing now and then you're looking at games you lost 0-1 or 1-2 that you might have been winning. We also went through a transition, we lost Alex Cropley, he was important in our midfield because he allowed myself and Frank to go forward. We weren't winning the games we should have. Don't forget we had the European games as well in the UEFA Cup. We got right up to the quarter-finals in Barcelona, we could have won that game. We started really well and we were looking comfortable.

We weren't consistent and if you look at the number of players that we used particularly in the midfield area; I remember playing with Tommy Craig, Alex Cropley, Terry Bullivant, just loads of players coming and going. Ron was struggling to find the balance of the team. Then we started having trouble with Gidman and Gray wanting to leave. And then we had the upheaval of the board, Bendall coming in; Harry Kartz was the chairman. But then we started having troubles when Ellis tried to divide the board and also the fans, by trying to imply that it was the manager's fault. The rest of the squad were saying it isn't about the manager, it's just about two players who want to leave the football club. Ron managed to get that out of the way and start to rebuild again. He knew the way he wanted the team to play with the players that were left there, he moved Allan Evans back to play alongside Ken McNaught and brought in Kenny Swain.

Every season I was optimistic that we'd win something. I'd been at the football club for one full season practically when we won the League Cup. I just thought there was something special about what was happening at Villa Park. It was disappointing that nothing else came in the next two or three seasons because I knew we had the players but the problem was, sometimes Ron was unable to put out what he thought was his best team for games, consequently sometimes it didn't quite work for us because the cohesion wasn't there. Remember when Tony Morley came to the football club, his first season he got injured very early on. He had a problem with his knee and only played 15 games, playing a lot of his games in the reserves, because he was struggling.

We started getting some of the young kids coming through, Colin Gibson and Gary Williams, Gary Shaw started to make an appearance and all of a sudden Ron's got the makings of what could be a great team. And so leading up to season 1980/81, when it all happened, the big jigsaw puzzle was put together now by Peter Withe. He was the piece we needed. In the pre-season games we played I did feel we've got something going. Everyone looked in great shape.

"Going into the new season 1980/81. Tony Morley had been brought into the football club because of what he could do and all of a sudden now he's fit, everyone looked really fit. There was myself, Des Bremner and Gordon Cowans raring to go in midfield. We had a nice balance there, from the point of view of Gordon with his passing ability and Des and putting the pressure on the other teams by making forward runs; we had Kenny Swain who was making tremendous runs from right back, Colin Gibson and Garry Williams who were great attacking full-backs and we had two really good centre-halves who were very solid and had now been working together for a couple of seasons, really bedding themselves into that role. In Jimmy Rimmer we had a solid goalkeeper, lots of experience.

Then we had this young Gary Shaw, who to me could have gone on to be as good as Kenny Dalglish. Gary was so much like Dalglish from the point of view of his positioning, the way he scored goals. He had this lovely knack of what I called caressing the ball into the back of the net, it wasn't always about pure power. When I put my foot through the ball, it was power and it was power that was going to get the ball in the back of the net most of the time. When you study Dalglish everything about him was guile and that's what Gary had. He could score goals from any angle, with his left or right foot, and here he is 19-years-old, coming into the team having had a few games the season before and he's playing up with Peter, the partnership was brilliant, it suited us down to the ground.

To me, it all came together in that Leeds game. I felt we deserved more than two goals. We went down very early on to a goal, a penalty, one of those dubious penalty appeals. It didn't stop us we took Leeds apart as we did most teams. I felt so good and thought this is the team that's going to do it. And obviously the rest is history.

We had a lot to do, if we had a little slump we always came back again and we put the games together, we won them and they were hard games. There was no other team in the country that had to play so many derby matches, fourteen in all, that's a lot of games. You're now up against your rivals but in a bigger way, you play the Liverpools, the Evertons, they're your rivals but the rivalry between local derbies, there's always more on those games. Having to play that many, our season was always going to be difficult as were the seasons before. So much more emphasis is put on the match itself.

We wanted to play a derby the way we always liked to play - to try and play football but sometimes the other teams came out with one intention and that was trying to put you off your game. You knew you had to overcome that but sometimes you couldn't depending on which way the game was going. One team might want to play football while another will try to kick you off the pitch. I think that was a big factor in winning the League, we overcame having to play so many local derbies, (Villa won eleven of those fourteen and drew the rest).

It was unique from the point of view of using so few players. I think it was testament to the fitness of the guys who played those games, we built up a really good resilience to play in that kind of atmosphere week in, week out. There was a good blend of experienced players and good youngsters coming through the ranks who had a number of games under their belts and started to really find their feet. The way we were playing complimented them. A lot of things came together that season.

The important thing from our point of view, as individual players was we'd never won the League and this was our opportunity to go forward and win this championship which had eluded us, which I thought we'd have been probably closer to after 1976/77. It had taken us another three years to get where we wanted to be. I'd seen Liverpool win it so many times I was chomping at the bit in a way.

We were now in a position where we could win the League, it was going through my mind that we've got a chance and I think we knew that as a team, because we all felt the same way now about what was happening on the pitch. That was why it was such a good, well knit squad, we all had a role to do and we all knew that role was important and we fulfilled it week in and week out.

Beating Liverpool was an important milestone. I felt in winning that game we put them off their stride and made everyone realise it wasn't going to be about them this season, it was going to be about Aston Villa and Ipswich Town. The only disappointment was losing to Ipswich three times, two League games and an F.A. Cup tie. If you look closely at the game, our first one at theirs, we hadn't lost up til then.

We played them off the park - and when you consider the quality that was on that pitch that day, not only in our side, but also in the Ipswich side which was this full of international players - we played some of the best football ever against a team that played some of their best football ever. That was a game for the purest, yet we came away with nothing but a lot of pats on the back. We thought OK then, we knew we were as good as them even though Ipswich had been knocking on the door the previous season. Robson was building a side there

a little bit like Ron was building our side, but the fact that their team was full of international players and we didn't have any was the sort of difference between the two teams. But, put us on the football pitch with them and there was no difference, we had the same about us as what they had from the point of view of being able to move the ball.

When you look at winning the championship, when we lost Peter Withe we had to bring in David Geddis. Now David was a totally different player to Peter, so in a way we had to change the way we played but he scored some important goals when he appeared in the first team and like one or two others their contribution was essential in the campaign.

Where Europe was concerned, you look at the competition and you know if you can put your best performance together, you're going to make it difficult for the opposition, you're going to have a chance. I remember Valur, we took them apart and scored five and there was a quote from the chairman or the guy who owned the football club, he said; "Just wait til you get back to our place." I thought what a stupid thing to say. Does he think he's going to overturn five goals when it could have been far more. And so we ended up in Iceland and we got the two-nil result, we played a professional game, made sure that we didn't give anything away and we got the two goals that we needed through Shawry.

We go into the next game, the next few are going to be difficult, because when you play against the Eastern Bloc teams you know you're up against more than just a team. The one thing that you knew you had to do, what you had to match, against those teams was their fitness and if we could, we had enough then to score goals – and we proved that. They were big strong teams, when you compared us to them, physical beasts some of them so beating Berlin and Kiev were fantastic results. And then obviously getting into the semi-final against Anderlecht, the games are never going to be won by big scores. If we'd ended up with Kiev in the first round maybe that would have been more difficult. But because we had a chance to score five and then two it gave us an opportunity to start building our team and our season and once we got going in the League we started to put a bit more consistency to the game. Then going into the European games was something special. You always think you can win a Cup competition and look forward to them. Sometimes you felt with the League that was probably just 42 games too many.

In the Final we weren't able to play our game because of the way Bayern Munich played. I can't remember ever getting behind the Bayern defence with a run because I couldn't, they played so deep. The likes of myself and Des, it was very difficult for us to get in to make runs forward and into those kinds of positions to get beyond them, and Kenny as well. The game was very open for them, it was open for us as well but it was only open from the point of view of playing in front of their back three or four. We couldn't get behind them and the one time we got that opportunity we took it and we scored with Tony beating the full-back, getting round him and turning him inside out and then crossing for Peter.

You felt maybe this is going to be your night because they couldn't score. They were huffing and puffing but they couldn't blow the house down. But we also got a great performance from Nigel Spink, he made some really good important saves and we came out one-nil winners, it never matters what score it is, it's just winning that matters. That's how I sum it up. I read a quote from Paul Breitner and he was quite complimentary about us, he said; "Villa play a different game to most English teams" I never saw that prior to the game, I only read that recently.

Dennis Mortimer also led his troops in the World Club Championship, a match played in Tokyo, Japan. The opposition, Penarol had already won the competition twice before.

I remember being disappointed with the playing surface for such a prestigious game. I think also the fact that no British club had won it yet, Liverpool had tried and Forest. It would have been a nice accolade to have gone over there and been the first English team to win it.

Overall I look back and it was an immense honour to play a part in the finest moment of Aston Villa's illustrious history.

DAVID PLATT

Having been released by Manchester United under manager Ron Atkinson, a young David Platt was starting to make a name for himself, his performances and his ability in front of goal during the next three seasons at Gresty Road was attracting the attention and bids from higher placed clubs. During Aston Villa's Second Division sojourn under Graham Taylor, the Midlands club showed their hand in early 1988, little would they know they'd land the Ace! Signed in relative obscurity from Fourth Division Crewe Alexandra, he rocketed to stardom and due to his exploits with the England World Cup side of 1990 and that extra-time winner against the Belgian's, David became the superstar of the time. His later transfers fees to Bari, Juventus, Sampdoria, Arsenal and Forest combined, made him the most expensive player in the history of the game. David himself recounts his time at the Villa.

The 1987/88 season for me personally started well, I was scoring goals at Crewe Alexandra and also playing at the top of my game. Media stories used to come out, Sunday newspapers had those little areas they had to fill with snippets. I was linked with all sorts of clubs and the most pleasing thing for me was that every time somebody did make a bid, Dario Gradi came and told me. Hull City and Hibernian came in with a bid as did a few others but Dario would say: "These have made a bid but I don't want to sell you to them. I would sooner you stay here until a proper bid comes in."

I think he thought he could get more money for me. But what he did say to me, and armed with that information that the club in question had made a bid for me, if I wanted to go, then he would try to negotiate a deal and make it happen. And what that gave to me was the ability to know that whatever was in the Sunday newspapers, it didn't turn my head in any way. If somebody was concrete with a bid, he was going to tell me. I was taking my guidance from him, I didn't have an agent, they weren't really commonplace, certainly for youngsters and League Two or League One players at that point.

My counsel in many ways was Dario, so when he was telling me that such and such a club had come in for me, but he didn't think it was necessarily the right move for me, I thought he was probably right. So I stayed where I was. I thought: "Okay, let's carry on." I was confident enough that if I continued to play well and carry on scoring goals somebody might come in. I might get my move, not that I was looking for one and my career might start going up. But I was totally au fait with who was in for me, because if he's telling me about those clubs, he wouldn't not tell me if a different club came in.

It happened very quickly Dario called me in one day and said: "Look, Aston Villa have made a bid, £150,000." I wouldn't say Crewe were going for promotion but we were having a better season than we had done in the past, there was an outside chance. What was evident, he didn't want me to go, he told me. He didn't want me to go at that point because things had changed for Alexandra. Yes, they wanted the money, but equally, there was a very slim chance of promotion and if I left, that slim chance went down to next to nothing because I was the one scoring the goals and making things happen.

He told me on the Friday. I played on the Saturday and then drove back home to Chadderton for the weekend. For the first time, the club in question was in my head. The other clubs, I just didn't picture myself at for all sorts of reasons; I was 22-years of age, my now wife but then girlfriend lived in the Nantwich area, near Crewe. I wasn't moving to Hibernian, I wasn't moving to Hull, if I joined Aston Villa I was going 45 minutes down the road. I was in a comfortable environment with friends because at Crewe none of us had houses that we owned,

hummel
mita

we didn't earn enough money. Three or four of us stayed in a club flat, we rented it at a cheap rate off one of the football club directors. After training we were still together, playing snooker etc. So it wasn't just on-field Aston Villa, but off-field too. Yes it was a big club in the old Second Division.

From that perspective do you wait? But they were top of the League in the Second Division. I don't know what swung it in the end, but basically, I went home to Chadderton and I remember that evening going into the local fish and chip shop. They had a portable TV behind the counter and for some reason Aston Villa was on, Match of The Day must have covered very briefly the Division Two games at the top of the League and the goals were being shown. Villa won easy, and it was like, hang on that's a big club, big crowd, I'd been to Villa Park when Manchester United had played there when my dad had taken me to watch the game.

So I went in on a Monday morning, knocked on Dario's door and said for the first time, I think I'd like the opportunity to speak to Villa. He said to me: "If they bid me another £50,000 I'll agree it." I walked out of the office and thought, that's it, they won't bid another 50 grand. I don't know what the bloody hell they're doing but they're already bidding 150, so I doubt they'll bid another 50!

It got to Tuesday or Wednesday, we hadn't done much training because the ground was really frosty. He pulled me into the office, we'd arranged a mid-season friendly at West Brom, more as a training session. Ironically managed by Ron Atkinson. Dario said to me: "Right you're not coming to West Brom, you're going to Villa this afternoon to talk to Graham Taylor they've bid the extra 50 grand."

So I said to him very naively: "West Brom's just around the corner, I'll come down play in the game and go from there." He said: "No you won't, I'm not having 200 grand's worth of player wandering around in a football match for 90 minutes." So I didn't go to West Brom. I went home, got showered and set off to go down to Villa quite early because I wanted to make a good impression.

Again no agent just me, so Graham showed me around the club. Then we sat in his office and he started to talk terms and I suppose the only real counsel I took at that time was my dad's, I ran everything past him. So when he finished talking he offered me basically £4000 less signing on fee than what I'd been advised I should be on.

I was brave enough to say I've been advised to ask for 10% of the transfer fee, which he said: "Yes, we'll do that, no problem." I said I'd like 48 hours to go away and think about it. So that was fine, he actually got Steve Stride to print the contract up, unsigned, but so it was there in writing. I took that back with me to Rachel's house and we sat there looking at it. I knew I was going so I told Dario. He rang Graham to tell him the deal was done. I then got on the phone to ask what he wanted me to do. He said: "Let's not do anything, we've got the Cup game against Liverpool on Sunday. Why don't you and your girlfriend come down and watch the game and then come back on Monday morning for training and we'll sign the contract." So that's what happened.

We sat in the press conference when I signed the contract on the Monday afternoon. Before I spoke, before any questions came, Graham laid out how the story unfolded and what was important to realise from a journalist's point of view was that I'd asked for 48 hours to think about things, but not once in that time did I come back and ask for more money, it was genuinely to think things over. He was pre-empting the potential perception that I hadn't signed immediately because I was holding out for more money.

I did my first training session on the Monday afternoon with the reserves, they were playing that week at Sheffield United. From that session, I went back to Villa Park, did the press conference and then into Birmingham to stay at the Midland Hotel where I was being put up. I remember feeling all of a sudden like going from being a big fish in a little pond to being a very, very little fish in a big pond. I'd been playing League football albeit in front of 2000 people, being the star of the show, enjoying my football, to going to Aston Villa, which is a much bigger club and at that time thinking, Christ I'm in the reserves. For me at that time - it wasn't but - there was the fear that this had been a backward step. I'd gone from being a reserve team player at Manchester United to playing League football and one of the reasons that I was quite happy to leave United and go to Crewe was because

I thought it was a step up in terms of football because I was playing in the League. Suddenly I've got four walls of a hotel room, on my own and thinking I'm a reserve team player again.

Over the next two weeks, I played for the reserves, I was then sub for the first-team against Leicester but never got on. Then I went up to Hull; Stuart Gray was coming back from injury, there were 13 players, it was the days of only one substitute and when he named the team and substitute, Stuart was on the bench. I was the 13th man. So for the first two weeks it almost confirmed I wasn't a first-team player. What was I here? Was I having to come here and develop my career again and had I made a mistake? The Midland Hotel was lovely but I was there on my own. I joined the club with players who had families, houses, etc, because they were earning more money. Yes you had your training ground camaraderie, don't get me wrong, but they went back to their houses and I went back to mine, just that mine was a hotel room and a bed to sit on.

Fortunately the fact it was only 45 minutes away from Rachel's, when I got a day off I started to leave training and go there and then come back that following night. It manifested itself, Graham never wanted you travelling that far to go into training but it was very rarely I stayed in the Midland Hotel, I'd go back, stay at Rachel's family's house and then set off early in the morning. I found a back route through Stone and Lichfield to Bodymoor Heath, the danger was much less of me being held up in traffic on the M6.

I started to do that and at least it gave me the comfort off the pitch. But still from a football perspective, things didn't feel right. Not because it was Villa, but just because I felt I'd taken a certain step back. We were training leading up to the Blackburn game. What stuck in my mind most was Alan McInally and Garry Thompson physically, they were things I'd never seen before really at Crewe Alexandra, and the speed of Tony Daley. Graham was doing some coaching and pulled alongside me, he'd taken four or five players away to do something a little bit different than what the rest of the group was doing. I was one of those four or five players and he just sidled up to me and said: "Let your parents know that you're playing at the weekend."And that was it.

But I go into a game against Blackburn thinking I'm a reserve team player, I've got an opportunity but I have to play well. We got beat 3-2 and I scored. So who knows what's going to happen in the next game at home to Plymouth. We won 5-2 and I score again. At Bournemouth we win 2-1 and I get another. From there that was it. I got one at Palace then the big game was the one against Bradford at home because it was like a six pointer. In the end the promotion came down to the point at Swindon Town with Middlesbrough and Bradford losing at home, strange results. It was very, very close.

Back in the First Division results were a mixed bag but it never felt that we were really the ones that didn't have a chance of staying up. I think we always knew it was in our own hands though in the end it took Liverpool beating West Ham to keep us safe. I have this vague recollection, I'd been named in the England B squad against Scandinavia and was driving down to meet up and listening to the Anfield game on the radio.

The second year Villa took off in September. Personally for me it was good, I was scoring goals, I got named in the England squad and yet it wasn't that far away from when I'd been in the hotel room, thinking I'd made a mistake and the next thing you know, leading into the Everton game I signed a new contract. Well, I actually didn't sign it, I agreed a new contract on the Friday and the other thing was, Stuart Gray was injured and Graham named me captain. So I had this express train of a career that was going on.

I was offered the new contract by Graham. I actually went in and didn't think it was a fair to be honest, not that I asked for ridiculous money but I'm guessing dressing room rumours, you know what other people are earning. I was scoring the goals and things so I went in and asked to up it a little bit.

On the Friday before the Everton game I'd had to go down to Villa Park with Graham and meet Doug Ellis. I suppose the interesting thing about it was that it was the Friday evening, we were playing on the Sunday and everything sort of got agreed at that meeting. I asked for something in the contract - I didn't have an agent so I'd spoken to the PFA - basically my mortgage was crippling me because the interest rates were very high at the time. Not crippling me in terms of debt, but there wasn't a great deal of spare money to reduce my mortgage. That was one of the clauses that I put into the contract when I got what they called a loyalty bonus at that time, just to clear some of the mortgage to make it more manageable on a monthly basis. I asked the PFA and they told me about it.

I remember Doug sending Steve Stride out to check the rules on whether they could or couldn't pay me. Steve came back in and said: "Yes, it's allowed." Doug said: "We'll agree it, will you sign the contract?" On the Friday I said: "No, I need to speak to my dad first." It was about six o'clock and Doug almost threw the phone at me saying: "Ring him now, ring him now." I said: "To be honest, it's a Friday night. You're not going to get a great deal of sense out of my old man after the week he'll have had at work." I said I'd speak to him over the weekend. So I'd agreed the contract, we trained on the Saturday, beat Everton 6-2 on the Sunday. Graham gave us the Monday off, I drove back up to Nantwich to stay with Rachel, all with a contract that's unsigned. And then on the Monday lunchtime I got named in the England squad. I can remember my mobile phone going off left, right and centre with Doug chasing me to come down and sign the contract. I think he felt that I was going to go in the following day and ask for even more money because now I was an England international. I went down on the Tuesday morning and signed it.

Only now do I look back over that runners-up season and think it's a little bit like the Italian World Cup as well. It's only a considerable time afterwards that you look back and think, if only, had we believed a bit more, had I scored that penalty against Wimbledon - still haunts me now - had this happened, had that happened because we were so, so close because I think at the time it was so unexpected for us to be even in the running for the League. You still feel, but we've had a very good season, an exceptional season and although you're disappointed that you haven't won the League, I don't think we ever expected to. That was the same as the Italian World Cup, we'd got to the semi-finals, the whole country was cock-a-hoop and it's only later when you look back and think, had we believed that we could win a bit more, potentially we might have done.

When Graham left to go and manage England, I think it was a big blow to the whole club that he'd gone. Whoever came in was going to have it very difficult. Jo Venglos having been the Czechoslovakian manager in the World Cup should probably have been given a lot more respect than he was, not just by the players, but by the media as well. In essence Jo was way ahead of his time in terms of getting a team physically correct and things like that. He came into a football club that, in many ways overachieved with a manager that everybody had bought into, so it was a going to be difficult for us to have a similar season to what we'd had the year before and he was going to get the blame for it. He had some big boots to fill and it was always going to be difficult to fill them. What could better the season before, the only thing he could do is go and win the League.

It was also a time straight after the World Cup, which had enthused me. I'd started to believe in myself as a player more and the Italian clubs had started to sniff around me and things and that was where football was played. Sid (Cowans) had had that experience, so to speak and we had a good bond at Villa because we complemented each other so well in midfield. I wouldn't say that we socialised much off the field other than when the team was together or when the team was away and things like that. There was a mutual respect between myself and Sid, I appreciated what he could do and he appreciated what I could do.

The best player I played with was Roberto Mancini at Sampdoria, just because he did things with a football that nobody else could but from my point of view, for me personally it would be Gordon Cowans, I didn't have to time runs with him because no matter where the ball was in and around him he had the ability to manipulate it to make the pass that counted. If the ball was at Sid's feet you could make the run and he'd find you and what that enabled me to do was score goals, he could find me on a sixpence, put it where I wanted it. I helped him by making those runs but he helped me by putting the ball where it needed to be. The other thing that goes unmentioned which is more a tactical thing is we had two midfield players, me and Gordon and I vacated the middle of the midfield very early from a tactical point of view

and he never complained once. If I disappeared I left holes and if Sid didn't find me we were really susceptible to the counter attack and that was quite a potent weapon because the be all and end all is you can't get hit on the counter unless you give the ball away - and he didn't.

The goal at home to Inter Milan is a prime example, it shows the telepathy that was there between us because I actually start my run when Tony Cascarino's got the ball. I start my run not to get the ball off Tony, I know he can't play me, I start my run because I can picture it being laid off to Sid and I know where it's going to go.

When I came back from the World Cup there were a couple of sniffs around me at that time from Italian clubs. When we drew Inter I remember John Ward saying: "Right we've got League games before the UEFA game," he actually banned the players from talking about the Inter game to the media because that was going to take over from our League games. I couldn't get it out of my mind, I was on such a high because this was a global game. I'd go out and give everything that I had in the games I played but the Inter game was very difficult not to think about. It gave me another opportunity to go up against what was arguably the best player in the world at that time, Lothar Matthaus, I'd played against him in the semi-finals of the World Cup. I went down to Villa Park to watch Inter train. I remember one of the directors of Inter Milan giving me a little pin badge and a wink on that night, the day before the game so it was clear that I was on Inter's radar. As I said, you knew the game would be seen all over. It's not that I wanted to leave Villa, don't get me wrong, but after the euphoria of the year before and what we'd done and then big clubs showing an interest....

Things get to you through your agents, by this time I did have one, and I knew that there were clubs interested. Equally the Italians didn't necessarily want to touch English players at that time as they'd had their fingers burnt with one or two of the other ones that hadn't learn the language, etc. So it was tentative. And then Bari started to make concrete noises. Literally it was a case of let's speak to them, let's go over. It never really felt right, like the right club. I was probably thinking that I should go to a different one in Italy but to be honest they chased and chased even when I turned them down, the president at that time, he's dead now, it became a mission of his, he just chased.

And then what became apparent, I came back for pre-season training when Ron Atkinson had taken over. I think Ron at the time probably wanted to keep me but at the same time, the money that he could get for me would enable him to rebuild a team basically, and a team that probably needed rebuilding.

ANDY GRAY

Andy Gray was a prolific scorer at Crystal Palace but when Ian Wright and Mark Bright were signed by The Eagles he was moved to a central-midfield role. Villa manager Graham Taylor saw the player's potential and moved for the maestro to boost the promotion push that was starting to gather momentum.

"I played in the Crystal Palace side at Villa in the mid-week (Oct '87) and I knew Villa were interested in me two weeks before that game." Gray had had a bit of a fall out at Palace in the summer and basically wanted to get away. "The players there at the time were old-school type players and the language was industrial but you just had to get on with it. The opportunity was there for me to go somewhere else where I felt I'd be appreciated. I thought the grass was greener on the other side. Graham Taylor wanted me to play alongside Kenny Jackett but that never happened. Stuart Gray joined from Barnsley.

"I knew how big Villa were because when I was a schoolboy at Crystal Palace I used to stay at John Burridge's house. I spoke with Andy Gray when I was 13-years-old on the phone because obviously Budgie played at the Villa and knew Andy well. I knew the players, Morley, Cowans the European side so of course I knew it was a massive club.

"I stayed in the Midland Hotel. You had eight weeks accommodation and in that time you had to find somewhere. I bought a flat in the Hagley Road. It's funny, because when I first signed, on the night before the game Mark Walters came round, to make sure that I was okay."

Stuart and Andy Gray (no relation) both debuted at top of the table Bradford City in late November, it was clearly a good combination as Villa put four past the division's leaders. Gray recalled: "We had a strong bond, that team. Even on a Friday, we would have a beer together. We were a good click. It was a good group of players."

In only his fourth game for his new club he played a big part in the demolition of Hull City. Villa put five past them, with no reply, to go top of the table. Andy Gray scored his first goal that afternoon. "It was a half-volley, Thommo (Garry Thompson) knocked it back to me, at the Holte End, I hit it from about 25 to 30 yards."

In the February Graham Taylor came calling to Gray's house. "What happened was crazy. I trained on the Tuesday for the Villa and then the same night the gaffer knocks on the door. My girlfriend at the time answered and tells me it's my boss. I'm thinking what the hell have I done? So he comes in and says: "Congratulations, you've been called up to play against Scotland." The gaffer left, I had to drive from Birmingham to London to get my passport, then up to Nottingham to the hotel. It was midnight by the time I got there. We trained in the morning, played against Scotland at Forest's ground, done well, and then played another game against France. It's on YouTube that game and I never knew Cantona played in it. That side they had was phenomenal and he scored."

The games were part of the UEFA Under 21 Championships. England beat Scotland 1-0 in the quarter-finals, Tony Dorigo who left Villa for Chelsea before Gray's arrival played in Nottingham. In the semi-finals England travelled to Besancon, Eastern France. The French ran out 4-2 winners with Cantona getting the second goal. Martin Keown, a Villa teammate of Andy also played in the game.

In Gray's first season he helped guide Villa back to the First Division. "We were the best side in the League even when we had them little blips, we were still the strongest team and we went up because we deserved it over a long season. It was the form from all the away games that basically got us up. Millwall overhauled us on the back of their astonishing run."

"There were circumstances, especially with Graham Taylor at the time, he was going for the England job so basically everyone had to be squeaky clean. I mean, I had a few problems when I was at Palace. They weren't really worried about me having any issues, they would deal with them - there was no one running for the top job. Basically anyone who was deemed trouble - not trouble in the sense of upsetting the team – Graham Taylor would get rid of them."

The tough tackling, no-nonsense Gray was expected to be a force in the top flight following promotion. "We started the season at home to Millwall and drew 2-2. Paul Birch a great, great guy slotted me through when we were 0-2 down. I went round the keeper, he knocked me down, Stuart Gray gets one from the penalty spot, McInally got the second. We then go to Highbury and beat them 3-2 and I scored a cracking free-kick from about 30 yards." His second of the campaign would be more fanatically celebrated by the Villa masses as he crashed home Villa's second of the evening to put Villa in the driving seat at St Andrew's in the Second Round first-leg of the League Cup.

"That season was okay up until maybe the Sheffield Wednesday game, where I got sent off and it basically went downhill from there. We played Queen's Park Rangers at home after Christmas and I played out wide. During the game Trevor Francis asked me: "Do you want to come back to London?" I said: "Yes." "From my sending off at Hillsborough things didn't seem quite right and I was travelling back to London. The gaffer said no one can travel. I lived on the Hagley Road, I was the only one who lived in town. After this particular day training he told everyone to go back home, no one was allowed to go anywhere other and here's me, I have driven back to London. I've got down to the bottom of the motorway and who do I see - the gaffer. We didn't fall out but we both knew I wasn't towing the line the way he wanted. I didn't fall out of love with the club but basically

there was just too much politics. I kind of lost focus and wanted to come back home. To be honest it was a massive club to be at but being a London boy I didn't settle. I've got regrets the club and the supporters didn't see the best of me. It was a short spell there, it was like I went in there and done the job, but there was more. I know I had more to give."

Andy Gray then got the move back to the capital and to QPR for £500,000 in February. "I went to a Palace 'Player of The Year' dance when the season had finished and Steve Coppell asked if I wanted to come back, Palace had got promoted. On the Monday morning I went in to Trevor Francis and said: "Listen gaffer, I want to go back to Palace." And he let me go back, he knew I wasn't happy but I had done well for them in the time I was there, scored, helped them stay up and they made a bit of a profit too." Gray helped Palace reach the 1990 F.A. Cup final and the following season they finished third in Division One, his performances led to a Tottenham Hotspur move for £900,000.

Graham Taylor came calling again, this time not on the player's door. Sadly an England call-up didn't do the ex Villa lad any favours. "It was the worst thing that ever happened to me. Prior to that I was playing the best football of my life, I was at Palace, we were doing well that season, I was on fire. I remember the day I got picked and where it was, Liverpool away, a screaming game, we beat them 2-1. Coppell comes into the dressing room and told me someone wanted to talk to me in the boot room. It was the gaffer, he said: "We are playing Poland in two weeks time, I announce the squad on Monday, you'll be playing."

I trained that week but had a slight hamstring problem, if I'm being honest I could have said to myself, you know what, you're not 110% fit, I knew it, but getting picked for England.... So I played in the game and I got dragged off after 45 minutes, but he did that regularly with debut players. But what done me was he didn't call me to tell me why he did it and I took it the wrong way. From there I lost my rhythm. Everything I did I tried harder but basically I just lost it. Over the years my credit of building my reputation was what got me the move to Tottenham and I was shit at Tottenham! These things happen, you either rise above it but I didn't have the answers. The only answer I had was to try harder but by doing that I was damaging myself. No one ever sat me down and said Andy look what you've achieved, you're a good player, so I dealt with this on my own. I look at how far I got in the game but I know I could have done more. I can't beat myself up, I played for some great clubs, Cup finals, I'm from an era where you had to suck it up and get on with it.

GARRY THOMPSON

Aston Villa fan Garry Thompson would get to play in the beloved claret and blue colours during the 80s decade, but not before having cut his teeth at Coventry City and spells at West Bromwich Albion and Sheffield Wednesday. In his own words Garry gives us a unique insight into his time at his team.

I was playing for Sheffield Wednesday, we'd had a good season although I hadn't scored loads of goals because Howard (Wilkinson) was playing me in a different position. We played the final game Sheffield Wednesday/Villa at Hillsborough. At the end we waved to the fans and I'm going up the tunnel, I was one of the last ones off the pitch. Ron Wylie's at the bottom of the tunnel and as I'm walking up he says:

"Big man would you come to Villa?"

"Like a shot, I'd walk there."

I'd been a Villa fan from being a kid, saw Santos play Villa, my dad's a big Villa fan, family's all Villa.

When I left West Brom for Sheffield Wednesday I was supposed to go to Villa and Graham Turner kept saying: "If you turn down every other club - there was Arsenal, QPR, Chelsea, Sheffield Wednesday, about six or seven clubs chasing me - they have to accept our offer." I said: "Albion hate Villa, there's no way they'll take less money than everyone else is offering." I thought well, that's not going to happen. So a year later, Ron pulls me, he says: Would you come?" After I'd said I'd walk there he says: "Okay leave it with me." We both start walking up the tunnel. Howard Wilkinsons at the top,

"Who are you f****** talking to?"

"He's my coach I've known him since I was 14-years of age."

"Get in that f****** dressing room Thompson!"

England were in the World Cup, Howard Wilkinson was doing the commentary for the BBC and he rang me from Mexico. Howard's a bit dour: "Now then, we've just had an offer from Aston Villa. You can stay or you can go, it's up to you." The moment he said that I was going to the Villa. Howard didn't even try to keep me, he made it easier for me. I had a bit of a problem because the wife, we'd moved to Sheffield and we ended up having a great social life, we were hanging with the Human League, and we're going out with different people, it was lovely. Off the field was brilliant but I wasn't enjoying the football because the way we were playing, but it was the first time we'd stood on our own two feet away from Birmingham so it was great.

I went straight down the Villa and agreed to sign but I had to go back and tell her - she was not happy. In the end she said she understood it was my dream, I'd always wanted to play for Aston Villa and I now had that opportunity. Because I'd been playing week in week out, I'd ask: "How did Villa get on today?" but I didn't study the team. I'd realised they'd got to the semi-final of the League Cup so as far as I'm concerned, they're still doing okay so I've never really checked the league position and that and then I joined. I think it was the first or second day and Gary Shaw, who I've known since we were kids, said to me: "You're three years too late big man, the place has gone to the dogs." I thought Gary was bitter because he'd been injured a lot.

The better kids had always gone to Villa and they'd get a good grounding because of how the club brought them on, but the biggest problem was, they gave them all a chance in the team too soon. Doug Ellis was trying to cut corners after the European and Super Cup wins, within three or four years Villa were relegated. You can only reduce the wage bill so far and still remain in the top division

THE
mita

and compete for honours. Doug thought the best way of doing it was blooding the youngsters but you can only bring them through if they've got good experienced players to help them along.

But within the first three or four training sessions I knew Shawry was right. The Aston Villa feeling that I always had playing against them just wasn't there. It wasn't like I'm a football expert, but when I was at Wednesday Howard Wilkinson used to play 11-aside every day, he'd break down the training to set pieces, breaking defensive work down, midfield work, full-back work, we were doing all that and I was bored shitless. Because I'm a centre-forward I just want to play 5-aside and score goals. Wednesday had finished fifth in the League and got to the F.A. Cup semi-final so it was a reasonably good season but a lot of it was because of the shape, the way we played and the organisation. I go to Aston Villa and there's no shape, no organisation, there's nothing.

My old man - a massive Villa fan who worked at Longbridge - said: "So, what's it like?"

"Well, it's not quite what I thought it would be dad."

"Come on, what you've got to do is get your head into it, get into the game son. This minute you're still disappointed because of the way Sheffield Wednesday went. You're at a club now that you want to play for, you've got to crack on with it."

I said "No, I'm desperate to play for Aston Villa but it's just not how I envisaged it."

We played a pre-season game – Port Vale I think - and Gary Shelton, Gary Megson, Lee Chapman and Mark Chamberlain came down from Sheffield to watch the game. They've watched us play this friendly and we're having a chat and a drink after. Shelly (Gary Shelton who used to play for Villa) pulled me and says:

"Big man unless you get some players in you could go down."

"F*** Off Shelly this is Aston Villa mate."

We played Liverpool at Anfield and we took the lead three times but if there'd been another five minutes in that game they would have beaten us 4-3. We came off the pitch and the Villa players were throwing punches and rowing with each other because we could have got beat. In those days Liverpool were the top team, no one went to Anfield and scored three goals. I thought, Jesus we're in trouble here.

When we played we were too deep and we were lacking in midfield. I could see all this because of the way Howard at Sheffield Wednesday had worked.

I'm shouting: "We've got to squeeze the play, you've got to get up and squeeze them." Then I'm getting back off them: "F*** Off when did you become a coach?" I'm hollering: "But there's too much space" and this was going on most of the year. Stevie Hunt was there, he knew me from Coventry as a kid and one of the best players I ever played with. We played Sheffield Wednesday around the Christmas time and he had a big bust up with Billy McNeill at full time.

To be honest it wasn't fair on Billy because people have asked me and I've said he was a poor manager. It wasn't that he was a poor manager, now I'm older I can see it for what it was. Billy McNeill had just had a horrendous time at Manchester City, he quit from there and walked straight into the Villa job. Billy should have gone away from football for a few months worked out what he'd done wrong and what hadn't worked... but to go straight from one job to another, to another club that was struggling, it was jumping out of the frying pan into the fire. It took me years to see that.

When Billy McNeill died and I was on the phone in, I was just talking away and I said, "Look I ain't speaking ill of the dead but I have to be honest, as a manager at Aston Villa at the time, it wasn't the right one." I was trying to be diplomatic and polite and the more I thought about it, it wasn't his fault. Richard Sydenham wrote the book about all the things that Villa decided to cut corners on, and all these decisions that were made after winning the European Cup. It was inevitable, Billy was just caught up in the flow of it. It could have been Alex Ferguson, it doesn't matter who was there, that club was always going down, we'd been edging towards that.

Steve Hodge bore the brunt of us going down yet he left at Christmas. Villa fans said he never tried a leg since coming back from the World Cup but he was always going to get his move. Hodgey did take a bit of abuse but to be fair he'd gone by then but people were still blaming him. It wasn't his fault that we were just rubbish. It was all of us collectively. As a midfield player Hodgey would break forward and join up with me or as a striker and get goals. He was like a poor man's Bryan Robson for an attacking midfield player and could score goals, good football logic. He came back from the World Cup and nothing really happened - he didn't sulk but he wasn't happy.

We got relegated. I'd been injured for a few months by then, the medical department had no idea what was wrong with me. Dave Norton had the same sort of injury, they took a bit of bone off his hip and placed it in between his pelvis, fusing it. So Dave had the operation and they were saying to me that could be the way forward. And then Doug spoke to me and tried to offer me £20,000 to retire.

"Why would I do that Mr Ellis when my contracts worth about four times that?"

"But we're not a wealthy club and it's not really worked out."

So basically, take the money and F*** Off and I was like, "I will stay here til the last day of my contract, then I'll retire if I can't play again." We were at a standoff.

Doug drove up to Bodymoor in the big Bentley, walks into the canteen and announces: "Gentlemen I introduce you to the new manager of Aston Villa." Graham Taylor comes in, smartly dressed in his club suit. He looks around at us all and the first thing he says: "You lot, you'll all look at me and go who's he played for, what's he ever done in his career? I'll tell you, I played for Grimsby and Scunthorpe" and he said how many games and his career ended at 28 through injury. Then he said: "So that's my career now let's look at you lot."

He then decided to eviscerate people.

"Paul Elliott, have you given your best for Aston Villa this year?"

"Yeah."

"So how come you've got a move lined up?"

"Tony Dorigo, I ask the same question."

"Yes."

"You've agreed to go to Chelsea."

Me and Steve Hunt were pissing ourselves laughing, he's getting into it. He's hammering people, some players are giggling a bit. We'd been saying things about these boys all year, to their faces. He didn't even look at me and he went:

"You, you wander about, you're too busy fighting with people, you get more bookings than goals, your socks round your ankles, they've spent a fortune on you, and now you're injured. You're no f****** good to me. You might as well just F*** Off."

That was my first meeting with Graham Taylor, he'd spoken for three hours and proceeded basically to say everything that was wrong, what he would do to change it and what he expected from us. He's laid down the law the first day. Me, Shawry, Steve Hunt and a few others go out, and we're like, "F*** me, there's going to be big changes at this place."

Andy Gray and Simon Stainrod left, he got rid of the big hitters as it were and the way he spoke to me I would imagine that if I'd been fit he'd have probably tried to oust me as well.

Our next meeting was the very next day. As I pulled up at the training ground, Warren Aspinall was walking back towards his car, so I know something's up. We call him George Formby because of the teeth and that. I said: "Forms what's happening?"And he just went: "Good luck" got in the car and drove off.

If you walk straight you go into the entrance but if you walk to the right there are all the football pitches. So I thought I'll be clever, I went onto the pitch picked up a bit of grass as if I'm checking the wind direction. They're busy chatting, there's Bobby Downs. Steve Harrison and Graham Taylor, they've all got their club suits on. I get round the back of them and just as I'm about to open the door and slide in he (GT) says:

"Can I ask your question?"

"Yeah."

"Where do you live?"

"Bassetts Pole, just down the road."

"What's your house like?"

"I've got a five bedroom detached, sauna, study, got foundations laid for a swimming pool, a third of an acre blah blah blah."

"It sounds very nice. What do you think your neighbours think when they see you in the mornings?"

"They probably think it's Thommo off to training."

"No, they think 'look at that scruffy twat' and he's going to represent Aston Villa. Look at you!" I was dressed in a white tee shirt, black leather jacket, blue jeans, trainers and no socks. I looked a million dollars.

So he's gone: "Look at you, you're dressed like the black Fonz. Get back in your car. When you come into work you wear a tracksuit, because your'e coming to work at a football club or you wear slacks, a shirt and shoes. Now F*** Off and get changed."

"Okay gaffer got it, in future..."

"No, go home now!"

I got back in the car and drove home, it's only five minutes away. As I went in the house my missus was like: "What's happened?" I told her and she pissed herself laughing. I've gone back, I'm all dressed up and then he proceeded to say: "Right you've got three sets of training kit, you'll clean your own boots, I'll get you back in love with wearing your kit."

Graham Taylor had this thing, we'd start training with the coaches, crack a few jokes, tell a few stories and then Graham would walk across the pitch after 20 minutes of the session. If the tempo didn't raise 10% when you saw the manager coming, he'd stop the whole thing. "They're working with you, they're training you but the moment you see me coming, you better raise your game."

So he actually got us washing our own kit, cleaning our own boots and training at the ground because the disconnect between the fans and the players was massive. He says: "They f****** hate you and rightly so. You have to get used to playing at Villa Park."

And he was right. I watched the first ten games or whatever because I was injured. We were expected to win but in the first few we struggled. Graham kept saying: "It will turn, it will turn, but you have to keep working hard." But the fans were waiting for the players to mess up. The players are shit scared. I've seen grown men playing them games thinking, oh my God.

Garry had to sit out the first Birmingham City derby in his time at the club due to injury.

I watched the game from an executive box in the Doug Ellis Stand with Gary Shaw. We'd been looking forward to watching it so much and it was a damp squib. The away fans clocked Shawry and gave him so much abuse. It capped off a horrendous day.

We'd been relegated and obviously as a local lad I'm taking abuse wherever I go. I'm injured as well and it looks like my career could be ending because no one knows what's happening. Graham Taylor came in, gets Jim Walker the physio in. Jim took me to see a guy called Paddy Harmer who sussed out my problem. I had the operation at Harley Street and within six weeks I was back playing.

Taylor to be fair to him, played me against Bradford City in the Simod Cup. He caught me on the morning, I'd been training for a couple of weeks and I thought I was going to play in the reserves.

He went to me: "What do you reckon then?"

I thought he meant sub and said: "That'd be nice."

He shouts: "Everybody stop." He gets everyone gathered around. "This is what's wrong with this f****** football club. We've got our centre-forward who's done f*** all since he's been here by the way and I say to him, big game tonight, what do you reckon? Expecting him to go, yes gaffer I'm all over it and he goes, ooooh that would be nice."

I said: "I didn't mean it like that."

"I'm f****** talking!"

He slaughtered me again. All the lads pissed themselves laughing. I played for an hour and then he took me off. We got beat 0-5. I know next day Graham will have us at the ground training. I'm thinking bath, massage, relaxing that sort of thing and a debrief with me. Gary Shaw goes to me: "Big man, first time you've played in 11 months. You've got to go out and have a little drink."

"Gaz, I'm knackered I just need to go to my bed."

He continues: "All this hard work to get yourself back playing, you've got to have at least one." Anyway weak man that I am I end up getting home at 4.30 in the morning.

I wake up in the morning I feel dreadful. I'm thinking, I'll get to training, have a bath etc and that'll be my day and I'll be back in bed by one o'clock to sleep it off. So I go into training and Jim Walker says: "Get your kit on, gaffer wants a word with you."

So I think Graham's going to say: "Look son you didn't do too bad or that was crap and we can work on that." A pep talk and that. He goes "Come on." He took me to Aston Park over the road, just the two of us and I'm walking over thinking what's he doing now? There's no balls or anything, then I think we're going to have a walk around and a talk about what's gone wrong and how I can improve and all that.

He ran me all over Aston Park, all over the f****** place, up and down, I saw parts of it I'd never seen before in my life. After I'm lying there on the floor dying, he's says: "Yeah, you're a game lad. You'll play in the first team if you keep your standards up, you'll play in the reserves - we'll get you fit." "He was true to his word, he ran the f*** out of me every chance he got, played me in the reserves, played me in the first team and I started scoring and it went really well.

We beat Bradford at theirs 4-2, we'd just signed Andy and Stuart Gray and I remember sitting on the floor with Birchy after I'd done the double one-two with Stuart Gray, he's bent it in the goal, and I'm laughing and saying: "I'll tell you what, we've got the final piece of the jigsaw, we're going up. I'd been out for so long it was great because as a Villa fan to score for my club, to actually start righting the wrongs because I was part of it and I felt guilty as, the way things had gone - it was brilliant.

We did ever so well away from home for so long then all of a sudden we faltered a bit towards the end but went up because of the game at Swindon, we should have gone up easy. We were doing well and I felt part of the collective group that was actually moving in the right direction. The likes of Kevin Gage, Steve Sims, Allan Evans, Warren Aspinall, big McInally, who's one of my best mates - we were all part of something. We're friends forever now because we went through something. Yes we got them back into the Premier League and I know me and Graham kind of fell out after that. There were different reasons for it but we did what we needed to do. We probably did need to go down to actually clear the decks and start again. I'm proud of my career anyway because I had highs and lows, good times and bad but over a 20 year career my worst days were better than most people's best days. I did something that many people want to do, but didn't or couldn't. It wasn't about the money. I played professional football for the club I love and supported and I managed to get a career out of it so I had a great time.

To gain promotion with Aston Villa wasn't the pinnacle, but one of the highest things I did because they were so low and then to get back and to play in what is the top league after that with Villa - it was special.

When I fell out with Graham I was put into the 'bomb squad,' players he's trying to get out of the club. Mark Lillis, Birchy, four of five of us had to train on our own. But in my head if I'm not playing I'm not staying. It was nothing about picking up money I wasn't going to stay and not play.

If getting promoted was all I did at Aston Villa I'll have that. I'd love to have won trophies whatever but we were part of something that was really wrong and we ended up righting it. I'm happy with that.

"Macca (Alan McInally) then pulls me, he says: "I've agreed to go to Bayern Munich, it's going to happen." Graham then signed Ormondroyd, the club was too big for him. Now when I look at it I was headstrong, stupid and I'm going. When he put Watford in front of me I just went. I sat in a hotel room after I signed and cried my eyes out, what the f*** have I done?

To be fair, everything Graham Taylor did, very good psychology, but very, very clued into what he was doing, what he wanted. When you look at it now he almost used the Villa as a stepping stone to get to the England job but he took a massive gamble taking a club that got relegated once, could have gone through it again, had to clear the decks, bring in hard working players and get us back up the table.

MARK BURKE

I first went to the club when I was ten. It was different in those days, basically another world. Villa had scouts like every other club looking at different players; Dave Richardson (head of youth football at Aston Villa) had sent some of his scouts out and a bloke called Fred Greenaway had seen me play. Dave then came to watch me in a big five-a-side tournament, 800 schools from Birmingham enter and we, St Gerards, Castle Vale, only a little school got to the Final, a great achievement for us even though we lost. Dave (who I still keep in touch with regularly) was giving the prizes out and he invited me down to train. From then on (about 1979) I was going every school holiday and twice a week to the Aston Villa Leisure Centre. They only invited so many, Phil Robinson was there the very first time I went, he was two years older than me and was there all the way through. People came and went, it was all very informal.

I was a big Villa fan so for me that was great. I was in the Clock End, Highbury when they won the League and I went to Rotterdam when Villa won the European Cup, my mom took me after I'd bugged her that much. A proper last minute job!

In those days you signed associate schoolboy forms at 14-years-old. I had a lot of clubs who wanted me, all the Midland ones, and Manchester United wanted me to go up there but I was always going to go to Villa. I signed for them in 1983. A year later I played for the England Schoolboys scoring a hat-trick at Wembley against Holland. Before that I'd played against Scotland, we beat them 1-0 and I got the goal, then we went up to Scotland a week later beat them one-nil and I scored again. Playing for the schoolboys was an amazing experience and pulling on the England shirt was unbelievable.

When I was 15-years-of-age I started to play some games for the youth team on a Saturday morning. I also got some games in the Midland Intermediate League, which in those days was an open-age league, totally different to now. It wasn't youth football, you were playing against pros. Teams like Derby, Forest and Leicester - if players weren't playing in the first team they were playing on the Saturday morning. Against teams like Forest you were lucky if you got a corner, they were so good!

For a young kid it was great, to play against internationals you'd only seen on the TV. I remember playing against John Robertson in the Intermediate League, he was one of my favourites – a brilliant player, I would be 15 or 16. I left school in 1985 and became an apprentice. Then I was playing in the reserves against top, top players. Liverpool, United and the others, if their players weren't in the first team they'd be in the reserves. In my group there was Gary Clipstone, Mark Mahoney, Steven Mead, Ian Bates but none of them came through. Ian Olney signed in 1986 and made a name for himself in the first team before going to Oldham for big money.

Mark Burke realised a childhood dream when he signed professional forms in February 1987 for his team. Billy McNeill was the manager and handed the youngster his debut against champions elect Everton on 18 April 1987.

I found out the day before I was playing. Everton were going for the League, they were the best in the country at the time. It was a big thing to do and Villa Park felt like a full house. The only things I remember about the game; early on I managed to get a shot off, Martin Keown had the ball and I was shouting at him to give it me back quick, by the time I got it I'd been closed down and my shot went wide. I thought, if only! If he'd played me in earlier I might have scored. I also remember being absolutely knackered and how good they were. I felt it went okay, it went as well as it could and my family were there to watch.

Pulling on a Villa shirt was great but we were really struggling by then and got relegated so it was a tough time. The club was in a bad way. When I think back now, where I've been after that, looking at the two and a half years I had at Villa, some of the things were absolutely ridiculous. From winning the European Cup three or four years before to going where it went was scandalous when you think about it. Shawry (Gary Shaw), he's a really good mate, he always says to me: "You were there in the worst two years of the club's history." I know what he means. It was a mess, they were great players, really top players but it was just so unorganised.

In the morning a bag of kit was dumped on the floor in the youth team dressing room and it would literally be a fight to get a good pair of shorts or socks, and I mean, a proper fight. All the balls were different, it was like an amateur club and in the next changing rooms you've got some of the top players in the country, Andy Gray, Steve Hodge, Mark Walters, Shawry, Simon Stainrod, Paul Elliott, Tony Dorigo, all these brilliant players. Because I'd been going there such a long time I knew a lot of them to say hello to but you showed them maximum respect as they were older pros and in the first team. When I was 16 I trained a few times with them, odd times we'd play games against them with the youth team or sometimes you'd be called over to train with them if someone was injured.

There were only three changing rooms, the first team in two, we were in the other. Everybody had lunch together so everybody knew each other but there was a massive respect towards the senior players. If an older player said: "Burkey go and get me a tea with two sugars" you just did it, you wanted to because they were great lads and we were in awe of them. They were good to the young pros, it was a great laugh. But when you look back at the club, at Aston Villa, it shouldn't have been like that.

When Graham Taylor came he saw the mess for himself and he actually said: "This is an absolute shambles." I was 18 but I wasn't thinking I've got to be in the first team this year. Villa's a big club and there were a lot of players ahead of me so I just wanted to do my best every day, improve and hopefully get a chance. I was talking to Phil Robinson the other day about when Graham came. Doug Ellis introduced him at the training ground, Bodymoor Heath. It was one building, you had the canteen, kit man's office, changing rooms, manager's office and boot room, that was it really, there was nothing else there. In the canteen Graham stood and talked for two or three hours. As a young kid I was impressed, he went into so much detail and about different players. One thing I remember he said very clearly, he asked a general question to everyone: "What do you do if you are one nil down with five minutes to go?" Nobody said anything so he asked it again and then someone said: "Well you launch it in the box." Graham replied: "Why don't you do that from the first minute?" Andy Gray and Simon Stainrod were sat behind me and I heard one of them go: "F****** Hell." I remember thinking it makes a lot of sense but that's a bit basic, you can't just do that but, he had a plan and he made us aware, if the ball was there, it's going to go there and so on, it was about thinking and reacting. It was a very rigid, strict plan, but it was a definite plan so everybody knew what they were doing. Whatever anyone says about his style of play he knew exactly what he wanted, he had fantastic success at Watford, what he did there was amazing, one of the great football stories, so nobody could really argue with him.

On the fitness side of it, he was really good; he brought Steve Harrison in who was a brilliant, brilliant coach, a top bloke as well and everybody loved him, he was great with the lads, we got massively fit. As I said Graham had his plan about how to actually play the game, whether you agreed or didn't - if you didn't you weren't getting in the team basically. People like Andy and Simon, great players and great blokes, but because they were big personalities for him coming they would be a challenge for him, he'd want his own men in so he was always going to get rid of them. I loved them but I don't think they were for him.

Under Taylor, Burke came on as a substitute away to Hull City. The manager saw enough in the youngster to play him from the start for the next three matches, the last one being at home to Middlesbrough.

[Above] Mark Burke and the Villa reserve team getting ready to board the coach at Bodymoor Heath, including the legendary former Villa player, Eric Houghton, on the far right

I look back now and don't think I was ready at 18 and to play the way Graham wanted, I wasn't ready physically either though I did okay. After the Boro match I was standing outside the changing rooms talking to Brian Little, he'd been my youth team coach before leaving to take up a similar role at Ayresome Park. As we chatted the Middlesbrough manager Bruce Rioch (a Villa legend) walked past and said something to Brian. I said: "What did he say?" Brian replied: "He likes you." Apparently Bruce had kept a tab on what was happening at Villa, he was up and down all the time watching the reserve games and he knew all the young players at Villa Park and that's why he took people like Kevin Poole, Paul Kerr and Dean Glover.

Mark Burke joined Boro in December 1987.

Brian probably rang me and told me of Middlesbrough's interest, though in all honesty I can't remember. I went into Bodymoor and Graham Taylor said: "Middlesbrough are interested, you should go and talk to them." I went to captain Allan Evans. Everyone looked up to and respected 'Evo' and I asked his advice. "If the manager is saying you should talk to them, then do it, it's always better to go where you're wanted."

It was bitter sweet leaving Villa because it was all I'd ever wanted and known. But, football was my profession and you go where you get the opportunities. Villa had changed, the club was changing, if you're not getting played and the manager says "You're a good player but the way I want the team to play might not suit you" then the decision is made for you. I was still a Villa fan, no problem there.

Bruce Rioch and Colin Todd came round my mom's house in Erdington. My uncle then drove myself and mom up. We were shown round Ayresome Park, you could tell there was something going on there. It was a really good set up, lively and impressive, a tiny squad of only 14 or 15 but very tight knit and they had the lads from Villa I'd known from being 10-years-old.

In February Mark came up against Villa - the first live game from Division Two that was on the TV.

Boro and Villa were going for the title, it was a big game. It was really strange, I'd been training with all these lads not long ago but once the game started I wanted to win.

In one of the closest finishes in Second Division history Aston Villa scraped through by the skin of their teeth to take the last automatic slot behind champions Millwall.

We played Leicester and Villa played Swindon and we only had to get a draw. Everybody just presumed we were going up and the whole town was getting ready for a massive party. I remember going out with Trevor Senior one night in that week and he said: "I don't like this." Everyone was coming up saying we are going to win and do this and that to Leicester on Saturday. We went out against them and just froze.

Looking back on my time at Villa it was fantastic, great people and a real family atmosphere but it's such a shame that the real team that won the League and the European Cup was broken up so soon and the club fell into a bit of a state. There were many changes along the way, when Graham Turner was manager, I think there was a lot going on behind the scenes politically which made it difficult for him to do the job unhindered. I always thought he was a decent man and he proved that when I played for him at Wolves.

The coming of Graham Taylor changed the club again and brought it steadily back to where it should always be.

Burke would stay on Teesside until 1991 before returning to the Midlands where he was reunited with Graham Turner at Wolverhampton Wanderers for three years. A short period followed at Port Vale before the footballer took his talents abroad where his clubs included Dutch outfit Fortuna Sittard, Omiya Ardija (Japan) and Rapid Bucharest one of the biggest clubs in Romania.

NIGEL SPINK

I recall vividly sitting high in the stand watching as the drama of Jimmy Rimmer leaving the field during the 1982 European Cup Final unfolded before me. There were gasps and who's he, who's that coming on? I was an anorak in those days too: "He's Nigel Spink our reserve keeper from Chelmsford City, he played for the first team back in 1979 at Forest!" I informed those around me.

What I didn't know at that time was that Nigel had turned out for West Ham previously. Back in the mid-seventies he played in a practise game, West Ham reserves versus their first team, a few youth team matches and one Football Combination reserve game against a Spurs side including a young Glenn Hoddle and striker Martin Chivers. Nigel, who'd knocked off early from his building site job conceded seven, four by that man Chivers. After the game the Upton Park hierarchy, Ron Greenwood and John Lyall, thanked the keeper but informed him not to give up the day job as they didn't think he'd become a professional footballer.

The lad only went on to become an England international, European Cup winner and a Villa legend - only five other Villa players throughout history have bettered his 460 appearances for the original claret and blue wearers.

Spink came on to Villa's radar totally by luck, assistant manager Tony Barton had gone down to Conference side Chelmsford City to watch Nicky Penn. The keeper was offered a trial but turned it down, wanting to stay in Essex. One of the Chelmsford directors told Tony: "Come back next week and see the other lad play, we don't know which one is the best out of the two of them." It turned out Penn and Spink alternated in goal as manager Bobby Kellard couldn't decide between them. Playing in that same side was a certain Jimmy Greaves: "He was something else, different gravy!" recalled Nigel.

Tony came back the following week and saw him play. "He obviously had a word with Ron Saunders because in October 1976 I was invited for a week's trial. I got the phone call on the Saturday night from Tony and on the Sunday I was on the train up to New Street Station where Jim Paul picked me up and took me to the club hostel on the Chester Road. Jim and his wife Sylvia ran the hostel but he was also the kitman at Villa having taking over from Walter Cowans (Sid's dad)."

He had a week's trial, didn't play any games, just training for the week and then went back home. "I got a call again, could I come up for another week's trial and at the end of that week they were going to play me in the reserves. I came up and had the week's training with the reserves and youth teams. On the Monday afternoon we jumped on the coach and were off up to Newcastle. The following day we played Newcastle United reserves at St James' Park. Those were the days when the Central League games were played in the stadiums when the first team were playing away so I was lucky enough to play at the likes of Villa Park, Maine Road, Anfield, Old Trafford and Elland Road etc."

Jake Findlay was the main reserve keeper with John Burridge also featuring but Nigel made the position his own when both the others moved on. With 57 Central League appearances under his belt Spink was unexpectedly handed his first-team debut on Boxing Day 1979 at Nottingham Forest's City Ground.

"Ron Saunders told me I was going along for the experience. We went to this hotel for the pre-match meal before making our way to the ground, I was sitting close to the front, Ron turned saying: "Do

you fancy a game today?" I replied: "Yes gaffer." And he went: "You're playing." Little did I know Jimmy Rimmer had a problem with his foot. I didn't have chance to tell anybody, there were no mobile phones then, couldn't put it on Facebook! Nobody knew about it til I was able to speak to my parents and friends after the game.

"Making my debut was awesome. The reserves didn't train anywhere near the first team so it was all new to me. The lads were brilliant but they were different company than what I was used to with the reserve team squad. When you get to the ground, look at the programme and see their team - holders of the European Cup and on the verge of winning it again, you think, wow, that's unbelievable. They were a top team. I remember quite a bit about the game, the pitch wasn't great, it was muddy but you just got on with it. Forest went one-nil up through Robertson and then Stan Bowles scored with a header which was very unusual, I don't think he headed many goals. Gary Shaw scored for us."

It would be three years before Nigel Spink would be back in the first-team line-up. Now this is where history could have been rewritten. Had Nicky Penn not turned down the Villa trial, then perhaps Spink might have found fleeting fame appearing on the silver screen. Penn and his Chelmsford teammates appeared in the 1979 Porridge film with Ronnie Barker, shot on location at Chelmsford Prison, Essex. Had that been the case, Penn might have become the household name on the evening of 26 May 1982 for exploits on a pitch in Rotterdam. As it was it the name Nigel Spink made the big headlines in papers all around the world.

"My next game was the '82 Final and that was an even shorter time to worry about it. It was a big enough game anyway but the circumstances of me playing were news on their own. I didn't have a clue what was about to unfold. When we got to the ground the build up to the game was quite relaxed. Me and the other four subs – in those days substitutions were for injuries they weren't tactical – decided we'd get changed quickly and go out and enjoy the atmosphere and do a proper warm-up because everybody was left to their own. The lads were shooting at me in goal and we were just

savouring it, we didn't think we'd get another sniff of it really. Little did I know when Jimmy decided he couldn't carry on... well it was just an amazing turn of events.

"I was gutted for Jimmy when he had to come off and felt for him after the game. He was disappointed but he was pleased for me, because we got on. Jimmy in his own way - when Jake Findlay and Budgie left - took me under his wing. I used to train with him, he used to get the youth team out before training for half an hour and they'd be shooting from al angles, peppering us with crosses coming into the box. It was before the specialised goalkeeper training, Jimmy had got this routine and he knew exactly how he wanted it to work to make himself better and that rubbed off on me. He was arguably one of the best, if not the best goalkeeper. How he never got to play for England on a regular basis I'll never know."

After the highs of Rotterdam it was back to reserve team football. "I didn't think any different of it, I thought that was how it would be at the end of the day."

"Ron was the first massive influence on me at the club because of his discipline, he showed us how you needed to be, how you needed to work. You had to put the hours in to get where you needed to be and then obviously working with Jimmy for that half an hour because once that time was up the first team came out to train and I then had to go over with the reserves. Bill Shorthouse was our reserve team coach at the time, he was another big influence on me, he had masses of respect from us, he'd played with Billy Wright at the Wolves and had a great career himself. He was a good coach and a good mentor, three afternoons a week we'd be out with the reserve team squad crossing and finishing, shooting practise, all things that would benefit me more than anybody else probably. I was improving all the time."

In December 1982 Spink was recalled to the side. "I don't really know what happened nor what the reasoning was, only Tony Barton and Roy MacLaren would know the answers. I just remember Tony calling me into the manager's office and saying: "Look we want to give you your chance, we think you're ready for the first team." Whether there was an influence from above, the thoughts of the senior players was they were being forced out by the chairman and Jimmy was one of those. Whether Jimmy being left out was the start of the end...it was just an opportunity for me. I remember coming in and having two epic battles in the Super Cup against mighty Barcelona. That really showed me; that and the Juventus quarter-final, the home-leg, showed me what an atmosphere you could get at Villa Park. When it's a full house it's amazing. Even going to Barcelona, they didn't generate the same passion as the Villa supporters can. They were two immense atmospheres and that just made me think, this is what I want. I want to experience this for a long time and I was lucky enough to have a good run at it.

"When the decline was happening, there was so much change in the club, personnel, managers, coaching staff, it was just too much really. The philosophies built by Ron Saunders and by Roy MacLaren, Dave Richardson looking after the youths and getting players in, and Keith Leonard there as youth team coach, it's like they were thrown up in the wind and blown away. The harder you tried the worse it got to arrest it and when that happens the players are unable to have any effect, in the end we weren't good enough to stay up. We were poor but that was the catalyst really that sprung us back into where I believe we are today. Graham Taylor's first season was absolutely marvellous. I know we were in the old Second Division but we had a squad and a team spirit the likes of which I really didn't see at Villa Park. The castle that Graham was starting to build there was magnificent, everybody loved and respected him and everyone was a little bit scared of him as well because he had a disciplined side to him. Only at Villa could they do things in a spectacular way - we're all sitting on the pitch in front of our supporters at Swindon waiting for the other games to finish and then to find out our miserly little draw had taken us up."

Nigel spink had a career at Villa Park that spanned almost two decades 1977 – 1996, and was the main keeper during Villa's exceptional top-flight runners-up seasons of 1989/90 and 1992/93. He did something right because this anorak is struggling to recall another player in Villa history that featured in the first team under no less than eight managers. Legend!

KEVIN GAGE

Kevin Gage never had aspirations to become a footballer, let alone represent his country. Originally from Chiswick before moving to Addlestone in Surrey, he never got to watch football. Fourth Division Aldershot was a 45 minute journey, but his dad worked Saturdays. He turned out for his school and district teams and was spotted as a 15-year-old by a Wimbledon scout. Kevin trained with the Fourth Division side, signed six months later and on making his debut become the youngest player in their history. He played five times in all for the England Youth team including the Youth World Cup in Australia.

I started my career for Wimbledon joining straight from school as a midfield player, but the way Wimbledon played in our rise through the divisions, we played the long ball game and basically the midfield didn't get an awful lot of the ball. The gaffer (Dave Bassett) wanted to go with taller, bigger and stronger midfield players so I was moved to full-back because my techniques were quite good and I could accurately deliver the ball into the areas that we wanted it. I was an attacking midfielder as well so I always liked to get forward. Graham Taylor bought me as full-back because he was aware of the Wimbledon rise and how well we had done. He wanted and needed to reshape his Villa team and he obviously looked at me and thought I'd be a good addition.

Aston Villa had just been relegated; Wimbledon had had their very first season in the old First Division (now the Premiership). In actual fact, I was leaving a club that had finished sixth in the top division, obviously a hugely successful season, to join a club in the lower league even though I'd spent all my career trying to get into the First Division.

Many people saw it as, not a strange move, but they questioned why I was going.

The reason I came to Aston Villa was purely because I had absolute faith in Graham Taylor and the way he sold the club to me. Well, he didn't have to sell the club to me, because it's Aston Villa for God's sake. I may not have got a chance to play for a club as historic and as large as Aston Villa in my career. I had supreme faith in him, given his track record with Watford and Lincoln, to get the club back on a sure footing and be part of the new Aston Villa.

I couldn't wait to come up and meet Graham. Obviously I met him during the summer and we chatted about it, he walked me around the ground, the main stand, the offices, everything. I met Doug Ellis and all the other Villa staff and he just sold the club to me. It was a very easy sell to be honest and I was absolutely delighted to join.

I had a couple of other bits of interest from clubs, one of them was Luton Town, quite a good team and in the top flight. Had I gone to look at them.... they were very much like Wimbledon, a 10,000 capacity. So if it was a choice between Aston Villa and Luton there's only going to be one winner even though they were in a lower division.

So I thought, Villa got relegated, obviously had a bad season but I've put my trust in Graham to build a side to get us back, to be part of it. Having experienced all the many promotions with Wimbledon and being part of something special, the old crazy gang team and squads to get us through those four divisions in such a short space of time, I got quite turned on by the idea of being part of something, building something new at Aston Villa. I didn't just want to go to a club that had a run of the mill, mid-table team. I wanted to go and be part of something again.

Gage dropped effortlessly into the right full-back berth with Bernie Gallacher doing the same on the opposite flank. Gallacher's only

[Above] Kevin Gage with Sheffield Wednesday's Franz Carr during Villa's 1-0 home win in February 1990

appearance in the first team had been in the last game of the previous season, a defeat at Old Trafford.

I didn't know Bernie until I got there and we kind of made both full-back spots our own. I think Graham Taylor let Tony Dorigo go, he was a bit of a big name. Now whether Graham knew that Bernie Gallacher was in the ranks and ready to step in I don't know? But, we had a quite a good full-back pairing and he was a youngster coming through and did really well in the season. It's one of the proudest things of my whole career in that I played every single minute of every single game that season which is quite a feat. It ended up being 51 games with the Cup games as well. That takes some doing because sometimes injuries take their toll, you can't always be that lucky. I mention that fact when anybody talks about Aston Villa because I was quite proud of that for a long time and it was a promotion season as well, which was the icing on the cake.

The first season back in the top flight was quite eventful for me because at the start of that season Graham Taylor signed Chris Price who was a specialist right-back. I was a little bit concerned thinking what the hell's going on here, what's going to happen to me, especially having played every single game, I thought I'd done all right. I didn't go storming in the office, I didn't even go and see Graham, I thought I'll see how it's going to pan out and bide my time. As it turned out he had an idea that I could play midfield. I think he wanted extra cover for right-back and to see how the season went with an idea of maybe using me occasionally in midfield. After a couple or three weeks we played Birmingham City in the League Cup and he gave me a run out in midfield.

I hadn't played midfield for a good spell of time or consistently for a couple of years and it really got my juices flowing again, I found myself rolling back the years to my early days of Wimbledon, in midfield and I really enjoyed it. I think I did all right and basically turned from right-back to a midfield position, myself and Gordon Cowans along with David Platt occasionally. So for a long part of that season I was used in the centre of midfield and I was doing really well.

Taylor changed the team throughout the campaign but Gage was consistently played in a central role due to the aggression and bite he brought to the midfield not to mention the telling passes he could deliver. Those attributes stemming from his Wimbledon days.

The way I was brought up there we liked to play forward whenever we could. People, even pundits assume we just whacked it forward, you don't get anywhere by just booting it upfield. When we got the ball we were looking forward all the time, rather than just playing a five or ten yard pass, square or backwards. Hopefully I injected a bit of positivity into the side and obviously I liked to get stuck in. Gordon Cowans liked to tackle as well, he's not physically the strongest, I probably added a little bit more physicality into the midfield.

I really found my feet and some form, scored a couple of goals as well, which is nice and everything was going brilliantly well until we get to Millwall away and I got badly injured. I got a late, over the top tackle from Kevin O' Callaghan and I was stretchered off in the first half. I'd ruptured all my knee ligaments and cartilage, that put me out for the rest of that season. Not a good time for me personally to be out of action, I was an integral part of the team so that's the last thing we needed. We stayed up and I was still injured at the start of next season because I had to have an operation on the knee so I was out of action for about six months.

There was a long period when I was injured where I thought I might not get back to the standard I wanted to. I remember the surgeon operating on me, my knee ligaments were completely ruptured, he said: "We've only just pioneered this kind of surgery in the last couple of years, five years ago your career might have struggled." It was just a relief to get back fully fit and back in the team and obviously the way the season went it was fantastic.

So obviously you miss pre-season and then you're playing catch up trying to get fit again until you can get back into first-team action. My first game back in the first team was Spurs at home, we beat them two-nil. I remember it because I was in midfield against Gascoigne

That season we got on a bit of a roller coaster. We hit on this formation with the three centre-backs. Tony Daley was flying up front and Ian Olney was playing fantastically well as a lone striker. He was crucial to our system because he held the ball up so well, not massively quick or fantastic in the air but just perfect for us, we could knock the ball up to him and he'd get hold of it and we could feed Daley or Ormondroyd; or Platt making his runs and scoring goals for fun. We had Cowans probing from midfield, I started off there then I was I moved to wingback, either on the right or the left hand side. Beating Manchester United, Arsenal and Chelsea was an amazing sequence and I remember them because I scored against United and at Chelsea."

After going top with a win at White Hart Lane in the week it was a given that Villa would extend their lead at the top to five points on the Saturday, the opposition Kevin's former side Wimbledon. Lawrie Sanchez brought Gage down for the penalty which Platt - who you'd bet your house on – hit down the middle and watched in horror as it was saved. "You can imagine how galling that was for me" said Gage.

It was a fantastic season for everybody connected with Aston Villa, though unfortunately it kind of petered out and we lost a bit of momentum at the end. For me personally, I was relieved just to get my career back. No matter what, it was a fantastic season for everybody involved.

Villa's meteoric runners-up season hadn't yet finished (the 3-3 draw at Goodison Park brought the curtain down on the 1989/90 campaign) but the supporters knew they would be losing their leader to the England job.

I was pleased for him but personally I was really disappointed, gutted to be honest. He was such a great manager and I got on so well with him, he obviously thought highly of me. Disappointed from a club point of view too, because we wanted to build on what we'd achieved in that season.

Graham leaving left everything up in the air. Who are we going to get? That summer wasn't fantastic because there was a lot of speculation as to who was coming in. Josef Venglos came, he'd managed the Czechoslovakian side in the summer's World Cup.

Unfortunately his communication skills were not good enough, on the training pitch, in team meetings, he just couldn't get across what he wanted to say. The difference between Graham Taylor's communication skills and his team talks and then moving straight to Josef Venglos – it was like chalk and cheese. It was so far apart from what we'd been used to with Graham it was very difficult for us.

For me personally I couldn't come to terms with Josef Venglos I have to be honest. I was a shadow of my former self. I was fit, I was doing the job and I would always give 100% but I couldn't get going and I don't think Dr Jo knew where to play me, he didn't know whether to play me as a full-back or whether I was a midfield player and I kept getting chopped and changed. There were a couple of niggly injuries as well. That season was a bit of a write off for me.

Under Dr Jo, Kevin's first three games were in the centre-forwards jersey. "I can hang my hat on the fact I followed in the line of great Villa No 9s" - even though he never played upfront. "That season was a bit of a wash out for me and then Venglos left after a year."

Ron Atkinson came in, again a lot of speculation as to what was going to happen. I was open minded. I obviously knew of him, he probably knew of me. But I think what happened with Ron Atkinson is he had preconceived ideas about who he wanted to get rid of, and who he wanted to remain in that team and within the squad. Very similar to what Graham Taylor had to do, he needed to rebuild the squad and the team with his own men.

I got myself super fit because I knew a new manager was coming in, I wanted to be absolutely right as rain. There was one pre-season game, we were in Germany, I played midfield and I thought I was outstanding, absolutely superb. Ron Atkinson didn't see that game. I know his coaches told him, and yet there were a couple of times at the start of the season, one game especially, where we were really struggling for midfield players. Kevin Richardson must have been injured, there must have been other injuries and there was literally no one else to play midfield but me. And what happened, the coaches told Ron Atkinson: "Just play Kevin Gage, Gagey can play midfield." "He didn't, he played Kent Nielson in central midfield in front of me. It became clear to me very quickly, that whatever I did, I wasn't going to get a place in the squad - as simple as that. It wasn't just myself, there was Stuart Gray, I think Mountfield was one of them, Ormondroyd, there were a couple of others as well, who were stuck in the reserves and just forgotten about. I thought well that's it, I'm finished here, completely wasting my time. I knew the writing was on the wall. And then he even stopped playing me in the reserves so I wasn't even getting a game in the last couple of weeks. It was a very frustrating time for me, bearing in mind, I'd done nothing to upset him.

I didn't go around throwing my weight about or moaning to the papers or anything, I just wanted to play. So unfortunately my time at Villa came to an end and not the way I wanted it to happen. Players don't get played, they get frozen out and then moved on and that's what happened to me. What made it difficult, it was the very first time it had happened to me because all the way through my career, being in the first team, playing and being part of successful teams, I'd never had to suffer being dropped and stuck in the reserves and going nowhere, so I took it quite hard to be honest - difficult times!

It doesn't sour my time at Villa. I look back and my overriding reactions are of fantastic times. I look back on it with fond memories all the way through. I don't even dwell on the times with Atkinson because I wasn't a Villa player - there in name only. I was never going to get a game so in my time at Villa I don't even count that last six months.

Jimmy Rimmer

Goalkeeper

Born; Southport, 10th February 1948

Made his mark at Old Trafford where he was an amateur before signing apprentice and professional contracts. Was on the bench when the Manchester side lifted the European Cup in 1968 so received a coveted medal. He spent three and a half years at Arsenal before Ron Saunders brought him to Villa Park in August 1977. He immediately displaced John Burridge between the posts. Missed only two league games in a five season spell. Was ever-present when Villa landed the title in 1981 and was instrumental when they lifted the European Cup in 1982, none more so than his vital penalty save away to Dynamo Berlin. Remembered for having to leave the Rotterdam pitch early in the Final to be replaced by Nigel Spink. Won Under 23 honours and a solitary full England cap.

287 appearances (0 sub) 0 goals

Kenny Swain

Inside-forward/full-back

Born; Birkenhead, 28th January 1952

Played in the same Kirkby Boys side as a certain Dennis Mortimer. Initially signed as a forward to play alongside John Deehan due to Brian Little being injured. Kenny cost the Villa £100,000 when he made the switch from Chelsea. When John Gidman left for Everton, Ron Saunders moved Swain to the right-back position where he is more fondly remembered by Villa supporters. Was one of seven ever-presents during Villa's title winning campaign of 1980/81 and starred in the 1982 European Cup final in Rotterdam where he headed one Bayern effort off the line! After being told regular first-team action couldn't be guaranteed under manager Tony Barton, Kenny was quickly snapped up by Brian Clough for his Nottingham Forest side.

179 appearances (inc 0 sub) 5 goals

Eamonn Deacy

Full-back

Born; Galway, Ireland, 1st October 1958

Signed from Galway Rovers in March 1979 after writing to Villa asking for a trial. Made his debut coming on for the injured David Geddis in a 2-1 win at White Hart Lane in December 1979. Featured in ten of Villa's matches during their title winning 1980/81 campaign. Scored his only goal in claret and blue during a 3-2 win at home to Norwich City, March '83. A humble guy, loved by his team-mates, who sadly passed away in Galway 2012. Galway FC's ground Terryland Park has since been renamed Eamonn Deacy Park in recognition of the area's famous son.

41 appearances (inc 11 sub) 1 goal

Gary Williams

Defender

Born; Wolverhampton, 17th June 1960

Came to Villa Park as an apprentice. Signed pro forms within two years at the time he captained Villa's Youth Cup final team (as a centre-half) who lost narrowly to Crystal Palace. Gary could also play in midfield but made his name at full-back. Spent numerous seasons vying for the left-back shirt with Colin Gibson before partnering him, Gary switching to the right. Williams won a First Division title medal in 1981 to go with future European Cup and Super Cup gongs. Had a brief loan spell at Walsall before leaving for Leeds United in 1987. Injury ruled out his chance of Under 21 honours with England.

302 appearances (inc 5 sub) 2 goals

Ken McNaught

Centre-half

Born; Kirkcaldy, Fife, 17th January 1955

The son of Scottish international Willie McNaught. Taken on as an apprentice at Goodison Park in July 1971 and made a pro within ten months. Totally dominating in the air Ken took no prisoners. His outstanding performances for Everton in the 1977 League Cup final matches – against you know who – led to Ron Saunders clinching his signature in a £200,000 move. Had his work cut out to win the Villa Park faithful around after taking Chris Nicholl's place in the side. Once McNaught was accustomed to, what for him was an alien role initially in Villa's defence alongside Leighton Phillips, he commanded respect. He and Allan Evans were possibly one of the best centre-half pairings throughout Europe. Ever-present in the 1981 title campaign and a stalwart in Villa's impressive European odyssey the following season. Captained the side to victory (and scoring) against the mighty Barcelona in the 1983 European Super Cup. Gained amateur and youth honours with Scotland. Still seen around B6 as he runs the 'Lions & Legends,' a team made up of former Aston Villa stars who play matches for charity.

260 appearances (inc 0 sub) 13 goals

Dennis Mortimer

Midfielder

Born; Liverpool, 5th April 1952

Started his career playing in the same Kirkby Boys team as future teammate Kenny Swain. He signed on apprentice terms at Highfield Road in 1967 and was rewarded with a pro contract two years later. He amassed over 200 appearances for Coventry City before Ron Saunders signed him in December 1975 as 'a present for the supporters.' A very underrated player, Dennis had the lot, vision, skill and determination. Picked up a League Cup winners gong in 1977 before leading the club to their first title in 71 years. Mortimer was one of seven ever-presents in that magical 1980/81 season. Eclipsed the title win by landing the European Cup at the first time of asking in 1982. Was capped at youth and Under 23 level with England yet amazingly he only gained an England 'B' cap at senior level. Only a handful of players (nine) have appeared more in the Villa jersey.

406 appearances (inc 1 sub) 36 goals

Des Bremner

Midfielder

Born; Aberchider, Aberdeenshire, 7th September 1962

The likable Scot came down from Hibernian in a deal that sent Joe Ward the other way. From making his debut in a home draw with Arsenal (September 1979), Des was an ever-present for the rest of the season. His work rate, tackling and passing very evident from the terraces and well received and respected by his team-mates. Capped only once at senior level with Scotland (a travesty) and a handful of appearances with the U23s. Bremner would be one of the final pieces of the Villa jigsaw that dominated football in the early 1980s, winning League championship, European Cup and Super Cup gongs in the process. Left the Villa for bitter rivals Birmingham in October 1984.

227 appearances (inc 5 sub) 10 goals

Gary Shaw

Striker

Born; Kingshurst, Birmingham, 21st January 1961

Prolific scorer at school and District level. Villa signed him on in July 1977 as an apprentice and as a professional 18 months later. After hitting the back of the net regularly for the reserves (22 all told during '78/79) he turned out a few times for the first-team but showed glimpses of his true potential when he was given an extended run the following year and rewarded Saunders faith by bagging goals in all three domestic competitions. His partnership with Peter Withe was key to Aston Villa's successful title bid of 1981 and the following year the pair took Europe by storm and landed the biggest trophy in club football. Gary was voted PFA 'Young Player of the Year' in 1981 and 'Outstanding Young European Player of the Year' in 1982. Sadly for Shaw, the Villa and football in general, the blonde haired striker was injured in September '83 in a league game at Nottingham Forest. He required operations on his damaged knee on no less than six occasions. He played on at Villa Park, but a former shadow of what he'd been, soldiered on albeit briefly at numerous other clubs before making a new career for himself working with OPTA (football match stats) and radio commentary. It was England's loss the lad was only capped at Youth and Under 21 level.

213 appearances (inc 9 sub) 79 goals

Peter Withe

Forward

Born; Liverpool 30th August 1951

Signed from Newcastle United in 1980 for a club record fee of £500,000, turning down his boyhood team Everton in the process. Described by manager Ron Saunders at the time as the 'last piece of the jigsaw.' Saunders was proved correct as Villa swept to the First Division championship in 1981, their first title in 70 years, Withe scoring 20 of the goals. His young partner in crime was Gary Shaw (scored 18) and they went together like bacon and eggs according to the club's video. Withe a journeyman played in many outposts; South Africa (Arcadia Shepherds), Wolverhampton (Wolves), USA (Portland Timbers), Birmingham City and also played under the magician Brian Clough at Nottingham Forest. Withe's name is part of Villa folklore having scored the decisive goal against the might of Bayern Munich to land the 1982 European Cup final. Later coached and managed in the game.

233 Appearances (inc 0 sub) 92 goals

Gordon Cowans

Midfielder

Born; Cornforth, Durham 27th October 1958

Cowans came through the Aston Villa youth team in the mid 1970s and questionably the best player to do so. Gordon rose quickly and in his second season he was part of the side that beat Ipswich Town 5-2 (over two legs) in the Southern Junior Floodlight Cup, also turning out for the reserves. In February 1976 Gordon made his first-team debut away to Manchester City coming on as substitute, this being his only appearance that season.1976/77 would start slowly for him but would finish with his second piece of silverware when he played in both replays of the League Cup final vs Everton. By the start of the 1980s Gordon was a fully fledged member of the team which went on to win the First Division championship followed by the European Cup 1982 and the European Super Cup 1983. During pre-season 1983 he broke his leg and missed the whole of the campaign before returning for 1984/85. At the end of that season he departed for Italian side Bari. After three seasons he returned to Villa Park and helped the team cement their place in the top flight following promotion. The side kicked on and made a charge for the title in 1989/90, finishing second to champions Liverpool. In November 1991 he was sold to Blackburn Rovers but returned for a third spell before playing his last match for the club in 1993.

527 appearances (inc 22 sub) 59 goals

Tony Morley

Winger

Born; Ormskirk, 26th August 1954

Started out at Preston North End. In his time at Deepdale he helped England Youth win the mini-World Cup - defeating East Germany in Italy – and gained Under 23 honours. Turned down the chance to go to Arsenal, instead landing up at Turf Moor. Had three successful seasons at Burnley before signing for the Villa in the summer of 1979. Played sporadically in his first season but was ever-present in Villa's title success of 1981, playing as an old fashioned left-winger though he was naturally right-footed, where he not only supplied the ammunition for the deadly partnership of Shaw and Withe but weighed in with vital league and cup goals (12 in all). Was Villa's leading scorer in the triumphant European Cup campaign of 1982 and supplied the cross for Withe to score the only goal in the Final versus Bayern Munich. A crowd favourite at B6 who like others, was pushed out of Villa Park far too soon.

180 appearances (inc 10 sub) 34 goals

Colin Gibson

Left-back/midfielder

Born; Bridport, 6th April 1960

Was a Youth Training Scheme product but signed pro within two years (Oct 1978). Weeks later Colin had a brief run-out in a Villa shirt at Bristol

City when he replaced Allan Evans. Had an extended run, playing in the remaining 11 fixtures of the season following injury to left-back Williams. Started both the following campaigns as first choice in the No 3 jersey ('79/80 & '80/81) earning a League champions medal for his efforts. Starred in the Charity Shield at Wembley, early rounds on the 1982 European Cup trail and also played in the Super Cup clashes with Barcelona. Moved to a midfield role as Williams claimed the left-back berth. Joined Manchester United in a big figure deal - £275,000 - in November 1985. Capped at three different levels for England, Youth U21 and 'B.'

238 appearances (inc 5 sub) 17 goals

Allan Evans
Forward/Centre-half
Born; West Calder, West Lothian, 12th October 1956

A promising striker signed from Dunfermline Athletic in June 1977, a steal at only £30,000. During a run of Central League appearances Allan rattled in 9 goals inc six in one match (Sheff Utd, Feb '78). This had Saunders sitting up and taking notice. Evans made his full league debut weeks later in a drab 0-0 draw with bottom side Leicester City, having come off the bench against Barcelona four days earlier in the UEFA Cup quarter-finals. In spite of his prowess in front of goal, the Villa boss pulled off a masterstroke pairing him with fellow Scot Ken McNaught at centre-half. These two would form the cornerstone of the future title and European Cup winning side's defence. Diagnosed with Crohn's Disease in his last year at the Villa, Graham Taylor wouldn't renew his contract. Allan gained his 'A' and UEFA Licences and coached for a time in Canada. After various other appointments he ended up back at Villa Park, along with John Gregory to assist new manager Brian Little. Only Charlie Aitken 660, Billy Walker 531, and Gordon Cowans 527 have bettered Allan's 475 first-class appearances in claret and blue!

475 appearances (inc 9 sub) 62 goals

Dave Geddis
Forward
Born; Carlisle, 12th March 1958

Won an F.A. Cup winners medal with Ipswich Town in their surprise victory over Arsenal, May 1978. Ron Saunders signed Geddis in September 1979 for a club record fee of £300,000 following the departures of strikers Gray and Deehan. Found goals hard to come by scoring only three in 24 appearances in his first campaign at Villa Park. Due to Peter Withe's arrival in May 1980, David found himself down the pecking order somewhat but when required he came up with the goods during the 1980/81 title winning season scoring four vital goals in only eight starts. Gained England caps at Youth and B-level.

57 appearances (inc 5 sub) 16 goals

Andy Blair
Midfielder
Born; Kirkcaldy, 18th December 1959

Joined the newly crowned champions in the summer of 1981 from Coventry City for a fee of £300,000, set by a Football League tribunal.

His competitive debut was as a sub in the Charity Shield, a result shared with Tottenham Hotspur after a 2-2 draw, so too the shield. Andy would finish the season with another winners medal as an unused sub in the European Cup final. Was used sparingly during his three seasons before moving to Sheffield Wednesday in the close season of 1984, before returning to Villa Park in March 1986 to help stave of relegation. During his second spell at the club would feature in less matches and suffered with injury. Would eventually retire from the game with knee issues.

69 appearances (inc 15 sub) 2 goals

Brendan Ormsby

Defender

Born; Birmingham, 1st October 1960

Initially arriving at Villa Park in 1976 joining the ranks as an apprentice before turning professional two years later. Made his debut April 1979 at home to Derby County in an entertaining 3-3 draw. During 1979/80 he would appear a total of 25 times in the first team during a transitional season for the club and wouldn't play the following season due to the partnership of Evans and McNaught when only 14 players were used. Brendan would come to the fore in 1983/84 when McNaught moved on to WBA. In an away match at West Ham United (1984/85) he scored a goal from just inside the Hammers' half with a 45-yarder. Ormsby left the club for Leeds United in February 1986.

140 appearances (inc 4 sub) 7 goals

Terry Donovan

Centre-forward

Born; Liverpool, 27th February 1958

Villa signed the prolific Grimsby Town striker in September 1979 at a cost of £75,000. Donovan had to wait until December of that year to make his first-team start for Villa though it was a dream debut, scoring the opener in the 3-0 home demolition of Coventry City. Emulated his father Don Donovan when he was called up for the Republic of Ireland, winning two caps in his time at Villa Park. Scored vital goals in the early stages of the European Cup as well as a phenomenal amount for the reserves in the Central League (70 in only 120 games) but left for pastures new before the final itself; a loan spell in the States with Portland Timbers among his many ports of call.

24 appearances (inc 0 sub) 11 goals

Ivor Linton

Midfielder

Born; West Bromwich, 20th November 1959

Following an initial trial and the mandatory apprenticeship Ivor was handed a pro contract in September 1977. The following term he was one of the stars of Villa's FA Youth Cup run which ended in Final defeat. Had a couple of first-team run outs at the tail end of the 1976/7 season and did likewise in the following two campaigns. During 1978/9 Linton featured in 16 league and cup matches before making the journey to Peterborough's London Road. Later made a bit of a name for himself in Finland where he played for a couple of sides.

30 appearances (inc 13 sub) 0 goals

Noel Blake

Defender

Born; Jamaica, 12th January 1962

Signed professionally in August 1979 after two years with local side Sutton Coldfield. Appeared over 30 times in the Central League during '79/80, scoring twice. Given his first-team start at home to Spurs (April '80) in that same season and also played in the remaining two games. Blake would make only one more appearance in claret and blue (December 1981) before joining near neighbours Birmingham City in September 1982 in a deal worth £55,000.

4 appearances (inc 0 sub) 0 goals

Terry Bullivant

Midfielder

Born; Lambeth, London, 23rd September 1956

Landed from Fulham, November 1979, in a deal worth £220,000 for 'The Cottagers.' Was used sparingly during the 1979/80 campaign (a total of only seven league and cup apps), didn't feature at all during the title win the following year and was only given limited games in his last season at Villa Park. Unsuccessful at landing a regular place in the side Terry moved back to London, signing for Brentford, July '83.

15 appearances (inc 4 sub) 0 goals

Gary Shelton

Midfielder

Born; Nottingham, 21st March 1958

Joined Walsall as an apprentice and signed professional forms two years later in 1976. Came to Villa's notice and signed in January 1978 for a fee of £60,000, but had to wait until the first game of the 1978/79 campaign (home to Wolves) to make his debut. Scored in the following game, a surprise 4-1 win at White Hart Lane when Villa upstaged the well documented arrival of Argentine World Cup stars Osvaldo Ardiles and Ricardo Villa. Shelton only featured four times in the 1979/80 season, none the following year when Villa won the title using only 14 players and after a solitary appearance during 1981/82 he left for Sheffield Wednesday. Gained an England U21 cap in his time at Hillsborough.

27 appearances (inc 1 sub) 8 goals

Mark Jones

Defender

Born; Warley, 22nd October 1961

Joined the club in the summer of 1977 as an apprentice before signing professional terms in summer 1979. Was part of the very successful youth team that won the 1980 Youth Cup with fellow future first-team players Noel Blake, Paul Birch, Robert Hopkins, Ray Walker and Mark Walters. Jones would make his first team debut in a 2-1 home win over Coventry City. The following season would be his most productive in claret and blue appearing 24 times including the first-leg of the European Super Cup final away to Barcelona.1983/84 would be his last season at Villa Park before transferring to Brighton in March 1984, being valued at £50,000 with Steve Foster coming in the other direction for £200,000.

33 appearances (inc 0 sub) 0 goals

Pat Heard

Defender

Born; Hull, East Riding of Yorkshire, 17th March 1960

Pat joined Villa from Everton in October 1979 as part of the deal that saw want-away full-back John Gidman go to Goodison. After turning in good performances in the Central League (1979/80), weighing in with a solitary goal, Pat was thrown in against Norwich City in the 2-0 home win in early April. He played well enough to remain in the side for the remaining eight fixtures of the season. Was unable to get a game during the halcyon title winning campaign but was back in the action for the 1981/82 season, scoring too. The pinnacle of his career undoubtedly was as a substitute (albeit unused) for the 1982 European Cup final in Rotterdam. A steady player who could always be relied on when called into the action. Left for Hillsborough, January 1983.

27 appearances (inc 6 sub) 2 goals

Mark Walters

Winger

Born; Birmingham, 2nd June 1964

Signed on as an apprentice in the summer of 1980 but had already played for the youth team the previous season where he was part of the side that lifted the F.A. Youth Cup. Signing professionally the following year having turned 17. Made his first-team debut at the end of 1981-82 season in a home defeat to Leeds United. Walters would start to be integrated into the side during 1982-83 and would come on as sub during the second leg at home to Barcelona in the European Super Cup final, won on the night 3-0 for a 3-1 aggregate victory. Mark would be the main man on the wing for the next five seasons once Tony Morley left for WBA, scoring many memorable goals from the wing. Moved to Rangers half way through 1987/88, gaining five winners medals during his time at Ibrox.

225 appearances (inc 18 sub) 48 goals

Nigel Spink

Goalkeeper

Born; Chelmsford, 8th August 1958

Was signed from Chelmsford City (a top Southern League side) for the sum of £4,000 in January 1977 after impressing Tony Barton. Behind both Burridge and Findlay, Spink was pushed further down the pecking order with the arrival of Jimmy Rimmer. Made his long-awaited debut away to European Cup winners Nottingham Forest on Boxing Day 1979. Ironically Nigel would wait another three years before getting a second game in

Villa colours, impressing Barton once again and seeing his name in the headlines all over the world. Replacing Rimmer after only nine minutes, Nigel was unfazed and held everything Bayern Munich could throw at him in the 1982 European Cup final. A superb shot-stopper, no keeper has played more in claret and blue (green technically speaking) though he came on as an outfield player for the injured Ian Taylor at QPR in his last game. Disgraceful he won only a solitary England cap!

460 appearances (inc 5 sub) 0 goals

Robert Hopkins

Midfielder

Born; Hall Green, Birmingham, 25th October 1961

Came to Villa Park as an apprentice and signed professional terms two years later in July 1979. Played over 20 times for the reserve side in his first season, scoring on the odd occasion. An F.A. Youth Cup winner with Aston Villa in 1980 and scored on his first-team debut at home to Norwich in March 1980 with his only kick of the game. Hopkins had a terrible disciplinary record and took great delight in broadcasting the fact he played for Villa with a Birmingham City badge pinned to his shirt! He joined Blues in 1983.

3 appearances (inc 2 sub) 1 goal

Alan Curbishley

Midfield

Born; Forest Gate, 8th November 1957

A classy midfield player who started his career with his local Club West Ham United where he spent four years before joining Villa's neighbours Birmingham City. He was there for four years also, making more than 100 appearances. In March 1983 he crossed the city to join Aston Villa in a deal that saw Blues get £100,000 and Robert Hopkins. Curbishley would play in the first team for the remainder of the season helping the club to reach Europe for 1983/84, qualifying for the UEFA Cup and play regularly in the side until the end of March during which time he scored his only goal in the away defeat to Watford. In 1984/85 he played only three times before moving to Charlton Athletic where he would end his playing career, though spending time at Brighton in-between his two spells at the Valley.

43 appearances (inc 2 sub) 1 goal

Ray Walker

Midfield

Born; North Shields, 28th September 1963

Joined Aston Villa as an apprentice July 1979 and in his first season would be an F.A. Youth Cup winner along with Birch, Hopkins and Walters. Ray would make his first-team debut in 1982/83 at West Ham United's Upton Park ground in a 0-2 loss. Over the next three seasons he played 17 times as well as nine from the sub's bench. He initially joined Port Vale on loan November 1984 before returning on a permanent move in July 1986 for a bargain £12,000 and would establish himself as a Port Vale legend spending the next 11 years at Vale Park before winding down with local non-League sides Leek Town and Newcastle Town.

27 appearances (inc 9 sub) 0 goals

Paul Birch

Midfield

Born; West Bromwich, 20th November 1962

Died Sutton Coldfield, 2nd February 2009

Another one of our successful youth products from the 1979/80 period. Initially joining as an apprentice in summer 1978 before turning professional two years later. Another player part of the victorious youth team that won the F.A. Youth Cup 1980. Made his first-team debut in the European Super Cup final second leg vs Barcelona when he came off the bench. A very underrated and tenacious player with a fair amount of skill, he became a mainstay of the team until end of 1987/88 season. In the last three seasons Paul was a bit-part player but during his last season 1990/91 he put in two magnificent performances when he nullified the threat of both Paul Gascoigne of Tottenham and Lothar Matthaus of Inter Milan. Moved to Wolverhampton Wanderers March 1991 staying five years at Molineux. Paul sadly died at the young age of 46 after a battle with bone cancer. His memory lives on in the "Spinky and Birchy, Alan McInally" chant that regularly rings round Villa Park.

223 appearances (inc 31 sub) 25 goals

Steve McMahon

Midfield

Born; Liverpool, 20th August 1961

Started as an apprentice with Everton in the summer of 1977, signing professional forms two years later, Steve played more than 100 times for The Toffees and would wear the captain's armband with distinction. In 1983 Tony Barton fought off a determined Liverpool to capture the combative McMahon for the Villa. During his time in Aston the team was in transition with the old guard of League and European champions being moved on to pastures new. Settling quickly into the side and establishing himself as a top-notch player the side could only finish in 10th place, which was also repeated the following season. With only three matches of the 1985/86 season played McMahon got the move he desired, Liverpool. Whilst at Anfield he would win three League titles, two F.A. Cups and play for England.

91 appearances (inc 1 sub) 7 goals

Paul Rideout

Striker

Born; Bournemouth, 14th August 1964

Signed from Swindon Town in the summer of 1983 along with Steve McMahon from Everton. Starting the 1980/81 season as a 16-year-old Paul was thrust into Swindon's first team, being their youngest ever player to do so. He appeared 16 times and find the back of the net on four occasions that first season. In his two seasons at Villa Park the club would finish 10th both campaigns. During his first season he was understudy to Peter Withe with five goals from 25 League appearances, the following season was much better when he scored 14 in 29 League matches. At the season's end he was sold along with Gordon Cowans to Italian club Bari who had been suitably impressed with Paul's displays during the season. Later on having returned to England he would score the winner for Everton in the 1995 F.A. Cup final.

63 appearances (inc 7 sub) 22 goals

Mervyn Day

Goalkeeper

Born; Chelmsford, 26th June 1955

He started out at West Ham United as a youth player in July 1971 before signing pro forms in February 1973. He played over 200 matches for The Hammers and was in the 1975 F.A. Cup final winning side. Later on he lost his place through injury and couldn't reclaim his spot due to Phil Parkes performances, so he moved to Leyton Orient where he remained for five years. From Brisbane Road he arrived at Villa Park in the close season of 1983. Was brought in to challenge Nigel Spink for the number one spot. At the end of his first season he got a run of 11 matches to showcase his ability and stayed in the side with another straight 18 appearances when he was suddenly dropped and sold to Leeds United. He established himself as number one at Elland Road for the next eight seasons.

33 appearances (inc 0 sub) 0 goals

Steve Foster

Defender

Born; Portsmouth, 24th September 1957

England defender Foster arrived from Brighton in March 1984, Mark Jones going in the other direction. A commanding centre-half which manager Tony Barton had been searching for ever since McNaught left for WBA. His career started at Portsmouth as an apprentice in 1973, turning pro in 1975, playing over 100 times before moving onto Brighton in July 1979. He established himself in the heart of Brighton's defence helping them to the 1983 F.A. Cup final which they lost in a replay to Manchester United. His stay with Villa was short lived, less than a year and only 15 appearances in the league before moving to Luton Town. A big signing at the time which didn't really work out.

17 appearances (inc 0 sub) 3 goals

Paul Kerr

Forward

Born; Portsmouth, 9th June 1964

Another product of the Aston Villa youth system having signed as an apprentice in June 1980, signing pro forms two years later. A prolific scorer for both youth and reserves. He made his debut as a sub in a 0-2 defeat at Leicester City 1983/84 and his full debut the next month. The following season he managed to score two goals in his first game of the campaign in a League Cup tie at Scunthorpe United in a 3-2 win.

Would be used sparingly over the next two seasons and in January 1987 moved to Middlesbrough, who he helped gain promotion finishing 2nd in Division Three.

35 appearances (inc 12 sub) 6 goals

Tony Dorigo

Defender

Born; Melbourne, Australia, 31th December 1965

Signed as an apprentice before turning professional with Villa in 1982 after having written letters to the club asking for a trial. After progressing through the youth and reserve teams he made his debut as a sub in the last match of the 1983/84 season away to Ipswich Town. The following three seasons saw Tony establish himself as first choice left-back in a side slowly sliding each year. After qualifying as a British citizen he was picked to play for the England U-21's and later for the full side, but only after leaving for Chelsea in the summer of 1987. Villa had been relegated at this stage. Chelsea would suffer the same fate 12 months later.

135 appearances (inc 6 sub) 1 goal

Dean Glover

Defender

Born; Birmingham, 29th December 1963

Centre-Half Dean initially joined as a 14-year-old schoolboy, would later sign as an apprentice and then professional forms in December 1981. He made his debut two years later versus Norwich City in a 3rd round F.A. Cup replay at Carrow Road. This his only appearance in 1983-84.

Dean's most prolific season was 1985/86 appearing 24 (+3 as sub) times and featuring in all but the 1st round of the League Cup, losing to Oxford United in the semis. He appeared a few times the following season as the club hurtled towards relegation. He moved to Middlesbrough in 1987 where in his second season he'd help them to promotion to the First Division before moving on again to Port Vale where he became a legend during his nine seasons at Vale Park.

39 appearances (inc 3 sub) 1 goal

Didier Six

Left Winger

Born; Lille, France, 21st August 1954

French superstar Didier Six arrived at Villa Park in October 1984 from French club Mulhouse having starred in the France team that won the Euros that summer. A very skilful and tricky left-winger whose signing was greeted with great excitement by the Villa Park faithful. His debut display at home to Manchester United as Villa won 3-0 was electrifying, unfortunately it wasn't sustained and would be the highlight of his career in claret and blue. Didier then suffered a bad ankle injury which led to Mark Walters taking his place in the side. His brief stay in English football ended that summer when he returned to French side Metz and led to a nomadic existence until he retired from playing in 1992.

18 appearances (inc 4 sub) 2 goals

David Norton

Defender

Born; Cannock, 3rd March 1965

David arrived at League Champions Aston Villa in June 1981 as an apprentice and would go onto sign a professional contract aged 18. An England Youth International, the club had high hopes and he made his debut in an away victory at Coventry City, then the following week in a home win vs Ipswich Town these being his only appearances in 1984-85. David appeared over 20 times, in both following seasons mainly playing at right-back in a struggling side which would suffer relegation in May 1987. During the promotion campaign he played only twice more for the club before being sold to Notts County during the close season of 1988. Also had a good career in the lower leagues with Hull City, Northampton Town and Hereford United.

57 appearances (inc 3 sub) 2 goals

Darren Bradley

Midfielder

Born; Birmingham, 24th November 1965

Darren joined newly crowned European Champions Aston Villa in June 1982 as an apprentice before joining the professional ranks 18 months later. Making his debut from the bench away to Norwich City in March 1985. His full debut came at Sunderland in a 2-0 win which helped send the Mackems down. 1985/86 would see Darren playing 18 (+3 sub) times, mainly in the No 6 shirt which Mortimer had made his own for the last decade. Bradley would be a makeweight in the deal to resign former player Steve Hunt from West Brom as the club fought a desperate battle with relegation. A mainstay at the Hawthorns over the next nine seasons and also captain before ending his career at Walsall.

23 appearances (inc 4 sub) 0 goals

Kevin Poole

Goalkeeper

Born; Bromsgrove, 21st July 1963

Goalkeeper Kevin joined Villa in the summer of 1979 as an apprentice before turning pro two years later. He didn't make his debut until the end of the 1984/85 season when he replaced Nigel Spink for seven of the last ten matches of the campaign, keeping four clean sheets. The following two seasons he battled with Spink to be the club's No 1 keeper. At the beginning of 1987/88 Kevin joined Middlesbrough where he tried and failed to establish himself as the main goalie. This was achieved at his next club, Leicester City where he helped win the 1997 League Cup. He retired from the game at the end of 2013/14 season whilst with Burton Albion.

32 appearances (inc 0 sub) 0 goals

Tony Daley

Winger

Born; Birmingham, 18th October 1967

Local boy Tony joined on a YTS (Youth Training Scheme) in June 1983 before signing professionally. Made his debut at Southampton

towards the end of 1984/85. An electrifying winger who terrified opposing full-backs. The following season he was gradually introduced into the side, playing on the opposite side to fellow local lad Mark Walters. During the relegation season he played three quarters of the matches whilst his Second Division campaign was hampered with injury. He returned to first-team duty and became a regular during the next three seasons, pushing his way into the England reckoning. His last season at Villa Park saw him win a League Cup winners medal as Villa denied Manchester United the treble. That summer he reunited with former boss Graham Taylor at Wolverhampton Wanderers.

290 appearances (inc 49 sub) 38 goals

Andy Gray

Striker

Born; Gorbals, Drumchapel, 30th November 1955

Joined the club from Dundee United for a club record fee of £110,000. Scored on his home debut in a League Cup defeat against Manchester United. The fans loved his cavalier attitude, he was the latest in a long line to grace the iconic No 9 shirt. His return of a goal every three games in a season when he was still finding his feet gave a clue to what his future held. The following season Andy took all that stood before him, he terrorised defences the length and breadth of the country. He plundered 25 league goals in 36 games as well as four in ten cup matches. He walked away with both 'Young Player' and 'Player of the Year' awards in the 1976/77 season, the first time this had been achieved. Behind the scenes all wasn't well in the corridors of B6 and in September 1979 Andrew Mullen Gray joined Wolverhampton Wanderers for a seven figure sum. Won honours at Wolves and Everton before playing for his boyhood team Rangers. Made a return to Villa Park in 1985.

210 appearances (inc 4 sub) 78 goals

Steve Hodge

Midfielder

Born; Nottingham, 25th October 1962

Hodge joined his local club Nottingham Forest as an apprentice in 1980 and rose through the ranks under Brian Clough before finding himself at Aston Villa following a big money move in August 1985. During his debut season in claret and blue Hodge fitted in well and scored ten goals in 48 appearances which culminated in being included in that summer's World Cup finals in Mexico. On his return to club football at Villa the shocking start to the season didn't bode well, nor did it improve after a change of managers with Billy McNeill replacing Graham Turner. Hodge was sold to Tottenham Hotspur in December 1986 for £650,000, wound up having a successful career and being a League title winner with Leeds United.

70 appearances (inc 0 sub) 16 goals

Simon Stainrod

Forward

Born; Sheffield, 1st February 1959

Stainrod was a well travelled forward who played for 11 clubs during a 20-year career plying his trade in France and Scotland as well. Started his career with home town club Sheffield United as a 16-year-old before moving to Oldham Athletic which in turn led to a big money move to Queens Park Rangers in November 1980, scoring 48 in 145 league matches. After a brief stint with Sheffield Wednesday he arrived at Villa Park in September 1985 and had a remarkable debut, scoring four times at Exeter City in a League Cup tie as Villa coasted to a 8-1 victory. In total scoring 21 times in 40 (+2 sub) appearances during his first season with the club. The following year his goal return was far less with only six as the club slid into bottom place and ultimately relegated. Stainrod made only four appearances in the Second Division and moved on to Stoke City.

82 appearances (inc 6 sub) 27 goals

Paul Elliott

Central Defender

Born; London, 18th March 1964

Elliott started his career with Charlton Athletic as an apprentice in the summer of 1980 and appeared 60 odd times before moving on to Luton Town in March 1983. He stayed at Kenilworth Road only two seasons before being prized away by Aston Villa in December 1985 to fill the troublesome slot next to Allan Evans in central defence. He played well during his spell at the club even though it was a struggling team which wound up relegated at the end of his second season. This led to him asking to leave and getting a move to Italian side Pisa for the same fee as was paid for his services. After a couple of seasons in Pisa Elliott returned to Britain and joined Celtic, again for only two seasons before his final move which was back to London and Chelsea before retiring in 1994 due to injury.

69 appearances (inc 1 sub) 7 goals

Steve Hunt

Midfielder

Born; Perry Barr, Birmingham, 4th August 1956

Joined Villa in July 1972 and turned pro in January '74. Made his first-team debut replacing Ian Hamilton at Hillsborough (April '75) in the historic 4-0 win that guaranteed Villa promotion back to the top-flight after an eight year absence. His full debut was in front of a 57,000 Villa Park crowd in the following game (home to Sunderland). Used sparingly over the next two seasons before heading Stateside to play with New York Cosmos of the NASL. After spells at the 'Sky Blues' and the 'Baggies' Steve returned to B6 having won two England caps but couldn't halt the club's slide into Division 2 under Turner and McNeill. Played regularly in the first half of the 1987/88 promotion campaign but was forced to retire prematurely due to recurring knee problems. Later had varying roles in management and coaching.

81 appearances (inc 5 sub) 9 goals

Garry Thompson
Forward
Born; Birmingham, 7th October 1959

Aston Villa fan Thompson started his career as a youth player with Coventry City in 1976 and soon appearing in the Coventry first team averaging just under a goal every three games before moving to West Bromwich Albion where he linked up up with future Villa player Cyrille Regis in a devastating strike partnership scoring 39 in 91 league appearances. After being with Sheffield Wednesday for 1985-86 Thompson joined the club he supported, Aston Villa, in the summer of 1986. Unfortunately his first season ended in relegation but he was an important cog in the squad that returned to Division One at the first time of asking and is fondly remembered for his brace at St Andrews in a 2-1 win. He would end his career at Northampton Town in 1997 having played nearly 500 league matches.

73 appearances (inc 4 sub) 19 goals

Martin Keown
Central Defender
Born; Oxford, 24th July 1966

Young central defender Keown joined Aston Villa in the summer of 1986 from Arsenal where he was highly thought of. He was seen as one for the future at B6. Even though Villa were relegated the experience helped mould him and the club returned at the first time of asking, gaining promotion on the last day of the season at Swindon Town. During his three seasons at Villa Park Keown matured tremendously as a player and moved to Everton at the end of the 1988/89 season, making Villa a big profit in the process. After four years at Goodison Park he returned to Arsenal in 1993 and would win a host of medals as part of the Invicibles.

132 appearances (inc 3 sub) 3 goals

Neale Cooper
Midfielder
Born; Darjeeling, West Bengal, India, 24th November 1963

Cooper grew up in Aberdeen, joined his local club straight from school and would be a first-team regular from the age of 18. Under Alex Ferguson Aberdeen broke the stranglehold the two Glasgow clubs held. Neale won six trophies during his five seasons at Pittodrie as the midfield enforcer. During the summer of 1986 Cooper was enticed to Villa Park but his chapter in English football suffered a faltering start as he was injured in pre-season and wouldn't make his debut until January 1987, a home draw with Nottingham Forest. The season ended in relegation for one of footballings founder members. The 1987/88 campaign started well for Cooper, featuring in seven of the nine matches before injury put paid to his season, his brief time in claret and blue over before it had barely started. Summer 1988 saw Cooper return to Scotland when he joined Rangers.

22 appearances (inc 1 sub) 1 goal

Warren Aspinall

Forward

Born; Wigan, 13th September 1967

Aspinall joined his home team club straight from school and signed pro forms as soon as he turned 17. Was thought of as something special by those in the know and it wasn't long before a very good offer arrived from Everton, joining for £150,000 though being immediately loaned back to Wigan. His career never took off at Goodison Park. Aspinall was signed for Aston Villa by then manager Billy McNeill for a fee of £300,000 whilst still a teenager. Brought in to help stop the club's slide towards relegation he played in 12 matches, notching three goals but it wasn't enough to stave off relegation. Graham Taylor took over the reins at Villa Park for the promotion push and Aspinall started the following season in the first team. Ultimately he would leave the club due to disciplinary problems in August 1988, joining Portsmouth.

50 appearances (inc 5 sub) 16 goals

Phillip Robinson

Midfielder

Born; Stafford, 6th January 1967

Another youth team product that reached the first team if only briefly. Joined the club as an apprentice in June 1983 and then signed professional terms January 1985. Robinson would only appear in the first team on three occasions and was on the losing side on all three. Made his debut in a 0-4 loss at Southampton and then featured in the last two matches of the season as the club slipped into the Second Division.That summer Robinson would move to Wolverhampton Wanderers where he helped them to success in winning both the Fourth and Third Division titles before moving on again, this time to Notts County. A solid lower division player appearing in more than 500 matches.

3 appearances (Inc 1 sub) 1goal

Mark Burke

Winger

Born; Solihull 12 February 1969

One of four young reserve players to make their debut during this very disappointing season of 1986-87. Burke would make his debut in the 0-1 home defeat against Everton this was his only involvement that season. He would be sub and play in a few early season Second Division matches and was transferred to the Villa colony at Ayresome Park. From there he would move to Wolverhampton Wanderers where again his manager was Graham Taylor before embarking on foreign fields playing in Holland, Japan, Romania, Sweden before finishing his career back in the Netherlands.

8 appearances (inc 3 sub) 0 goals

Bernie Gallacher

Left Back

Born; Johnstone, Perthshire Scotland, 22nd March 1967

Joined in June 1983 as an apprentice coming down from Scotland straight from school and signed professionally March 1985. It would be two more years before he made his debut in the first team

when he was played at left-back in the the last match of the season at Manchester United, the club already relegated. The following season Graham Taylor entrusted the young Scot to be his first choice left-back and only missed the one match which was the 1-2 home loss to Oldham Athletic. Over the next three seasons Gallacher was used sparingly in the first team before moving to Doncaster Rovers in 1991, staying only briefly before moving again that year to Brighton and Hove Albion. He retired in 1994 aged 27 due to injury.

72 appearances (inc 3 sub) 1 goal

Stuart Ritchie

Midfielder

Born; Southampton, 20th May 1968

First played for the youth team in 1983/84 making only the one appearance. Ritchie signed apprentice forms summer 1984 before turning professional in 1986. Stuart made his only appearance in the first-team on the last day of the season when he came on for the second half at Manchester United in a 1-3 defeat.That summer he was released and signed for Crewe Alexandra making no first-team appearances before moving to Irish side Waterford United. He returned to England and played non-League football in the south east before becoming a manager.

1 appearance (inc 1 sub) 0 goals

Kevin Gage

Right Back

Born; Chiswick, London, 21st April 1964

One of Graham Taylor's first signings as manager when he came in to sort out the shambles that the club was in. He arrived from Wimbledon having come through their ranks straight from school, making his debut just after his 17th birthday and becoming a fully fledged member of the Crazy Gang. Gage was a mainstay of the side as promotion was gained at the first attempt and would play regularly until injury during 1990-91 season. Gage never figured under Ron Atkinson who promptly sold him to Sheffield United where he teamed up with his old Wimbledon boss Dave Bassett. He retired at the end of 1998-99 season after a 19 year career.

145 appearances (inc 2 sub) 12 goals

Steve Sims

Central Defender

Born; Lincoln, 2nd July 1957

Experienced central defender Sims was brought to Villa Park by old boss Graham Taylor (who signed him for the third time in his career) to help shore up the gaps in a relegated defence. Initially signing for Leicester City in 1973 as an apprentice he played in their first team for three seasons before hooking up with Taylor at Watford. By the time he arrived at Villa Park he was a seasoned professional and would play his part in gaining promotion and establishing the club back in the First Division before moving to non-League Burton Albion after two seasons at Villa Park.

47 appearances (inc 0 sub) 0 goals

David Hunt

Midfielder

Born; Leicester, 17th April 1959

Another experienced player brought in during the summer of 1987 by new manager Taylor having played 336 league games for unfashionable Notts County. A solid unassuming midfield player who featured in the early part of the promotion season until injury prevented him playing. He would not reappear in the first team until March 1989 when he made his only appearance of the season and ultimately his last for the club. That summer Hunt then moved onto pastures new with Mansfield Town.

15 appearances (inc 1 sub) 0 goals

Malcolm Allen

Forward

Born; Deiniolen, Gwynedd, Wales, 21st March 1967

Brought in on loan for a month in September 1987 from Watford by his old manager Graham Taylor. Made his debut alongside other new boy Mark Lillis away to Leicester City, the Villa's first win of the season. He only played four times for the club before returning to Watford, from there he would move on to Norwich City and Millwall, finishing at Newcastle United. Allen represented Wales on 14 occasions scoring three times.

4 appearances (inc 0 sub) 0 goals

Mark Lillis

Forward

Born; Manchester, 17th January 1960

Signed for the club September 1987 from Derby County, going straight into the side to face Leicester City. Lillis scored the second goal in a 2-0 win at Filbert Street.This was the first of four goals he would score for the club all coming in the 1987/88 season during 36 appearances. He would only feature twice the following season, spending exactly two years at Villa Park before moving to Scunthorpe United.

38 appearances (inc 1 sub) 4 goals

Alan McInally

Forward

Born; Ayr, Scotland, 10th February 1963

Scottish forward McInally arrived at Villa Park in the summer 1987 being one of six players signed by new manager Graham Taylor. He got injured in pre-season and would miss the first ten matches of the season before making his debut against Blackburn Rovers at home. McInally would only score six goals in all competitions

in his first season but would take the First Division and Cup competitions by storm in 1988/89 hitting 19 goals in total. One against Millwall in the League Cup was as audacious as it was enthralling and is still talked about in the Villa Park stands to this day. The German giants Bayern Munich came calling the following summer to prise the swashbuckling forward away.

71 appearances (inc 8 sub) 28 goals

Andy Gray

Midfielder

Born; Lambeth, London, 22nd February 1964

Andy joined Aston Villa in November 1987 from his first professional club Crystal Palace. Along with other new signing Stuart Gray he went straight into the side, slotting with ease into the centre of midfield and played a big part in Villa's resounding 4-2 win at Division Two leaders Bradford City. His stay at Villa Park was fairly short, only 18 months in duration before leaving to return to London and joining Queens Park Rangers and making the club a profit of £300,000 in the process. Gray would win one England cap two years after leaving Villa Park when his former manager Taylor picked him.

46 appearances (inc 6 sub) 6 goals

Stuart Gray

Defender/Midfielder

Born; Withernsea, 19th April 1960

Stuart joined at the same time as his namesake Andy Arthur Gray, from Barnsley and starred on his debut away to Bradford City, scoring twice in a thrilling 4-2 win over the division's pacesetters. Stuart would win promotion with Villa at the end of the season when they were runners-up to Champions Millwall. The season back in the top-flight was one of consolidation, with the club staying up by the skin of their teeth. But, the following campaign was a revelation as they pressed Liverpool all the way for the title, but had to settle for second place. Gray was now playing in a defensive role. 1990/91 would see another battle against relegation with new manager Dr Jozef Venglos brought in after Graham Taylor's England calling. He would be be sold in September 1991 by new manager Ron Atkinson who decided on whole scale changes.

132 appearances (inc 7 sub) 15 goals

David Platt

Midfielder

Born; Chadderton, 10th June 1966

David Platt joined his boyhood team Manchester United directly from school. Unable to make the breakthrough he was released by Ron Atkinson in 1985 and joined Crewe Alexandra where he shone as an attacking midfield player. Graham Taylor purchased Platt in early 1988 for £200,000. A figure he claims was over the top as Watford's interest pushed the price up. Five goals in 11 games helped Villa achieve promotion from Division Two. Was the club's leading scorer in 1989/90 with 24 goals as Villa ran out runners-up to Liverpool for the title. He had another good season as Villa struggled under Jozef Venglos putting himself in the shop window with an outstanding display against Inter Milan. Sold for a club record £5.5m as Atkinson took the manager's job at Villa Park. One of the finest players to grace the famous Villa ground.

155 appearances (inc 0 sub) 68 goals

Gareth Williams

Winger

Born; Cowes Isle of Wight, 12th March 1967

Gareth was signed by manager Graham Taylor from non-League Gosport Town for an initial £10,000 in January 1988. A tricky winger, he made his first team debut in a friendly match at Villa Park against a Monaco side which included the likes of Glenn Hoddle and Mark Hateley and managed by the up and coming Arsenal Wenger. Villa ran out 3-0 winners with Gareth scoring one of them. He would play just the once in the league when he turned out at Crystal Palace in a 1-1 draw during the promotion campaign. The following season he would make just two appearances, one as a sub.1989/90 was his best season in the Villa colours, playing a part as Villa beat Manchester United, Arsenal and Chelsea in a fondly remembered purple patch. He would start six with an additional seven appearances from the bench as Villa contended the Division One title. away winning all three. Reserve team football was Gareth's lot in 1990/91 before being sold to Barnsley the following season.

16 appearances (inc 8 sub) 0 goals

Chris Price

Right back

Born; Hereford, 30th March 1960

Chris, an experienced right-back and one of two players that joined Aston Villa in the summer of 1988 on the clubs return to the top flight,the other being Derek Mountfield. Chris started his professional career with home town club Hereford United in 1978 and joined the Villa from Blackburn Rovers after two seasons with them. When making his debut for the club it would be his first taste of top flight football and he took to it like a duck to water. In his first three seasons he played 40+ matches each campaign, his last being 1991/92 where he appeared only four times before being sold back to the Ewood Park outfit. Fondly remembered by the Villa Park faithful in the "Chris Price... he has no hair... but we don't care" terrace anthem.

144 appearances (inc 3 sub) 2 goals

Derek Mountfield

Centre back

Born; Liverpool, 2nd November 1962

Signed in 1988, the vastly experienced central defender Mountfield was part of the very successful Everton side that won a plethora of trophies in the mid 1980s. Derek was an infectious sort of personality who slotted straight into the side as the club battled to

stay up in their first season back in the top flight. In his second season he made up a fantastic back three line with fellow defenders Paul McGrath and Kent Nielsen as they strived for the title but ultimately came in short to Liverpool. The 1990/91 season was one of struggle under new manager Dr Venglos and would last only one season before being replaced by Ron Atkinson. The new boss made sweeping changes, Derek would appear twice more before being shipped out to near neighbours Wolverhampton Wanderers in November 1991, staying three and a half years.

120 appearances (inc 2 sub) 17 goals

Ian Olney

Striker

Born; Luton, 17th December 1969

Ian Olney came through the youth ranks at Villa Park having joined the club in June 1986 as a YTS and signing professional terms in July 1988, having scored 77 goals for the youth and reserve sides during 1986/88. Ian was promoted to the first team during the 1988/89 season when he appeared 18 times, half of those from the bench and finding the net three times. During 1989/90 he spearheaded the attack as the team came second in the league but lost his place in the team when the club decided to buy Tony Cascarino. During his two final seasons at B6 he was primarily the back up centre-forward and would leave to join Oldham Athletic for £700,000.

114 appearances (inc 31 sub) 21 goals

Nigel Callaghan

Winger

Born; Singapore, 12th September 1962

Having been born abroad Nigel was then raised in Watford where he played schools football. Upon leaving he joined local club Watford, breaking into their first team during 1980/81. He would amass over 200 appearances for Watford including an F.A. Cup final when they lost to Everton. During 1986/87 he moved to Derby County and would score four goals in 18 appearances as they won the 2nd Division championship and would be an ever present the following season for The Rams. In February 1989 he moved to Villa Park reuniting with his first manager Graham Taylor. This move worked out for neither club or player, he would make 31 appearances and score the one goal for the first team in a four year spell. During his time at Aston he would be loaned out to both former clubs as wall as Huddersfield Town. Callaghan would finally leave on a free transfer to Stafford Rangers.

31 appearances (inc 4 sub) 1 goal

Ian Ormondroyd

Winger

Born; Bradford, 22nd September 1964

Ian joined Aston Villa on the same day as Nigel Callaghan in February 1989 and was the club's record signing (which had stood since 1980 when Peter Withe signed). He was a tall lanky looking winger who posed a threat on the flank during his first full season as

Villa finished runners-up. Ormondroyd spent only two and a half years at Villa Park before moving to Derby County. This was fairly short lived before becoming Leicester City's record signing, playing at Wembley helping The Foxes achieve Premier League football.

74 appearances (inc 18 sub) 10 goals

Lee Butler

Goalkeeper

Born; Sheffield, 30th May 1966

Lee joined the club in August 1987 from Lincoln City as back up to Nigel Spink and wouldn't make his debut until the following season, finally deputising for Spink who at that time was in great form. During his time at Villa Park he made ten first team appearances and in 1991 moved on to Barnsley where he played most first-team games as their first-choice goalkeeper after which he travelled around before retiring in 2008. Later became a goalkeeping coach.

10 appearances (inc 0 sub) 0 goals

Darrell Duffy

Defender

Born; Birmingham, 18th January 1971

Darrell had joined the ranks at Villa Park straight from school signing on as a YTS in June 1987, turning professional in July 1989. Prior to signing professionally Darrell had made his first-team debut away to Derby County in May 1989 deputising for Chris Price. This would be his only first team appearance. He would be a regular for the reserves before being given a free transfer whereupon he joined non-League Moor Green. In 1991 he joined Scunthorpe United, back in the league for a little over a year in 1993. He later joined the West Midlands Police.

1 appearance (inc 0 sub) 0 goals

Paul McGrath

Central Defender

Born; Ealing, 4th December 1959

Paul McGrath was a master stroke of a signing by manager Graham Taylor when joining the club in August 1989 from Manchester United. Although deemed to be past his best due to injuries suffered, Taylor's faith in him proved to be correct. The tailored training and care paid dividends as he would play over 300 matches for the Villa Park outfit. This silky smooth performer was voted PFA Player's Player of the Year at the end of 1992-93 season. Initially coming over from Dublin McGrath would join Manchester United where he'd spend seven years, gaining an F.A. Cup winners medal in 1985 and playing over 150 times for the Old Trafford side. During his first season at Villa Park the club finished runners-up to Liverpool. Under his former Old Trafford manager Ron Atkinson the club yet again came second this time in the inaugural Premier League season. Further campaigns brought two League Cup winners medals in 1994 and 1996. Time finally caught up with this magnificent player and he would move to Derby County in 1996/97, finally retiring the next year.

323 appearances (inc 8 sub) 9 goals

Kent Nielsen

Central defender

Born; Brondby, Denmark, 28th December 1961

After the narrow escape of relegation in 1988/89 manager Graham Taylor decided to overhaul the defence and brought in Kent Nielsen to partner Paul McGrath. Shortly into the season the manager decided to add Derek Mountfield, the three of them forming a formidable barrier. Kent joined from Danish club IF Brondby and was a Danish international, winning the European Championship in 1992 just a few months after leaving Villa Park. During his B6 stay he was a solid performer, remembered for his thunderbolt of a goal against an outstanding Inter Milan side at Villa Park during 1990/91.

102 appearances (inc 6 sub) 5 goals

Adrian Heath

Forward

Born; Stoke on Trent, 11th January 1961

Adrian came to Villa Park with a big reputation and big price tag from RCD Espanyol. Started his career at local club Stoke City before a move to Everton where he won two League titles and an F.A. Cup medal. Staying only one season in Spain he was one of three major signings made by Taylor but after only seven months with the Villa he was signed by his former Everton boss Howard Kendall for Manchester City. During his unmemorable time at Villa Park he made only a dozen appearances, scoring no goals.

12 appearances (inc 3 sub) 0 goals

Andy Comyn

Defender

Born; Wakefield, 2nd August 1968

Andy was another player plucked from non-League football arriving from Alvechurch in August 1989. Initially starting his football with Manchester United in their youth team but was released and went to University in Birmingham and playing with Alvechurch. Within days of signing on at Villa Andy would be thrown straight into first-team action against Liverpool in a 1-1 draw. In total that season he would only start three games and come off the bench in two others. The 1990/91 season was more fruitful, making 14 starts and two as substitute before being sold to Derby County for a big profit. Comyn stayed just two years but would feature far more before moving yet again, Plymouth Argyle the next port of call.

21 appearances (inc 4 sub) 0 goals

Mark Blake

Midfielder

Born; Nottingham, 16th December 1970

Mark Blake would be the last player to reach the senior side via the club's youth policy. Joining the club as an apprentice and turning professional in July 1989, making is debut during 1989/90 away

to Luton Town. Mark only played sporadically during his first two seasons whilst his third was his most productive with 19 appearances and two goals to his credit. Season 1992/93 was his last, making only one substitute appearance at the beginning of the season before being sold to Portsmouth for £400,000. Blake wouldn't see the campaign out, moving back to the Midlands and Leicester City in March 1994. During his time at Villa he was a regular for the England U-21s.

37 appearances (inc 6 sub) 2 goals

Tony Cascarino

Forward

Born; Orprington, 1st September 1962

Tony was a club record buy for Aston Villa at £1.1 million when signed from Millwall in March 1990. Seen as the man to help Villa over the line in their quest for the title. Unfortunately, Villa being Villa, things didn't go according to plan for club or player, his two goals in the ten matches proved insufficient. The following season was a little better with ten goals from 44 matches as the club returned to Europe for the first time since the Heysel blanket ban. At the end of the season he would move north to Scottish giants Celtic, but wasn't there long before being enticed back to England, namely Chelsea in February 1992 and staying two seasons before moving to France, playing for Marseille, Nancy and Red Star 93. He retired after two games with the latter, in 2000.

54 appearances (inc 4 sub) 12 goals

Dwight Yorke

Forward

Born; Canaan Tobago, 3rd November 1971

The precociously talented 18-year old Dwight was spotted on a tour (allegedly by Sir Doug) when the club visited Trinidad & Tobago. Later signed that year, December 1989 and would make his first team debut only three months later as a substitute at Crystal Palace. The following season he was gently introduced into the first-team fold, scoring the first of his many goals for the Villa and continuing his development into a first rate player. Yorke would score many wonderful goals which culminated in the 1996 League Cup final win over Leeds United. Always playing with a smile on his face he moved onto Manchester United for a record £12.6 million fee and would land the treble with them.

287 appearances (inc 40 sub) 98 goals

[Right] Allan Evans and Colin Gibson in chefs' hats messing around in the kitchen – January 1985

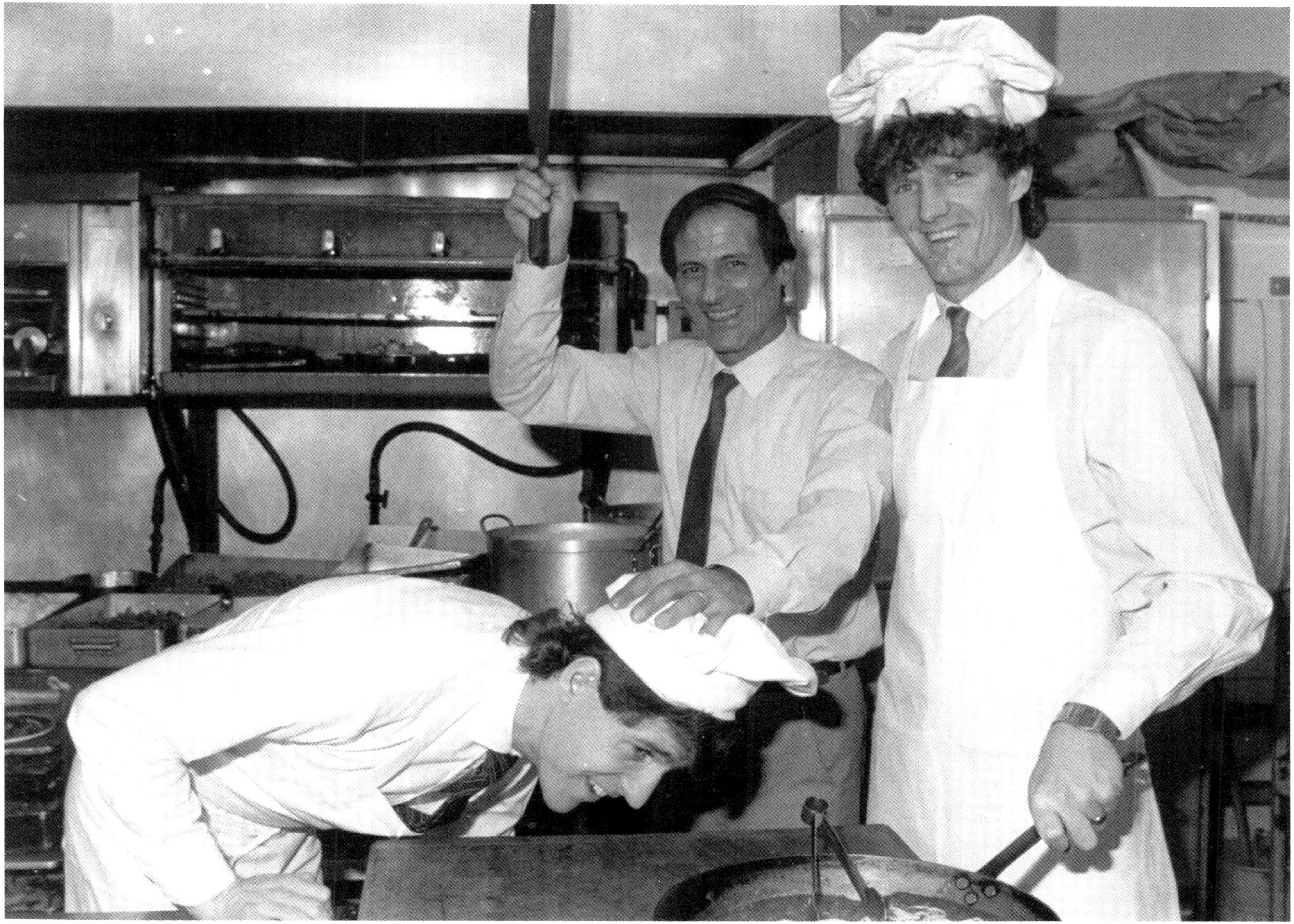

[Right] The Villa team, featuring George Best, who played a benefit match for the victims of the Bradford Fire in May 1985. [Back Row] Ray Walker, Gordon Cowans, Steve McMahon, Brendan Ormsby, Allan Evans, Kevin Poole, Peter Withe, [Front Row] Paul Rideout, George Best, Gary Williams, Tony Dorigo.

OTHER FIXTURES

FRIENDLIES, TESTIMONIALS AND NON-COMPETITIVE MATCHES

mita

1980-81 PRE-SEASON FRIENDLIES AND OTHER NON-COMPETITIVE MATCHES

Pre-Season Tour (Germany)

Friendly — **Wed 30th July**
FC Bochult 0 — **Aston Villa 1**
Withe
Rimmer, Swain, Gibson, Williams, McNaught, Mortimer, Bremner, Shaw, Withe, Cowans, Deacy (Geddis).

Friendly — **Sat 2nd August**
Nuremberg 2 — **Aston Villa 1**
Morley
Rimmer, Swain, Gibson, Evans (Williams), McNaught, Mortimer, Bremner (Donovan), Shaw (Morley), Withe, Cowans, Deacy (Heard).

Friendly — **Tue 5th August**
VFL Bochum 1 — **Aston Villa 1**
Morley
Rimmer, Swain, Gibson, Evans (Williams), McNaught, Mortimer, Bremner, Morley, Withe, Cowans, Deacy (Shaw).

Friendly — **Date unknown**
Kidderminster 2 — **Aston Villa 2**
Donovan, Shelton

Friendly — **Sat 9th August**
Aston Villa 2 — **VFL Bochum 1**
Morley, Shaw
Att 6,000
Rimmer, Swain, Gibson, Williams, McNaught, Mortimer, Bremner, Shaw, Withe, Cowans, Morley.

Friendly **Tue 30th September**
Willenhall Town 2 **Aston Villa 4**
Williams, Stirland, Young, Shelton
Att 2,600

As listed on programme; Spink, Linton, Ormsby, Williams, Blake, Deacy, Shelton, Bullivant, Cropley, Heard, Donovan, Little, Young, Stirland.

Friendly **26th January**
Aston Villa 4 **Rapid Vienna 0**
Withe 2, McNaught, Deacy
Att 6,285

Rimmer, Swain, Gibson (Deacy), Evans, McNaught, Mortimer, Bremner, Shaw, Withe, Cowans, Morley, Subs Geddis, Jones, Spink.

Joe Gallagher Testimonial **Tue 5th May**
Birmingham City 3 **Aston Villa 6**
Bremner, Gibson, Shaw, Mortimer, Morley, Cowans
Att 9,656

Rimmer, Swain, Gibson, Evans, McNaught, Mortimer, Bremner, Shaw, Withe, Cowans, Morley, Subs Spink, Deacy, Geddis, Hopkins.

Ian Paul Benefit **Wed 6th May**
Walsall 1 Aston Villa 1
Cropley
Att 5,446

Spink, Jones, Deacy, Bullivant, Blake, Glover, Hopkins, Walters, Geddis, Cropley, Shelton, Subs Young, Walker, Stirland.

End of Season Tour (France & Spain)

Nantes 4 Aston Villa 0 **Sat 16th May**
Real Vallodolid 4 Aston Villa 4 **Mon 18th May**

1981-82 PRE-SEASON FRIENDLIES AND OTHER NON-COMPETITIVE MATCHES

Pre-Season Tour (Switzerland & Greece)

Friendly — **Tue 4th August**
Servette 2 — **Aston Villa 1**
Mortimer
Att 9,500
Rimmer, Swain, Gibson, Evans, Williams, Mortimer, Bremner, Shaw (Geddis), Withe, Cowans, Morley.

Friendly — **Fri 7th August**
Frauenfeld (Zurich) 0 — **Aston Villa 4**
Withe 2, McNaught, Gibson

Friendly — **Mon 10th August**
AEK Athens 2 — **Aston Villa 2**
Bremner, Evans
Att 40,000

Friendly — **Wed 12th August**
Olympiakos 1 — **Aston Villa 1**
Shaw
Att 40,000

Friendly — **Mon 17th August**
Aston Villa 4 — **German Democratic Republic XI 2**
Mortimer, Cowans (pen), Withe 2
Att 9,748
Rimmer, Swain, Gibson, Evans, McNaught, Mortimer, Bremner, Shaw (Geddis), Withe, Cowans, Morley.

Brian Little Testimonial — **Tue 18th May**
Aston Villa 3 — **England XI 2**
Little 2, Morley
Att 9,229
*Rimmer, Swain, *Williams, Evans, *McNaught, Mortimer, Bremner, *Little, *Withe, Cowans, Morley, Subs Geddis, Spink, Gibson, Heard, Walters all used.

Friendly — **Sun 23rd May**
Moroccan League Select XI 3 — **Aston Villa 2**

Neutral Tetouan Morocco — **Sunday 30th May**
Aston Villa 1 — **Kuwait 1**
Des Bremner

1982-83 PRE-SEASON FRIENDLIES AND OTHER NON-COMPETITIVE MATCHES

Friendly **Sun 8th August**
Shrewsbury Town 1 **Aston Villa 3**
Shaw, Mortimer, Withe

Pre-Season Tour (Germany)

Friendly **Tue 10th August**
FC Kaiserslautern 5 **Aston Villa 1**
Withe
Rimmer, Swain, Williams, Evans, McNaught, Mortimer, Bremner, Shaw, Withe, Cowans, Morley.

Friendly **Fri 13th August**
Werder Bremen 2 **Aston Villa 0**

Friendly **Mon 16th August**
Shalke 04 4 **Aston Villa 2**
Withe, Walters

Friendly **Sat 21st August**
Aston Villa 1 **Dukla Prague 2**
Mortimer
Att 3,746
Rimmer, Swain, Gibson, Williams, McNaught, Mortimer, Bremner, Shaw, Withe, Cowans, Morley, Subs Heard, Walters, Birch, Spink.

Alex Cropley Testimonial **Mon 23rd August**
Portsmouth 3 **Aston Villa 4**
Withe, Walters 2, Mortimer
Att 4,519
Rimmer, Swain, Gibson, Williams, McNaught, Mortimer, Bremner, Walters, Withe, Cowans, Morley.

Friendly **Sat 18th September**
Arsenal 1 **Aston Villa 1**
Donovan
Spink, Swain, Gibson, Walker, Ormsby, Glover, Birch, Deacy, Donovan, Walters, Geddis.

Friendly **Mon 4th October**
Aston Villa 5 **Tottenham Hotspur 0**
Walters 3, Ormsby, Swain
Spink, Swain, Gibson, Birch, Ormsby, Glover, Rees, Deacy, Geddis, Walters (Rogers), Hutchinson.

Tommy Hughes Testimonial **Mon 11th October**
Hereford United 1 **Aston Villa 2**
Att 3,710
Hopkins, Geddis
Spink, Swain, Gibson, Birch, Ormsby, Glover, Hopkins (Rees), Deacy (Walker), Geddis, Walters (Kerr), Heard (Jones).

Sports Argus Cup **Sat 23rd October**
Aston Villa Res 2 **West Brom Res 0**
Walters, Walker
Spink, Blair, Rogers, Glover, Ormsby, Walker, Hopkins, Walters, Donovan, Hutchinson, Heard.

Richard Finney Testimonial — **Mon 15th November**
Rotherham United 1 — **Aston Villa 3**
Att 3,007
Evans, Geddis, Walters

Spink, Jones, Gibson, Smith, Glover, Evans, Blair, Shaw, Geddis, Cowans, Walters, Subs (all used) Ormsby, Hopkins, Heard, Deacy.

Sports Argus Cup — **Wed 12th Jan**
Wolves Res 1 — **Aston Villa Res 2**
Kerr, Donovan

Poole, Deacy, Rogers, Birch, Ormsby, Glover, Hopkins, Blair, Donovan, Kerr, Walker, Sub Hutchinson.

Kevin Bird Testimonial — **Wed 4th May**
Mansfield Town 1 — **Aston Villa 3**
Walters, Palin, Rees

Poole, Jones, Dorigo, Walker, Ormsby, Shipley, Blair, Birch, Kerr, Walters, Hutchinson. Subs used: Rees, Palin, Langford

1983-84 PRE-SEASON FRIENDLIES AND OTHER NON-COMPETITIVE MATCHES

Aston Villa 4 **Peterborough United 3**
at Bodymoor Heath

Ian Twitchin Testimonial **Mon 8th August**
Torquay United 2 **Aston Villa 1**
Rideout
Att 3,500
As listed on programme; From Spink, Gibson, Jones, McNaught, Evans, Williams, Bremner, Cowans, Mortimer, McMahon, Curbishley, Withe, Rideout, Shaw, Morley, Walters.

Brian Johnson Testimonial **Wed 10th August**
Plymouth Argyle 0 **Aston Villa 3**
Shaw 3
Att 3,562
Spink, Williams, Gibson, Evans, McNaught, McMahon, Curbishley, Shaw, Withe, Cowans, Walters, Sub Glover.

Pre-Season Tour (Spain, Zaragosa)

Friendly **Thur 18th August**
FC America 2 **Aston Villa 2**
(Villa lose 2-4 on penalties)
McMahon, Evans
Spink, Williams, Gibson, Evans, McNaught, McMahon, Curbishley, Shaw, *Withe, *Cowans, *Walters, Subs Rideout, Jones, Mortimer all used.

Friendly **Fri 19th August**
Polytechnica 1 **Aston Villa 1**
(Villa won 4-2 on penalties)
Withe
Spink, Williams, Gibson (Jones), Evans, Ormsby, Mortimer, Curbishley, Shaw (Withe), Rideout, McMahon, Walters.

Friendly **Mon 22nd August**
Derby County 1 **Aston Villa 3**
Att 4,436
Shaw 2, Withe
Spink, Williams, *Gibson, *Evans, Ormsby, Mortimer, Curbishley, Shaw, Withe, McMahon, *Bremner, Subs Walters, Jones, Glover all used.

Opening of Floodlights **Mon 14th November**
Chelmsford City 0 **Aston Villa 1**
Att 4,500
Evans

Friendly **Tue 28 December**
Aston Villa 5 **Paget Rangers 0**
Bremner, Shaw 2, Birch, Kerr
Day, Walker, Gibson (Dorigo), Bremner, Bradley, Glover, Birch, Shaw, Kerr (Greenhalgh), Norton, Obi (Palin).

Friendly **Mon 23rd January**
Bideford 1 **Aston Villa 2**
Evans, Withe
Spink (Day), Bremner, Gibson, Evans, Ormsby, Walker, Curbishley, Shaw, Withe, Blair, Rideout.

Friendly **Tue 10th April**
Poole Town 0 **Aston Villa 1**
Att 500
Evans
As listed on programme; Spink, Williams, Gibson, Evans, Foster, Mortimer, Curbishley, Rideout, Withe, Shaw, Walters, Subs Bremner, McMahon

Friendly **Fri 13th April**
Aston Villa 5 **Valur Reykjavik 0**
Gibson, Withe, Walker, Glover, Curbishley
Poole, Norton, Gibson (Howell), Bradley, Glover, Curbishley, Walker, Dorigo, Withe (Greenhalgh), Palin, Obi.

Friendly **Thur 24th April**
Walsall Borough 1 **Aston Villa 6**
McMahon 2, Williams, Ormsby, Kerr, Walker
As listed on programme; From Day, Williams, Gibson, Dorigo, Ormsby, Evans, Foster, Deacy, Glover, Bradley, Birch, Blair, Walker, Curbishley, Norton, Palin, Obi, Kerr, Walters, Rideout

Brendan Batson Testimonial **Mon 30th April**
West Bromwich 1 **Aston Villa 2**
Kerr, Walker
Att 4,800
Day, Williams, Deacy, Ormsby, Foster, Mortimer, Blair, Shaw, Withe, Birch, Kerr, Sub Walker.

Malcolm Phelps Testimonial **Mon 14th May**
Worcester City 4 **Aston Villa 6**
Att 1,342
Foster, Bremner, Curbishley, Ormsby, Shaw (pen), Kerr
As listed on programme, Day, Williams, Deacy, Evans, Ormsby, Mortimer, Blair, Birch, Withe, McMahon, Walters.

Friendly **Wed 16th May**
Fr Portsmouth 0 **Aston Villa 1**
Att 2,652
Foster
Day, Bremner, Deacy, Ormsby, Foster, Mortimer, Blair, Shaw, Walker, Birch, Curbishley. Subs Spink, Glover, Bradley, Kerr.

Friendly **Sat 19th May**
Udinese 1 **Aston Villa 1**
Att 7,000
Mortimer
Day, Williams, Dorigo, Ormsby, Foster (Bremner), Mortimer, Blair, Shaw (Kerr), Withe, Birch, Walker.

Friendly **Sat 26th May**
Verona 1 **Aston Villa 1**
Att 10,000
Birch
Spink, Williams, Dorigo, Ormsby, Bremner, Mortimer, Blair, Shaw (Kerr), Withe, Birch, Walker (Curbishley).

Friendly **Sun May 27th**
Citadella 0 **Aston Villa 8**
Blair 2, Dorigo, Birch, Kerr, Mortimer, Curbishley, Spink (pen)

1984-85 PRE-SEASON FRIENDLIES AND OTHER NON-COMPETITIVE MATCHES

Friendly **Sat 4th August**
Millwall 2 **Aston Villa 4**
Att 2,692
Evans, McMahon, Rideout, Bremner
Day (Spink), Williams, Gibson, Evans, Ormsby, McMahon, Curbishley, Rideout, Withe, Cowans, Birch, Sub Bremner.

Friendly **Sat 11th August**
Rotherham United 2 **Aston Villa 1**
Rideout
Spink, Williams, Gibson, Evans, Foster, McMahon, Bremner, Mortimer, Rideout, Cowans, Walters.

Friendly **Tue 14th August**
Shrewsbury Town 1 **Aston Villa 1**
Att1,788
Foster
Day, Williams, Gibson, Evans, Foster, McMahon, Birch, Curbishley, Rideout, Mortimer, Walters, Subs Cowans, Ormsby, Bremner.

Friendly **Wed 15th August**
Wolverhampton Wanderers 1 **Aston Villa 0**
Spink, Williams, Gibson, Evans, Foster, McMahon, Bremner, Walters, Rideout, Cowans, Mortimer, Subs Day, Ormsby, Curbishley, Birch.

Pre-Season Tour (Spain)

Friendly **Tue 21st August**
Bayern Munich 2 **Aston Villa 1**
McMahon
Day, Williams, Gibson, Evans, Foster, McMahon, Bremner, Walters, Rideout, Cowans (Curbishley), Mortimer.

Friendly **Wed 22nd August**
Boca Juniors 2 Aston Villa 0
Att 90,000
Day, Gibson, Dorigo, Ormsby, *Foster, *McMahon, *Bremner, Walters, Rideout, Curbishley, Mortimer, Subs Evans, Cowans, Walker all used.

Mike Barrett Memorial **Tue 11th September**
Bristol Rovers 2 **Aston Villa 1**
Att 4,949
McMahon
Poole, Norton, Dorigo, Bradley, Foster, McMahon, Birch, Palin (Hutchinson), Withe, Cowans, Walters (Daley).

Friendly **Sun 25th November**
Aston Villa 2 **Australia 0**
Att 2,550
Curbishley, Birch
Spink, Williams (Norton), Gibson (Dorigo), Glover, Ormsby, Curbishley, Birch, Walters, Kerr (Palin), Cowans (Bradley), Daley (Gibson).

Gibson who was captain for the game was replaced by Tony Dorigo, only to come back on later in place of Tony Daley.

SHREWSBURY TOWN FOOTBALL CLUB

PRE SEASON PRACTICE MATCH

SHREWSBURY TOWN v. ASTON VILLA

Tuesday, 14th August, 1984. K.O. 7.30 p.m.

OFFICIAL PROGRAMME Price 2p

SHREWSBURY TOWN Blue and Gold		ASTON VILLA All White
RON GREEN	1.	MERVYN DAY
WAYNE WILLIAMS	2.	GARY WILLIAMS
PAUL JOHNSON	3.	COLIN GIBSON
ROSS MACLAREN	4.	ALAN EVANS
COLIN GRIFFIN	5.	STEVE FOSTER
STEVE CROSS	6.	STEVE McMAHON
BERNARD McNALLY	7.	PAUL BIRCH
PAUL PETTS	8.	ALAN CURBISHLEY
GARY STEVENS	9.	PAUL RIDEOUT
GERRY NARDIELLO	10.	DENIS MORTIMER
GARY HACKETT	11.	MARK WALTERS
COLIN ROBINSON	12.	GORDON COWANS
PAUL TESTER		BRENDON ORMSBY
ANDY KERR		DES BREMNER
CHIC BATES		

REFEREE

M. IBBOTSON, Shrewsbury

LINESMEN

Red Flag - E. FELTON
Yellow Flag - R. L. GROOME

NEXT MATCH AT THE GAY MEADOW

Sat. 1st Sept. Div. II. CRYSTAL PALACE. Kick off 3 p.m

Joe Jopling Testimonial — **Tue 27th November**
Aldershot 1 — **Aston Villa 4**
McMahon, Gibson, Evans, Palin
Att 2,320
As listed on programme; From Day, Williams, Gibson, Evans, Ormsby, Birch, McMahon, Cowans, Six, Withe, Walters, Kerr, Dorigo, Curbishley, Hutchings

Jeff Hemmerman Testimonial — **Mon 3rd December**
Cardiff City XI 3 — **Aston Villa 0**

Ethiopia Appeal Charity Match — **Tue 15th January**
Leeds United 1 — **Aston Villa 3**
Att 1,781
McMahon, Gibson 2
Spink, Norton, Dorigo, Glover, Ormsby, McMahon, *Birch, Rideout, Withe, *Gibson, Walters, Subs Cowans, Bradley both used.

Mid-Season Tour (Bermuda)

Friendly — **Wed 23rd January**
Hotels International 0 — **Aston Villa 6**
Att 6,000

Friendly — **Fri 25th January**
Somerset Trojans 0 — **Aston Villa 12**
Att 7,000

Friendly | **Wed 13th February**
Fr Central Wales League 1 | **Aston Villa 6**
Kerr 4, Williams pen, Walker
Poole, Williams (Robinson), Dorigo, Walker, Ormsby (Bradley), Glover, Birch, Cowans (Hellin), Kerr, Norton, Palin.

Friendly | **Sat 16th February**
Fr Exeter City 0 | **Aston Villa 3**
Att 2,590
Gibson, Rideout 2
Spink, Williams, Dorigo, Evans, Ormsby (Glover), McMahon, Gibson (Birch), Rideout, Withe, Cowans, Walters.

Dennis Mortimer Testimonial | **Tue 14th May**
England XI 4 | **Aston Villa 1**
Att 5,451
Withe
Poole, Swain, Dorigo, Evans, McNaught, Mortimer, Ormsby, Shaw, Withe, Cowans, Morley.

Bradford Fire Appeal | **Fri 17th May**
Aston Villa 3 | **West Brom 3**
Att 5,664
McMahon, Evans, Six
Poole, Williams, Dorigo, Evans, Ormsby, McMahon, Walker, Rideout (Shaw), Withe, Cowans, Best (Six).

[Left] The iconic George Best wearing an Aston Villa shirt during the Bradford Fire Appeal match in May 1985

1985-86 PRE-SEASON FRIENDLIES AND OTHER NON-COMPETITIVE MATCHES

Friendly — **Mon 29th July**
Hereford United 1 — **Aston Villa 6**

Pre-Season Tour (West Country)

Friendly — **Sat 3rd August**
Plymouth Argyle 1 Aston Villa 4
Att 3,325
Gray, Ormsby, McMahon, Gibson
Spink, Williams, Dorigo, Evans, Ormsby, McMahon, Birch, Daley, Gray (Shaw), Gibson, Walters.

Friendly — **Mon 5th August**
Liskeard 2 — **Aston Villa 6**

Friendly — **Tue 6th August**
Exeter City 1 — **Aston Villa 3**

Friendly — **Sat 10th August**
Aston Villa 2 — **Sunderland 1**
Att 2,500
Walters, Scorer needed
Spink, Williams, Dorigo, Evans, Ormsby, McMahon, Birch, Daley, Gray (Shaw), Gibson, Walters.

Billy Morris Testimonial — **Mon 14th October**
Hednesford 0 — **Aston Villa 4**
Scorers unknown
As listed on programme; From Spink, Williams, Dorigo, Ormsby, Birch, Gibson, Stainrod, Hodge, Walters, Daley, Bradley, Norton, Glover, Shaw.

John Powell Testimonial — **Mon 11th November**
John Powell XI 2 — **Aston Villa 6**
Att 1,500
Scorers unknown
As listed on programme; Spink, Williams, Dorigo, Evans, Glover, Gibson, Daley, Stainrod, Gray, Hodge, Walters, Sub Walker.

Friendly — **Sat 15th February**
Shrewsbury Town 0 — **Aston Villa 3**

Brian Kendall Testimonial — **Mon 21st April**
Atherstone Town 2 — **Aston Villa 4**
Kerr 3, Shaw
As listed on programme; From Poole, Norton, Dorigo, Evans, Elliott, Blair, Birch, Hunt, Gray, Stainrod, Daley, Spink, Williams.

Kevin Broadhurst Testimonial — **Mon 5th May**
Birmingham City Select XI 3 — **Aston Villa 3**
Att 7,010

End of Season Tour (Indian Ocean)

Friendly — **Sun 18th May**
Mauritius Select XI 0 — **Aston Villa 4**

1986-87 PRE-SEASON FRIENDLIES AND OTHER NON-COMPETITIVE MATCHES

Bass Charity Soccer Vase — **Wed 30th July**
Burton Albion 2 — **Aston Villa 2**
Howell, Daley
Spink, Keown, Dorigo, Robinson, Elliott, Cooper, Birch, Ritchie, Kerr, Howell (Burke), Daley.

Friendly — **Sat 2nd August**
Celtic 1 — **Aston Villa 0**
Att 18,000
Poole, *Keown, Dorigo, Evans, Elliott, Birch, *Hunt, Stainrod, Thompson, *Cooper, *Walters, Subs Daley, Williams, Norton, Hodge all used.

Pre-Season Tour (Italy)

Friendly — **Wed 6th August**
Pisa 0 — **Aston Villa 0**

Friendly — **Sat 9th August**
Lamporecchio 0 — **Aston Villa 8**
Stainrod 2, Walters 2, Thompson, Blair, Hodge, own goal

Friendly — **Wed 13th August**
Port Vale 0 — **Aston Villa 1**
Att 2,104
Birch
*Spink, *Williams, Dorigo, Keown, Elliott, Blair, Birch, Thompson, *Gray, Hodge, *Walters, Subs Daley, Stainrod, Poole, Evans all used.

Friendly **Sat 16th August**
Leeds United 1 **Aston Villa 3**
Att 3,200
Hodge, Thompson, Kerr
Poole, Keown, Dorigo, Cooper, Elliott, Blair, Birch, Stainrod, Thompson, Hodge, Daley, Subs Evans, Kerr.

Friendly **Mon 18th August**
Atherstone 0 **Aston Villa 9**
Scorers unknown
As listed on programme; Spink, Williams, Gallacher, Keown, Evans, Hunt, Birch, Thompson, Gray, Hodge, Blair, Subs Stainrod, Kerr, Robinson, Norton, Poole.

Friendly **Fri 30th January**
Sheffield United 1 **Aston Villa 0**
abandoned at half time
Att 1,236

End of Season Tour (Jamaica)

Friendly **Tue 26th May**
Caribbean Select XI 0 **Aston Villa 2**
Burke, Evans

Friendly **Sun 31st May**
West Indies Select XI 2 **Aston Villa 4**
Walters, Gray

1987-88 PRE-SEASON FRIENDLIES AND OTHER NON-COMPETITIVE MATCHES

Pre-season Tour (Scandanavia)

Friendly — **Sun 26th July**
BK Vargarna (Nortalje) 1 — **Aston Villa 5**
Stainrod 4, Gallacher
Spink (Poole), Hunt D, Gallacher, Keown, Sims, Cooper, Birch, Shaw, McInally (Stainrod), Hunt S, Walters, Subs Burke, Evans.

Friendly — **Tue 28th July**
Gullringen GolF 2 — **Aston Villa 2**
Cooper, Aspinall
Spink, Gage, Gallacher, Evans (Keown), Sims, Cooper (Hunt D), Birch, Aspinall, Stainrod, Hunt S, Walters, Subs Burke, Poole.

Friendly — **Thur 30th July**
Enkopings 0 — **Aston Villa 2**
Walters 2
Spink, Gage, Gallacher, Keown, Sims, Hunt D, Burke, Aspinall, Shaw, Hunt S, Walters, Subs Poole, Evans, Birch, Harrison.

Friendly — **Sun 2nd August**
Varmbols Golf 0 — **Aston Villa 8**
Aspinall 3, Burke 2, Walters, Stainrod, Shaw
Spink (Poole), Gage, Gallacher, Cooper, ?, Hunt D , Birch (Daley), Aspinall, Stainrod (Shaw), Burke, Walters. Player missing

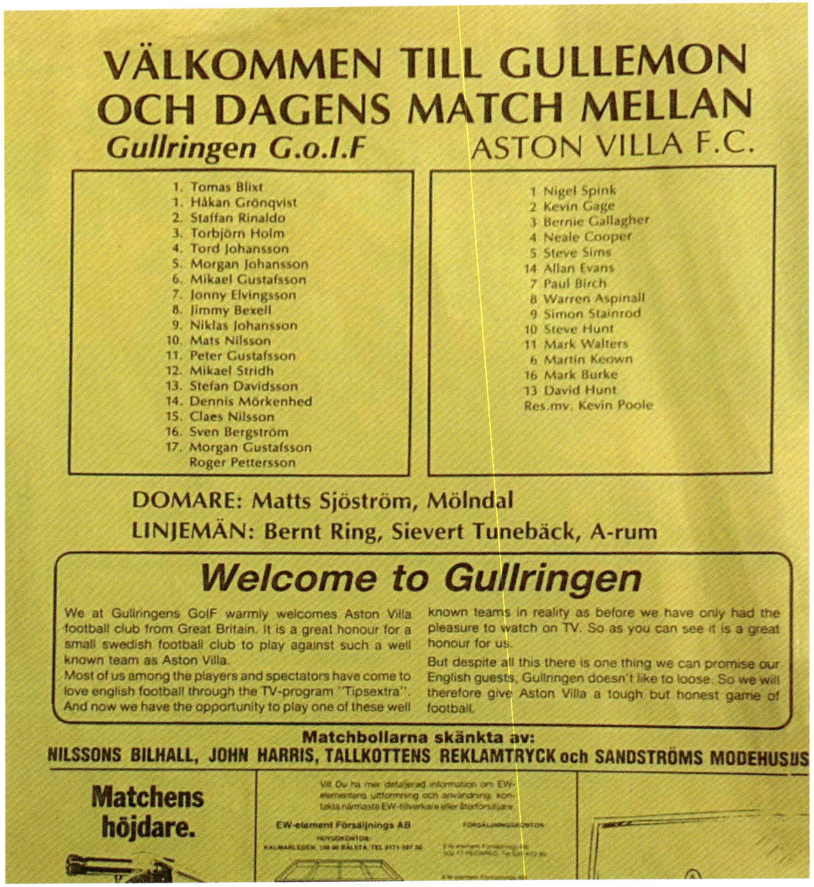

VÄLKOMMEN TILL GULLEMON
OCH DAGENS MATCH MELLAN
Gullringen G.o.I.F — ASTON VILLA F.C.

Gullringen G.o.I.F	Aston Villa F.C.
1. Tomas Blixt	1 Nigel Spink
1. Håkan Grönqvist	2 Kevin Gage
2. Staffan Rinaldo	3 Bernie Gallagher
3. Torbjörn Holm	4 Neale Cooper
4. Tord Johansson	5 Steve Sims
5. Morgan Johansson	14 Allan Evans
6. Mikael Gustafsson	7 Paul Birch
7. Jonny Elvingsson	8 Warren Aspinall
8. Jimmy Bexell	9 Simon Stainrod
9. Niklas Johansson	10 Steve Hunt
10. Mats Nilsson	11 Mark Walters
11. Peter Gustafsson	6 Martin Keown
12. Mikael Stridh	16 Mark Burke
13. Stefan Davidsson	13 David Hunt
14. Dennis Mörkenhed	Res.mv. Kevin Poole
15. Claes Nilsson	
16. Sven Bergström	
17. Morgan Gustafsson	
Roger Pettersson	

DOMARE: Matts Sjöström, Mölndal
LINJEMÄN: Bernt Ring, Sievert Tunebäck, A-rum

Welcome to Gullringen

We at Gullringens GolF warmly welcomes Aston Villa football club from Great Britain. It is a great honour for a small swedish football club to play against such a well known team as Aston Villa.
Most of us among the players and spectators have come to love english football through the TV-program "Tipsextra". And now we have the opportunity to play one of these well known teams in reality as before we have only had the pleasure to watch on TV. So as you can see it is a great honour for us.

But despite all this there is one thing we can promise our English guests, Gullringen doesn't like to loose. So we will therefore give Aston Villa a tough but honest game of football.

Matchbollarna skänkta av:
NILSSONS BILHALL, JOHN HARRIS, TALLKOTTENS REKLAMTRYCK och SANDSTRÖMS MODEHUS

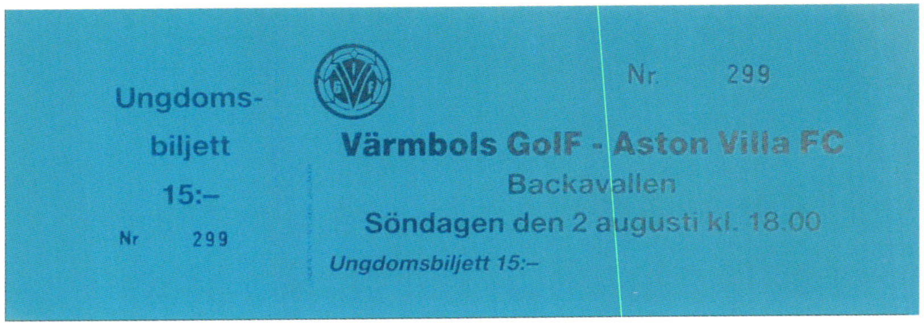

[Above] Football League Founders Centenary match which was played against Birmingham City

Friendly **Tue 4th August**
Fr Nykopings BIS/IFK Eskilstuna 2 **Aston Villa 4**
Walters 2, Aspinall, Shaw
Spink, Gage, Gallacher, Cooper (Burke), Keown, Evans (Shaw) (Stainrod for Shaw), Birch, Aspinall, Shaw, Hunt D, Walters.

Friendly **Thur 6th August**
Highgate United 1 **Aston Villa 1**
Details unknown

Friendly **Sat 8th August**
Aston Villa 3 **Coventry City 2**
Birch, Aspinall, Walters
Spink, Gage, Gallacher, Cooper, Sims, Keown, Birch, Aspinall, Stainrod (Shaw), Hunt D, Walters, Subs Poole, Burke.

Gordon Guthrie Testimonial **Mon 10th August**
Derby County 0 **Aston Villa 1**
Att 2,737
Aspinall
Spink, Gage, Gallacher, Cooper, Sims, Keown, Birch, Aspinall, Hunt S (Hunt D), Shaw (Burke), Walters.

Friendly **Mon 8th February**
Aston Villa 3 **AS Monaco 0**
Att 5,285
Williams G, Gray AA, Birch
Spink, Gage, Gallacher, Gray AA, Evans, Sims, *Daley, *Lillis, McInally, Platt, Williams G, Subs Birch, Norton both used.

Founders Centenary Match **Wed 13th April**
Aston Villa 5 **Birmingham City 2**
Att 6,645
Platt 2, Williams, Daley, Olney
Butler, Gage, Norton, Evans, Sims, Birch, Daley, Platt, Thompson, Aspinall, Williams, Sub Olney.

League Centenary Tournament Wembley **Sat 16th April**
Blackburn Rovers 0 **Aston Villa 0**
Evans,
won 2-1 on pens

League Centenary Tournament Wembley **Sun 17th April**
Nottingham Forest 0 **Aston Villa 0**
Lost 0-1 on pens

Nigel Spink Testimonial **Wed 11th May**
Aston Villa 2 **Wolves 1**
Att 7,258
Shaw, Gray AA

1988-89 PRE-SEASON FRIENDLIES AND OTHER NON-COMPETITIVE MATCHES

Geoff Moss Testimonial **Sat 30th July**
Halesowen Harriers 1 **Aston Villa 2**
Att 1,600
Aspinall, Thompson
Butler, Williams M (Hunt), Gage, Lillis (Olney), Evans, Keown, Gray A (Cooper), Aspinall (Morris), Thompson, Gray S, Williams G.

Friendly **Sat 6th Aug**
Derby County 1 **Aston Villa 0**
Butler, Williams, Small, Lillis, Sims, Duffy, Blair, Jones, Blake, Hunt D, Morris (Parrott).

Pre-Season Tour (Scotland)

Friendly **Thur 4th August**
St Johnstone 1 **Aston Villa 2**
Platt, Mountfield
Spink, Gage, Gray S, Evans, Mountfield, Cooper (Birch), Daley, Platt, McInally (Thompson), Cowans, Williams G (Gray A).

Friendly **Sat 6th August**
St Mirren 1 **Aston Villa 0**
Spink, Price, Gage (Platt), Gray A (Cooper), Mountfield, Keown, Birch (McInally), Aspinall, Thompson (Cowans), Gray S, Daley (Williams G).

Friendly **Mon 8th August**
Greenock Morton 2 **Aston Villa 3**
McInally, Birch, Thompson
Spink, Price, Gray S, Cooper (Olney), Evans, Keown, Birch, Platt (Gray A), McInally (Thompson), Cowans, Williams G.

Bass Charity Vase 3rd place play off **Wed 10th August**
West Brom 1 **Aston Villa 2**
Olney, Aspinall,
Butler, Hunt, Small, Lillis, Sims, Cooper, Blair, Aspinall, Olney, Cowans, Williams G, Sub Blake.

Friendly **Sat 13th August**
Notts County 3 **Aston Villa 2**
Att 2,034
Cowans, Williams
Spink, Price, Gray S, Platt, Mountfield, Evans, Birch, *McInally, *Thompson, Cowans, Williams G, Subs Aspinall, Gray AA both used.

Friendly **Tue 16th August**
Gosport Borough 1 **Aston Villa 5**
Platt 2, Williams, Daley, Gray S
Spink, Price, Gray S, Lillis, Mountfield, Keown, Daley, Platt, McInally, Cowans, Williams G.

Allan Evans Testimonial **Fri 19th August**
Aston Villa 4 Walsall 2
Att 7,789
Gray A, Evans, McInally, Gray S
Spink, Price, Gage, Gray A (Cooper), Mountfield (Keown), Evans, Birch, Platt, McInally, Cowans, Gray S.

Friendly **Sat 20th August**
Hull City 1 **Aston Villa 1**
Gray S
Spink, Price (Gallacher), Gage, Gray A, Evans, Keown, Birch, Platt, McInally, Cowans, Gray S.

Friendly	**Tue 23rd August**
Halesowen Town	**Aston Villa**
Details unknown	

As listed on programme; Butler, Williams M, Gallacher, Lillis, Sims, Hunt D, Morris, Blair, Olney, Cooper, Williams G, Subs Duffy, Blake

Kevin Pressley Testimonial	**Tues 11th October**
Harworth	**Aston Villa**
Details unknown	

As listed on programme; Butler, Williams M, Moore, Lillis, Sims, Duffy, Blair, Williams G, Thompson, Hunt D, Morris, Subs Jones, Parrott.

Opening of Floodlights	**Tue 15th November**
Barnstable 0	**Aston Villa 6**
Olney, McInally, Daley, Gallacher, Platt 2	

Spink, Gray S, Mountfield, Evans, Gage, Daley, *Olney, *Thompson, McInally, Cowans, Gallacher, Subs Platt, Gray AA both used

Friendly	**Tue 20th December**
Israel 1	**Aston Villa 0**
Att 5,000	

Spink, Price, Gray S, Gage, Evans, Mountfield, Gray AA, Platt, McInally, Cowans, Daley.

Mid-Season Tour (West Indies)

Friendly	**Sat 4th March**
Fr Trinidad & Tobago 0	**Aston Villa 1**

Friendly	**Sun 5th March**
Fr Tobago XI 0	**Aston Villa 5**
Att 4,000	

Friendly	**Mon 3rd April**
Fr Banks' Brewery League XI 1	**Aston Villa 4**
Att 1,000	
Scorers Unknown	

As listed on programme; From Butler, Spink, Birch, Callaghan, Daley, Gage, Evans, Hunt D, Platt, Keown, Lillis, Sims, Ormondroyd, Williams G, Gray S, McInally, Cowans, Mountfield, Price, Morris, Olney, Williams M.

1989-90 PRE-SEASON FRIENDLIES AND OTHER NON-COMPETITIVE MATCHES

Pre-Season Tour (Switzerland)

Friendly | **Sat 15th July**
Servette Geneve 1 | **Aston Villa 0**
Spink, Price, Gallacher, Cowans, Nielsen, Mountfield, Birch, Platt, Olney, Gray, Callaghan, Subs Sims, Daley, Ormondroyd, Blake used. Butler not used

Friendly | **Sun 16th July**
Reinal Select (Regional Select XI) 2 | **Aston Villa 0**
Butler, Gage, Gray S, Platt, Sims, Mountfield, Daley, Spink D, Ormondroyd, Cowans, Williams G, Subs Price, Olney used. Spink N, Birch, Blake not used.

Friendly | **Tue 18th July**
Winterthur 4 | **Aston Villa 4**
Platt 2 (1 pen), Mountfield, Birch
Spink, Price, Gallacher, Gage, Sims, Mountfield, Birch, Platt, Olney, Gray, Callaghan, Subs Spink D, Ormondroyd, Daley, Cowans used. Butler not used.

Friendly | **Wed 19th July**
FC Solothurn 0 | **Aston Villa 6**
Spink D 3, Daley, Olney, Price
Butler, Price, Williams, Platt, Mountfield, Gray, Callaghan, Daley, Spink D, Cowans, Ormondroyd, Subs Olney, Birch, Sims, Blake used. Spink N not used.

Friendly | **Fri 21st July**
Fr Echallens 0 | **Aston Villa 9**
Platt 3, Ormondroyd 2, Olney, Spink D, Callaghan, Cowans
Spink N (Butler), Gage, Gray, Platt, Sims, Mountfield, Birch, Olney, Ormondroyd, Cowans, Callaghan, Subs Spink D, Blake, Price, Daley.

David Okorhi Benefit | **Thur 3rd August**
Paget Rangers 0 | **Aston Villa 7**
Att 2,000
Daley 2, Parrott 2, Blake, Spink D, Butler M
As listed on programme; Spink, Price, Gray S, Lillis, Sims, Mountfield, Callaghan, Platt, Olney, Cowans, Ormondroyd, Subs, Blake, Duffy, Parrott, Jones D.

Friendly | **Sat 5th August**
Aston Villa 1 | **Hibernian 0**
Att 6,622
Nielsen
Spink N, Price, Gray S, Platt, Mountfield, McGrath, Birch, Olney (Nielsen), Ormondroyd (Daley), Lillis, Parrott.

Friendly | **Tue 8th August**
Bromsgrove Rovers 0 | **Aston Villa 4**
Ormondroyd 2, Daley, Olney
Butler, Duffy, Darke, Blake, Sims, Comyn, Daley, Olney, Ormondroyd, Lillis, Parrott, Sub Jones.

Friendly | **Wed 9th August**
Chester City 0 | **Aston Villa 5**
Cowans 2, Daley, Platt, Olney
Spink N, Price, Williams G, McGrath, Mountfield, Nielsen (Daley), Birch, Heath (Olney), Platt, Cowans, Callaghan.

Friendly **Sat 12th August**
Crewe Alexandra 4 **Aston Villa 3**
Platt 2, Gray S
Spink N, Williams, Price, Nielsen, McGrath, Cowans, Callaghan (Daley), Gray, Platt, Heath, Birch.

Kenny Jackett Testimonial **Mon 14th August**
Watford 1 **Aston Villa 6**
Daley 2, Heath, Nielsen, Cowans, Price
Spink N, Price, Gray S, McGrath, Mountfield, Nielsen (Callaghan), Birch, Heath (Ormondroyd), Platt, Cowans, Daley, Sub Williams not used

Friendly **Wed 1st November**
Hinckley Athletic 2 **Aston Villa 5**
Details unknown
As listed in programme; Butler, Duffy, Williams M, Comyn, Sims, Blake, Jones, Small, Parrott, Birch, Callaghan, Spink D, Ormondroyd

Opening of Floodlights **Wed 20th December**
Nettleham 1 **Aston Villa 5**
Abandoned due to floodlights after 65mins
Att 1,000

Penn & Johnson Testimonials **Wed 9th May**
Halesowen Town 1 **Aston Villa 6**
Att 3,518
Platt 3, Olney 3

[Right] Villa's 1984/85 reserves win Birmingham Senior Cup [Back Row] Paul Birch, Matt Hellin, Leigh Palin, Dennis Mortimer, Ray Walker, Paul Kerr, Bill Shorthouse (Coach), [Front Row] Kevin Poole, Dean Glover, Darren Bradley, David Norton, Tony Obi.

RESERVES

mita copiers
TSB
TSB
Evening Mail
mita

1980/81

Central League

Sat 16th August
Huddersfield Town (H) Won 3-0
Donovan 2, Hopkins
Spink, Linton, Jones, Heard, Blake, Bullivant, Hopkins, Stirland, Donovan, Cropley, Young, Sub Shelton.

Tue 19th August
Liverpool (A) Won 2-0
Donovan 2
Spink, Linton, Jones, Blake, Ormsby, Shelton, Hopkins, Stirland (Young), Donovan, Cropley, Heard.

Sat 23rd August
Coventry City (H) Lost 1-4
Geddis
Spink, Linton, Deacy, Heard, Ormsby, Cropley, Shelton, Stirland, Geddis, Bullivant (Hopkins), Young.

Sat 30th August
Manchester City (A) Drew 2-2
Little 2
Spink, Linton, Deacy, Williams, Ormsby, Shelton, Hopkins, Little, Donovan, Cropley, Young, Sub Jones.

Sat 6th September
Derby County (H) Drew 1-1
Hopkins
Spink, Linton, Jones, Blake, Ormsby, Bullivant, Hopkins, Geddis, Donovan, Cropley, Young, Sub Shelton.

Sat 13th September
Everton (A) Lost 1-2
Little
Spink, Deacy, Jones, Bullivant, Ormsby, Heard, Hopkins, Little, Geddis, Cropley, Shelton. Young

Tue 17th September
Huddersfield Town (A) Won 4-2
Geddis 3, Cropley
Spink, Linton, Jones, Shelton, Ormsby, Williams, Hopkins, Little, Geddis, Cropley, Young.

Thur 25th September
Blackburn Rovers (A) Lost 0-1
Spink, Linton, Jones, Bullivant, Ormsby, Williams, Young, Stirland, Donovan, Cropley, Heard (Hopkins).

Sat 27th September
Wolverhampton Wanderers (H) Drew 2-2
Donovan, Little
Spink, Deacy, Jones, Blake, Ormsby, Bullivant, Hopkins, Little, Donovan, Cropley, Heard, Sub Stirland.

Wed 8th October
Sheffield United (H) Won 1-0
Jones
Spink, Linton, Jones, Shelton, Ormsby, Heard, Hopkins, Little, Geddis, Cropley, Young.

Sat 11th October
Manchester United (H) Won 4-3
Cropley, Heard, Donovan 2
Spink, Linton, Jones, Blake, Ormsby, Bullivant, Hopkins, Geddis, Donovan, Cropley, Heard, Sub Shelton.

Sat 18th October
Bury (A) Won 3-0
Ormsby, Donovan, Geddis
Spink, Linton, Jones, Bullivant, Ormsby, Williams, Hopkins, Geddis, Donovan, Heard, Shelton, Sub Young.

Wed 22 October
Preston North End (A) Draw 2-2
Geddis, Little
Kendall, Linton, Jones, Bullivant, Ormsby, Heard, Hopkins, Little, Geddis, Cropley, Young, Sub Shelton.

Sat 25th October
Leeds United (H) Won 3-1
Shelton, Young, Cropley,
Kendall, Linton, Jones, Bullivant, Ormsby, Heard, Shelton, Little, Stirland, Cropley, Young, Sub Hopkins.

Sat 1st November
Burnley (A) drew 1-1
Geddis
Kendall, Linton, Heard, Bullivant, Ormsby, Blake, Geddis, Little, Donovan, Cropley, Shelton, Sub Hopkins.

Sat 8th November
Sheffield Wednesday (H) Lost 1-2
Donovan
Kendall, Linton, Jones, Heard, Ormsby, Blake, Geddis, Little, Donovan, Cropley, Young, Sub Birch.

Wed 12th November
Liverpool (H) Lost 0-3
Kendall, Linton, Jones, Bullivant, Ormsby, Blake, Hopkins, Little, Geddis (Stirland), Heard, Young.

Sat 22nd November
Bolton Wanderers (H) Won 5-1
Donovan 2, Geddis 2, Hopkins
Kendall, Deacy, Jones, Bullivant, Ormsby, Heard, Hopkins, Geddis, Donovan, Cropley, Young, Sub Stirland.

Wed 26th November
West Bromwich Albion (A) Drew 1-1
Geddis
Kendall, Deacy, Gibson, Bullivant, Ormsby, Heard, Hopkins (Jones), Geddis, Donovan, Cropley, Shelton.

Sat 29th November
Nottingham Forest (A) Lost 1-5
Own goal
Kendall, Deacy, Gibson, Birch, Blake, Heard, Hopkins, Little, Donovan, Cropley, Shelton.

Wed 3rd December
Blackpool (A) Lost 1-2
Little
Kendall, Deacy, Gibson, Bullivant, Ormsby, Blake, Heard, Little, Donovan, Cropley, Shelton.

Sat 6th December
Newcastle United (H) Lost 1-2
Cropley
Lowe, Taylor, Gibson, Blake, Ormsby, Birch (Shelton), Hopkins, Little, Donovan, Cropley, Young.

Mon 15th December
Sheffield United (A) Won 3-0
Hopkins, Donovan, Young
Kendall, Deacy, Gibson, Bullivant, Blake, Heard, Hopkins, Little, Donovan, Shelton, Young.

Sat 20th December
Preston North End (H) Won 2-1
Little 2
Spink, Taylor, Jones, Shelton, Blake, Mail, Hopkins, Little, Donovan, Cropley, Young, Sub Heard.

Sat 27th December
Stoke City (H) Won 2-0
Donovan, Walters
Spink, Taylor, Jones, Bullivant, Blake, Heard, Shelton, Walters, Donovan, Cropley, Young, Sub Hopkins.

Sat 10th January
Bolton Wanderers (A) Won 3-0
Walters, Cropley 2
Spink, Shelton, Jones, Bullivant, Blake, Heard, Hopkins, Birch (Young), Donovan, Cropley, Walters.

Sat 17th January
Manchester City (H) Drew 1-1
Bullivant
Spink, Shelton, Jones, Bullivant, Blake, Heard, Hopkins, Deacy, Donovan, Cropley, Walters.

Tue 3rd February
Coventry City (A) Lost 2-4
Hopkins, Shelton
Spink, Linton, Jones, Heard, Mail, Bullivant, Hopkins, Shelton, Geddis, Cropley, Walters, Sub Stirland.

Sat 7th February
Everton (H) Won 2-1
Hopkins, Walters
Spink, Linton, Shelton, Bullivant, Blake, Heard, Hopkins, Walters, Donovan, Birch, Young, Sub Mail.

Sat 14th February
Derby County (A) Lost 1-2
Walters
Spink, Deacy, Gibson, Jones, Blake, Mail, Hopkins, Walters, Donovan, Birch, Heard (Young).

Sat 21st February
Wolverhampton Wanderers (A) Drew 1-1
Heard
Spink, Deacy, Jones, Mail, Blake, Shelton, Birch, Walters, Donovan, Heard, Hopkins, Sub Linton.

Sat 28th February
Blackburn Rovers (H) Won 2-0
Hopkins, Donovan
Spink, Deacy, Jones, Bullivant, Blake, Mail, Hopkins, Geddis, Donovan, Cropley, Sub Shelton.

Sat 14th March
Manchester United (A) Won 1-0
Bullivant
Spink, Deacy, Jones, Nebbeling, Blake, Bullivant, Hopkins, Geddis, Donovan, Heard, Shelton, Sub Linton.

Sat 21st March
Bury (H) Won 4-2
Donovan, Walters (pen), Bullivant, Young
Spink, Linton, Shelton, Bullivant, Blake, Nebbeling, Hopkins, Walters, Donovan, Heard, Young, Sub Birch.

Wed 25th March
Blackpool (H) Won 7-0
Donovan 2, Hopkins, Young, Walters 2, Bullivant
Spink, Gibson, Deacy, Bullivant, Blake, Nebberling, Hopkins, Walters, Donovan, Heard, Young.

Sat 4th April
Burnley (H) Won 1-0
Walters
Spink, Deacy, Gibson, Bullivant, Blake, Walker F, Shelton, Walters, Donovan, Birch, Hopkins, Sub Jones.

Mon 13th April
Sheffield Wednesday (A) Lost 1-2
Donovan
Spink, Jones, Rogers, Birch, Walker, Glover, Shelton, Walters, Donovan, Cropley, Hopkins.

Thur 16th April
Leeds United (A) Drew 0-0
Spink, Jones, Rogers, Bullivant, Blake, Glover, Shelton, Geddis, Donovan, Deacy, Hopkins.

Mon 20th April
West Bromwich Albion (H) Drew 2-2
Cropley 2
Spink, Jones, Rogers, Blake, Walker, Bullivant, Hopkins, Walters, Linton, Cropley, Young.

Wed 22nd April
Stoke City (A) Drew 1-1
Donovan
Spink, Jones, Shelton, Bullivant, Blake, Glover, Hopkins, Walters, Donovan, Cropley, Young.

Thur 30th April
Newcastle United (A) Won 1-0
Geddis
Spink, Deacy, Shelton, Bullivant, Blake, Jones, Hopkins, Geddis, Donovan, Cropley, Young.

Central League Table 1980 - 81

	P	W	D	L	F	A	Pts
Liverpool	42	29	9	4	98	26	67
W.B.A.	42	22	14	6	68	31	58
Newcastle	42	23	9	10	74	40	55
Wolves	42	21	13	8	67	40	55
Man. City	42	17	18	7	74	51	52
Aston Villa	**42**	**20**	**11**	**11**	**79**	**54**	**51**
Nott'm Forest	42	19	11	12	60	43	49
Everton	42	17	11	14	58	53	45
Burnley	42	16	12	14	45	45	44
Coventry	42	16	10	16	75	74	42
Sheffield Wed	42	15	10	17	52	60	40
Leeds United	42	10	20	12	42	56	40
Bury	42	14	11	17	53	58	39
Stoke City	42	14	11	17	51	57	39
Man. United	42	11	16	15	47	54	38
Preston	42	12	12	18	51	72	36
Huddersfield	42	11	12	19	40	48	34
Sheffield Utd	42	9	16	17	44	61	34
Derby County	42	9	14	19	57	65	32
Bolton	42	9	9	24	40	85	27
Blackpool	42	6	12	24	28	85	24
Blackburn	42	7	9	26	33	78	23

Sat 2nd May
Nottingham Forest (H) Won 2-0
Hopkins, Stirland
Spink, Jones, Shelton, Bullivant, Blake, Glover, Hopkins, Stirland, Donovan (Walker), Cropley, Young.

1981/82

Central League

Sat 29th August
Leeds United (A) Won 2-0
Donovan 2
Spink, Linton, Jones, Mail, Blake, Heard, Shelton, Bullivant, Donovan, Stirland, Young, Sub Birch.

Wed 2nd September
Sheffield United (H) Drew 0-0
Spink, Linton, Williams, Mail, Blake (Birch), Heard, Hopkins, Bullivant, Walters, Stirland, Shelton, Sub Birch.

Sat 5th September
Manchester United (H) Won 2-0
Stirland, Walters
Spink, Linton, Jones, Mail, Blake, Bullivant, Hopkins, Blair, Stirland, Walters, Heard, Sub Shelton.

Sat 19th September
Liverpool (H) Drew 1-1
Shelton
Spink, Linton, Deacy, Blake, Ormsby, Heard, Hopkins, Shaw, Geddis, Bullivant, Shelton, Sub, Stirland.

Sat 26th September
Preston North End (A) Won 5-2
Shaw 2, own goal, Geddis 2
Spink, Deacy, Williams, Mail, Blake, Heard, Shelton, Shaw, Geddis, Bullivant, Hopkins, Sub Young.

Sat 3rd October
Sheffield Wednesday (A) Drew 0-0
Spink, Linton, Williams, Heard, Blake, Jones, Shelton, Stirland, Geddis, Bullivant (Deacy), Young.

Sat 10th October
Coventry City (H) Drew 0-0
Spink, Linton, Jones, Mail, Blake, Heard, Shelton, Stirland, Donovan, Birch, Deacy, Sub Hutchinson.

Tue 13th October
Bury (A) Won 4-3
Mail, Birch, Stirland 2
Poole, Deacy, Jones, Mail, Blake, Heard, Birch, Stirland, Donovan, Bullivant, Shelton, Sub ???

Sat 17th October
Newcastle United (A) Lost 1-3
Shelton
Spink, Linton, Jones, Mail, Blake, Heard, Shelton, Donovan (Rogers), Bullivant, Birch.

Sat 24th October
Blackpool (H) Lost 1-2
Stirland
Spink, Linton, Jones, Mail, Blake, Heard, Shelton, Stirland, Geddis, Bullivant, Deacy, Sub Birch.

Sat 31st October
Wolverhampton Wanderers (A) Lost 1-2
Geddis
Kendall, Linton, Jones, Walker, Blake, Heard, Hopkins, Blair, Donovan, Geddis, Bullivant, Sub Deacy.

Sat 7th November
Derby County (A) Lost 0-1
Kendall, Deacy, Jones, Birch, Blake, Ormsby, Hopkins, Geddis, Donovan, Heard, Shelton, Sub Stirland.

Sat 21st November
Nottingham Forest (H) Won 3-2
Donovan, Geddis 2
Kendall, Linton, Rogers, Blair, McNaught, Ormsby, Shelton, Geddis, Donovan, Heard, Hopkins, Sub Stirland.

Tue 24th November
Sheffield United (A) Lost 2-5
Blair, Donovan
Kendall, Mail, Jones, Blair, McNaught, Ormsby, Hopkins, Geddis, Donovan, Heard, Shelton, Sub Stirland.

Sat 28th November
Manchester City (A) Won 2-0
Donovan, Shelton
Spink, Jones, Rogers, Blair, Blake, Ormsby, Shelton, Geddis, Donovan, Bullivant, Heard, Sub Birch.

Sat 5th December
Bolton Wanderers (H) Won 7-1
Hopkins, Shelton, Donovan 2, Heard 2, Geddis
Spink, Linton, Jones, Blair, Blake, Ormsby, Hopkins, Shelton, Donovan, Birch, Heard, Sub Mail.

Wed 23rd December
Everton (A) Lost 1-3
Shelton
Spink, Deacy, Jones, Blair, McNaught, Ormsby, Hopkins, Mortimer, Walters, Heard, Shelton, Sub Birch.

Sat 30th January
Liverpool (A) Won 2-0
Donovan 2
Spink, Deacy, Jones, McNaught, Ormsby, Heard, Hopkins, Bullivant, Donovan, Walters, Shelton, Sub Blake.

Tue 2nd February
Coventry City (A) Lost 0-1
Spink, Linton, Jones, McNaught, Blake, Heard, Hopkins, Birch, Donovan, Walters, Deacy, Sub Walker.

Sat 6th February
Bury (H) Won 6-1
Own goal, Donovan 2, Walters 2, Heard
Spink, Deacy, Rogers, McNaught, Ormsby, Heard, Hopkins, Birch, Donovan, Walters, Hutchinson, Sub Blake.

Tue 9th February
Stoke City (A) Won 5-3
Kerr, Linton, Shelton 2, Blake
Spink, Deacy, Jones, Glover, Blake, Heard, Hopkins, Kerr, Linton, Birch, Shelton, Sub ???

Sat 13th February
Sheffield Wednesday (A) Won 5-2
Shaw, Heard, Donovan 3
Spink, Deacy, Rogers, Glover, Blake, Heard, Hopkins, Birch, Donovan, Shaw, Shelton, Sub Stirland.

Sat 20th February
Preston North End (H) Won 4-0
Donovan 2, Walters 2
Spink, Deacy, Jones, Blake, Ormsby, Heard, Hopkins, Blair, Donovan, Walters, Shelton, Sub Birch.

Mon 22nd February
Blackburn Rovers (H) Won 4-0
Hopkins, Donovan, Shelton, Heard
Spink, Deacy, Gibson, Blake, Ormsby, Heard, Hopkins, Bullivant, Donovan, Geddis, Shelton, Sub Jones.

Mon 1st March
Manchester United (A) Drew 1-1
Walters
Kendall, Brown, Jones, Blake, Ormsby, Heard, Hopkins, Birch, Donovan, Walters, Walker, Sub Norton.

Sat 6th March
Newcastle United (H) Won 6-0
Walters, Ormsby, Donovan 2, Shelton, Birch
Spink, Linton, Deacy, Blake, Ormsby, Heard, Hopkins, Birch, Donovan, Walters, Shelton, Sub Stirland.

Sat 13th March
Blackpool (A) Won 3-0
Heard 2, Walters
Spink, Linton, Deacy, Blake, Ormsby, Heard, Hopkins, Bullivant, Kerr, Walters, Shelton, Sub Birch.

Mon 22nd March
West Bromwich Albion (H) Drew 1-1
Ormsby
Spink, Jones, Deacy, Blake, Ormsby, Birch, Hopkins, Linton, Kerr, Geddis, Shelton, Sub Walker.

Sat 27th March
Derby County (H) Won 2-1
Donovan, Stirland
Spink, Linton, Deacy, Walker, Ormsby, Birch, Hopkins, Blair, Donovan, Geddis, Stirland, Sub Hutchinson.

Tue 30th March
Burnley (A) Won 1-0
Donovan
Spink, Deacy, Jones, Walker, Ormsby, Birch, Hopkins, Blair, Donovan, Geddis,Walters. sub

Sat 3rd April
Blackburn Rovers (A) Lost 0-1
Spink, Deacy, Jones, Walker, Glover, Bullivant, Hopkins, Bremner, Donovan, Geddis, Walters, Sub Birch.

Mon 12th April
West Bromwich Albion (A) Lost 2-3
Donovan, Deacy,
Spink, Linton, Deacy, Walker, Glover, Birch, Hopkins, Blair, Donovan, Walters, Bullivant. sub

Sat 17th April
Nottingham Forest (A) Drew 0-0
Spink, Linton, Deacy, Glover, Ormsby Birch, Hopkins, Walker, Donovan, Walters, Hutchinson, Sub Stirland.

Sat 24th April
Manchester City (H) Won 3-1
Heard, Donovan, Geddis
Spink, Deacy, Jones, Blake, Ormsby, Heard, Hopkins, Birch, Donovan, Geddis, Hutchinson, Sub Walker.

Mon 26th April
Leeds United (H) Lost 1-2
Walters
Spink, Linton, Jones, Blake, Glover, Walker, Hopkins, Birch, Kerr, Walters (Stirland), Hutchinson.

Thurs 29th April
Stoke City (H) Won 2-1
Birch, Bullivant
Spink, Linton, Jones, Blake, Glover, Walker, Hopkins, Bullivant, Stirland, Kerr (Hutchinson), Birch.

Sat 1st May
Bolton Wanderers (A) Won 3-1
Donovan, Stirland, Hopkins
Spink, Deacy, Jones (Hutchinson), Blake, Glover, Walker, Hopkins, Linton, Donovan, Stirland, Birch.

Wed 5th May
Burnley (H) Won 1-0
Donovan
Spink, Deacy, Gibson, Blake, Ormsby, Walker, Linton, Bullivant (Kerr), Donovan, Geddis, Hutchinson.

Sat 8th May
Everton (H) Won 1-0
Geddis
Spink, Deacy, Gibson, Blake, Ormsby, Walker, Linton, Bullivant, Donovan, Geddis, Hutchinson, Sub Norton.

Mon 10th May
Huddersfield Town (H) Won 3-0
Own goal, Blake, Birch (pen)
Spink, Jones, Gibson, Blake, Ormsby, Walker, Hopkins, Deacy, Geddis, Walters (Linton), Birch.

Thurs 13th May
Wolverhampton Wanderers (H) Won 3-0
Geddis, Stirland 2
Spink, Jones, Gibson, Blake, Ormsby, Linton, Hopkins, Stirland, Geddis, Deacy (Blair), Birch.

Central League Table 1981 - 82

	P	W	D	L	F	A	Pts
Liverpool	42	29	9	4	87	30	67
Everton	42	30	3	9	98	32	63
Aston Villa	**42**	**25**	**7**	**10**	**94**	**45**	**57**
Nott'm Forest	42	23	10	9	102	37	56
Newcastle United	42	19	10	13	61	57	48
Wolverhampton	42	19	10	13	79	69	48
W.B.A.	42	17	13	12	57	44	47
Sheffield United	42	16	14	12	51	43	46
Manchester Utd	42	18	8	16	58	44	44
Derby County	42	18	8	16	60	54	44
Leeds United	42	18	5	19	60	53	41
Sheffield Wed	42	18	5	19	75	76	41
Coventry City	42	15	11	16	49	59	41
Stoke City	42	11	15	16	50	61	37
Bury	42	13	9	20	48	74	35
Blackpool	42	14	7	21	56	85	35
Blackburn Rovers	42	10	14	18	58	81	34
Manchester City	42	12	9	21	43	73	33
Preston N. E.	42	12	8	22	60	86	32
Huddersfield Town	42	12	5	25	45	87	29
Burnley	42	7	11	24	42	88	25
Bolton Wanderers	42	6	9	27	54	109	21

Sat 15th May
Huddersfield Town (A) Won 3-1
Geddis 3
Spink, Jones, Gibson, Blake, Ormsby, Linton, Hopkins, Stirland (Walker), Geddis, Deacy, Birch.

1982/83

Central League

The format has changed with the Central League being split into two divisions of 16 clubs, giving a total of 30 matches instead of the previous 42.

Wed 1st September
Wolverhampton Wanderers (A) Won 3-1
Geddis 2, Rees
Spink, Jones, Deacy, Blake (Rees), Ormsby, Walker, Birch, Blair, Geddis, Kerr, Heard.

Sat 4th September
Liverpool (H) Lost 1-3
Kerr
Spink, Swain, Rogers, Walker, Ormsby, Glover, Hopkins, Birch, Rees, Kerr, Hutchinson, Sub McKenzie.

Wed 8th September
Huddersfield Town (A) Won 3-0
Hutchinson, Kerr, Hopkins
Spink, Swain, Gibson, Walker, Ormsby, Glover, Hopkins, Kerr, Donovan, Birch, Hutchinson, Sub Rogers.

Wed 22nd September
Leeds United (H) Won 2-0
Donovan (pen), Geddis
Spink, Swain, Gibson, Birch, Ormsby, Glover, Hopkins, Deacy, Donovan, Geddis, Heard, Sub Hutchinson.

Wed 13th October
Everton (H) Drew 1-1
Walters
Spink, Swain, Gibson, Birch, McNaught (Glover), Ormsby, Hopkins, Deacy, Geddis, Walters, Heard.

Sat 30th October
Blackburn Rovers (A) Lost 2-3
Walters, Donovan
Spink, Blair, Rogers, Walker, Ormsby, Glover, Hopkins, Geddis, Donovan, Walters, Heard, Sub Hutchinson.

Wed 10th November
Blackpool (A) Won 2-0
Walters 2
Spink, Jones (Deacy), Rogers, Walker, Ormsby, Glover, Hopkins, Blair, Donovan, Walters, Heard.

Wed 17th November
Stoke City (A) Drew 2-2
Glover, Walters
Spink, Jones, Ormsby, Glover, Gibson (Walker), Blair, Smith, Heard, Hopkins, Walters, Geddis.

Wed 1st December
Newcastle United (H) Won 2-1
Donovan, Glover
Spink, Walker, Gibson, Smith, Ormsby, Glover, Hopkins, Blair, Donovan, Walters, Heard, Sub Birch.

Sat 18th December
Liverpool (A) Won 2-1
Donovan, Gibson
Spink, Deacy, Gibson, Birch, Ormsby, Glover, Blair, Walker, Donovan, Kerr, Heard, Sub Hutchinson.

Wed 22nd December
Sheffield United (A) Won 2-1
Blair 2
Spink, Deacy, Gibson, Birch, Ormsby, Glover, Hopkins, Blair, Donovan, Kerr, Heard, Sub Walker.

Wed 5th January
Huddersfield Town (H) Won 2-1
Kerr, Birch
Poole, Deacy, Rogers, Birch, Ormsby, Glover, Hopkins, Blair, Donovan, Kerr (Walker), Heard.

Sat 22nd January
West Bromwich Albion (A) Won 4-0
Donovan, Geddis, Hopkins, Walters
Poole, Deacy, Rogers, Walker, Ormsby, Glover, Hopkins, Geddis, Donovan, Birch, Walters, Sub Kerr.

Mon 24th January
Bury (A) Lost 0-1
Poole, Deacy, Rogers, Walker, Ormsby, Glover, Hopkins, Geddis, Donovan, Birch, Kerr (Hutchinson).

Tue 1st February
Sheffield Wednesday (A) Lost 2-3
Walters 2
Poole, Jones, Rogers, Walker, Ormsby, Glover, Hopkins, Walters, Kerr, Birch, Hutchinson, Sub Bradley.

Wed 16th February
Blackpool (H) Won 4-1
Kerr 3, Hopkins
Poole, Jones, Rogers, Birch, Ormsby, Glover, Hopkins, Kerr, Geddis, Deacy, Hutchinson, Sub Norton.

Tue 22nd February
Everton (A) Won 1-0
Kerr
Rimmer, Deacy, Rogers, Walker, Ormsby, Glover, Hopkins, Kerr, Geddis, Birch, Hutchinson, Sub Obi.

Sat 26th February
Manchester United (H) Lost 1-3
Geddis
Rimmer, Deacy, Rogers, Norton, Ormsby, Glover, Hopkins, Kerr, Geddis, Birch, Hutchinson, Sub Dorigo.

Tue 8th March
Coventry City (A) Won 5-1
Kerr, Birch, Hutchinson, Geddis 2
Rimmer, Jones, Rogers, Walker, Ormsby, Glover, Hopkins, Kerr, Geddis, Birch, Hutchinson, Sub Bradley.

Wed 23rd March
Sheffield Wednesday (H) Won 3-1
Ormsby, Blair, Geddis
Rimmer, Jones, Deacy, Walker, Ormsby, Glover, Hopkins, Blair, Geddis, Kerr, Birch, Sub Hutchinson.

Wed 30th March
West Bromwich Albion (H) Drew 0-0
Rimmer, Jones, Dorigo, Walker, Ormsby, Glover, Blair, Curbishley, Geddis, Kerr (Birch), Morley.

Wed 6th April
Stoke City (H) Won 8-0
Walker, Ormsby, Kerr, Morley 3, Geddis 2
Poole, Jones, Deacy, Walker, Ormsby, Glover, Birch, Blair, Geddis, Kerr, Morley, Sub Norton.

Mon 11th April
Sheffield United (H) Won 6-1
Walker, Glover, Kerr 2, Geddis 2
Poole, Jones, Deacy, Walker, Ormsby, Glover, Blair, Curbishley, Geddis, Kerr, Morley, Sub Birch.

Sat 16th April
Newcastle United (A) Lost 0-2
Poole, Jones, Deacy, Walker, Ormsby, Bradley, Birch, Blair, Geddis, Kerr (Norton), Hutchinson.

Mon 25th April
Blackburn Rovers (H) Won 2-0
Kerr, Birch
Rimmer, Jones, Dorigo, Blair, Bradley, Bremner, Rees, Birch, Kerr, Walters, Hutchinson, Sub Palin.

Sat 30th April
Manchester United (A) Won 2-1
Norton, Birch
Rimmer, Jones, Dorigo, Birch, Ormsby, Glover, Blair, Norton, Geddis, Kerr, Hutchinson, Sub Rees.

Thur 5th May
Coventry City (H) Lost 1-3
Bremner
Rimmer, Jones, Dorigo, Birch, Ormsby, Glover, Bremner, Rees (Norton), Kerr, Walker, Hutchinson.

Sat 7th May
Leeds United (A) Won 2-0
Walker, Norton
Rimmer, Jones, Dorigo, Birch, Ormsby, Glover, Blair, Norton, Bradley, Walters, Walker, Sub Hutchinson.

Wed 11th May
Wolverhampton Wanderers (H) Won 2-0
Walters 2 (1pen)
Poole, Jones, Dorigo, Walker, Ormsby, Glover, Blair, Birch, Kerr, Walters, Hutchinson, Sub Palin.

Mon 16th May
Bury (H) Won 4-2
Geddis 2,Ormsby, own goal
Rimmer, Deacy, Gibson, Walker, Ormsby, Glover, Blair, Geddis, Withe, Birch, Walters, Sub Curbishley.

Central League Table 1982 - 83

	P	W	D	L	F	A	Pts
West Bromwich Albion	30	19	6	5	53	18	44
Aston Villa	**30**	**20**	**3**	**7**	**71**	**33**	**43**
Everton	30	17	8	5	47	20	42
Manchester United	30	18	5	7	60	28	41
Sheffield Wednesday	30	16	6	8	59	39	38
Liverpool	30	16	5	9	63	37	37
Stoke City	30	14	6	10	54	57	34
Newcastle United	30	12	9	9	41	34	33
Blackburn Rovers	30	12	6	12	49	53	30
Sheffield United	30	11	8	11	42	48	30
Leeds United	30	6	11	13	30	49	23
Bury	30	8	6	16	44	66	22
Coventry City	30	7	5	18	34	63	19
Huddersfield Town	30	6	5	19	32	53	17
Blackpool	30	7	1	22	35	74	15
Wolverhampton W.	30	3	6	21	19	61	12

1983/84

Central League

Wed 31st August
Stoke City (H) Won 2-1
Rideout, Morley (pen)
Day, Jones, Deacy, Walker, Glover, Dorigo, Norton, Palin, Rideout, Geddis, Morley, Sub Kerr.

Thur 8th September
Burnley (A) Lost 0-1
Day, Jones, Deacy, Walker, Geddis, Glover, Blair, Birch, Rideout (Kerr), Kennedy, Morley.

Sat 17th September
Manchester United (H) Drew 1-1
Kennedy
Day, Jones, Deacy, Walker, Bradley, Glover, Bremner, Blair, Geddis, Kennedy, Norton, Sub Kerr.

Tue 20th September
Sheffield Wednesday (A) Won 4-2
Blair, Kerr, Geddis 2
Belford, Jones, Deacy, Blair, Walker, Glover, Bremner, Kerr, Geddis, Birch, Morley, Sub Norton.

Sat 1st October
Liverpool (H) Lost 1-3
Blair
Day, Jones, Dorigo, Bradley, Walker, Glover, Blair, Norton, Rideout, Kerr, Obi, Sub Howell.

Wed 5th October
Leeds United (H) Won 2-0
Blair (pen), Rideout
Day, Jones, Dorigo, Blair, Walker, Glover (Bradley), Obi, Norton, Rideout, Kerr, Morley.

Wed 12th October
Blackburn Rovers (A) Drew 1-1
Palin
Day, Jones, Dorigo, Walker, Bradley, Glover, Blair, Norton, Rideout, Kerr, Palin (Hutchings).

Wed 9th November
Bolton Wanderers (A) Won 4-0
Kerr 2, Norton, Greenhalgh
Day, Shipley, Dorigo, Walker, Bradley, Glover, Obi, Norton, Greenhalgh, Kerr, Palin, Sub Hellin.

Wed 16th November
Sunderland (A) Won 4-1
Walker, Kerr, Norton 2
Day, Robinson, Shipley, Bremner, Walker, Glover, Obi, Norton, Palin, Kerr, Morley, Sub Hutchings.

Wed 23rd November
Sheffield United (H) Won 2-1
Norton, Walker
Day, Norton, Shipley, Bremner, Bradley, Glover, Curbishley (Hutchings), Walker, Greenhalgh,Kerr, Morley.

Wed 7th December
Everton (H) Lost 0-1
Day, Jones, Shipley, Norton, Bradley, Glover, Obi, McMahon, Kerr, Palin, Curbishley, Sub Greenhalgh.

Wed 14th December
Newcastle United (A) Lost 2-3
Norton, Obi
Day, Jones, Dorigo, Curbishley, Bradley, Glover, Bremner, Shaw, Kerr, Norton, Obi, Sub Palin.

Wed 21st December
Burnley (H) Won 3-0
Kerr, Shaw, Birch
Day, Jones (Norton), Dorigo, Bremner, Bradley, Glover, Birch, Shaw, Kerr, Walker, Obi.

Sat 7th January
West Bromwich Albion (A) Won 2-0
Glover, Rideout
Day, Jones, Dorigo, Norton, Bradley, Glover, Blair, Kerr, Rideout, Palin, Obi (Howell).

Wed 11th January
Derby County (H) Won 1-0
Williams
Day, Jones, Gibson, Williams, Bradley, Norton, Blair, Kerr, Greenhalgh, Palin, Dorigo, Sub Hutchings.

Sat 14th January
Manchester United (A) Won 2-1
Greenhalgh, Dorigo
Day, Jones, Dorigo, Norton, Bradley (Hutchings), Glover, Blair, Birch, Greenhalgh, Kerr, Palin.

Mon 16th January
Nottingham Forest (H) Drew 2-2
Kerr 2
Poole, Jones, Dorigo, Norton, Bradley, Glover, Blair, Birch, Greenhalgh (Walker), Kerr, Palin.

Sat 4th February
Liverpool (A) Lost 0-1
Day, Jones, Deacy, Norton, Ormsby, Glover, Birch, Blair, Kerr, Palin (Bradley), Dorigo.

Wed 8th February
Blackburn Rovers (H) Won 1-0
Birch
Day, Jones, Deacy, Norton, Ormsby, Glover, Birch, Blair, Bradley, Kerr (Obi), Walker.

Tues 6th March
Derby County (A) Lost 1-3
Greenhalgh
Day, Deacy, Dorigo, Norton, Bradley (Greenhalgh), Glover, Blair, Walters, Kerr, Walker, Obi.

Tue 13th March
Leeds United (A) Won 1-0
Bradley
Day, Deacy, Dorigo, Norton, Bradley, Glover, Blair, Kerr, Greenhalgh (Hutchings), Palin, Obi.

Wed 21st March
Stoke City (A) Drew 2-2
Obi, Greenhalgh
Poole, Deacy, Dorigo, Blair, Walker, Norton, Bremner, Kerr, Greenhalgh, Palin, Obi, Sub Hutchings.

Sat 24th March
Sheffield Wednesday (H) Lost 2-3
Greenhalgh, Obi
Poole, Norton, Deacy, Mortimer, Walker, Shipley, Blair, Kerr, Greenhalgh, Palin, Obi, Sub Hutchings.

Wed 28th March
Sunderland (H) Won 2-0
Norton (pen), Mortimer
Spink, Norton, Dorigo, Walker, Bradley, Glover, Bremner, Mortimer, Greenhalgh (Hutchings), Kerr, Obi.

Wed 4th April
Sheffield United (A) Won 6-0
Obi, Kerr, Blair 2, Palin, Walker
Spink, Norton, Deacy, Walker, Bradley, Glover, Blair, Kerr, Greenhalgh, Palin, Obi, Sub Dorigo.

Wed 9th April
West Bromwich Albion (H) Lost 0-2
Spink, Norton, Gibson, Bradley, Foster, Glover, Palin, Walker, Kerr, Dorigo, Obi, Sub Greenhalgh.

Wed 25th April
Newcastle United (H) Drew 0-0
Spink, Norton, Dorigo, Walker, Bradley, Glover, Curbishley, Kerr (Hutchings), Greenhalgh, Palin, Obi.

Sat 28th April
Everton (A) Drew 0-0
Spink, Norton, Dorigo, Hellin, Bradley, Glover, Hutchings, Curbishley, Greenhalgh, Kerr, Palin, Sub Gallacher.

Thurs 3rd May
Bolton Wanderers (H) 1-0
Foster
Spink, Norton, Gallagher, Bremner, Bradley, Glover, Curbishley, Shaw (Howell), Foster K, Kerr, Palin.

Central League Table 1983 - 84

	P	W	D	L	F	A	Pts
Liverpool	30	18	7	5	57	33	61
Manchester Utd	30	17	6	7	64	34	57
Aston Villa	**30**	**16**	**6**	**8**	**50**	**29**	**54**
Nott'm Forest	30	14	10	6	60	38	52
Everton	30	16	3	11	53	35	51
WBA	30	14	7	9	46	35	49
Newcastle Utd	30	14	7	9	44	37	49
Derby County	30	11	7	12	45	42	40
Stoke City	30	11	6	13	52	59	39
Sheffield Wed	30	11	5	14	52	61	38
Blackburn	30	10	6	14	38	46	36
Sheffield Utd	30	10	6	14	38	59	36
Sunderland	30	9	3	18	36	54	30
Leeds United	30	7	7	16	37	51	28
Bolton	30	8	3	19	35	63	27
Burnley	30	5	9	16	19	45	24

Thurs 10th May
Nottingham Forest (A) Won 1-0
Shaw
Spink, Shipley, Dorigo, Walker, Bradley, Glover, Bremner, Shaw, Foster K, Curbishley, Obi, Sub Kerr.

1984/85

Central League

Sat 25th August
Nottingham Forest (A) Won 1-0
Birch
Poole, Norton, Dorigo, Walker, Ormsby, Glover, Birch, Kerr, Greenhalgh, Palin, Obi, Sub Gallacher.

Wed 29th August
Newcastle United (H) Won 5-0
Birch, Ormsby, Rideout 2, Walker
Poole, Norton, Dorigo, Walker, Ormsby, Glover, Birch, Curbishley, Rideout, Kerr, Obi, Sub Bradley.

Tue 4th September
Derby County (A) Drew 1-1
Kerr
Poole, Norton, Dorigo, Bradley, Ormsby, Walker, Birch, Curbishley, Rideout (Glover), Kerr, Obi.

Wed 12th September
Sheffield United (H) Won 2-0
Hutchings 2
Poole, Norton, Williams, Bremner, Ormsby, Glover, Daley, Mortimer, Bradley (Palin), Hutchings, Obi.

Tues 18th September
Coventry City (A) Drew 1-1
Kerr
Poole, Williams, Norton, Bremner, Ormsby, Glover, Curbishley, Mortimer, Kerr, Palin, Obi, Sub O'Connell.

Wed 26th September
Nottingham Forest (H) Drew 1-1
Norton (pen)
Poole, Norton, Dorigo, Mortimer, Ormsby, Glover, Obi, Howell, Hutchings, Palin, Daley, Sub Hellin.

Wed 3rd October
Barnsley (A) Drew 0-0
Poole, Norton, Dorigo, McKenzie, Hellin, Glover, Obi, Kerr, Greenhalgh (Hutchings), Palin, Daley.

Thurs 11th October
Everton (H) Won 2-0
Daley, Obi
Spink, Norton Gallacher, Mortimer, Hellin, Glover, Obi, Kerr, Hutchings, Palin, Daley, Sub Greenhalgh.

Tues 16th October
Notts County (A) Won 3-1
Dorigo 2, Obi
Stink, Norton, Gallacher, Mortimer, Foster, Glover, Obi, Howell, Dorigo, Kerr, Palin, Sub Hellin.

Wed 24th October
Bradford City (H) Won 3-0
Kerr 2, Dorigo
Poole, Norton, Dorigo, Mortimer, Hellin, Glover (Hutchings), Obi, Curbishley, Palin, Kerr, Daley.

Wed 7th November
Stoke City (A) Won 3-1
Norton, Walker, Palin
Stink, Norton, Gallacher, Mortimer, Foster, Glover, Hutchings, Greenhalgh, Palin,Walker, Obi, Sub Hellin.

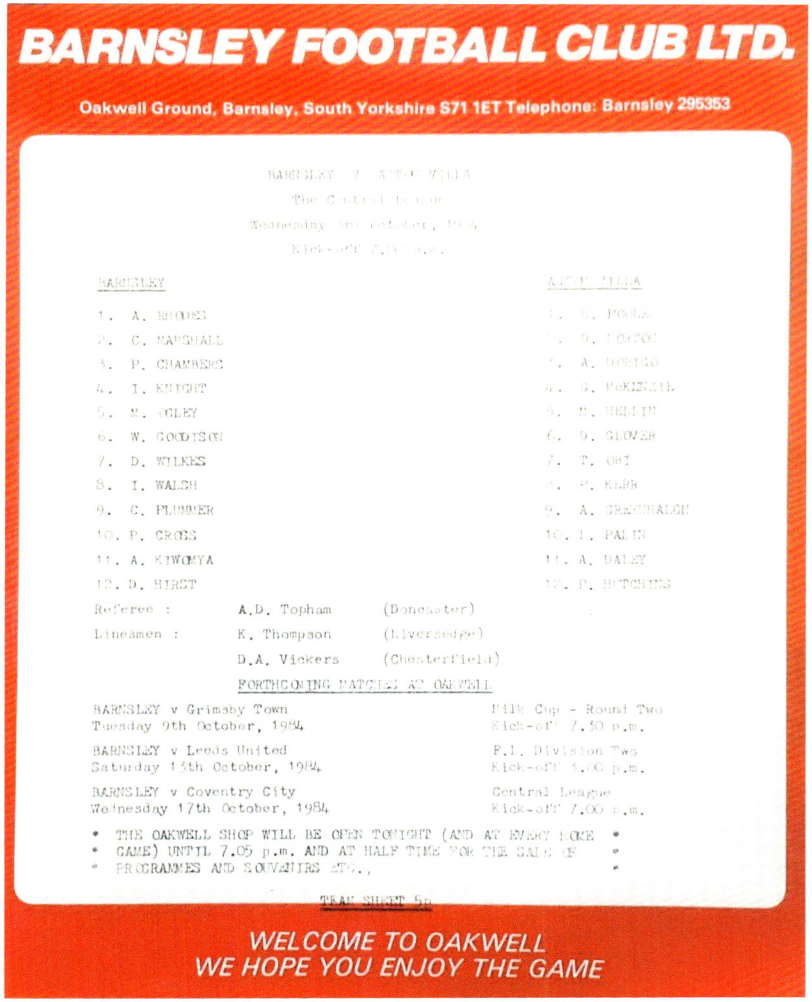

BARNSLEY FOOTBALL CLUB LTD.

Oakwell Ground, Barnsley, South Yorkshire S71 1ET Telephone: Barnsley 295353

BARNSLEY V ASTON VILLA

The Central League

Wednesday [illegible] October, 1984

Kick-off [illegible] p.m.

BARNSLEY	ASTON VILLA
1. A. RHODES	1. E. POOLE
2. C. MARSHALL	2. D. NORTON
3. P. CHAMBERS	3. A. DORIGO
4. I. KNIGHT	4. G. McKENZIE
5. M. OGLEY	5. M. HELLIN
6. W. GOODISON	6. D. GLOVER
7. D. WILKES	7. T. OBI
8. I. WALSH	8. P. KERR
9. C. PLUMMER	9. A. GREENHALGH
10. P. CROSS	10. I. PALIN
11. A. KIWOMYA	11. A. DALEY
12. D. HIRST	12. P. HUTCHINS

Referee : A.D. Topham (Doncaster)

Linesmen : K. Thompson (Liversedge)

D.A. Vickers (Chesterfield)

FORTHCOMING MATCHES AT OAKWELL

BARNSLEY v Grimsby Town — Milk Cup - Round Two
Tuesday 9th October, 1984 — Kick-off 7.30 p.m.

BARNSLEY v Leeds United — F.L. Division Two
Saturday 13th October, 1984 — Kick-off 3.00 p.m.

BARNSLEY v Coventry City — Central League
Wednesday 17th October, 1984 — Kick-off 7.00 p.m.

* THE OAKWELL SHOP WILL BE OPEN TONIGHT (AND AT EVERY HOME GAME) UNTIL 7.05 p.m. AND AT HALF TIME FOR THE SALE OF PROGRAMMES AND SOUVENIRS ETC., *

TEAM SHEET 5p

WELCOME TO OAKWELL
WE HOPE YOU ENJOY THE GAME

Wed 14th November
West Bromwich Albion (H) Won 2-0
Curbishley, Walters
Spink, Norton, Gallacher, Curbishley, Foster, Glover, Obi, Walters, Rideout, Palin, Dorigo, Sub Hutchings.

Wed 21st November
Liverpool (H) Won 5-1
Walters 2, Rideout 2, Daley
Spink, Norton, Dorigo, Mortimer, Foster, Glover, Obi, Bradley, Rideout, Walters, Daley, Sub Hutchings.

Sat 24th November
Manchester United (A) Lost 0-2
Spink, Norton, Gallacher, Mortimer, Foster, Bradley, Obi, Curbishley, Rideout, Hutchings, Palin, Sub Hellin.

Wed 28th November
Huddersfield Town (A) Won 2-1
Bradley, Rideout
Spink, Norton, Dorigo, Mortimer, Hellin (Gallacher), Glover, Curbishley, Kerr, Rideout, Bradley, Palin.

Wed 5th December
Sheffield Wednesday (H) Won 2-0
Kerr, Norton (pen)
Poole, Norton, Dorigo, Mortimer, Bradley (Gallacher), Glover, Obi, Walker, Palin, Kerr, Six.

Wed 12th December
Blackburn Rovers (A) Lost 0-1
Day, Norton, Gallacher, Walker, Bradley, Glover, McKenzie (English), Forman, Hutchings, Ritchie, Dorigo.

Wed 19th December
Manchester City (H) Won 1-0
Kerr
Day, Bradley, Gallacher, Mortimer, Walker, Glover, Hutchings, McMahon, Kerr, Cowans, Obi, Sub Howell.

Wed 30th January
Coventry City (H) Lost 0-3
Poole, Bradley, Gallacher, Evans, Glover, Walker, Obi, Hutchings, Kerr, Palin, Daley (Robinson).

Wed 6th February
Barnsley (H) Drew 1-1
Walker
Poole, William, Gallacher, Walker, Bradley, Glover, Obi, Howell (Hutchings), Kerr, Palin, Six.

Wed 27th February
Stoke City (H) Lost 2-3
McMahon, Kerr
Poole, Norton, Gallacher, Walker, Bradley, Glover, Hutchings, McMahon, Kerr, Palin, Six, Sub Robinson.

Mon 4th March
Sheffield United (A) Won 4-0
Kerr, Norton (pen), Bradley, Howell
Poole, Norton, Gallacher, Walker, Hellin, Glover, Hutchings, Howell, Kerr, Bradley, Palin, Sub Robinson.

Sat 9th March
Manchester United (H) Lost 0-1
Poole, Norton, Robinson, Forman, Hellin, Glover, Hutchings, Mortimer, Howell, Walker, Palin, Sub Ritchie.

Tues 12th March
Bradford City (A) Lost 0-3
Poole, Norton, Gallacher, Robinson, Hellin, Glover, Hutchings, Mortimer, Howell, Forman, Palin, Sub Ritchie.

Mon 18th March
Derby County (H) Won 1-0
Gibson
Poole, Norton, Gallacher, Birch, Bradley, Glover, Hutchings, Howell, Rideout (Forman), Gibson, Palin.

Wed 20th March
Notts County (H) Won 5-0
Palin 2, Howell, Birch, Norton
Poole, Norton, Gallacher, Robinson, Bradley, Glover, Hutchings, Mortimer, Howell, Birch, Palin, Sub Forman.

Fri 22nd March
Liverpool (A) Drew 1-1
Norton
Poole, Norton, Gallacher, Robinson, Bradley, Glover, Hutchings, Mortimer, Kerr, Birch, Palin, Sub Hellin.

Tues 26th March
Everton (A) Won 1-0
Gallagher
Poole, Norton, Gallacher, Walker, Bradley (Howell), Glover, Hutchings, Mortimer, Kerr, Birch, Robinson.

Wed 10th April
Huddersfield Town (H) Won 9-0
Palin 3, Daley 2, Obi 2, Kerr, Norton
Belford, Norton, Gallacher, Birch, Glover, Bradley, Obi, Palin, Kerr, Cowans, Daley, Sub Robinson.

Sat 13th April
West Bromwich Albion (A) Lost 1-2
Palin
Spink, Norton, Gallacher, Walker, Bradley, Glover, Birch, Palin, Kerr, Cowans, Daley, Sub Obi.

Tues 16th April
Sheffield Wednesday (A) Lost 2-4
Kerr, own goal
Poole, Norton, Gallacher, Cowans, Bradley, Robinson, Hutchings (Howell), Mortimer, Kerr, Palin, Obi.

Tues 23rd April
Manchester City (A) Won 2-1
Mortimer, Howell
Poole, Norton, Gallacher, Mortimer, Bradley (Robinson), Glover, Obi, Howell, Kerr, Cowans, Palin.

Wed 1st May
Blackburn Rovers (H) Won 3-1
Kerr 2, McMahon
Purkiss, Hellin, Robinson, Walker, Ormsby, Evans, Obi, Mortimer, Kerr, McMahon (Howell), Palin.

Wed 8th May
Newcastle United (A) Lost 1-2
Mortimer
Belford, Hellin, Robinson, Mortimer, Bradley, Walker, Hutchings, Howell, Kerr, Palin, Obi, Sub Forman.

Central League Table 1984 - 85

	P	W	D	L	F	A	Pts
Liverpool	34	21	8	5	66	37	71
Manchester Utd	34	22	3	9	76	32	69
Aston Villa	**34**	**19**	**6**	**9**	**67**	**34**	**63**
Nott'm Forest	34	17	10	7	70	50	61
Derby County	34	18	5	11	53	45	59
Sheffield Wed	34	18	4	12	69	55	58
Blackburn	34	17	7	10	57	43	58
Manchester City	34	16	6	12	53	52	54
Everton	34	16	3	15	73	59	51
Huddersfield	34	12	7	15	54	64	43
Sheffield United	34	12	3	19	49	60	39
Newcastle	34	10	9	15	45	62	39
WBA	34	11	4	19	35	53	37
Barnsley	34	9	9	16	39	53	36
Coventry	34	10	4	20	45	61	34
Bradford City	34	10	4	20	45	69	34
Stoke	34	8	6	20	43	72	30
Notts County	34	8	6	20	40	78	30

1985/86

Central League

Sat 24th August
Manchester United (A) Won 2-1
Howell, Kerr
Poole, Bates, Gallacher, Ritchie, Hellin, Forman, Spark, Palin, Kerr, Howell, Burke, Sub Clipston.

Wed 28th August
Liverpool (H) Lost 0-2
Poole, Ritchie, Gallacher, Walker, Hellin, Forman, Gibson (Spark), Palin, Shaw, Howell, Kerr.

Thurs 5th September
Leeds United (H) Won 5-0
Kerr 3, Walker, Shaw
Poole, Norton, Gallacher, Walker, Hellin, Glover, Howell, Forman, Shaw, Kerr, Palin, Sub Ritchie.

Wed 11th September
Hull City (A) Won 3-1
Shaw, Kerr 2
Poole, Norton, Gallacher, Walker, Hellin, Glover, Howell, Shaw, Kerr, Gibson, Palin, Sub Forman.

Wed 18th September
Blackburn Rovers (H) Drew 1-1
Shaw
Poole, Norton, Gallacher, Walker, Hellin, Glover, Howell, Shaw, Kerr, Bradley, Palin, Sub Forman.

Thurs 26th September
Barnsley (A) Won 3-2
Shaw, Kerr, Forman
Poole, Norton, Gallacher, Ritchie, Hellin, Glover, Forman, Shaw, Kerr, Howell, Palin, Sub Grainger.

Wed 2nd October
Nottingham Forest (Home) Lost 3-4
Kerr 2, Shaw
Poole, Norton, Clipston, Walker, Hellin, Glover, Howell, Shaw, Kerr, Palin (Forman), Daley.

Wed 9th October
Newcastle United (A) Lost 3-4
Shaw, Kerr, Ritchie
Poole, Norton, Robinson, Ritchie, Hellin, Glover, Forman, Shaw, Kerr, Palin, Howell, Sub Burke.

Wed 16th October
Everton (H) Won 1-0
Shaw
Belford, Norton, Gallacher, Walker, Bradley (Robinson), Glover, Howell, Shaw, Kerr, Palin, Daley.

Wed 23rd October
Sheffield United (A) Lost 0-2
Poole, Robinson, Gallacher, Forman, Bradley, Glover, Howell, Shaw (Hellin), Kerr, Palin, Grainger.

Wed 6th November
Sheffield Wednesday (H) Won 2-0
Gallacher (pen), Shaw
Poole, Robinson, Gallacher, Walker, Ormsby, Bradley, Birch, Shaw, Kerr (Forman), Norton, Howell.

Tues 12th November
Manchester City (A) Lost 0-2
Poole, Robinson, Gallacher, Bradley (Clipston), Ormsby, Norton, Birch, Howell, Shaw, Ritchie, Forman.

Tues 19th November
Wigan Athletic (A) Won 2-1
Shaw 2
Poole, Robinson, Gallacher, Norton, Hellin, Bradley, Forman, Shaw, Howell, Ritchie, Burke, Sub Bates.

Tues 26th November
Huddersfield Town (A) Drew 0-0
Poole, Bates, Gallacher, Norton, Hellin, Robinson, Forman, Howell, Kerr, Ritchie, Burke, Sub Clipston.

Tues 3rd December
Leicester City (A) Lost 3-8
Kerr, Shaw, Howell
Poole, Robinson, Gallacher, Forman, Hellin, Ritchie, Howell, Shaw, Kerr, Norton, Burke (Clipston).

Wed 11th December
West Bromwich Albion (H) 4-1
Howell, Shaw 2, own goal
Poole, Robinson, Gallacher, Norton, Hellin, Spark, Forman, Shaw, Kerr, Ritchie, Howell, Sub Burke.

Mon 16th December
Leeds United (A) Lost 1-7
Howell
Purkiss, Robinson, Gallacher, Forman, Ormsby, Hellin, Spark, Burke, Howell, Ritchie, Norton, Sub Clipston.

Sat 18th January
Manchester United (H) Lost 0-1
Poole, Robinson, Gallacher, Ritchie, Ormsby, Hellin, Forman, Burke, Howell, Callaghan (Bowen), Clipston.

Thur 30th January
Liverpool (A) Won 3-2
Shaw, Ormsby, Gallacher (pen)
Belford, Robinson, Gallacher, Forman, Ormsby, Hellin, Howell, Shaw (Burke), Kerr, Bradley, Daley.

Thus 20th February
Blackburn Rovers (A) Won 1-0
Forman
Spink, Williams, Gallacher, Hellin, Ormsby, Robinson, Ritchie, Forman, Burke, Walker, Clipston, Sub Bates.

Wed 5th March
Nottingham Forest (A) Lost 0-2
Poole, Bates, Gallacher, Walker, Hellin, Robinson, Forman, Shaw, Daley, Ritchie, Burke, Sub Clipston.

Thur 13th March
Newcastle United (H) Lost 0-1
Poole, Ritchie, Gallacher, Walker, Robinson, Hellin, Forman, Shaw, Stainrod (Burke), Norton, Daley.

Sat 15th March
Barnsley (H) Won 3-2
Burke 2, Forman
Poole, Ritchie, Gallacher, Walker, Robinson, Hellin, Daley, Forman, Burke, Norton, Clipston, Sub Spark.

Thur 20th March
Sheffield Wednesday (A) Won 3-1
Kerr 2, Forman
Poole, Robinson (Burke), Gallacher, Norton, Hellin, Glover, Birch, Forman, Kerr, Ritchie, Daley.

Thur 27th March
Derby County (H) Won 3-1
Birch, Kerr, Stainrod
Poole, Robinson, Gallacher, Norton Hellin, Glover, Walters (Forman), Stainrod, Kerr, Walker, Birch.

Wed 2nd April
Manchester City (H) Lost 0-2
Spink, Williams, Gallacher, Walker, Hellin, Glover, Birch, Shaw, Forman, Callaghan, Daley, Sub Clipston.

Mon 7th April
Huddersfield Town (H) Drew 1-1
Forman
Spink, Mahoney (Callaghan), Gallacher, Walker, Robinson, Glover, Forman, Shaw, Kerr, Ritchie, Daley.

Sat 12th April
Everton (A) Lost 1-4
Kerr
Belford, Bates, Gallacher, Walker, Forman, Robinson, Spark, Ritchie, Kerr, Burke, Clipston, Sub Clarke.

Mon 14th April
Hull City (H) Won 2-0
Shaw, Kerr
Spink, Forman, Gallacher, Walker, Robinson, Glover, Burke, Shaw, Kerr, Ritchie, Clipston, Sub Callaghan.

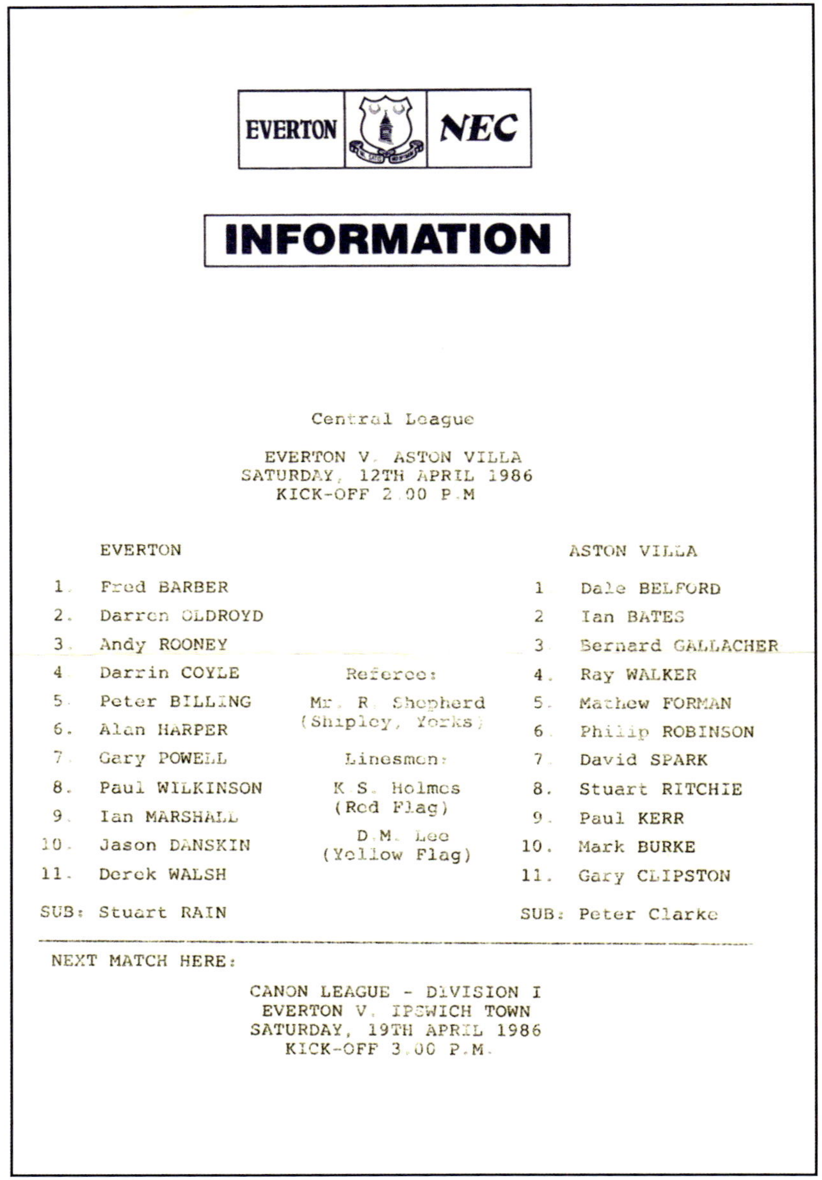
EVERTON NEC

INFORMATION

Central League

EVERTON V. ASTON VILLA
SATURDAY, 12TH APRIL 1986
KICK-OFF 2.00 P.M

EVERTON		ASTON VILLA
1. Fred BARBER		1 Dale BELFORD
2. Darren OLDROYD		2 Ian BATES
3. Andy ROONEY		3 Bernard GALLACHER
4 Darrin COYLE	Referee:	4. Ray WALKER
5. Peter BILLING	Mr. R. Shepherd (Shipley, Yorks)	5. Mathew FORMAN
6. Alan HARPER		6. Philip ROBINSON
7. Gary POWELL	Linesmen:	7. David SPARK
8. Paul WILKINSON	K.S. Holmes (Red Flag)	8. Stuart RITCHIE
9. Ian MARSHALL		9. Paul KERR
10. Jason DANSKIN	D.M. Lee (Yellow Flag)	10. Mark BURKE
11. Derek WALSH		11. Gary CLIPSTON
SUB: Stuart RAIN		SUB: Peter Clarke

NEXT MATCH HERE:

CANON LEAGUE - DIVISION I
EVERTON V. IPSWICH TOWN
SATURDAY, 19TH APRIL 1986
KICK-OFF 3.00 P.M.

Mon 21st April
Sheffield United (H) Lost 0-2
Belford, Mahoney, Gallacher, Bennett, Hellin, Robinson, Spark, Forman, Burke, Ritchie, Clipston, Sub Bates.

Wed 23rd April
Leicester City (H) Lost 2-5
Forman, Burke
Belford, Mahoney, Gallacher, Birch, Hellin, Robinson, Spark, Forman, Burke, Ritchie, Clipston, Sub Bates.

Sat 26th April
West Bromwich Albion (A) Lost 1-2
Shaw (pen)
Belford, Forman, Clipston, Walker, Clarke, Robinson, Burke, Shaw, Kerr, Ritchie, Bowen, Sub Spark.

Mon 28th April
Derby County (A) Lost 0-5
Belford, Forman, Clipston, Walker, Clarke, Glover, Spark, Shaw, Burke, Ritchie, Daley, Sub Callaghan.

Fri 2nd May
Wigan Athletic (H) Won 2-0
Ritchie 2
Spink, Forman, Gallacher, Robinson, Walker, Spark, Burke, Bowen, Kerr Ritchie, Clipston, Sub Bennett.

Central League Table 1985 - 86

	P	W	D	L	F	A	Pts
Derby County	34	21	3	10	81	35	66
Manchester Utd	34	19	5	10	55	32	62
Liverpool	34	19	4	11	85	53	61
Nott'm Forest	34	17	5	12	76	54	56
Manchester City	34	16	8	10	58	40	56
Sheffield Wed	34	16	4	14	55	47	52
Leeds United	34	16	3	15	63	70	51
Hull City	34	15	4	15	52	53	49
Aston Villa	**34**	**15**	**3**	**16**	**55**	**67**	**48**
Blackburn Rovers	34	14	4	16	57	49	46
Leicester City	34	12	10	12	60	58	46
Newcastle Utd	34	13	7	14	52	61	46
Everton	34	12	6	16	36	44	42
Sheffield Utd	34	12	5	17	44	76	41
Barnsley	34	12	4	18	44	60	40
WBA	34	9	10	15	41	65	37
Huddersfield Town	34	8	11	15	51	68	35
Wigan Athletic	34	11	2	21	44	77	35

1986/87

Central League

Sat 27th August
Nottingham Forest (H) Lost 1-2
Kerr
Spink, Keown, Clipston (Callaghan), Glover, Clarke, Robinson, Birch, Shaw, Gray, Ritchie, Kerr, Sub Olney.

Tue 2nd September
Sunderland (A) Drew 0-0
Spink, Norton, Gallacher, Glover, Cooper (Burke), Callaghan, Olney, Shaw, Gray, Ritchie, Clipston, Sub Mahoney.

Sat 13th September
Manchester United (H) Lost 0-7
Spink, Mahoney, Gallacher, Glover, Clarke (Morris), Callaghan (Bennett), Burke, Greene, Olney, Ritchie, Clipston.

Fri 26th September
Liverpool (H) Won 4-3
Walters, Shaw, Gallacher pen, Howell
Poole, Mahoney, Gallacher, Williams G, Glover, Ritchie, Daley, Shaw, Kerr (Howell), Robinson, Walters, Sub Clipston.

Wed 1st October
Hull City (H) Won 4-1
Walters 2, Kerr, Olney
Poole, Williams G, Gallacher, Robinson, Glover (Olney), Ritchie, Howell, Shaw, Gray, Kerr, Walters, Sub Callaghan.

Wed 8th October
Blackburn Rovers (A) Won 1-0
Olney
Poole, Mahoney, Gallacher, Williams G, Bates, Robinson, Howell (Burke), Ritchie, Olney, Callaghan, Shaw, Sub Clipston.

Wed 15th October
Newcastle United (H) Won 7-1
Walters 4, Kerr, Cooper, Shaw
Poole, Williams G, Ritchie, Keown, Glover, Cooper, Daley (Howell), Shaw, Kerr, Stainrod, Walters (Burke).

Wed 22nd October
Sheffield United (A) Lost 2-4
Olney, Burke
Poole, Williams G, Clipston, Bates, Cooper (Robinson), Ritchie, Howell (Burke), Shaw, Olney, Stainrod, Daley.

Mon 27th October
Leicester City (A) Won 2-1
Stainrod, Olney
Poole, Bennett, Clipston, Kerr, Bates, Stainrod (Burke), Mahoney, Shaw, Olney, Callaghan, Howell, Sub Brady.

Thur 6th November
Manchester City (H) Won 4-2
Shaw 3 (1 pen), Kerr
Poole, Williams G, Clipston, Ritchie, Elliott, Kerr, Howell (Callaghan), Shaw, Olney (Mahoney), Burke, Walters.

Tue 11th November
Coventry City (A) Lost 2-4
Howell, Burke
Poole, Mahoney, Clipston, Bates, Cooper, Ritchie, Callaghan (Morris), Kerr (Claxton), Howell, Bennett, Burke.

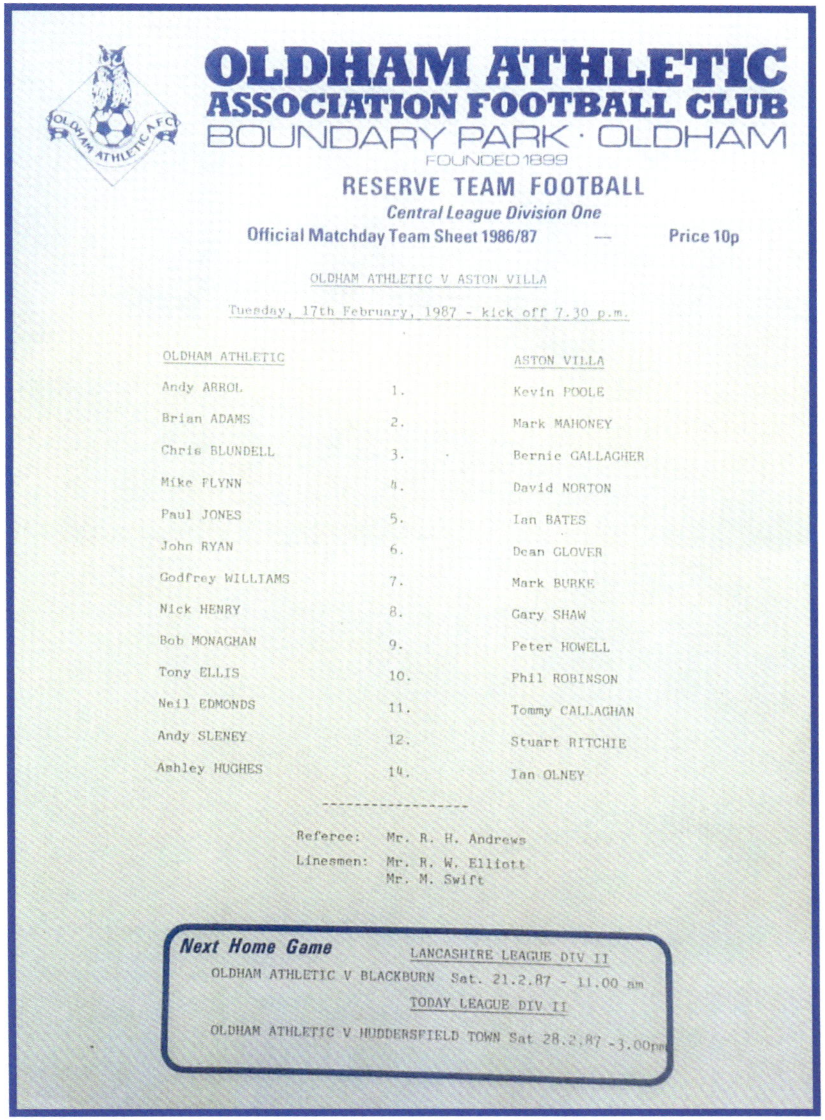
OLDHAM ATHLETIC
ASSOCIATION FOOTBALL CLUB
BOUNDARY PARK · OLDHAM
FOUNDED 1899

RESERVE TEAM FOOTBALL
Central League Division One
Official Matchday Team Sheet 1986/87 — Price 10p

OLDHAM ATHLETIC V ASTON VILLA
Tuesday, 17th February, 1987 - kick off 7.30 p.m.

OLDHAM ATHLETIC		ASTON VILLA
Andy ARROL	1.	Kevin POOLE
Brian ADAMS	2.	Mark MAHONEY
Chris BLUNDELL	3.	Bernie GALLAGHER
Mike FLYNN	4.	David NORTON
Paul JONES	5.	Ian BATES
John RYAN	6.	Dean GLOVER
Godfrey WILLIAMS	7.	Mark BURKE
Nick HENRY	8.	Gary SHAW
Bob MONAGHAN	9.	Peter HOWELL
Tony ELLIS	10.	Phil ROBINSON
Neil EDMONDS	11.	Tommy CALLAGHAN
Andy SLENEY	12.	Stuart RITCHIE
Ashley HUGHES	14.	Ian OLNEY

Referee: Mr. R. H. Andrews
Linesmen: Mr. R. W. Elliott
Mr. M. Swift

Next Home Game
LANCASHIRE LEAGUE DIV II
OLDHAM ATHLETIC V BLACKBURN Sat. 21.2.87 - 11.00 am
TODAY LEAGUE DIV II
OLDHAM ATHLETIC V HUDDERSFIELD TOWN Sat 28.2.87 -3.00pm

Wed 19th November
Oldham Athletic (H) Lost 2-5
Walters 2
Dudley, Callaghan, Clipston, Glover, Cooper, Ritchie, Howell, Burke, Olney, Hodge, Walters, Subs Bennett, Morris.

Wed 26th November
Sheffield Wednesday (A) Lost 1-4
Olney
Dudley, Bates (Bennett), Clipston, Robinson, Glover, Ritchie, Callaghan, Howell, Stainrod, Burke, Walters, Sub Olney.

Wed 3rd December
Derby County (H) Lost 2-4
Olney, Stainrod
Poole, Ritchie, Clipston, Robinson, Bates, Callaghan, Burke, Kerr (Greene), Olney, Stainrod, Howell, Sub Bennett.

Thur 11th December
Everton (A) Lost 1-3
Kerr
Poole, Callaghan, Clipston, Bates, Cooper, Ritchie, Kerr, Shaw (Olney), Howell, Robinson, Burke, Sub Bennett.

Mon 15th December
Coventry City (H) Drew 3-3
Walters, Williams G, Elliott
Poole, Williams G, Clipston, Keown, Elliott, Cooper, Birch, Kerr, Olney (Howell), Robinson, Walters, Sub Ritchie.

Wed 7th January
Middlesbrough (H) Won 4-0
Burke 2, Howell, Robinson
Poole, Norton, Ritchie, Cooper (Clipston), Elliott, Glover, Birch, Howell, Gray (Greene), Robinson, Burke.

Tue 3rd February
Liverpool (A) Drew 0-0
Poole, Norton, Gallacher, Ritchie, Elliott, Glover, Daley (Clipston), Shaw, Howell, Robinson, Burke, Sub Greene.

Wed 11th February
Leeds United (H) Lost 1-4
Elliott
Poole, Norton, Gallacher, Mitchell (Callaghan), Elliott, Glover, Ritchie (Olney), Shaw, Howell, Robinson, Burke.

Tue 17th February
Oldham Athletic (A) Won 3-1
Robinson, Shaw 2
Poole, Mahoney, Gallacher, Norton, Bates, Glover, Burke, Shaw, Howell, Robinson, Callaghan, Subs Ritchie, Olney.

Wed 25th February
Sheffield Wednesday (H) Lost 1-2
Olney
Poole, Bates (Ritchie), Gallacher, Norton, Evans, Glover, Mahoney, Greene (Claxton), Olney, Callaghan, Burke.

Mon 9th March
Sheffield United (H) Won 4-1
Birch 2, Aspinall, Burke
Poole, Norton, Gallacher, Ritchie, Cooper, Glover, Birch, Aspinall, Stainrod, Robinson, Burke, Subs Olney, Mahoney.

Wed 11th March
Newcastle United (A) Won 4-0
Olney, Howell, Burke, Evans (pen)
Poole, Williams G, Gallacher, Evans, Glover, Cooper, Birch, Howell, Olney, Robinson, Burke, Subs Ritchie, Mahoney.

Tue 17th March
Blackburn Rovers (H) Drew 0-0
Poole, Mahoney, Gallacher, Williams G, Glover, Robinson, Walters, Howell, Olney, Callaghan, Burke, Subs Ritchie, Clipston.

Sat 21st March
Manchester United (A) Lost 0-5
Poole, Mahoney, Clipston, Bennett, Glover, Ritchie, Morris (Claxton), Howell, Greene (Blake), Callaghan, Burke.

Thur 26th March
Hull City (A) Lost 1-2
Howell
Poole, Mahoney, Gallacher, Evans, Glover, Ritchie, Howell, Aspinall, Olney, Robinson, Burke, Subs Bennett, Clipston.

Tues 31st March
Manchester City (A) Lost 1-4
Olney
Poole, Bennett, Gallacher, Evans, Glover, Ritchie, Howell, Aspinall, Olney, Robinson (Clipston), Burke, Sub Brady.

Wed 8th April
Leicester City (H) Lost 1-2
Daley
Poole, Ritchie, Gallacher, Evans, Glover, Robinson, Howell (Clipston), Shaw (Olney), Aspinall, Burke, Daley.

Tue 14th April
Derby County (A) Lost 1-3
Olney
Poole, Bennett, Clipston, Evans, Glover, Ritchie, Howell, Shaw, Olney, Robinson, Burke, Subs Williams M, Claxton.

Tue 21st April
Leeds United (A) Lost 2-5
Howell, Olney
Poole, Mahoney, Gallacher, Evans (Bennett),Glover, Ritchie, Olney, Shaw, Stainrod, Robinson, Burke (Howell).

Thur 23rd April
Nottingham Forest (A) Lost 0-3
Poole, Bennett, Gallacher, Ritchie (Blake), Elliott, Glover, Walters, Shaw (Olney), Stainrod, Robinson, Burke.

Thur 30th April
Sunderland (H) Won 5-3
Mahoney, Walters 2, Olney 2
Ward, Mahoney, Gallacher, Evans, Glover, Ritchie, Daley (Blake), Walters (Bates), Olney, Robinson, Clipston.

Wed 6th May
Everton (A) Drew 0-0
Spink, Mahoney, Gallacher, Bates, Blake, Ritchie, Burke, Greene, Olney, Bennett, Robinson, Subs Morris, Brady.

Mon 11th May
Middlesbrough (A) Lost 0-2
Poole, Mahoney (Clipston) Gallacher, Robinson, Blake, Glover, Ritchie, Bates, Olney, Bennett, Burke, Sub Morris.

Central League Table 1986 - 87

	P	W	D	L	F	A	Pts
Manchester C	34	23	4	7	83	46	73
Derby County	34	19	11	4	65	31	68
Manchester U	34	21	5	8	65	35	68
Liverpool	34	20	7	7	70	41	67
Everton	34	17	8	9	58	31	59
Nottm Forest	34	17	5	12	68	38	56
Sunderland	34	16	6	12	57	47	54
Leeds United	34	17	3	14	64	61	54
Sheff United	34	16	5	13	66	66	53
Sheff Wed	34	13	10	11	57	51	49
Coventry C	34	12	8	14	61	61	44
Aston Villa	**34**	**11**	**5**	**18**	**64**	**81**	**38**
Leicester City	34	10	7	17	48	65	37
Hull City	34	10	6	18	47	69	36
Oldham Ath	34	10	5	19	51	63	35
Newcastle U	34	8	5	21	38	67	29
Blackburn R	34	5	8	21	27	72	23
Middlesbrough	34	5	4	25	33	97	19

1987/88

Central League

Tue 18th August
Manchester City (A) Lost 2-3
Bennett, Shaw
Poole, Williams, Claxton, Bennett, Blake, Duffy, Turley (Morris), Shaw, Olney, Hunt S, Burke, Sub Brady.

Wed 26th August
Hull City (H) Lost 1-2
Shaw
Butler, Williams, Claxton, Blair (Mead), Blake, Duffy, Daley, Shaw (Olney), Turnbull, Hunt S, Blake.

Wed 2nd September
Sheffield United (H) Lost 1-3
Mead
Butler, Williams (Brady), Blake, Blair, Reeve, Duffy, Mead, Olney, Turnbull, Bennett, Robinson (Morris).

Wed 9th September
Everton (A) Lost 0-5
Butler, Williams, Claxton, Blair, Blake, Maitland, Morris, Olney, Turnbull, Bennett, Robinson A, Subs Wile, Brady.

Thur 17th September
Leicester City (H) Won 3-1
Allen, Stainrod, Robinson S
Ward, Pearson, Cooper, Blair, Maitland (Olney), Hunt D, Burke, Allen, Turnbull, Stainrod, Robinson S, Sub Bennett.

Wed 23rd September
Huddersfield Town (A) Lost 2-3
Allen 2
Ward, Pearson, Cooper R, Blair, Blake, Bennett, Daley, Shaw, Allen, Brady, Robinson, Subs Olney, Morris.

Tue 6th October
Sunderland (A) Drew 0-0
Butler, Pearson, Cooper R, Blair, Evans (Olney), Hunt D, Murphy, Shaw, Turnbull, Stainrod (Blake), Burke.

Wed 14th October
Liverpool (H) Lost 0-4
Butler, Pearson, Cooper R, Blair, Hunt D, Blake, Murphy (Morris), Shaw, Turnbull (Olney), Bennett, Burke.

Thur 29th October
Coventry City (A) Drew 2-2
Morris, Olney
Butler, Pearson, Cooper R, Blair, Bennett, Blake, Murphy (Jones), Shaw, Olney, Burke, Morris, Sub Williams.

Wed 25th November
Sheffield Wednesday (H) Won 2-0
Shaw 2
Butler, Pearson, Cooper R, Blair, Evans, Blake, Murphy (Olney), Shaw, Thompson, Stainrod, Burke, Sub Duffy.

Tue 1st December
Manchester United (A) Lost 0-3
Butler, Pearson, Cooper R, Blair, Evans, Duffy (Olney), Bennett, Shaw, Thompson, Walters, Burke, Sub Parrott.

[Above] Local lad, Gavin Ward, began his career at Aston Villa before moving on to Shrewsbury Town

Wed 9th December
Grimsby Town (H) Won 5-1
Shaw 2, Olney, Norton, Burke
Butler, Bennett, Cooper R, Blair, Evans, Whittingham, McInally, Shaw, Olney, Norton, Burke, Subs Blake, Jones.

Wed 16th December
Nottingham Forest (A) Lost 1-2
Shaw
Butler, Bennett, Cooper R, Blair, Evans, Blake, McInally, Shaw, Williams G, Norton, Parrott (Olney), Sub Jones.

Wed 6th January
Bradford City (H) Won 3-0
Shaw 2, Williams G
Butler, Pearson, Cooper R, Blair, Whittingham, Duffy, Bennett, Olney, Shaw, Norton, Williams G, Subs Williams M, Jones.

Wed 20th January
Manchester City (H) Won 3-1
Williams G, Olney, Jones
Butler, Bennett, Pearson, Blair, Sims, Cooper N, Daley, Jones, Olney, Norton, Williams G, Subs Williams M, Blake.

Sat 30th January Hull City (A) Lost 0-4
Butler, Bennett, Cooper R, Blair, Sims, Duffy (Blake), Morris (Jones), Shaw, Olney, Hunt D, Williams.

Wed 3rd February
Sheffield United (A) Drew 4-4
Daley, Aspinall, Platt, Williams G
Butler, Pearson, Cooper R, Blair, Sims, Hunt, Daley, Aspinall, Platt, Norton, Williams G, Subs Blake, Olney.

Wed 10th February
Huddersfield Town (H) Drew 1-1
Williams G
Butler, Bennett, Cooper R, Blair, Sims, Hunt, Olney, Aspinall, Platt, Norton, Williams G (Blake), Sub Jones.

Mon 15th February
Leicester City (A) Lost 2-3
Platt 2
Butler, Bennett, Cooper R, Blair, Sims, Hunt, Olney, Aspinall, Platt, Norton, Gray S, Subs Williams M, Jones.

Tue 23rd February
Liverpool (A) Lost 0-4
Butler, Norton, R. Cooper, Blair, Sims, Hunt, Daley, Aspinall, McInally, Gray S, Williams G, Subs Morris, Bennett.

Mon 29th February
Leeds United (H) Won 3-1
Olney, McInally 2
Butler, Bennett, Cooper R, Blair, Sims, Hunt, Morris, Olney, McInally, Norton, Williams G, Subs Blake, Greene.

Wed 2nd March
Sunderland (H) Won 2-0
Norton, Blair
Butler, Bennett, Cooper R, Blair, Sims, Hunt, Morris, Olney, Greene, Norton, Parrott, Subs Blake, Jones.

Tue 8th March
Leeds United (A) Won 2-0
McInally, Aspinall
Butler, Bennett, Claxton, Blair, Sims, Hunt, Shaw, Lillis, McInally, Norton, Aspinall, Subs Olney, Blake.

Fri 11th March
Derby County (A) Lost 0-1
Ward, Bennett, Claxton, Blair, Blake, Hunt, Morris, Shaw, Olney, Norton, Aspinall, Subs Duffy, Brady.

Wed 16th March
Coventry City (H) Won 1-0
McInally
Butler, Bennett, Claxton, Lillis, Sims, Hunt, Blair, Aspinall, McInally, Norton, Williams G, Subs Olney, Blake.

Sat 19th March
Everton (H) Lost 0-1
Butler, Bennett, Claxton, Blake, Duffy, Hunt, Morris, Aspinall, Shaw, Norton, Williams G, Subs Olney, Greene.

Tue 22nd March
Blackpool (A) Won 3-1
McInally, Aspinall 2
Butler, Bennett, Claxton, Lillis, Sims, Hunt, Aspinall, Shaw, McInally, Norton, Williams G, Subs Olney, Blake.

Mon 28th March
Derby County (H) Won 2-0
Aspinall 2
Butler, Bennett, Claxton, Gray A, Sims, Hunt, Morris, Shaw, Aspinall (Olney), Norton, Williams G, Sub Blake.

Tue 12th April
Bradford City (A) Lost 1-3
Norton
Butler, Bennett, Claxton, Norton, Sims, Cooper N, Aspinall, Shaw, McInally, Hunt, Daley, Subs Blake, Duffy.

Tue 19th April
Grimsby Town (A) Won 2-0
Aspinall 2
Butler, Norton, Claxton, Gray A (Lillis), Sims, Hunt, Daley, Aspinall, Olney, Cooper N, Williams G, Sub Bennett.

Wed 27th April
Nottingham Forest (H) Lost 0-6
Butler, Bennett, Claxton (Blake), Blair, Sims, Hunt, Daley, Shaw, Olney, Cooper N, Williams G, Sub Morris.

Fri 29th April
Blackpool (H) Won 8-0
Olney 3, Blair, Shaw, Cooper, Williams G, Morris
Butler, Bennett, Claxton, Blair, Sims (Morris), Hunt, Daley (Blake), Shaw, Olney, Cooper N, Williams G.

Wed 4th May
Manchester United (H) Lost 2-3
Cooper N, Shaw
Butler, Bennett, Claxton, Norton, Blair, Deane (Blake), Cooper N, Daley, Shaw, Olney, Hunt, Subs Morris.

Mon 9th May
Sheffield Wednesday (A) Drew 4-4
Olney 2, Daley, Williams
Butler, Gage, Gallacher, Gray A, Sims, Cooper N, Daley, McInally, Olney, Gray S, Williams G, Subs Duffy, Morris.

Central League Table 1987 - 88

	P	W	D	L	F	A	P
Nottingham Forest	34	25	2	7	81	37	77
Liverpool	34	23	3	8	91	31	72
Derby	34	21	3	10	79	41	66
Manchester City	34	20	4	10	74	51	64
Sheffield United	34	17	6	11	68	55	57
Leeds	34	15	5	14	58	56	50
Sunderland	34	14	8	12	51	54	50
Everton	34	14	5	15	57	46	47
Sheffield Wed.	34	13	8	13	54	52	47
Manchester United	34	13	8	13	49	48	47
Coventry	34	11	13	10	51	37	46
Leicester	34	14	3	17	61	55	45
Huddersfield	34	13	6	15	44	63	45
Aston Villa	34	13	5	16	62	69	44
Hull	34	12	6	16	53	61	42
Bradford	34	9	6	19	45	77	33
Grimsby	34	6	3	25	29	100	21
Blackpool	34	3	6	25	23	97	15

1988/89

Central League

Wed 31st August
Huddersfield Town (H) Won 2-0
Daley, Williams G
Butler, Williams M, Gallacher, Cooper, Sims, Hunt, Blair, Daley, Thompson, Lillis, Williams G, Subs Olney, Duffy.

Wed 7th September
Newcastle United (A) Drew 2-2
Olney, Lillis
Butler, Williams M, Gallacher, Lillis, Sims, Hunt, Birch, Olney, Thompson, Cooper (Morris), Williams G, Sub Duffy.

Wed 14th September
Manchester City (H) Won 6-2
Mountfield, Blair 2, Olney, Thompson, Williams G
Butler, Hunt, Gallacher, Lillis, Sims, Mountfield, Blair, Olney, Thompson, Cooper, Williams G, Subs Morris, Duffy.

Wed 21st September
Blackburn Rovers (A) Won 3-1
Birch, Olney, Lillis
Butler, Williams M (Blair), Gallacher, Cooper, Sims, Hunt, Birch Olney, Thompson, Lillis, Morris (Williams G).

Wed 28th September
Sheffield Wednesday (H) Drew 1-1
Blair
Butler, Williams M, Small, Lillis, Sims, Hunt, Blair, Olney, Williams G, Cooper, Morris, Subs Blake, Duffy.

Wed 5th October
Sunderland (A) Won 3-0
Blair 2, Hunt
Butler, Duffy, Gallacher, Lillis, Sims, Evans, Blair, Olney, Williams G, Hunt, Morris, Subs Blake, Williams M.

Tue 18th October
Everton (A) Lost 0-7
Butler, Williams M, Gallacher, Blair, Sims (Parrott), Duffy, Blake, Olney, Williams G, Hunt, Morris, Sub Jones.

Wed 26th October
Manchester United (H) Lost 1-2
Olney
Butler, Williams M, Gallacher, Blake, Sims, Duffy, Morris, Olney, Williams G, Hunt, Parrott, Subs Jones, Liddle.

Tue 8th November
Coventry City (A) Won 4-2
Gray A, Olney 2, Lillis
Butler, Hunt, Small, Gray A, Sims, Duffy, Morris, Olney, Thompson, Lillis, Williams G, Subs Blake, Jones.

Thur 1st December
Liverpool (A) Drew 0-0
Butler, Duffy, Hunt, Lillis, Sims, Evans, Birch, Olney, Thompson, Morris, Williams G, Subs Blake, Williams M.

Thur 8th December
Derby County (H) Won 1-0
Olney
Butler, Hunt, Gallacher, Lillis, Sims, Mountfield, Birch, Olney, Thompson, Morris, Williams G, Subs Duffy, Williams M.

[Above] Carl Morris spent five seasons at Villa – he later played non-League football with Atherstone United and Moor Green

Wed 14th December
Barnsley (H) Won 7-2
Olney 3, Williams G 3, Birch
Butler, Williams M, Small, Lillis, Sims, Duffy, Birch, Olney, Thompson, Hunt, Williams G, Subs Morris, Blake

Wed 21st December
Nottingham Forest (A) Lost 0-4
Butler, Duffy, Small, Lillis, Sims, Hunt, Birch, Olney, Thompson, Morris, Williams G, Subs Williams M, Blake.

Wed 4th January
Newcastle United (H) Won 2-1
Lillis, Gray A
Butler, Williams M, Small, Gray A, Sims, Hunt, Birch, Williams G, Lillis, Blake, Morris, Subs Jones, Parrott.

Wed 11th January
Huddersfield Town (A) Won 7-1
Olney 3, Birch 3 (1 pen), Daley
Butler, Williams M, Small, Lillis, Sims, Duffy, Birch, Daley, Olney, Hunt, Williams G (Morris), Sub Blake.

Thur 19th January
Liverpool (H) Lost 1-3
Williams G
Butler, Duffy, Small, Hunt, Sims, Evans (Williams M), Birch, Williams G, Jones David, Blake, Morris, Subs Parrott.

Mon 23rd January
Leicester City (A) Drew 2-2
Birch (pen), Daley
Butler, Liddle, Small, Birch, Smith, Hunt, Morris, Daley, Olney, Blake, Williams G, Subs Mooney, Crisp.

Mon 30th January
Sheffield Wednesday (A) Drew 1-1
Olney
Butler, Williams M, Hunt, Birch, Sims, Duffy, Morris, Lillis, Olney, Blake, Williams G, Subs Jones David, Liddle.

Wed 8th February
Sunderland (H) Won 3-2
Daley 2, Williams G
Butler, Duffy, Small, Blake, Sims (Morris), Keown, Birch, Daley, Olney, Hunt, Williams G, Sub Williams M.

Wed 15th February
Everton (H) Drew 0-0
Butler, Williams M, Duffy, Keown, Small, Birch, Blake, Hunt, Williams G, Olney, Daley, Subs Morris, Parrott.

Thur 23rd February
Manchester United (A) Won 3-0
Daley, Olney 2
Butler, Hunt, Small, Blake (Morris), Sims, Keown, Birch, Daley, Olney, Lillis, Williams G (Williams M).

Thur 9th March
Sheffield United (H) Won 3-0
Olney 2, Williams G
Butler, Liddle, Williams M, Blake, Duffy, Evans, Morris, Daley, Olney, Hunt, Williams G, Subs Parrott, Mooney.

Mon 13th March
Blackburn Rovers (H) Won 2-0
Evans 2 (1 pen)
Spink, Williams M, Smith(Duffy), Hunt, Evans, Mountfield, Morris, Daley, Olney, Cowans, Williams G, Sub Blake.

Thur 16th March
West Bromwich Albion (H) Won 7-2
Olney 2, Williams G 2, Cowans, Lillis, Morris
Spink, Hunt, Williams M, Lillis, Mountfield, Evans, Morris, Williams G, Olney, Cowans, Parrott, Subs Blake, Duffy.

Mon 20th March
Leeds United (A) Won 4-3
Daley 3, Morris
Spink, Hunt, Williams M , Lillis, Mountfield, Evans, Morris, Daley, Olney, Blake, Williams G, Subs Parrott, Duffy.

Wed 22nd March
Barnsley (A) Won 4-1
Williams G 3, Daley
Spink, Hunt, Williams M, Lillis, Mountfield, Evans, Birch, Daley (Morris),
Williams G, Blake, Parrott, Sub Duffy.

Tue 28th March
Manchester City (A) Lost 0-2
Butler, Liddle, Small, Blake, Duffy, Hunt, Callaghan, Daley, Lovell (Parrott), Birch, Williams G, Sub Morris.

Thur 30th March
Coventry City (H) Lost 1-2
Ormondroyd
Butler, Williams M, Small, Lillis, Hunt, Duffy, Birch, Lovell (Parrott), Ormondroyd, Blake, Williams G, Sub Morris.

Tue 4th April
Nottingham Forest (H) Won 1-0
Ormondroyd
Butler, Duffy, Small, Lillis, Mountfield (Williams M), Hunt, Birch, Williams G, Ormondroyd, Blake, Williams G, Sub Morris.

Tue 11th April
Derby County (A) Lost 0-2
Butler, Price, Gray, Blake, Hunt, Duffy, Birch, Platt, Ormondroyd, Cowans, Williams G, Subs Morris, Parrott.

Wed 19th April
Leeds United (H) Won 2-1
Hunt, Ormondroyd
Butler, Williams M, Small, Blake, Hunt, Duffy, Birch, Williams G, Ormondroyd, Lillis, Morris, Subs Liddle, Mooney.

Wed 26th April
West Bromwich Albion (A) Drew 0-0
Butler, Liddle, Williams M, Blake, Hunt, Duffy, Birch, Daley, Ormondroyd,
Lillis, Williams G, Subs Morris, Parrott.

Wed 3rd May
Leicester City (H) Lost 0-1
Butler, Williams M (Liddle), Smith, Blake, Duffy, Hunt, Birch, Mooney, Williams G, Lillis, Morris (Parrott).

Wed 10th May
Sheffield United (A) Lost 0-3
Butler, Williams M, Small, Blake, Smith, Liddle, Morris, Jones, Mooney, Williams G (Carruthers), Parrott, Sub Crisp.

Central League Table 1988 - 89

	P	W	D	L	F	A	Pts
Nottingham F.	34	20	6	8	83	45	66
Everton	34	19	7	8	70	35	64
Aston Villa	34	18	7	9	73	50	61
Liverpool	34	16	9	9	64	40	57
Coventry	34	17	6	11	66	52	57
Derby	34	15	11	8	44	33	56
Sheffield Utd	34	14	9	11	67	74	51
Huddersfield	34	12	12	10	51	54	48
Leeds	34	13	7	14	59	59	46
Leicester	34	13	6	15	65	63	45
Manchester C.	34	12	9	13	64	65	45
Blackburn	34	13	2	19	55	62	41
Manchester U.	34	10	10	14	61	62	40
Newcastle	34	10	10	14	51	58	40
W.B.Albion	34	10	8	16	55	76	38
Barnsley	34	8	9	17	46	80	33
Sheffield Wed.	34	8	8	18	40	70	32
Sunderland	34	6	8	20	40	76	26

1989/90

Central League

Mon 21st August
Huddersfield Town (H) Won 2-1
Gallacher, Ormondroyd
Butler, Comyn, Gallacher, Blake, Sims, Lillis, Jones, Spink D, Ormondroyd, Williams G, Small, Subs Carruthers, Mooney.

Tue 5th September
Liverpool (A) Won 3-1
Olney 2, Callaghan
Butler, Comyn, Williams G, Gage, Sims, Lillis, Callaghan, Olney, Spink D (Parrott), Blake, Ormondroyd, Sub Jones.

Mon 11th September
Nottingham Forest (H) Lost 1-3
Cowans (pen)
Butler, Lillis, Comyn, Blake, Nielsen, Sims, Daley, Spink D, Ormondroyd, Cowans, Williams G, Subs Jones, Parrott.

Tue 19th September
Bradford City (A) Drew 0-0
Butler, Liddle, Small, Blake, Sims, Duffy, Birch, Spink D, Jones (Carruthers), Cowans, Parrott, Sub Froggatt

Mon 25th September
Leicester City (H) Won 5-1
Jones 4, Ormondroyd
Butler, Duffy, Comyn, Blake, Sims (Small), Nielsen, Birch, Jones, Spink D, Cowans, Ormondroyd, Sub Small.

Thur 5th October
Sheffield United (A) Lost 1-2
Spink D
Butler, Duffy, Small, Gage, Nielsen, Comyn, Birch, Heath (Parrott), Spink D (Jones), Williams G, Ormondroyd.

Mon 9th October
Everton (H) Won 4-3
Ormondroyd 2, Birch, Parrott
Butler, Duffy, Williams G, Gage, Sims, Comyn, Callaghan (Liddle), Jones (Parrott), Spink D, Birch, Ormondroyd.

Wed 18th October
Notts County (A) Won 6-0
Sims, Daley, Spink D, Williams G, Ormondroyd, own goal
Butler, Duffy, Gage, Blake, Sims (Small), Comyn, Callaghan, Daley, Spink D, Williams G, Ormondroyd, Sub Jones.

Thur 26th October
Manchester City (A) Lost 2-3
Jones 2
Butler, Liddle, Small, Heath, Comyn, Duffy, Callaghan, Jones, Spink D, Williams L (Crisp), Mooney (Carruthers).

Mon 30th October
Oldham Athletic (H) Won 3-0
Ormondroyd 2, Birch
Butler, Liddle (Small), Williams G, Blake, Comyn, Duffy, Callaghan Nigel, Jones, Ormondroyd, Birch, Callaghan Noel (Spink D).

Mon 6th November
Coventry City (H) Drew 1-1
Spink D
Butler, Liddle, Small, Callaghan Nigel, Smith, Comyn, Crisp, Jones, Spink D, Williams G, Parrott, Subs Mooney, Elliott.

[Above] Tommy Mooney went on to enjoy a long professional career, most notably with Watford and Birmingham City

Tue 14th November
Derby County (A) Lost 1-2
Spink D
Butler, Liddle, Gallacher, Blake, Comyn, Duffy, Birch, Heath, Spink D, Gray, Williams G, Subs Parrott, Jones.

Mon 20th November
Blackburn Rovers (H) Won 3-0
Williams, Heath, Jones
Butler, Duffy, Gray, Blake, Sims, Comyn, Callaghan, Jones, Heath, Cowans, Williams G, Subs Walker, Morgan.

Wed 29th November
Newcastle United (A) Lost 0-1
Butler, Duffy, Sims, Comyn, Small, Callaghan, Blake, Williams G, Mooney (Carruthers), Heath, Jones, Sub Liddle.

Wed 6th December
Hull City (A) Won 3-1
Callaghan 2, Heath
Butler, Duffy, Small, Gage (Jones), Sims, Comyn, Birch, Callaghan, Heath, Blake, Williams G, Sub Liddle.

Mon 11th December
Leeds United (H) Won 4-2
Callaghan 2, Heath, own goal
Butler, Duffy, Small, Gage, Sims, Comyn, Birch, Heath, Williams G, Blake, Callaghan, Subs Jones, Liddle.

Tue 19th December
Manchester United (H) Drew 2-2
Comyn, Spink D
Butler, Liddle, Small, Heath, Sims, Comyn, Birch, Williams G, Spink D, Blake (Yorke), Callaghan, Sub Jones.

Tue 2nd January
Liverpool (H) Won 6-3
Spink D, Yorke, Blake, Comyn, Callaghan (pen), Sims
Butler, Duffy, Gallacher, Heath, Sims, Comyn, Birch, Yorke, Spink D, Blake, Callaghan, Subs Jones, Small.

Thur 18th January
Huddersfield Town (A) Lost 2-3
Spink D, Heath
Butler, Duffy, Gallacher, Heath, Sims, Comyn, Jones, Yorke, Spink D, Blake, Callaghan, Subs Mooney, Carruthers.

Mon 22nd January
Bradford City (H) Lost 1-3
Spink D
Butler, Duffy, Gallacher, Heath, Sims, Comyn, Yorke, Williams G, Spink D, Birch, Callaghan, Subs Jones, Small.

Wed 7th February
Blackburn Rovers (A) Drew 2-2
Callaghan 2 (1 pen)
Butler, Duffy, Gallacher, Heath, Sims, Comyn, Birch, Williams G, Yorke, Blake, Callaghan, Subs Small, Jones.

Mon 12th February
Newcastle United (H) Won 5-0
Birch 2, Heath 2, own goal
Butler, Duffy, Gallacher, Heath, Comyn, Gray, Birch, Jones, Yorke, Blake, Callaghan, Subs Crisp, Mooney.

Mon 19th February
Leicester City (A) Lost 0-1
Butler, Duffy, Gallacher, Heath (Mooney), Comyn, Gray, Birch, Jones, Yorke, Blake, Callaghan, Sub Small.

Tue 6th March
Everton (A) Lost 1-2
Spink D
Butler, Liddle (Crisp), Small, Blake, Comyn, Duffy, Yorke (Mooney), Jones, Spink D, Williams G, Callaghan.

Mon 12th March
Notts County (H) Won 5-0
Yorke 2, Callaghan, Birch, Spink D
Butler, Liddle (Small), Gallacher, Callaghan, Smith, Comyn, Birch, Yorke, Spink D, Blake, Ormondroyd, Sub Jones.

Mon 19th March
Manchester City (H) Drew 0-0
Butler, Liddle, Gallacher, Blake, Comyn, Duffy, Crisp (Carruthers), Jones, Yorke, Williams G, Mooney (Williams L).

Tue 27th March
Oldham Athletic (A) Won 2-1
Williams G, Comyn
Butler, Crisp, Gallacher, Blake, Comyn, Duffy, Birch, Yorke, Olney, Williams G, Callaghan, Subs Jones, Williams L.

Mon 2nd April
Hull City (H) Won 5-0
Callaghan (pen), Birch, Jones, Williams G, Gallacher
Butler, Liddle, Gallacher, Blake, Comyn, Duffy, Birch, Jones, Yorke, Williams G, Callaghan, Subs Carruthers, Small.

Mon 9th April
Nottingham Forest (A) Lost 0-2
Butler, Liddle, Gallacher, Blake, Mountfield, (Elliott), Duffy, Callaghan, Yorke, Olney, Small, Ormondroyd, Sub Jones.

Wed 11th April
Leeds United (A) Won 5-1
Olney 2, Callaghan, Ormondroyd, Jones
Butler, Liddle, Gallacher, Small, Mountfield, Duffy, Callaghan, Olney, Ormondroyd, Williams G, Parrott (Jones), Sub Elliott.

Wed 18th April
Manchester United (H) Drew 0-0
Butler, Liddle, Gallacher, Small, Duffy, Comyn, Callaghan, Yorke, Olney, Williams G, Ormondroyd, Subs Jones, Carruthers.

Tue 24th April
Coventry City (A) Won 5-1
Jones 2, Olney 2, Ormondroyd
Butler, Liddle, Gallacher, Blake, Comyn, Duffy, Jones (Carruthers), Olney, Ormondroyd, Williams G, Callaghan, Sub Williams L.

Thur 26th April
Sheffield United (H) Drew 0-0
Butler, Liddle (Crisp), Gallacher, Williams L, Comyn (Froggatt), Duffy, Birch, Carruthers, Ormondroyd, Williams G, Callaghan.

Wed 2nd May
Derby County (H) Won 4-0
Blake, Ormondroyd, Callaghan (pen), own goal
Butler, Crisp, Gallacher, Blake, Mountfield, Duffy, Birch, Olney, Ormondroyd, Williams G, Callaghan, Subs Small, Williams L.

Central League Table 1989 - 90

	P	W	D	L	F	A	Pts
Liverpool	34	24	4	6	74	42	76
Nottingham Forest	34	19	6	9	79	48	63
Aston Villa	**34**	**17**	**7**	**10**	**84**	**42**	**58**
Manchester United	34	17	7	10	54	39	58
Derby County	34	16	7	11	64	47	55
Manchester City	34	18	3	13	64	51	57
Leicester City	34	16	8	10	51	48	56
Everton	34	16	5	13	58	53	53
Leeds United	34	14	8	12	62	49	50
Blackburn Rov.	34	14	8	12	69	59	50
Newcastle Utd	34	15	5	14	42	50	50
Sheffield Utd	34	14	5	15	47	46	47
Coventry City	34	12	5	17	50	64	41
Huddersfield	34	11	5	18	40	64	38
Notts County	34	8	9	17	44	90	33
Bradford City	34	8	6	20	41	64	30
Hull City	34	6	6	22	47	74	24
Oldham Ath.	34	6	6	22	34	74	24

[Right] Villa's 1982 youth side showing off their Southern Junior Floodlit Cup and Mannheim trophy. [Back Row] Tim Langford, Darren Bradley, Leigh Palin, Kevin Rogers, Kevin Poole, Dean Glover, Tony Rees, Mark Hutchinson, Stephen Barnes [Front Row] David Norton, Paul Birch, Mark Walters Ray Walker, Martin McKenzie, Paul Kerr, Tony Obi.

JUNIOR + YOUTH COMPETITIONS

DAVENPORTS

SOUTHERN JUNIOR FLOODLIT CUP

1980/81

Mon 29th September
Oxford United (H) 1st round Won 2-0
Hill, Kerr
Lowe, Taylor, Rogers, Walker, Glover, McKenzie, Kerr, Hutchinson, Hill, McClair, Walters, Sub Rees.

Wed 29th October
Colchester United 2nd round (H) Won 3-0
Birch 2, McKenzie
Lowe, Taylor, Rogers, Walker, Mail, Birch, Rees, Hutchinson, Hill, McKenzie, Walters, Subs Glover, McClair.

Wed 26th November
Fulham 3rd round (A) Drew 0-0

Tue 16th December
Fulham (H) 3rd round replay Won 3-2
McClair, Walters, Hill
Lowe, Taylor, Rogers, Glover, Mail, Walker, Rees, Hutchinson, Hill, McClair, Walters, Subs McKenzie, Kerr.

Tue 17th February
Arsenal (A) semi-final Won 2-1
Birch, Walters,
Poole, Mail, Walker, Glover, Rogers, Rees, Hutchinson, Birch, McKenzie, Walters, McClair, Subs Hill, Kerr.

Mon 27th April
West Ham United (A) Final 1st leg Won 2-0
Rees, Mail
Poole, Mail, Walker, Glover, Rogers, Rees, Hutchinson, Birch, McKenzie, McClair, Walters, Subs Hill, Kerr.

Thurs 30th April
West Ham United (H) Final 2nd leg Lost 0-1
As per programme: Poole, Mail, Rogers, Walker, Glover, McClair, Hutchinson, Birch, Norton, Rees, Walters, Kerr, McKenzie, Hill, Brown.

1981/82

Thurs 17th September
Plymouth Argyle (H) preliminary round Won 4-1
Rees, Kerr, Walters, own goal
Harrison, Barnes, Brown, Walker, Glover, Hutchinson, Rees, Kerr, Palin, Norton, Walters, Subs Obi, Bradley.

Wed 14th October
Bournemouth (H) 1st round Won 6-0
Rees 3, Palin 2, Hutchinson
Harrison, Brown, Rogers, Walker, Glover, Hutchinson, Norton, Palin, Kerr, Rees, Walters, Subs Bradley, Obi.

Wed 11th November
Southend United (H) 2nd round Won 1-0
Rees
Harrison, Brown, Rogers, Walker, Glover, Hutchinson, Norton, Palin, Kerr, Rees, Walters, Subs Bradley, Obi.

[Above] David Mail celebrating the Southern Junior Floodlit Cup win over West Ham United

Mon 25th January
Chelsea (H) quarter-final Won 2-0
Kerr, Hutchinson (pen)
Harrison, Bradley, Rogers, Walker, Glover, Hutchinson, Obi, Norton, Palin, Kerr, Walters, Subs Langford, Dorigo.

Thurs 25th March
Birmingham City (H) semi-final Drew 1-1
Hutchinson (pen)
Harrison, Bradley, Glover, Walker, Rogers, Obi, Hutchinson, Norton, Brown, Kerr, Walters, McKenzie, Palin, Langford, Dorigo.

Wed 21st April
Birmingham City (A) semi-final replay Won 2-1
Glover, Walters
Harrison, Bradley, Glover, Walker, Rogers, Obi, Hutchinson, Norton, Brown, Kerr. Walters, Subs McKenzie, Palin.

Thur 13th May
West Ham United (A) Final 1st leg Drew 0-0

Wed 19th May
West Ham United (H) Final 2nd leg Lost 0-2
Harrison, Brown, Rogers, Walker, Glover, Hutchinson, Obi, Kerr, Palin, Norton, Walters, Subs Bradley, McKenzie.

1982/83

Mon 4th October
Oxford United (A) 1st round Won 4-0
Langford, Rees, Palin, Norton (pen)
Belford, Barnes, Dorigo, Bradley, Shipley, Norton, Palin, Giles, Obi, Rees, Langford, Subs Hellin, Hutchins.

Mon 8th November
Watford (H) 2nd round Lost 1-2
Dorigo
Belford, Hellin, Shipley, Bradley, Dorigo, Norton, Palin, McMahon (Hutchins), Obi, Rees, Langford, Sub Kentish.

1983-84

Thurs 29th September
Oxford United (H) 1st round Won 3-0
Palin (pen), Howell 2
Belford, Shipley (McMahon), Robinson, Hellin, Dorigo, Palin, Bradley, O'Connell, Greenhalgh, Howell, Obi, Sub Hutchings.

Mon 14th November
Watford (H) 2nd round Won 3-2
Bradley 2, Greenhalgh
Belford, Robinson, Dorigo, Hellin, Shipley, Bradley, Mitchell, Palin, Greenhalgh, Howell (Hutchings), Obi, Sub O'Connell.

Mon 13th February
Norwich City (H) quarter-final Lost 1-2
Howell
Belford, Robinson, Dorigo, Hellin, Shipley, Bradley, Hutchings, McKenzie, Greenhalgh, Howell, Obi, Subs Mitchell, Gallacher.

1984/85

Tues 18th September
Watford (A) 1st round Won 2-1
Forman, Howell
Belford, Mitchell, Gallacher, Hellin, Robinson, McKenzie, Hutchings, Forman, Grainger, Howell, Daley, Subs Burke, Ritchie.

Tues 30th October
Arsenal (A) 2nd round Drew 2-2
Forman, Hutchings
Belford, Mitchell, Gallacher, Hellin, Robinson, McKenzie, Hutchings, Forman, O'Connell, Howell, Daley, Subs English, Burke.

Tues 6th November
Arsenal (H) 2nd round replay Won 3-2 AET
Forman, Ritchie, Hutchings
Belford, English, Gallacher, Hellin, Robinson, McKenzie, Hutchings, Forman, Ritchie, Howell, Daley, Subs Vacanti, Grainger.

Thurs 7th February
Portsmouth (A) 3rd round Drew 2-2 AET
Howell, Daley
Belford, English (Denoon), Gallacher, Hellin, Robinson, Ritchie, Hutchings, Forman, Burke, Howell, Daley, Sub Clipston.

Mon 11th March
Portsmouth (H) 3rd round replay Drew 1-1
Ritchie
Belford, Vacanti, Gallacher, Hellin, Robinson, Ritchie, Hutchings, Forman, Grainger, Howell, Burke, Subs Denoon, Clipston.

Fri 29th March
Portsmouth (A) 3rd round 2nd replay Lost 1-2
Hutchings
Belford, Ritchie (Vacanti), Gallacher, Hellin, Robinson, Grainger, Hutchings, Forman, Burke, Howell, Daley.

[Above] The 1987 youth team: [Back Row] Paul Brady, Andy Robertson, Mark Blake, Robert Greene, Derek Dudley, Darrell Duffy, Ian Olney, Lewis Claxton, Wesley Robb, John Wile, [Front Row] Mark Parrott, Stephen Meade, Tommy Bennett, Bobby Downes (Coach), Mark Williams, Carl Morris, David Jones.

1985/86

Mon 7th October
Reading (A) 1st round Drew 1-1
Daley
Purkiss, Bates, Clipston, Forman, Clarke, Grainger, Spark, Ritchie, Greene, Burke, Daley. Subs Byrne, Denoon P.

Mon 21st October
Reading (H) 1st round rep Won 2-0
Grainger, Bowen
Purikiss, Bates, Clipston, Forman (Mahoney), Clarke, Grainger, Spark, Ritchie, Greene, Daley, Sub Meade.

Mon 2nd December
Southend United (H) 2nd round Drew 3-3 AET
Greene, Ritchie (pen), Clipston
Purkiss, Bates, Clipston, Forman, Clarke, Ritchie, Spark, Callaghan (Bowen), Greene, Burke, Daley, Sub Mahoney.

Thurs 19th December
Southend United (A) 2nd round replay Lost 1-2
Bates
Purkiss, Callaghan, Clipston, Bates, Clarke, Ritchie, Forman, Byrne, Greene, Burke, Daley, Subs Bowen, Spark

1986/87

Wed 17th September
Arsenal (H) 1st round Drew 3-3
Morris, Greene, Olney
Ward, Mahoney, Clipston, Bates, Clarke, Bennett, Morris, Greene, Olney, Callaghan, Burke, Subs Claxton, Robb.

Wed 24th September
Arsenal (A) 1st round replay Drew 1-1 AET
Bennett
Dudley, Mahoney, Clipston, Bates, Clarke, Bennett, Morris, Greene, Olney, Robb, Burke, Subs Claxton, Mead.

Tues 30th September
Arsenal (A) 1st round 2nd replay Lost 2-5
Olney, Claxton
Dudley, Mahoney, Clipston, Bates, Clarke, Bennett, Morris, Greene (Claxton), Olney, Callaghan, Burke, Sub Robb.

1987/88

Mon 7th September
Bristol City (A) 1st round Won 5-2
Greene, Olney 2, Morris, Claxton
Ward, Wile, Claxton, Bennett, Blake, Duffy, Mead, Greene (Jones), Olney (Richardson), Brady, Morris.
Mon 2nd November
Reading (H) 2nd round won 6-1
Bennett (pen), Williams, Olney 2, Greene, own goal
Ward, Williams, Claxton, Brady, Blake, Bennett, Mead, Jones, Olney, Morris, Parrott, Subs Greene, Wile.

Mon 11th January
Charlton Athletic (A) 3rd round Won 3-0
Jones, Olney, Brady
Ward, Williams, Claxton M, Bennett, Blake, Duffy, Mead, Jones, Olney, Brady, Morris, Subs Greene, Wile.

Mon 22nd February
Luton Town (H) semi-final Lost 2-4
Greene 2
Ward, Williams, Claxton M, Bennett, Blake, Duffy, Jones, Greene, Olney, Brady, Morris, Subs Parrott, Small.

1988/89

Mon 12th September
Northampton Town (A) 1st round Won 1-0
Parrott
Livingstone, Williams M, Small, Blake, Smith, Duffy, Slocombe, Jones, Hemmings, Liddle, Parrott, Subs Yates, Crisp.

Mon 24th October
Bristol City (H) 2nd round Won 4-0
Blake, Jones, Liddle, Crisp
Livingstone, Williams M, Small, Blake, Smith, Duffy, Yates, Jones, Hemmings (Crisp), Liddle, Parrott, Sub Slocombe.

Mon 9th January
Gillingham (H) 3rd round Won 2-0
Jones, Parrott
Livingstone, Williams M, Small, Blake, Smith, Duffy, Williams L (Crisp), Jones, Mooney (Carruthers), Liddle, Parrott.

Sat 8th April
Brentford (Away) semi-final Won 1-0 AET
Carruthers
Livingston, Williams M,Small, Blake, Smith, Duffy, Crisp, Jones (Carruthers), Mooney, Liddle, Parrott, Sub Slocombe.

Mon 17th April
Southampton (H) Final 1st leg Lost 2-3
Mooney, Duffy
Livingston, Williams M, Small, Blake, Smith, Duffy, Crisp (Carruthers), Jones, Mooney, Liddle, Parrott, Sub Slocombe.

Mon 8th May
Southampton (A) Final 2nd leg Drew 0-0
Livingstone, Williams M, Small, Blake, Smith, Duffy (Williams L), Jones, Carruthers, Mooney, Liddle, Parrott, Sub Crisp.

1989/90

Wed 13th September
Luton Town (H) 1st round Lost 0-1
Livingstone, Liddle, Bullivant, Williams L, Smith, Elliott, Morgan (Travis), Mooney, Carruthers, Small, Froggatt, Sub Crisp.

FA YOUTH CUP

1980/81

Thur 4th December
Sheffield United (A) 2nd round Drew 2-2
Hutchinson, Birch
Lowe, Taylor, Rogers, Walker, Mail, Birch, Rees, Hutchinson, Hill, McClair, Walters, Sub Glover.

Thur 9th December
Sheffield United (H) 2nd round Won 3-2
Walters 2, Rees
Poole, Taylor, Rogers, Glover, Mail, Walker, Rees, Hutchinson, Hill, McClair, Walters, Sub McKenzie.

Mon 22nd December
Shrewsbury (A) Lost 1-3
Walters (pen)
Lowe, Taylor, Mail, Glover, Rogers, Kerr, Walker, Hutchinson, McClair, Walters, Hill, Sub McKenzie.

1981/82

Saturday 23rd January
Cardiff City (H) 4th round Drew 3-3
Walters, Palin, Hutchinson
Belford, Brown, Rogers, Walker, Glover, Hutchinson, Obi, Norton, Dorigo, Kerr, Walters, Sub Palin.

Tues 16th February
Cardiff City (A) 4th round replay Won 5-2
Kerr, Walker, Walters, Norton, Hutchinson
Harrison, Brown, Rogers, Walker, Glover, Hutchinson, Obi, Kerr, Palin, Norton, Walters, Sub McKenzie.

Thurs 4th March
Sunderland (H) quarter-final Lost 1-2
Walters
Harrison, Brown, Rogers, Walker, Glover, Hutchinson, Obi, Kerr, McKenzie, Norton, Walters, Sub Bradley.

1982/83

Tues 30th November
Hereford United (A) 2nd round Won 3-1
Palin, Obi, Hutchins
Belford, Barnes, Dorigo, Bradley, Shipley, Robinson, Norton, Hutchins, Palin, Hellin, Obi, Sub O'Connell.

Wed 5th January
Norwich City (A) 3rd round Lost 2-5
Dorigo, Norton (pen)
Belford, Barnes, Dorigo, Shipley, Bradley, Norton, Hellin, Obi, Palin, Langford, Hutchings, Sub Robinson.

1983/84

Mon 5th December
West Bromwich Albion (A) 2nd round Won 3-0
Obi, Dorigo, Howell
Belford, Robinson, Dorigo (Gallacher), Hellin, Shipley, Bradley, Hutchings, Palin, Greenhalgh, Howell, Obi.

Tues 3rd January
Chesterfield (A) 3rd round Won 2-0
Greenhalgh, Howell
Belford, Mitchell, Gallacher, Hellin, Dorigo, Bradley, Hutchings, O'Connell, Greenhalgh, Howell, Obi, Sub McKenzie.

Mon 30th January
West Ham United (H) 4th round Won 2-0
Greenhalgh, Dorigo
Belford, Robinson, Dorigo, Hellin, Shipley, Bradley (Mitchell), Hutchings, Palin, Greenhalgh, Howell, O'Connell.

Tues 21st February
Arsenal (A) quarter-final Lost 1-2
Bradley
Belford, Shipley, Gallacher, Hellin, Dorigo, Bradley, Hutchings, McKenzie, Greenhalgh, Howell (Mitchell), Obi.

1984/85

Tues 4th December
Chesterfield (A) 2nd round Won 2-0
Howell, Burke
Belford, English, Gallacher, Hellin, Robinson, McKenzie, Hutchings, Forman, Ritchie, Howell, Burke, Sub Vacanti.

Sat 26th January
Mansfield Town (A) 3rd round Lost 0-2
Belford, English, Gallacher, Hellin, Robinson, Grainger, Hutchings, Forman, Ritchie, Howell, Daley, Sub Vacanti.

[Above] Martin Carruthers enjoyed a long professional career before moving into non-League management

1985/86

Thurs 5th December
Luton Town (A) 2nd round Lost 2-4
Ritchie (pen), Greene
Purkiss, Spark, Clipston, Bates, Clarke, Ritchie, Bowen, Forman, Greene, Burke, Byrne P, Sub Callaghan.

1986/87

Mon 8th December
Ipswich Town (A) 2nd round Lost 1-4
Claxton
Dudley, Williams M, Clipston, Greene, Bates, Bennett, Burke, Brady, Callaghan, Claxton, Subs Mead, Morris.

1987/88

Mon 9th November
Peterborough United (A) 1st round Drew 1-1
Jones
Ward, Williams, Claxton, Bennett, Blake, Duffy, Mead, Jones, Olney, Brady (Parrott), Morris, Sub Greene.

Mon 16th November
Peterborough United (H) 1st round replay Drew 2-2 AET
Morris, Jones
Ward, Williams, Claxton, Bennett, Blake, Duffy, Mead (Jones), Greene (Brady), Olney, Morris, Parrott.

Mon 23rd November
Peterborough United (A) 1st round 2nd replay Won 2-0
Morris, Olney
Dudley, Williams, Claxton, Bennett, Blake, Duffy, Morris, Jones, Olney, Brady, Parrott, Subs Mead, Wile.

Mon 7th December
Crewe Alexander (A) 2nd round Lost 1-2
Bennett (pen)
Dudley, Williams, Claxton (Parrott), Bennett, Blake, Morris, Jones, Olney, Brady, Greene, Sub Mead.

1988/89

Mon 14th November
Chester City (A) 1st round Won 2-0
Liddle, Yates
Livingstone, Williams M, Hoban (Yates), Blake, Smith, Duffy, Williams L (Crisp), Jones, Hemmings, Liddle, Parrott.

Sat 17th December
Luton Town (H) 2nd round Lost 1-3
Parrott
Livingston, Williams M, Small, Blake, Smith, Duffy, Williams L, Jones, Hemmings (Crisp), Liddle, Parrott, Sub Slocombe.

1989/90

Wed 1st November
Hednesford Town (H) 1st round Won 9-0
Liddle 2, Crisp 2, Carruthers 2, Williams L, Mooney, Tyrrell
Livingston, Liddle (Morgan), Bullivant, Williams L, Smith, Elliott, Crisp, Mooney, Carruthers, Froggatt, Small (Tyrrell).

Tue 21st November
Watford (A) 2nd round Lost 1-2
Elliott
Livingstone, Crisp, Bullivant, Liddle, Smith, Elliott, Williams L, Mooney, Carruthers, Froggatt, Small, Subs Morgan, Walker.

[Right] Gary Shaw slides in to tackle Tottenham's Chris Hughton during the defeat at White Hart Lane in March 1981

FIRST TEAM INFORMATION

APPEARANCES

SEASON 1980-1981

	LEAGUE		FAC		LC		TOTALS	
NAME	P	G	P	G	P	G	APPS	GOALS
Des Bremner	42	2	1		3		46	2
Gordon Cowans	42	5	1		3		46	5
Ken McNaught	42		1		3		46	
Tony Morley	42	10	1		3	2	46	12
Dennis Mortimer	42	4	1		3		46	4
Jimmy Rimmer	42		1		3		46	
Kenny Swain	42		1		3		46	
Gary Shaw	40	18	1		2+1	2	43+1	20
Allan Evans	38	7	1		3		42	7
Peter Withe	36	20	1		3	1	40	21
Colin Gibson	19+2				3		22+2	
Garry Williams	21+1		1				22+1	
Davis Geddis	8+1	4	+1		1		9+2	4
Eamonn Deacy	5+5				+1		5+6	

NUMBER OF PLAYERS USED: 14
NUMBER OF GOALSCORERES: 8

[Right] David Geddis clashes with Cambridge United's Jamie Murray during the F.A. Cup third round defeat at the Abbey Stadium

SEASON 1981-1982

NAME	LEAGUE P	LEAGUE G	FAC P	FAC G	LC P	LC G	Euro P	Euro G	Charity Shield P	Charity Shield G	Total APPS	Total GOALS
Gordon Cowans	42	6	3	1	6	4	9		1		61	11
Jimmy Rimmer	42		3		6		9		1		61	
Des Bremner	38	3	2		6	1	9		1		56	4
Allan Evans	38	2	3		6		8		1		56	2
Kenny Swain	39		3		5		8		1		56	
Tony Morley	36+1	6	3		6	1	8	4	1		54	11
Peter Withe	35	10	2		6	2	9	3	1	2	53	17
Dennis Mortimer	32	2	3		4		9		1		50	2
Garry Williams	28		3		5		7				43	
Gary Shaw	26	9	2	2	6		8	3			42	14
Colin Gibson	23		2		6		4		1		36	
Ken McNaught	22	2	1				5	1	1		29	3
David Geddis	14	6	2	3					1		17	9
Brendan Ormsby	12				2		3				17	
Andy Blair	9+9		1		+2	1	2+1		+1		12+13	1
Terry Donovan	8	4					1	2			9	6
Pat Heard	6+3	2									6+3	2
Eamonn Deacy	4				2						6	
Terry Bullivant	4+3				+1						4+4	
Mark Jones	2										2	
Mark Blake	1										1	
Gary Shelton	1										1	
Ivor Linton	+1						+1				+2	
Nigel Spink							+1				+1	
Mark Walters	+1										+1	

NUMBER OF PLAYERS USED: 25

NUMBER OF GOALSCORERES: 12

[Right] Dennis Mortimer leads the Villa team out ahead of the Charity Shield final with Tottenham Hotspur

SEASON 1982-1983

	LEAGUE		FAC		LC		Euro		Super Cup		Total	
NAME	P	G	P	G	P	G	P	G	P	G	APPS	GOALS
Gordon Cowans	42	10	4	1	2		6	1	2	1	56	13
Ken McNaught	41	2	3		2		6		2	1	54	3
Dennis Mortimer	39	4	3		2		6	1	1		51	5
Gary Shaw	39	17	3	1	2		6	5	2	1	50	24
Des Bremner	36+1		3		2		6		2		49+1	
Allan Evans	39+1	4	4				4		2		49+1	4
Garry Williams	35+1		4		2		5		2		48+1	
Peter Withe	35	16	3	1	1		6	2	2		47	19
Tony Morley	29+4	5	4	1	2		5	1	2		42+4	7
Colin Gibson	23	1	3	1	1		4		1+1		32+1	1
Nigel Spink	22		4				2		2		30	
Jimmy Rimmer	20				2		4				26	
Mark Jones	17		1		2		2		1		23	
Mark Walters	18+4	1	2+1	1			1+1	1	+1		21+7	1
Andy Blair	6+1		2				2		1		11+1	
Pat Heard	5+2						1				6+2	
Alan Curbishley	6+1										6+1	
Eamonn Deacy	4	1	1				+1				5+1	1
David Geddis	2+2				1						3+2	
Kenny Swain	2										2	
Robert Hopkins	1										1	
Brendan Ormsby					1						1	
Ray Walker												

NUMBER OF PLAYERS USED: 24
NUMBER OF GOALSCORERES: 10

[Right] Peter Withe finds the net during the F.A. Cup win over Wolves in January 1983

SEASON 1983-1984

	LEAGUE		FAC		LC		UEFA		Total	
NAME	P	G	P	G	P	G	P	G	APPS	GOALS
Dennis Mortimer	37	5	2		7	2	4		50	7
Garry Williams	40				7		3		50	
Allan Evans	36	7	2		7	3	4		49	10
Steve McMahon	37	5	2		6		4		49	5
Peter Withe	36	16	2	1	7	1	4	4	49	22
Mark Walters	33+4	8	2		5	2	3+1	1	43+5	11
Brendan Ormsby	34	2	1		4		4	1	43	3
Nigel Spink	28		2		7		4		41	
Colin Gibson	28	1			7	2	4	2	39	5
Alan Curbishley	25+1	1			5		2		32+1	1
Paul Rideout	22+3	5	+1		3+1	2	1		26+5	7
Paul Birch	22	2	2		2				26	2
Des Bremner	14+3		2		4+1		2		22+4	
Gary Shaw	11+1	5	2		4	1			17+1	6
Mervyn Day	14								14	
Eamonn Deacy	12+1				+1				12+2	
Tony Morley	6+1	1			1		3+1		10+2	1
Andy Blair	9						1		10	
Ray Walker	5+3		2		+1				7+4	
Steve Foster	7	1							7	1
Mark Jones	5				1		1		7	
Paul Kerr	1+1								1+1	
Dean Glover			1						1	
Tony Dorigo	+1								+1	

NUMBER OF PLAYERS USED: 24
NUMBER OF GOALSCORERES: 13

[Right] Tony Morley blasts a shot at the Southampton goal during September's 1-0 home win over The Saints

SEASON 1984-1985

	LEAGUE		FAC		LC			Total
NAME	P	G	P	G	P	G	APPS	GOALS
Colin Gibson	40	4	1		3	2	44	6
Peter Withe	40	12	1		2		43	12
Garry Williams	38		1		3		42	
Allan Evans	38	6			2		40	6
Steve McMahon	34+1	2	1		3		38+1	2
Mark Walters	35+1	10	1		2		37+1	10
Brendan Ormsby	32	2	1		2		35	2
Gordon Cowans	29+1	1	1		3	1	33+1	2
Paul Rideout	28+1	14	1		1+1	1	30+2	15
Tony Dorigo	27+4		1		1+1		29+5	
Paul Birch	24+1	3	1		3		28+1	3
Nigel Spink	19		1				20	
Mervyn Day	16				3		19	
Didier Six	13+3	2			1+1		14+4	2
Steve Foster	8	2			2		10	2
Paul Kerr	6+4				2	2	8+4	2
Kevin Poole	7						7	
Dennis Mortimer	5+1						5+1	
Dean Glover	5						5	
Ray Walker	4+3						4+3	
Tony Daley	4+1						4+1	
Des Bremner	4	1					4	1
Ian Curbishley	3						3	
David Norton	2						2	
Darren Bradley	1+1						1+1	

NUMBER OF PLAYERS USED: 25 NUMBER OF GOALSCORERES: 13

[Right] Mark Walters about to score the first of his two goals at an icy Highfield Road during Villa's 3-0 win against Coventry City

mita

SEASON 1985-1986

	LEAGUE		FAC		LC		TOTALS	
NAME	P	G	P	G	P	G	APPS	GOALS
Mark Walters	40	10	4		9	3	53	13
Tony Dorigo	38	1	4		8		50	1
Allan Evans	35	3	4	1	9	2	48	6
Steve Hodge	36	8	4	1	8	1	48	10
Andy Gray	35	5	4		7	2	46	7
Nigel Spink	31		3		8		42	
Simon Stainrod	29+1	10	4	2	7+1	9	40+2	21
Paul Birch	25+2	2	4	1	7+1	3	36+3	6
Garry Williams	25		2		7	2	34	2
Paul Elliott	23	2	4		4		31	2
David Norton	20	2	2+1		3		25+1	2
Dean Glover	15+3		2		7	1	24+3	1
Tony Daley	16+7	2			2+1		18+8	2
Darren Bradley	15+3				3		18+3	
Brendan Ormsby	14				2	2	16	2
Kevin Poole	11		1		1		13	
Steve Hunt	12	2					12	2
Andy Blair	12						12	
Gary Shaw	10+2	1			+1		10+3	1
Paul Kerr	5+1	1	2	1	3		10+1	1
Colin Gibson	7	2			3		10	2
Ray Walker	5+2				1		6+2	
Steve McMahon	3						3	

NUMBER OF PLAYERS USED: 23
NUMBER OF GOALSCORERES: 17

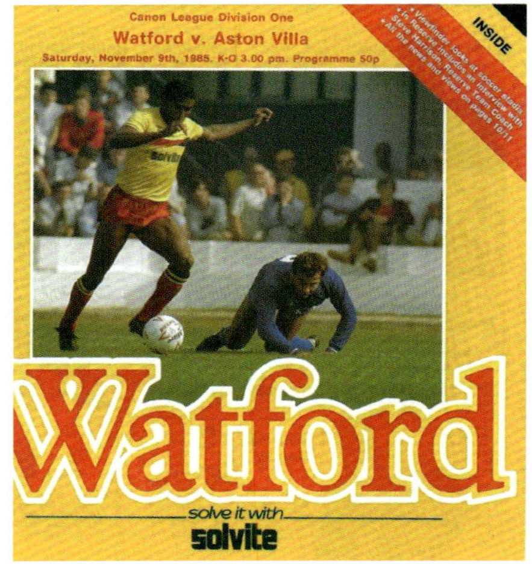

[Right] Tony Dorigo tackles Nigel Callaghan during the 1-1 draw at Vicarage Road in November 1985

11
IVECO

SEASON 1986-1987

	LEAGUE		FAC		LC		Full Members		TOTALS	
NAME	P	G	P	G	P	G	P	G	APPS	GOALS
Tony Dorigo	41		2		5		2		50	
Steve Hunt	39	2	2	2	5		1		47	4
Martin Keown	35+1		2		4				41+1	
Nigel Spink	32		2		4		1		39	
Paul Elliott	33+1	5			3		1		37+1	5
Garry Thompson	30+1	6	2		4	1	1		37+1	7
Allan Evans	25+1	6	2		5	1	2	1	34+1	8
Paul Birch	26+3	3	1+1		4	1	1		32+4	4
Simon Stainrod	25+4	6	2		4		1		32+4	6
Tony Daley	25+8	3	1+1		3	1	2	1	31+9	5
Gary Williams	26		2		1		1		30	
David Norton	19+1				5		2		26+1	
Mark Walters	18+3	3	2		2+1	1	2		24+4	4
Steve Hodge	17	4			4	2	1		22	6
Andy Gray	18+1		+2		1	2	1		20+3	2
Neale Cooper	13		2	1					15	1
Warren Aspinall	12	3							12	3
Kevin Poole	10				1		1		12	
Dean Glover	5						1		6	
Paul Kerr	4+2	2			+2				4+4	2
Andy Blair	4								4	
Paul Robinson	2+1								2+1	1
Gary Shaw	1						1	2	2	2
Mark Burke	1								1	
Bernie Gallacher	1								1	
Simon Ritchie	+1								+1	

NUMBER OF PLAYERS USED: 26 NUMBER OF GOALSCORERES: 15

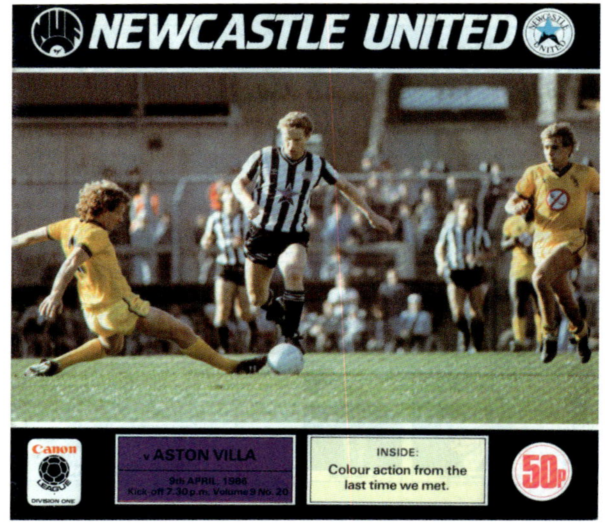

[Right] Warren Aspinall scored the Villa goal during the 2-1 defeat to Arsenal at Highbury in May 1987

mita

SEASON 1987-1988

	LEAGUE		FAC		LC		Simod Cup		TOTALS	
NAME	P	G	P	G	P	G	P	G	APPS	GOALS
Kevin Gage	44	2	2		4		1		51	2
Nigel Spink	44		2		4		1		51	
Bernie Gallacher	43		2		4		1		50	
Martin Keown	42	3	2		4				48	3
Paul Birch	38	6	2		4	1	1		45	
Mark Lillis	28+1	4	2		4		1		35+1	4
Steve Sims	29				4		1		34	
Warren Aspinall	28+4	11	1+1		4	2			33+5	13
Garry Thompson	24	11	2		1	1	1		28	12
Mark Walters	24	7			3		1		28	7
Alan McInally	18+7	4	2	1	3	1	1		24+7	6
Andy Gray	19	1	2	1					21	2
Allan Evans	18+2	1	2		+2				20+4	1
Stuart Gray	19+1	5							19+5	5
Davis Hunt	11+1				2				12+1	2
Tony Daley	10+4	3	1						11+4	3
David Platt	11	5							11	5
Neale Cooper	6+1								6+1	
Andy Blair	3+1	1			1		1		5+1	1
Mark Burke	4+2						+1		4+3	
Malcolm Allen	4								4	
Simon Stainrod	4								4	
Gary Shaw	1+3						1		2+3	
David Norton	1+1								1+1	
Gareth Williams	1								1	

NUMBER OF PLAYERS USED: 26
NUMBER OF GOALSCORERES: 15

[Right] Team Line up prior to Nigel Spink's Testimonial match

M&B
2.KEVIN
Ever
mita
copiers

SEASON 1988-1989

	LEAGUE		FAC		LC		Simod Cup		TOTALS	
NAME	P	G	P	G	P	G	P	G	APPS	GOALS
David Platt	38	7	2	1	5	6	2	1	47	15
Chris Price	36		1		5		2		44	
Nigel Spink	34		2		5		1		42	
Gordon Cowans	32+1	2	2		5		2		41+1	2
Martin Keown	32+2		2		4		2		40+2	
Stuart Gray	35	4	2		3		+1		40+1	4
Alan McInally	32+1	14	2	1	3	4	2	3	39+1	22
Kevin Gage	27+1	3	2	1	5	3	2		36+1	6
Tony Daley	25+4	5	2		5	1	1+1		33+5	6
Allan Evans	26+1		2		2		2	1	32+1	1
Derek Mountfield	22+2	1	2		5	1	2	1	31+2	3
Andy Gray	15+3	3	1+1		3	1	+2		19+6	4
Nigel Callaghan	15+1								15+1	1
Steve Sims	12				1				13	
Ian Olney	8+7	2	+1		1+1	1			9+9	3
Ian Ormondroyd	9+3	1							9+3	1
Bernie Gallacher	3+1				2+1		2	1	7+2	1
Paul Birch	6+6								6+6	
Lee Butler	4							1	5	
Garry Thompson	2+3				1		1		4+3	
Mark Lillis	2								2	
Darrell Duffy	1								1	
Davis Hunt	1								1	
Gareth Williams	1								1	

NUMBER OF PLAYERS USED: 24
NUMBER OF GOALSCORERES: 13

[Right] Chris Price taking a shot, but there would be no goals for him in his 44 appearances for Villa during the 1988-89 campaign

mita copiers
McEWANS

SEASON 1989-1990

	LEAGUE		FAC		LC		Zenith		TOTALS	
NAME	P	G	P	G	P	G	P	G	APPS	GOALS
David Platt	37	19	5	1	4	1	5	3	51	24
Nigel Spink	38		5		4		4		51	
Gordon Cowans	34	4	5		3		5		47	4
Paul McGrath	35	1	5		3		4		47	1
Kent Nielsen	34+2	2	4		2+1		5		45+3	2
Derek Mountfield	32	4	4	1	4	1	5	2	45	8
Chris Price	33+1	1	4		4		4+1		45	1
Tony Daley	31+1	6	4	2	3		4+1		42+2	8
Ian Olney	27+8	9	5	2	4		5		41+8	11
Kevin Gage	22	3	5		4		4		35	3
Stuart Gray	26+3		1+1	2	3	1	3+1		33+5	5
Ian Ormondroyd	19+6	4	4	2	1+1		5		29+7	6
Tony Cascarino	10	2							10	2
Paul Birch	6+6		1+2	2	1		1+1	1	9+9	3
Bernie Gallacher	6+1		1		2				9+1	
Adrian Heath	8+1		+1		1+1				8+3	
Nigel Callaghan	7+1				1+1				8+2	
Gareth Williams	4+6		2				+1		6+7	
Mark Blake	6+3				+1				6+4	
Andy Comyn	3+1				+1				3+2	
Lee Butler							1		1	
Dwight Yorke	+2								+2	

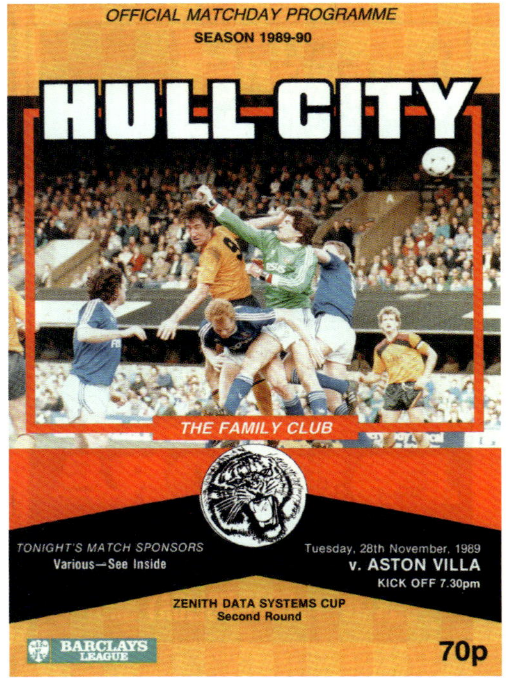

NUMBER OF PLAYERS USED: 22
NUMBER OF GOALSCORERES: 13

[Right] David Platt can do nothing as Cyrille Regis takes a shot at goal during the 2-0 defeat at Coventry in March 1990

PIUGEOT

DEDICATIONS

Russell Homer
Ray Homer
Talia Homer
Harry Homer
Charlie Homer
Colin J Abbott
Tree Day
Kyle & Sammy Abbott
Ryan, Leon & Kacy
Graydon Abbott
Brad Abbott
Tilly Abbott
Ieuan Brno-Evans
Bob Abbott
Ruby Rose Wilson
Sandra & Geoff Abbott
Julie & Des Richardson
Jon Farrelly
Mat Kendrick
Samuel Kendrick
Sue and Mick Tilt
Andy 'Turnstile' Ullah
John Whittaker
Lyndon Oxford
Jason Peters
Helen & Gary Parsons
John Pallister
Stuart Rimmer
Sue & Mike Quinlan
Reg Evans RIP
Michael Parker
Bob Gough (Northampton)
Greg Upton
Steve Knott
Andy Woodhull
Mark Homer
Paul Martin
Richard Birkin
Mark Austin
Paul Smith
Mark Clarke
Christopher Barton
Nick Howells
Robert Wilson
Craig Hodkiss
Peter Tennant
Lee Downing
Robert Smith
Tom Robertson
Andreas Meier Eide
Pete Doolan
Clive Capewell
David Pettitt
Ian Wiseman
Mark Green
Philip Lapthorne
Mick Crampton
John Uttley
Alex Langley
Jason 'Brummiewebbie' Webb
Paula Jones
Simon Wiggin
Nick Danks
Margaret Danks
Robert Garratt
Daniel Rainsford
Mark Stanford
Phil Stanford
Paul Stanford
Michael Atkinson
Nick Harper
Cliff Dubberley
Ray Geary
Stephen Barney
Wayne Bullock
Keith Roberts
Calvin Priest
David J. Taylor
Graham Biggs
Charlie (Chan) Harris
Adrian Casha
Michael David Ault
Gregory Shutt
David Clift
Darren Woolley
Mark Pearce
Garry Buckley
Sean Collins
Mike Davis
Lawrence Smith
David Hodges (Southam)
Martin Heavey
Steve McDonald
Jonathan Duffill
Matthew Carder
Stuart Giles
Michael Painting
Gary Cooke
John Holder
Richard Jenkins
David Clayton
Chris Greaves
Michèle Astbury
Steven Riddick
Stephen Hill
Leslie Edward Mason
Phillip Christopher Mason
James Phillip Edward Mason
Vittorio Sorci
Robert Mason
Paul Williams
Martin Lucas
Keith Burrows
Carl Withers
Michael Martin Lindsay
Lyndon Willetts
John Rooker
Steve Mann
Ray Geary
Clive Capewell
Melvyn Horton
Adam Colvin
Phil Coldicott
Paul Farrington
Keith Falconer
Andrew Cockburn

Bernadette Mackie
Steve Wall
Tim Cookson
Michael 'Archie' Hall
Michael Lindsay
Keith Rickett
Neil James
Kevin Rollason
Robert Ford
The Heaney Villans
Stephen Barney
Vaughan Ellis
David Bridgewater
Pam Bridgewater
Kevin Heaney
Sarah James
Jimmy Giles
Robin Wilkes
Michael Reidy
Colin O'Connor
Ian Wiseman
Christian Russ
Ian Wragg
Mark Policarpo
Mark Bevan
Derek Day
John Holder
Brod Mason
Ian Hucker
Patrick Drummey
Ray Biddle
Thomas Cole
Ian Wragg
Ian Hunter
Christopher Willey
Andrew Willey
Jason Reed
Thomas Hunter
John Foster
Will Hughes
Ron Dovey
Kalvin Davies
Peter Day
Thaness Sean Himathongkom
Alberto Zaliani
Paul Baker
Graham Farmer
David Birt
Kevin Gage
Andy Dale
Brian Seadon
Lee Bickerton
Andrew Toy
John Crawford
Steven Garbutt
Tony Bennett
David Smith
Arthur Bent
Colin Brown
Nigel Shaw
Steven Seatherton
Timothy Evans
Christopher Turner
Leon James
Andy Hooper
Andrew Webb
Nigel Parsons
Mark Thornley
David Lawlor
Keith Powell
Mark Hudson
Louis Aston Hudson
Ian Kenny
Andrew Mills
Derek Bignell
Cliff Dubberley
Paul Matthews
Martin Greenslade
Martin Childs
Philip Gray
Christine Rossiter
Simon Foxall
Paul Williams
Stephen Gough
Gregory Shutt
Grant Danskine
Roger Bunn
Ian Richards
Mark Davies
Keith Feaver
Gary Costello
Roger Levicki
Adam Levicki
Tim Levicki
Steve Fletcher-Turnstiles
Zoe Beal
Kathryn Burston
Ian Watson
Pauline Griffiths
Carl Withers
Timothy Cookson
Jason Donnelly
Ian Wragg
David Chick
John 'Villa' Power
Mark Reynolds
Christopher O'Connor
Rob Edwards
Amelia Edwards
Doug O'Brien
Roy Barrett
Anthony Hynes
Chris Ashmore
Dean Watson
Brian Watson
Mark Howell
Riccardo Rossi
Shaun Cope
Darren Monaghan
James Foat
Gordon Nicklin
Daniel Moss
Glenn Douglas
Allan Goodall
Thomas Goodall
Clayton Delaney
Clarkey AVFC
Victoria Ross
Julian Walker
Alan Jewhurst
Alan Bales
Mark Flanagan
David Coley
Richard King
James Steele
Steve Hughes
Paul Smith
Kevin Smith

THANKS AND ACKNOWLEDGMENTS

With the success of The Big Aston Villa Book of The Seventies; Aston Villa The First One Hundred and Fifty Years Vol I and Barton's Army, Conquering Europe with Aston Villa it gives me great pleasure to be putting this Thanks & Acknowledgements together as this is the latest journey completed. Legends Publishing's David Lane's continued faith in me means this, The Big Aston Villa Book of The Eighties has materialised. A big thank you for the belief and trust shown mate.

A big thank you to former Villa players Dennis Mortimer, David Platt, Andy Gray, Garry Thompson, Kevin Gage, Nigel Spink and Mark Burke for the lengthy interviews that have been included within these pages.

Jon Farrelly for being onboard yet again
Mick Tilt for support and friendship
Mat Kendrick for his continued support for our books
Andy 'Turnstile' Ullah
Chris Barton
Alan Hipkiss
Neil Morrison
Leigh Douglas
Greg Upton
Tree Day for the continued support.
Paul Faulkner, had it not been for his support during his role as CEO of Aston Villa none of my books would ever have seen the light of day.
Andy Blair and Mark Walters
Paul Collins

To the countless others who have assisted, you know who you are.

Lastly, you the supporters of Aston Villa who get behind and support the publications we produce. I am no different to each and any of you, a fan at heart. I write the books, not as an academic but as someone who fell in love with Aston Villa Football Club and want to preserve the history of this fine institution.

Colin J Abbott

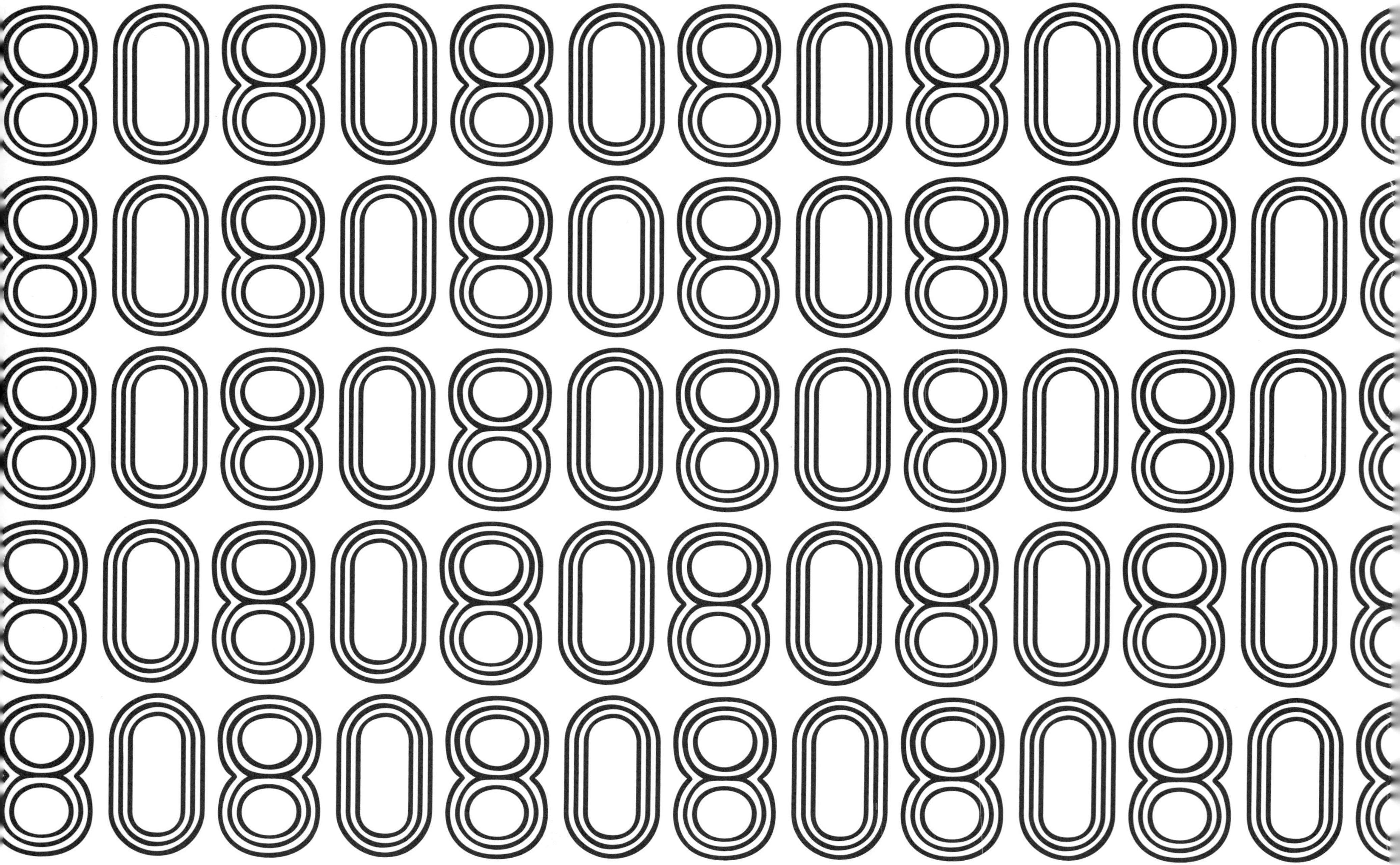
808080808080
808080808080
808080808080
808080808080
808080808080